The Tale of the Outcasts

5

story & art by
Makoto Hoshino

The tale of outcasts

5

Contents

Night 38 Dark Gaze

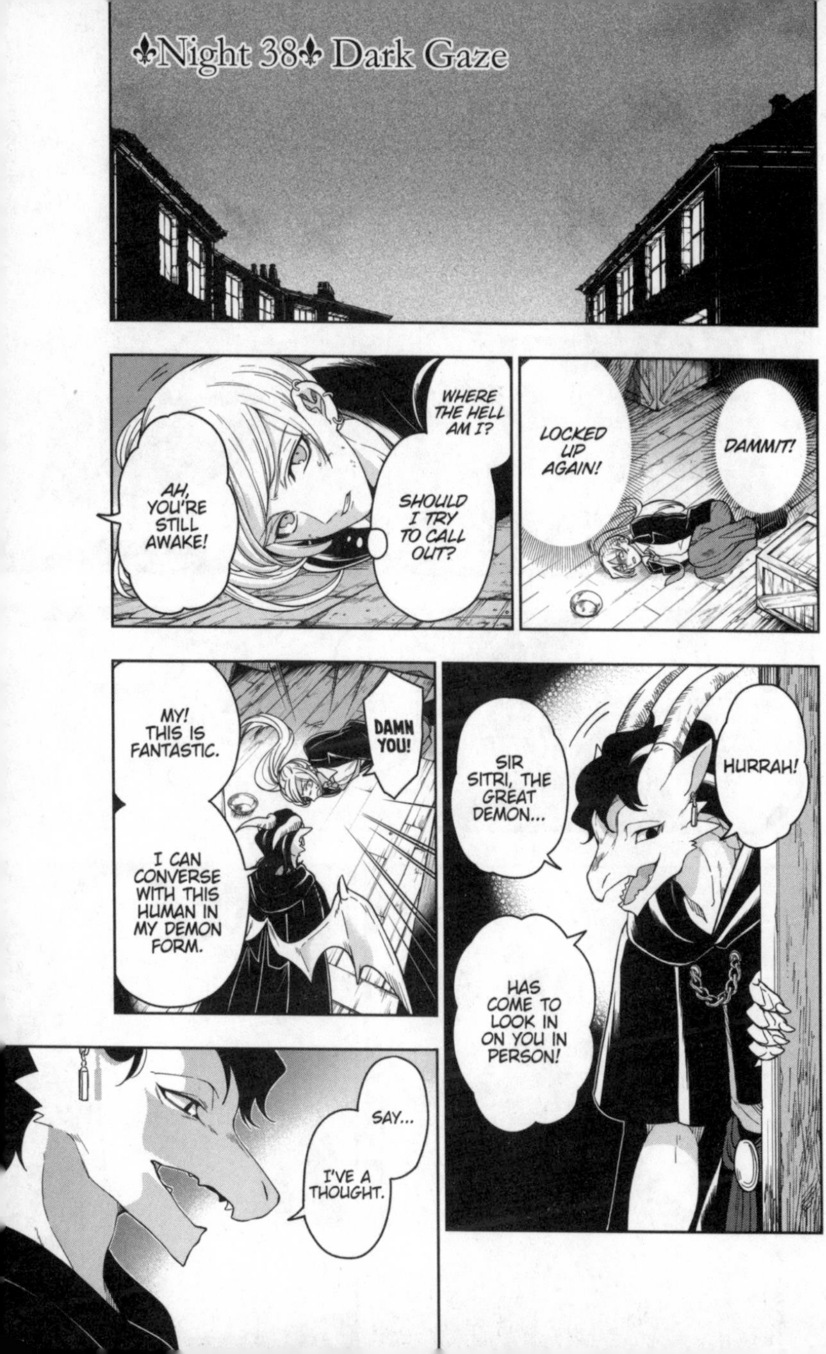
DAMMIT!
LOCKED UP AGAIN!
WHERE THE HELL AM I?
SHOULD I TRY TO CALL OUT?
AH, YOU'RE STILL AWAKE!
HURRAH!
SIR SITRI, THE GREAT DEMON...
HAS COME TO LOOK IN ON YOU IN PERSON!
DAMN YOU!
MY! THIS IS FANTASTIC.
I CAN CONVERSE WITH THIS HUMAN IN MY DEMON FORM.
SAY...
I'VE A THOUGHT.

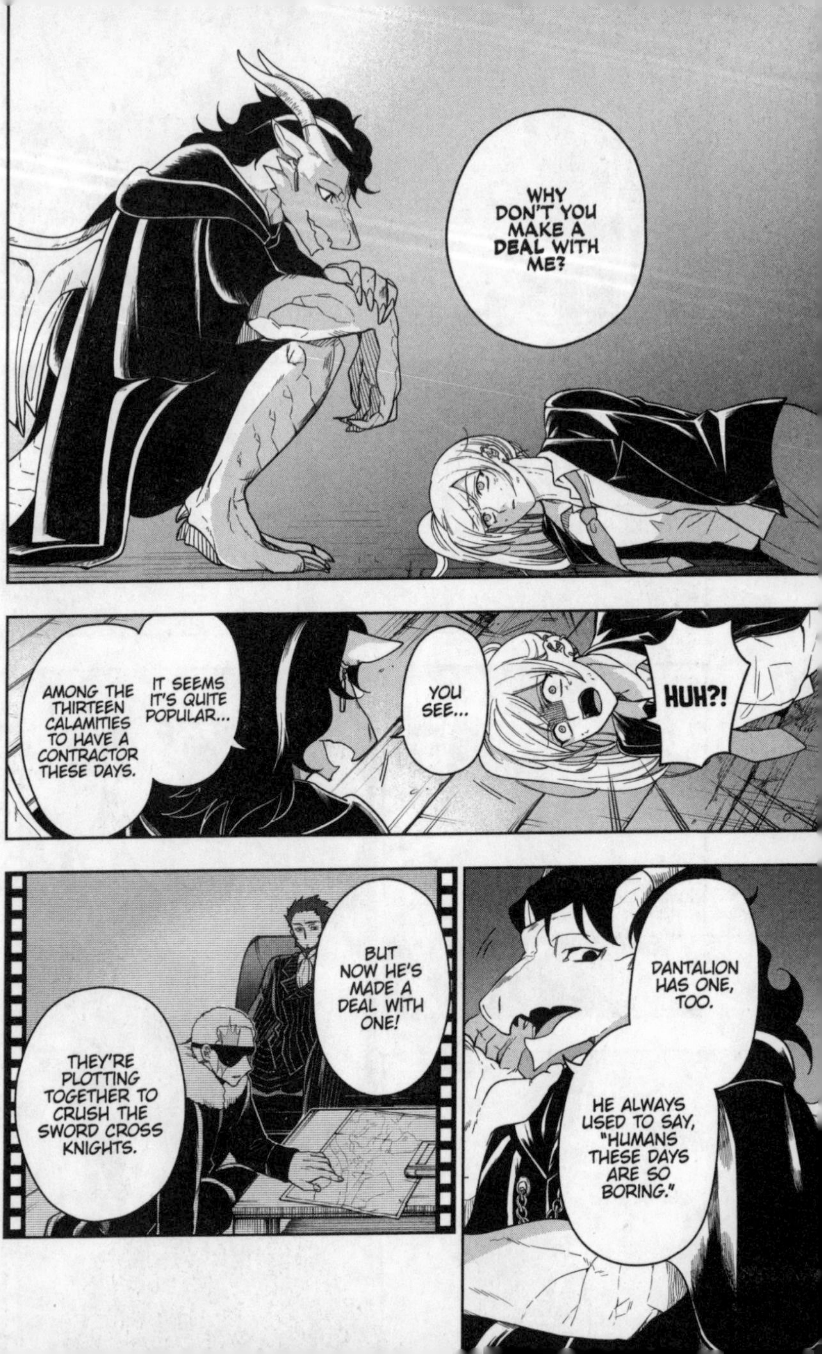
WHY DON'T YOU MAKE A DEAL WITH ME?
HUH?!
YOU SEE...
IT SEEMS IT'S QUITE POPULAR...
AMONG THE THIRTEEN CALAMITIES TO HAVE A CONTRACTOR THESE DAYS.
DANTALION HAS ONE, TOO.
HE ALWAYS USED TO SAY, "HUMANS THESE DAYS ARE SO BORING."
BUT NOW HE'S MADE A DEAL WITH ONE!
THEY'RE PLOTTING TOGETHER TO CRUSH THE SWORD CROSS KNIGHTS.

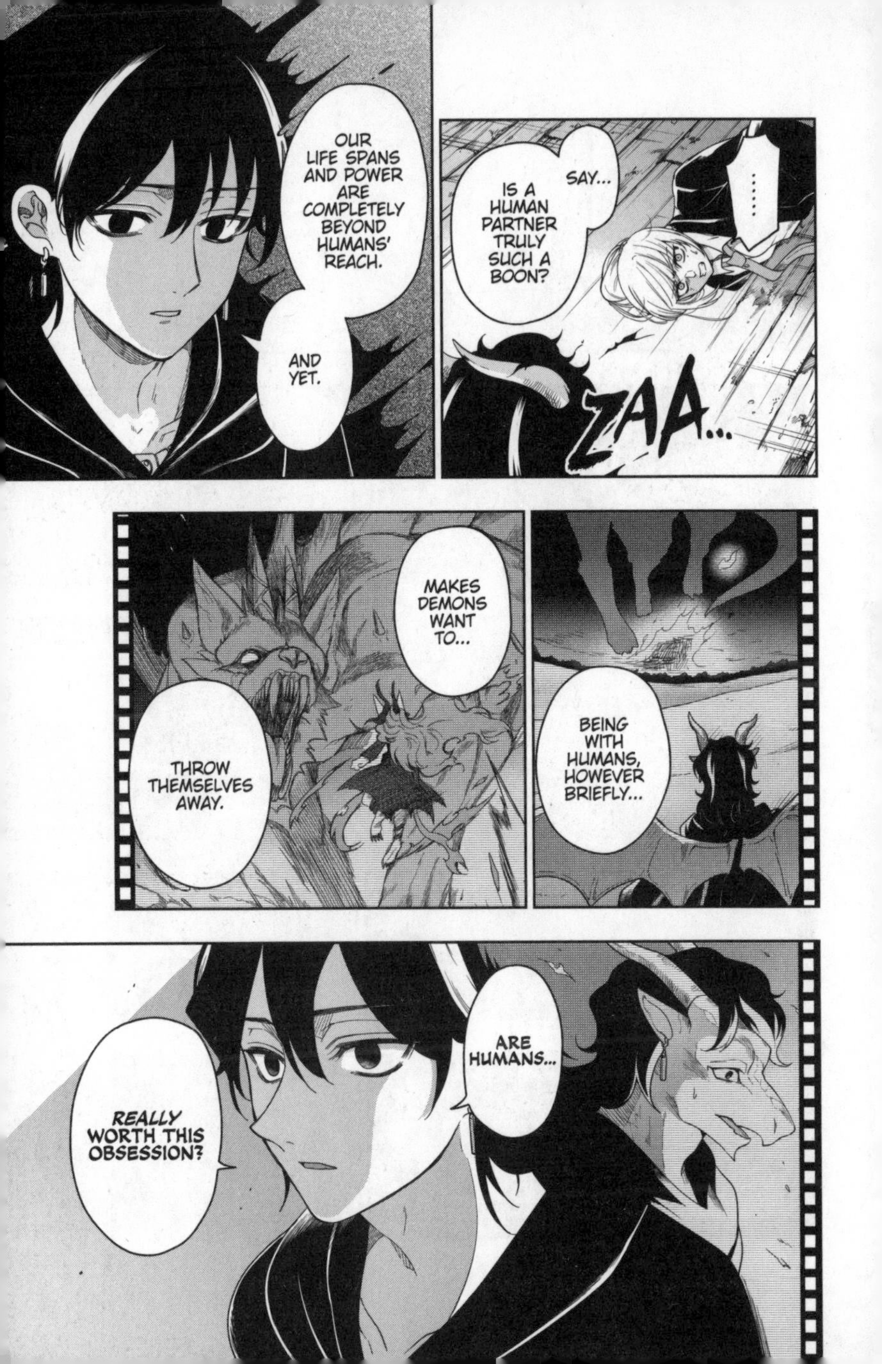

......
SAY...
IS A HUMAN PARTNER TRULY SUCH A BOON?
ZAA...
OUR LIFE SPANS AND POWER ARE COMPLETELY BEYOND HUMANS' REACH.
AND YET.
BEING WITH HUMANS, HOWEVER BRIEFLY...
MAKES DEMONS WANT TO...
THROW THEMSELVES AWAY.
ARE HUMANS...
REALLY WORTH THIS OBSESSION?

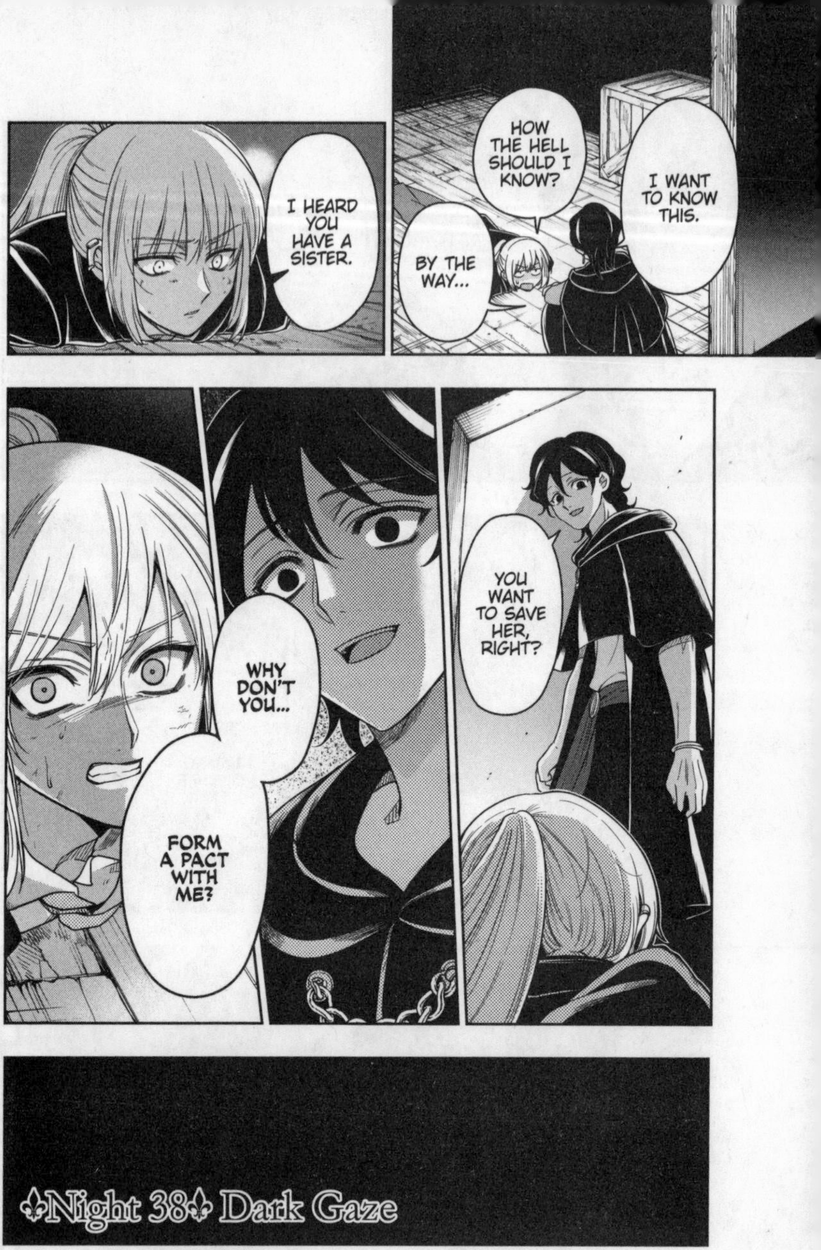
I WANT TO KNOW THIS.
HOW THE HELL SHOULD I KNOW?
BY THE WAY...
I HEARD YOU HAVE A SISTER.
YOU WANT TO SAVE HER, RIGHT?
WHY DON'T YOU...
FORM A PACT WITH ME?
Night 38 Dark Gaze

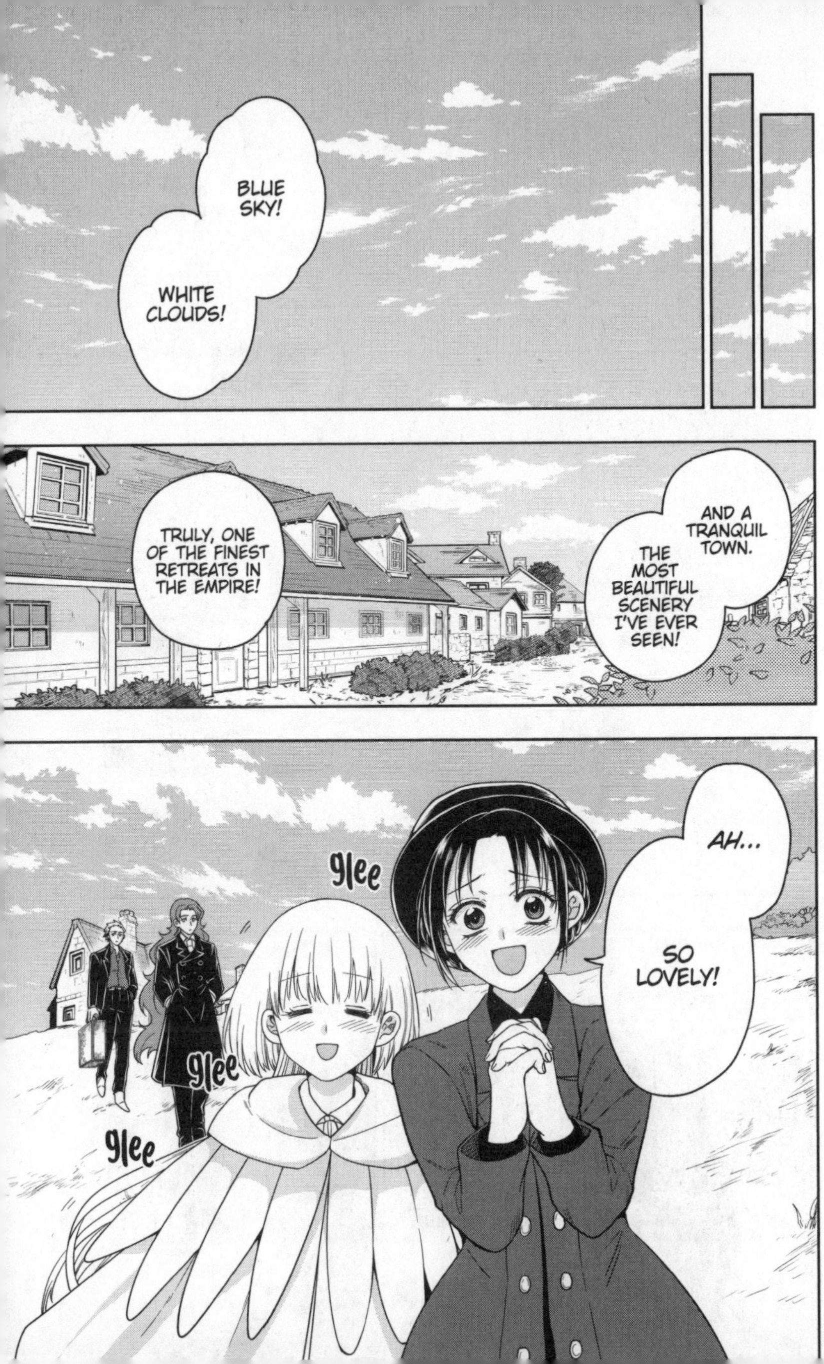
BLUE SKY!
WHITE CLOUDS!
AND A TRANQUIL TOWN.
THE MOST BEAUTIFUL SCENERY I'VE EVER SEEN!
TRULY, ONE OF THE FINEST RETREATS IN THE EMPIRE!
AH... SO LOVELY!
glee
glee
glee

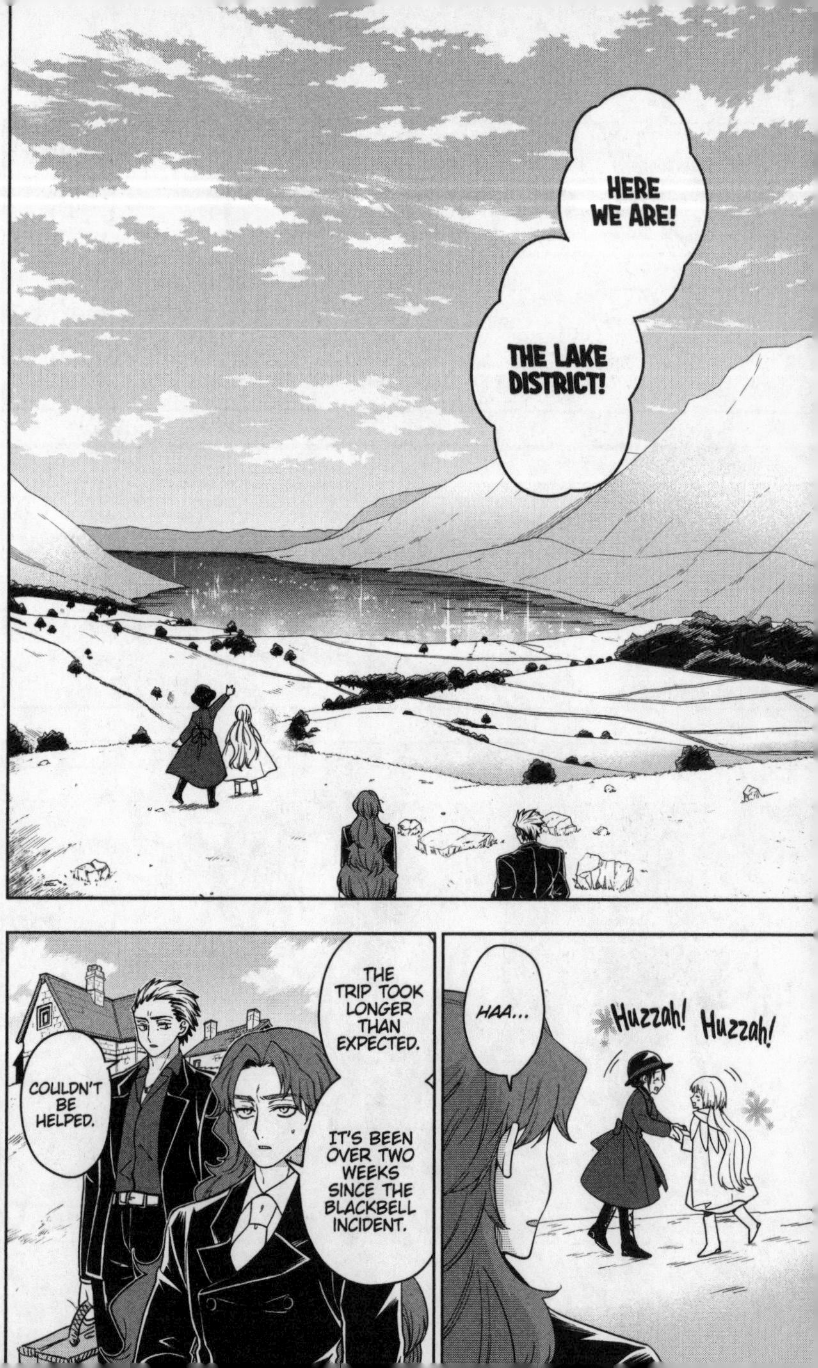
HERE WE ARE!
THE LAKE DISTRICT!
Huzzah!
Huzzah!
HAA...
THE TRIP TOOK LONGER THAN EXPECTED.
IT'S BEEN OVER TWO WEEKS SINCE THE BLACKBELL INCIDENT.
COULDN'T BE HELPED.

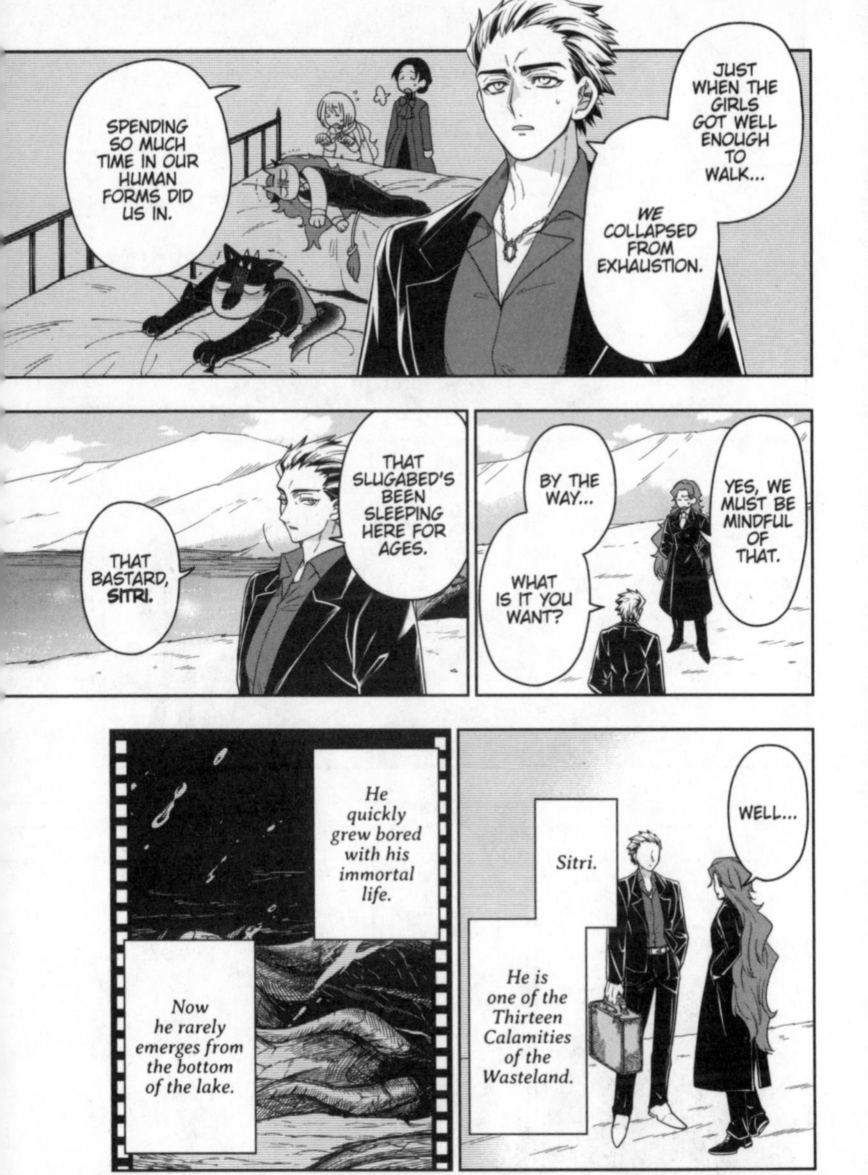
JUST WHEN THE GIRLS GOT WELL ENOUGH TO WALK...
WE COLLAPSED FROM EXHAUSTION.
SPENDING SO MUCH TIME IN OUR HUMAN FORMS DID US IN.
YES, WE MUST BE MINDFUL OF THAT.
BY THE WAY...
WHAT IS IT YOU WANT?
THAT SLUGABED'S BEEN SLEEPING HERE FOR AGES.
THAT BASTARD, SITRI.
WELL...
Sitri.
He is one of the Thirteen Calamities of the Wasteland.
He quickly grew bored with his immortal life.
Now he rarely emerges from the bottom of the lake.

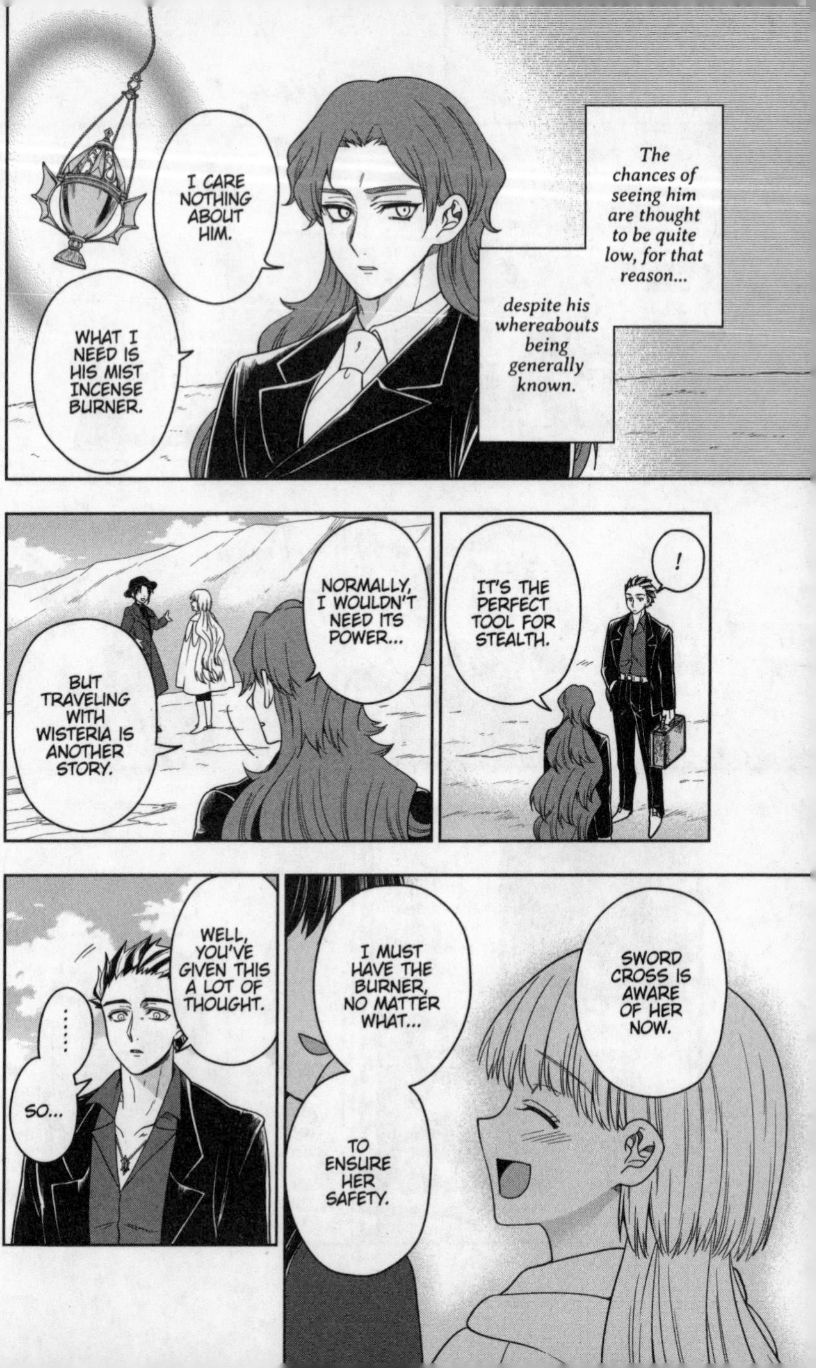

The chances of seeing him are thought to be quite low, for that reason...
despite his whereabouts being generally known.
I CARE NOTHING ABOUT HIM.
WHAT I NEED IS HIS MIST INCENSE BURNER.
!
IT'S THE PERFECT TOOL FOR STEALTH.
NORMALLY, I WOULDN'T NEED ITS POWER...
BUT TRAVELING WITH WISTERIA IS ANOTHER STORY.
SWORD CROSS IS AWARE OF HER NOW.
I MUST HAVE THE BURNER, NO MATTER WHAT...
TO ENSURE HER SAFETY.
WELL, YOU'VE GIVEN THIS A LOT OF THOUGHT.
......
SO...

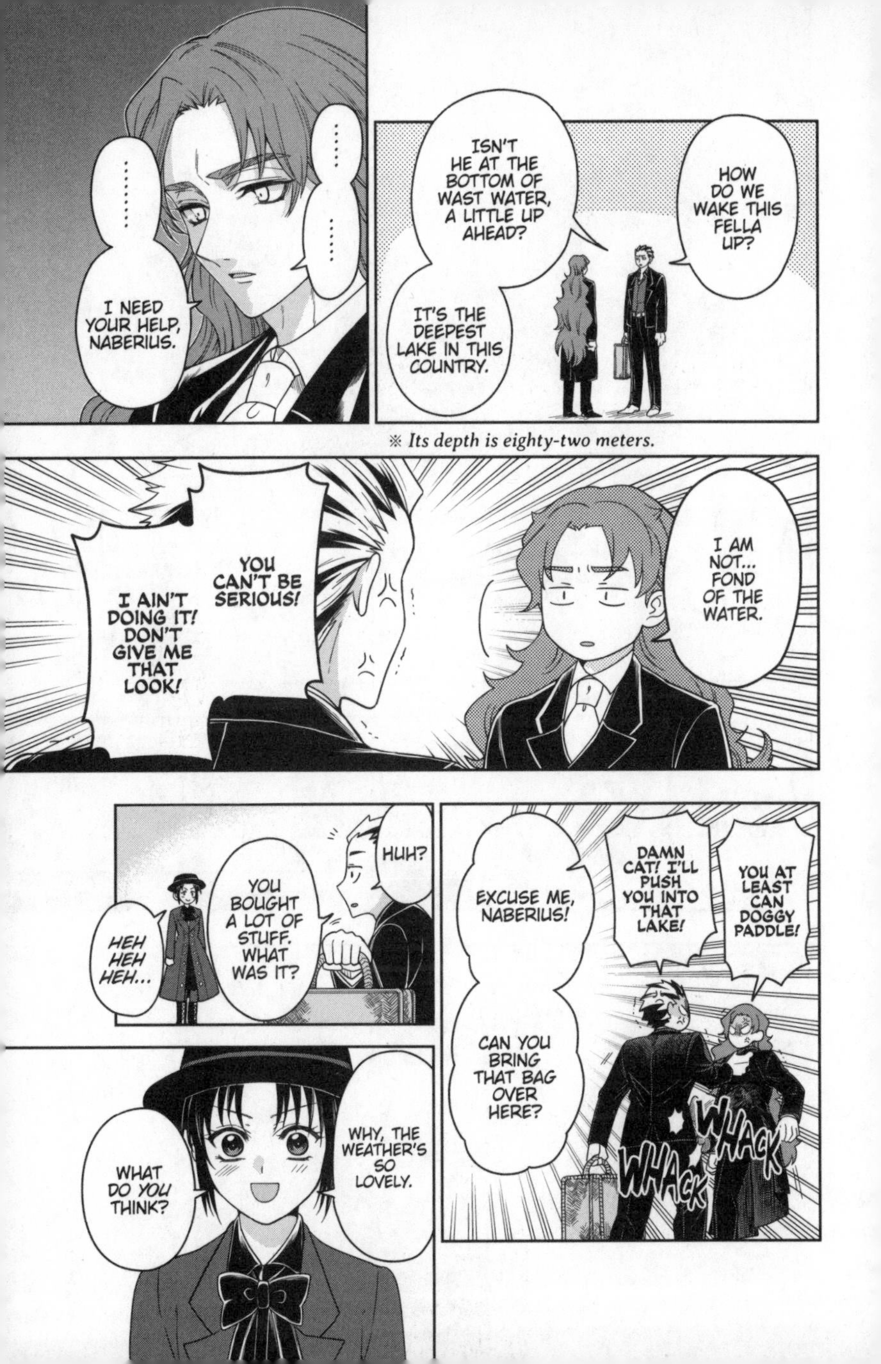
HOW DO WE WAKE THIS FELLA UP?
ISN'T HE AT THE BOTTOM OF WAST WATER, A LITTLE UP AHEAD?
IT'S THE DEEPEST LAKE IN THIS COUNTRY.
......
......
I NEED YOUR HELP, NABERIUS.
※ *Its depth is eighty-two meters.*
I AM NOT... FOND OF THE WATER.
YOU CAN'T BE SERIOUS!
I AIN'T DOING IT! DON'T GIVE ME THAT LOOK!
YOU AT LEAST CAN DOGGY PADDLE!
DAMN CAT! I'LL PUSH YOU INTO THAT LAKE!
EXCUSE ME, NABERIUS!
CAN YOU BRING THAT BAG OVER HERE?
WHACK
WHACK
HUH?
YOU BOUGHT A LOT OF STUFF. WHAT WAS IT?
HEH HEH HEH...
WHY, THE WEATHER'S SO LOVELY.
WHAT DO YOU THINK?

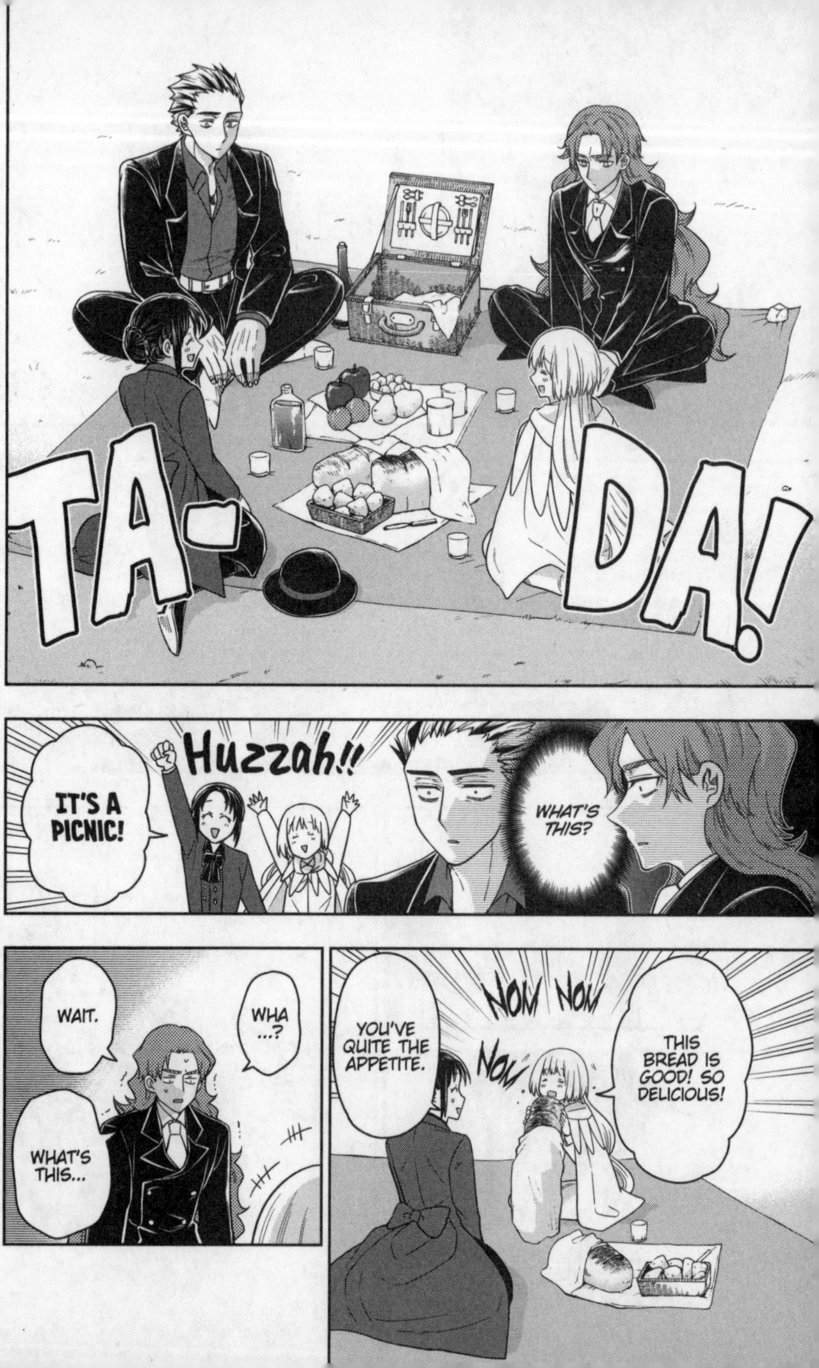
TA-DA!
WHAT'S THIS?
Huzzah!!
IT'S A PICNIC!
THIS BREAD IS GOOD! SO DELICIOUS!
NOM NOM
NOM
YOU'VE QUITE THE APPETITE.
WHA ...?
WAIT.
WHAT'S THIS...

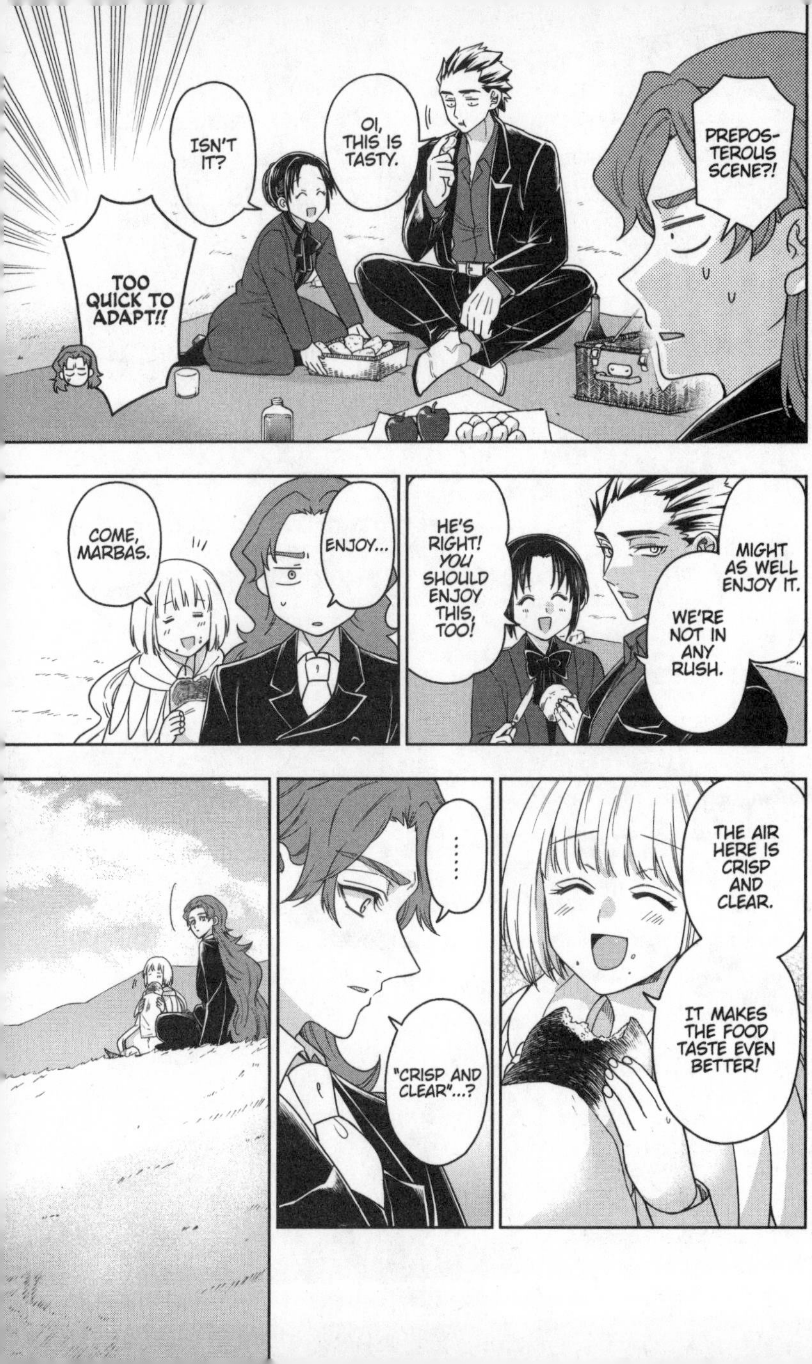
PREPOSTEROUS SCENE?!
OI, THIS IS TASTY.
ISN'T IT?
TOO QUICK TO ADAPT!!
MIGHT AS WELL ENJOY IT.
WE'RE NOT IN ANY RUSH.
HE'S RIGHT! *YOU* SHOULD ENJOY THIS, TOO!
ENJOY...
COME, MARBAS.
THE AIR HERE IS CRISP AND CLEAR.
IT MAKES THE FOOD TASTE EVEN BETTER!
......
"CRISP AND CLEAR"...?

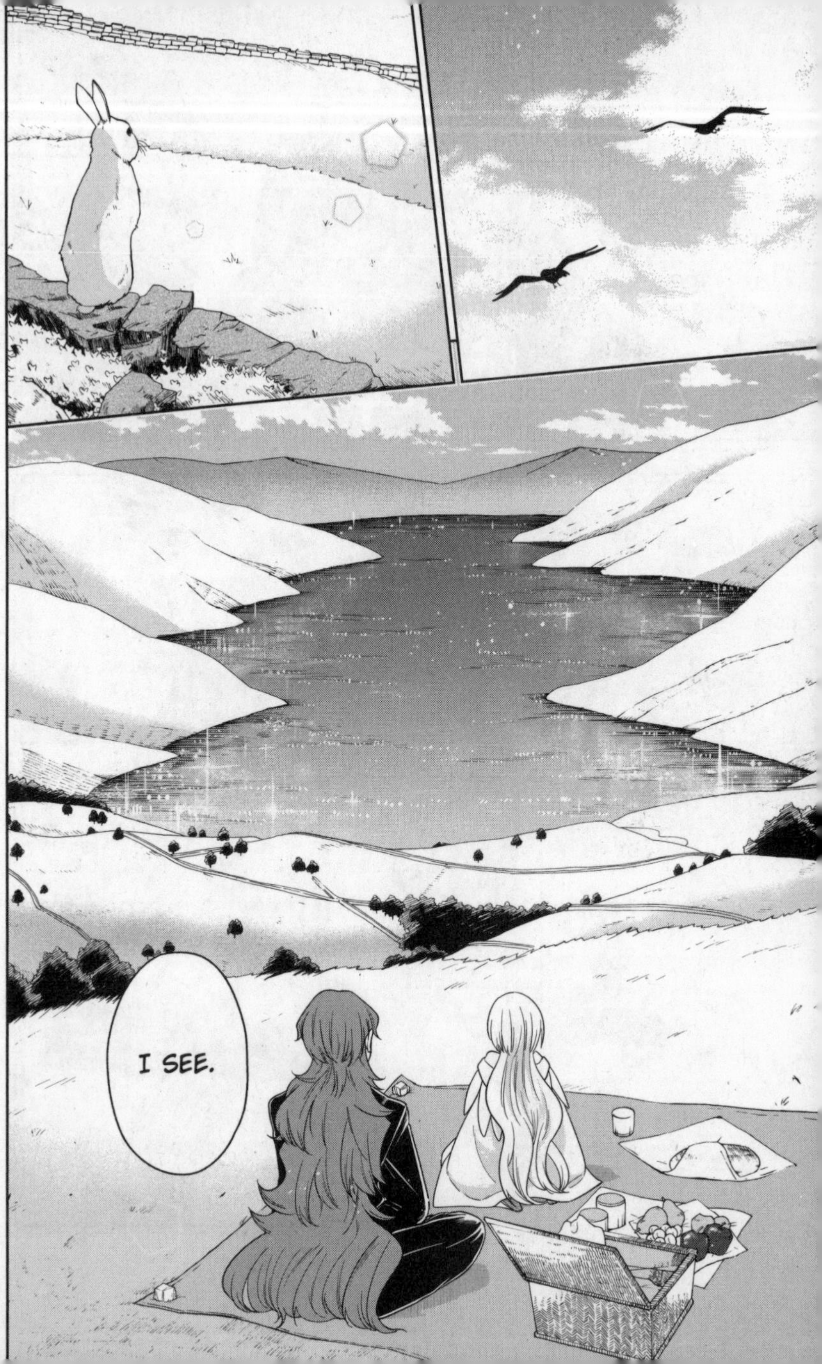
I SEE.

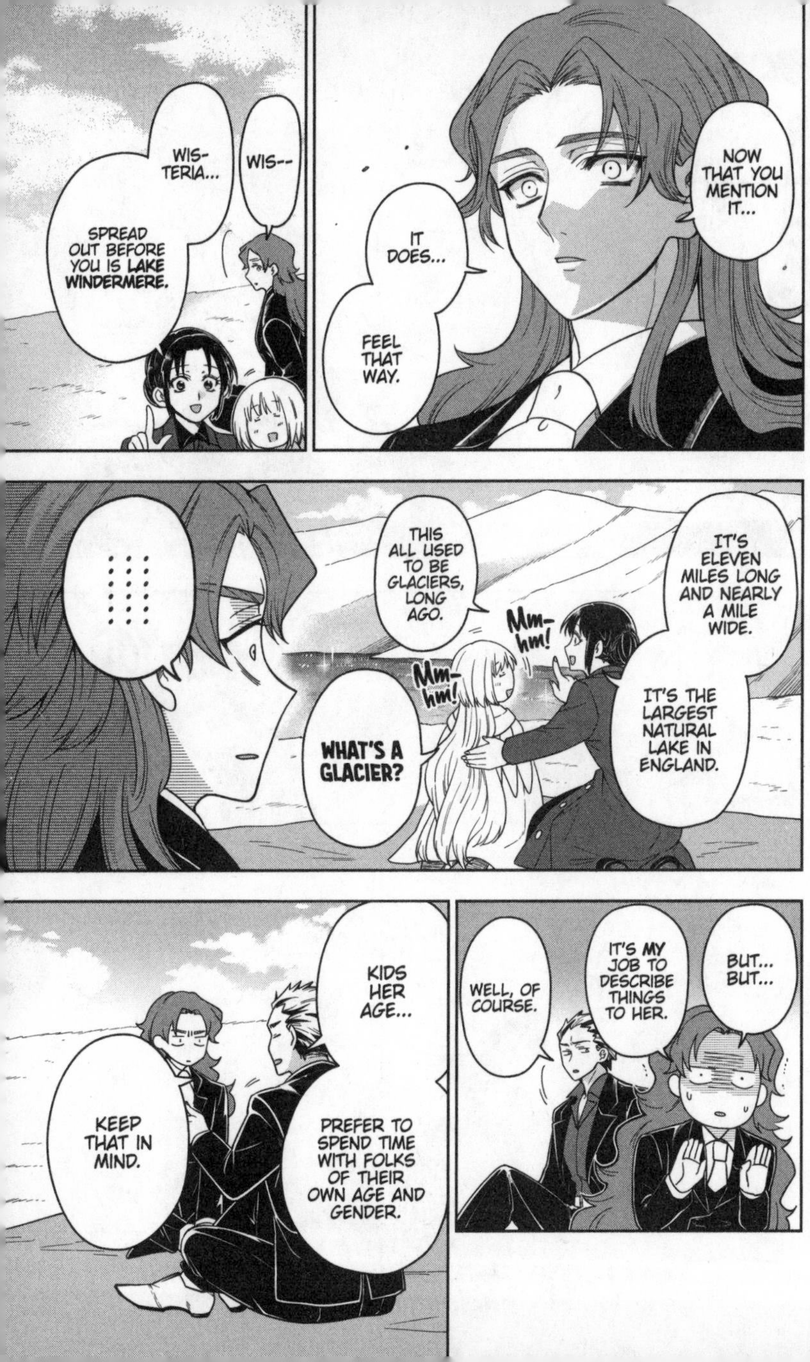
NOW THAT YOU MENTION IT...
IT DOES... FEEL THAT WAY.
WIS--
WIS-TERIA...
SPREAD OUT BEFORE YOU IS LAKE WINDERMERE.
IT'S ELEVEN MILES LONG AND NEARLY A MILE WIDE.
IT'S THE LARGEST NATURAL LAKE IN ENGLAND.
THIS ALL USED TO BE GLACIERS, LONG AGO.
Mm-hm!
Mm-hm!
WHAT'S A GLACIER?
......
BUT... BUT...
IT'S MY JOB TO DESCRIBE THINGS TO HER.
WELL, OF COURSE.
KIDS HER AGE... PREFER TO SPEND TIME WITH FOLKS OF THEIR OWN AGE AND GENDER.
KEEP THAT IN MIND.

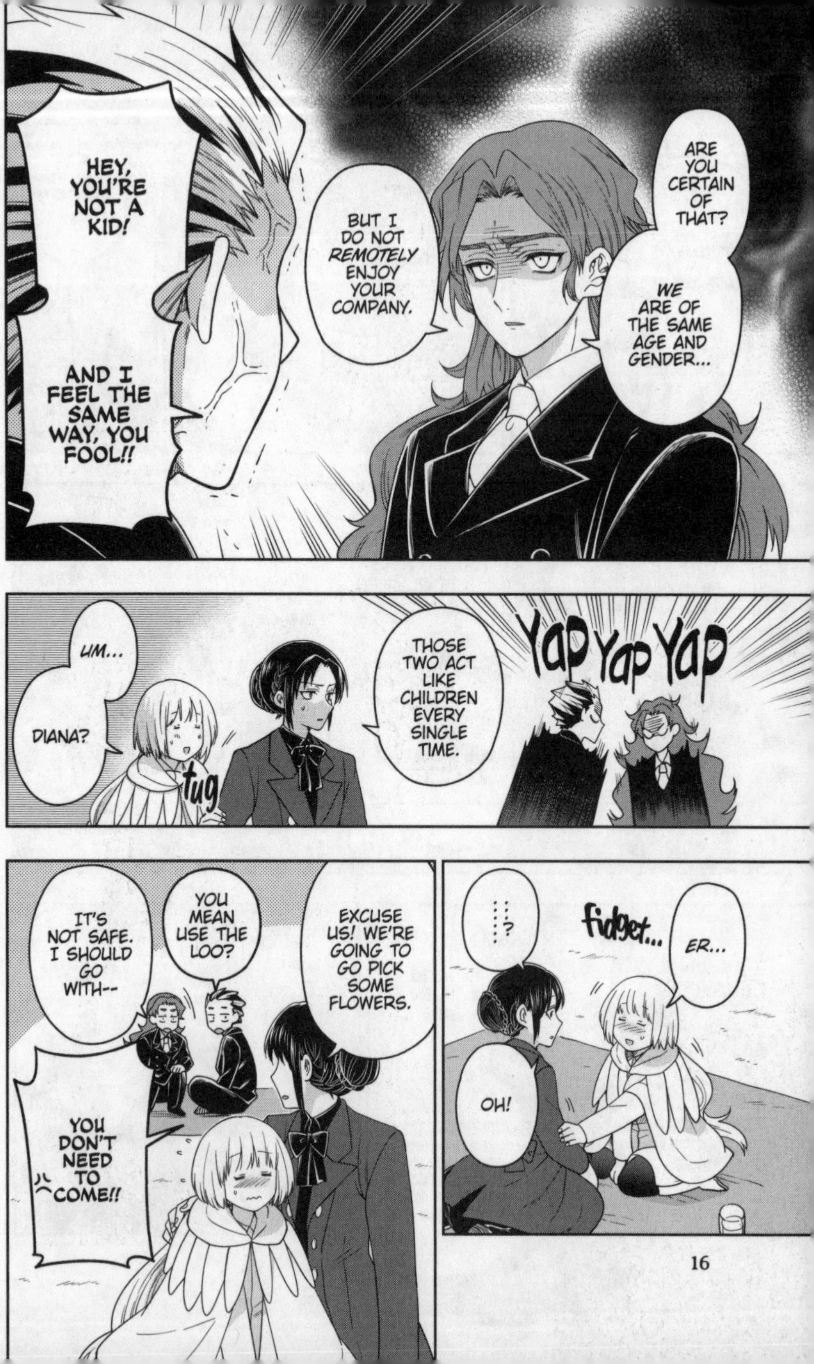
ARE YOU CERTAIN OF THAT?
WE ARE OF THE SAME AGE AND GENDER...
BUT I DO NOT REMOTELY ENJOY YOUR COMPANY.
HEY, YOU'RE NOT A KID!
AND I FEEL THE SAME WAY, YOU FOOL!!
Yap Yap Yap
THOSE TWO ACT LIKE CHILDREN EVERY SINGLE TIME.
tug
UM...
DIANA?
ER...
fidget...
...?
OH!
EXCUSE US! WE'RE GOING TO GO PICK SOME FLOWERS.
YOU MEAN USE THE LOO?
IT'S NOT SAFE. I SHOULD GO WITH--
YOU DON'T NEED TO COME!!

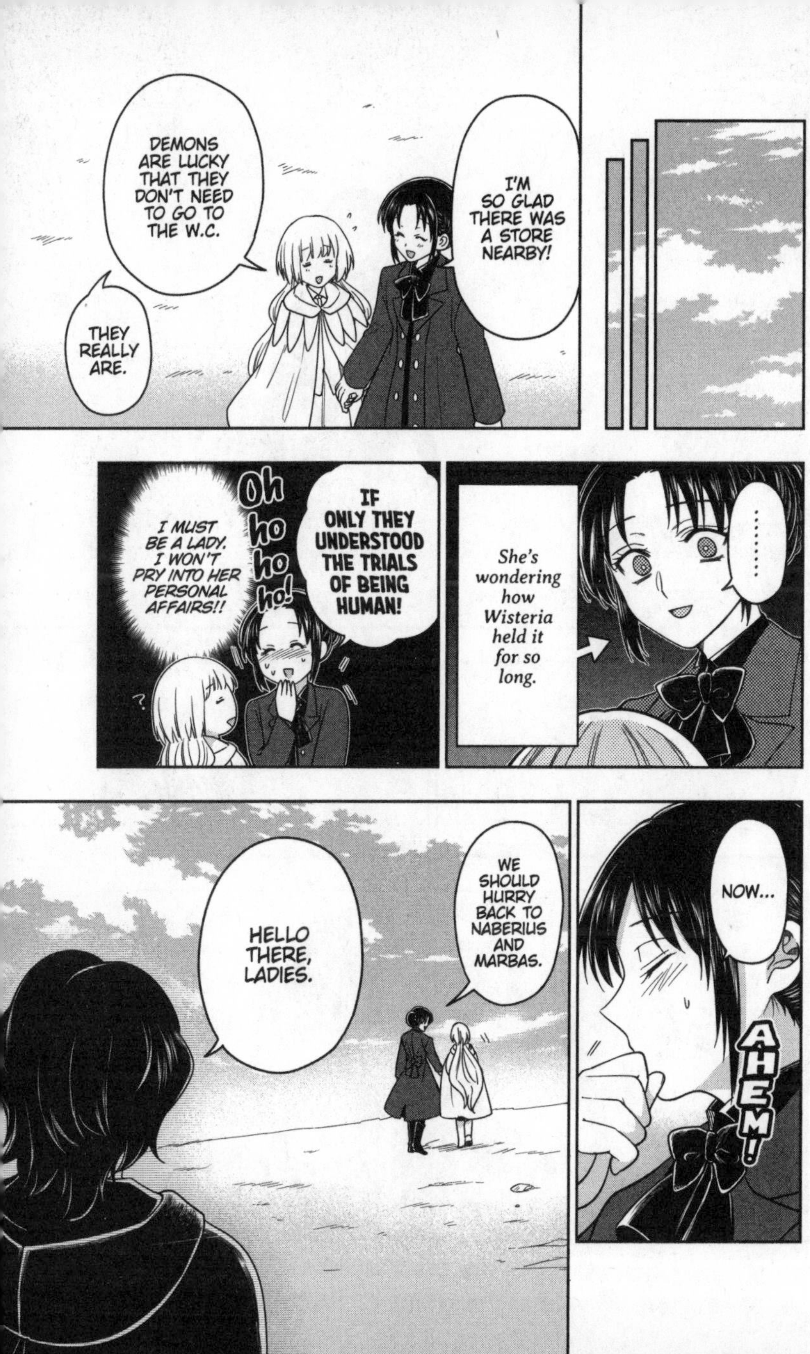
I'M SO GLAD THERE WAS A STORE NEARBY!
DEMONS ARE LUCKY THAT THEY DON'T NEED TO GO TO THE W.C.
THEY REALLY ARE.
......
She's wondering how Wisteria held it for so long.
IF ONLY THEY UNDERSTOOD THE TRIALS OF BEING HUMAN!
Oh ho ho ho!
I MUST BE A LADY. I WON'T PRY INTO HER PERSONAL AFFAIRS!!
?
NOW...
AHEM!
WE SHOULD HURRY BACK TO NABERIUS AND MARBAS.
HELLO THERE, LADIES.

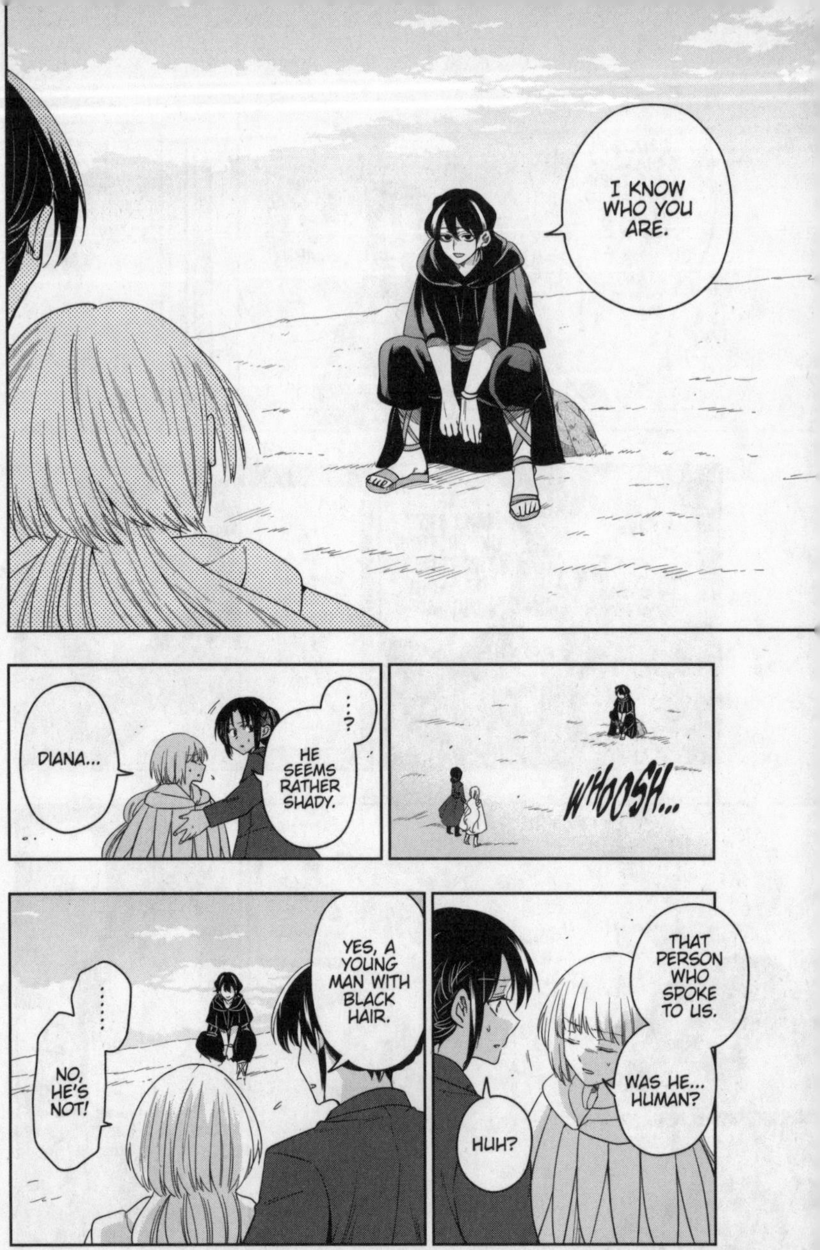
I KNOW WHO YOU ARE.
WHOOSH...
...? HE SEEMS RATHER SHADY.
DIANA...
THAT PERSON WHO SPOKE TO US.
WAS HE... HUMAN?
HUH?
YES, A YOUNG MAN WITH BLACK HAIR.
......
NO, HE'S NOT!

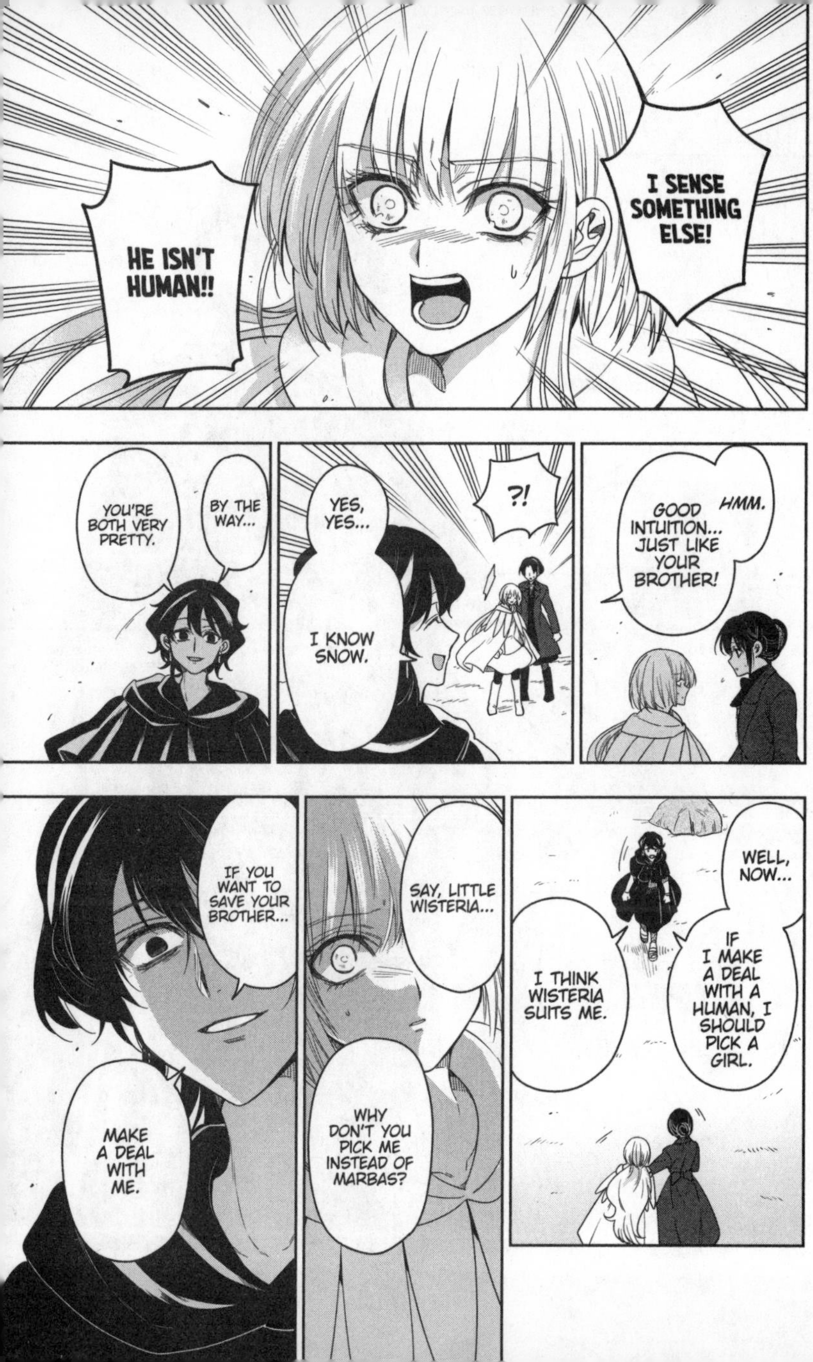
I SENSE SOMETHING ELSE!
HE ISN'T HUMAN!!
HMM.
GOOD INTUITION... JUST LIKE YOUR BROTHER!
?!
YES, YES...
I KNOW SNOW.
BY THE WAY...
YOU'RE BOTH VERY PRETTY.
WELL, NOW...
IF I MAKE A DEAL WITH A HUMAN, I SHOULD PICK A GIRL.
I THINK WISTERIA SUITS ME.
SAY, LITTLE WISTERIA...
WHY DON'T YOU PICK ME INSTEAD OF MARBAS?
IF YOU WANT TO SAVE YOUR BROTHER...
MAKE A DEAL WITH ME.

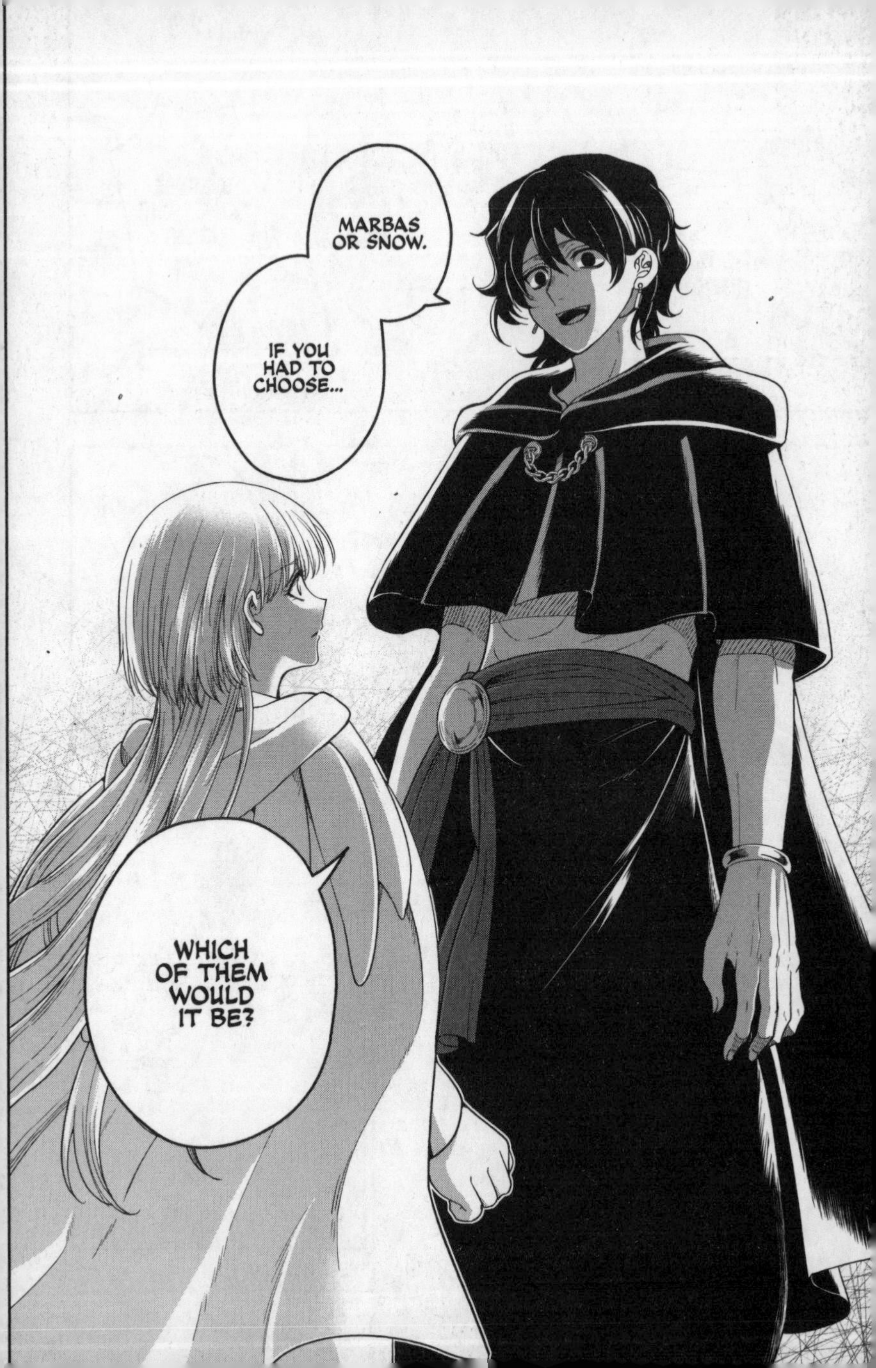
MARBAS OR SNOW.
IF YOU HAD TO CHOOSE...
WHICH OF THEM WOULD IT BE?

⚜Night 39⚜ Invitation to Battle

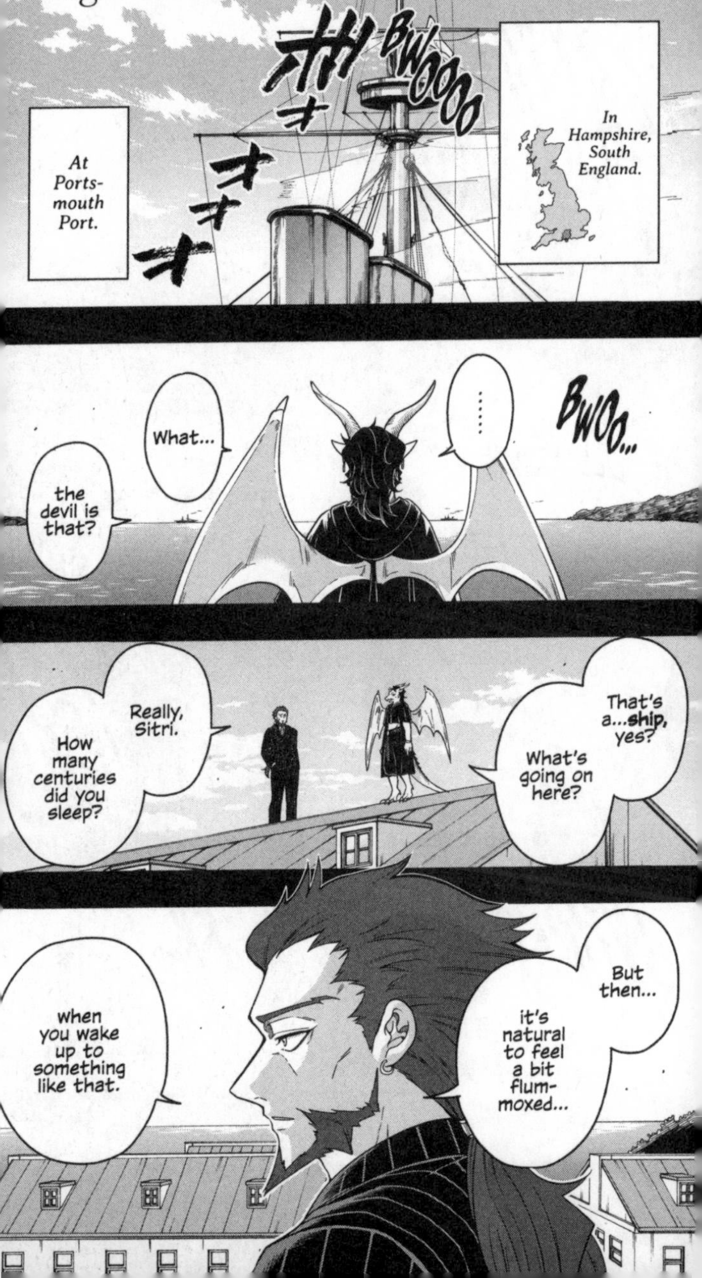

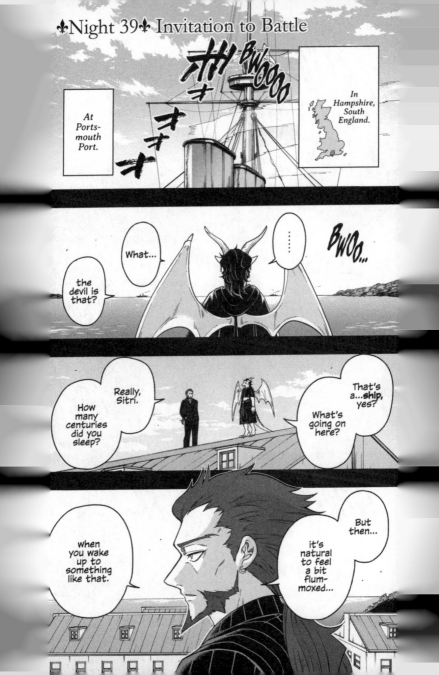

In Hampshire, South England.
BWOOOOO
At Portsmouth Port.
BWOO...
......
What...
the devil is that?
That's a...**ship**, yes?
What's going on here?
Really, Sitri.
How many centuries did you sleep?
But then...
it's natural to feel a bit flum-moxed...
when you wake up to something like that.

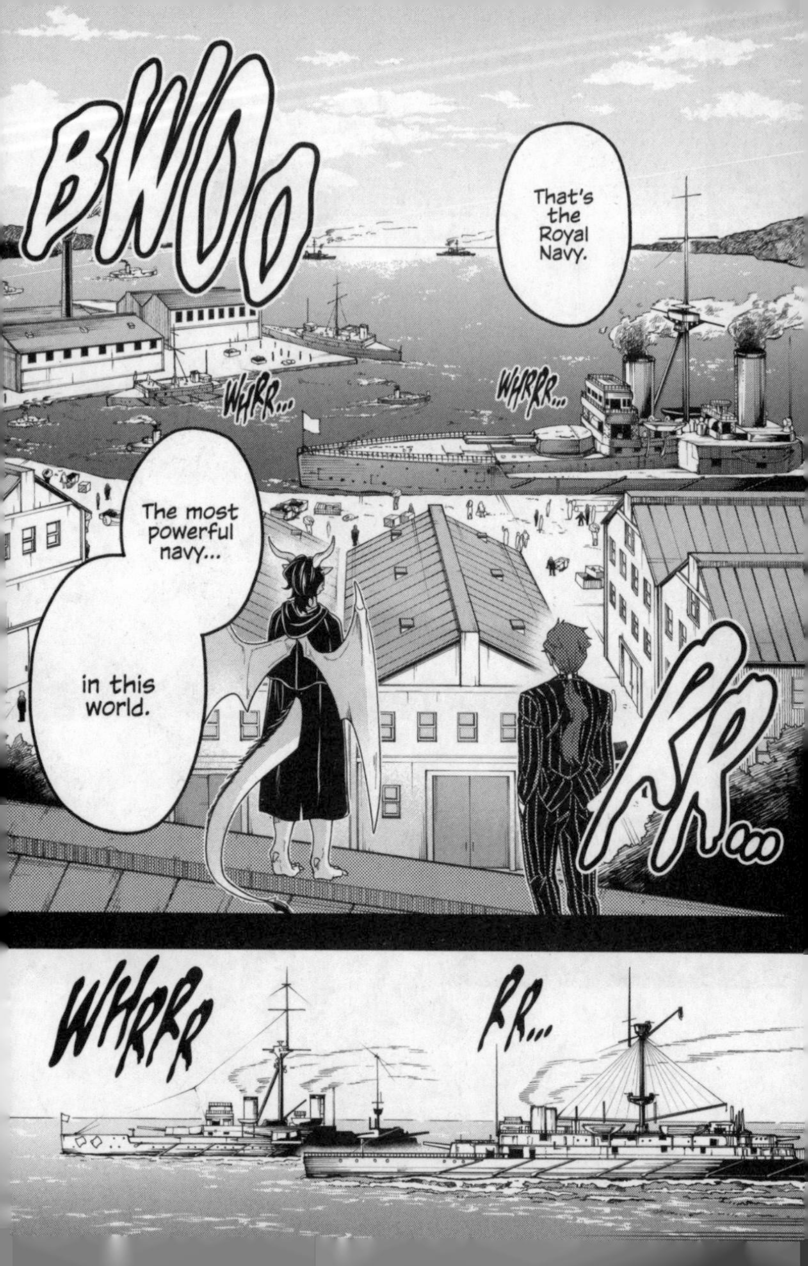
That's the Royal Navy.
BWOO
WHRRR...
WHRR...
The most powerful navy...
in this world.
RR...
RR...
WHRRR

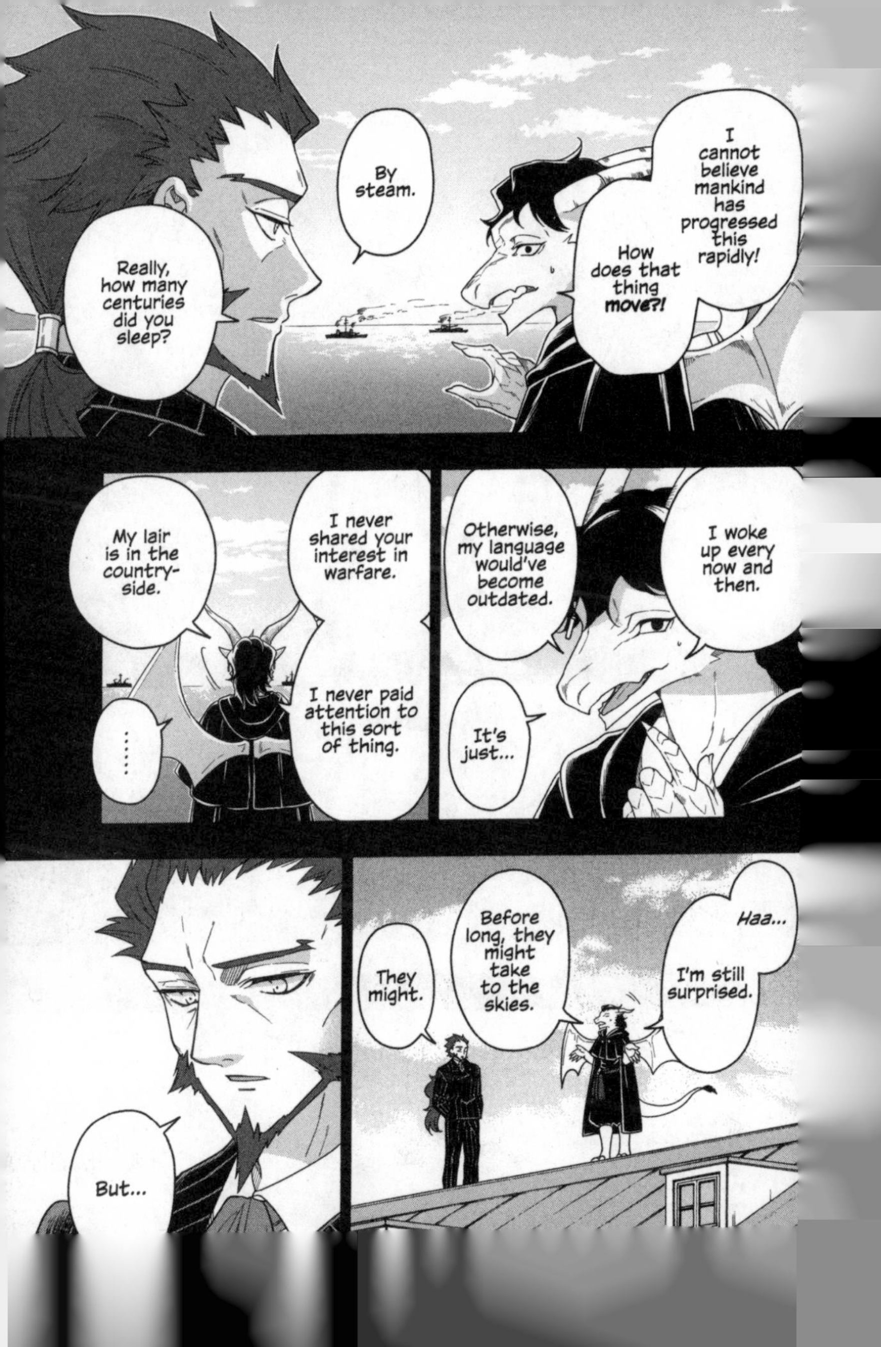
I cannot believe mankind has progressed this rapidly!
How does that thing move?!
By steam.
Really, how many centuries did you sleep?
I woke up every now and then.
Otherwise, my language would've become outdated.
It's just...
I never shared your interest in warfare.
I never paid attention to this sort of thing.
My lair is in the countryside.
......
Haa...
I'm still surprised.
Before long, they might take to the skies.
They might.
But...

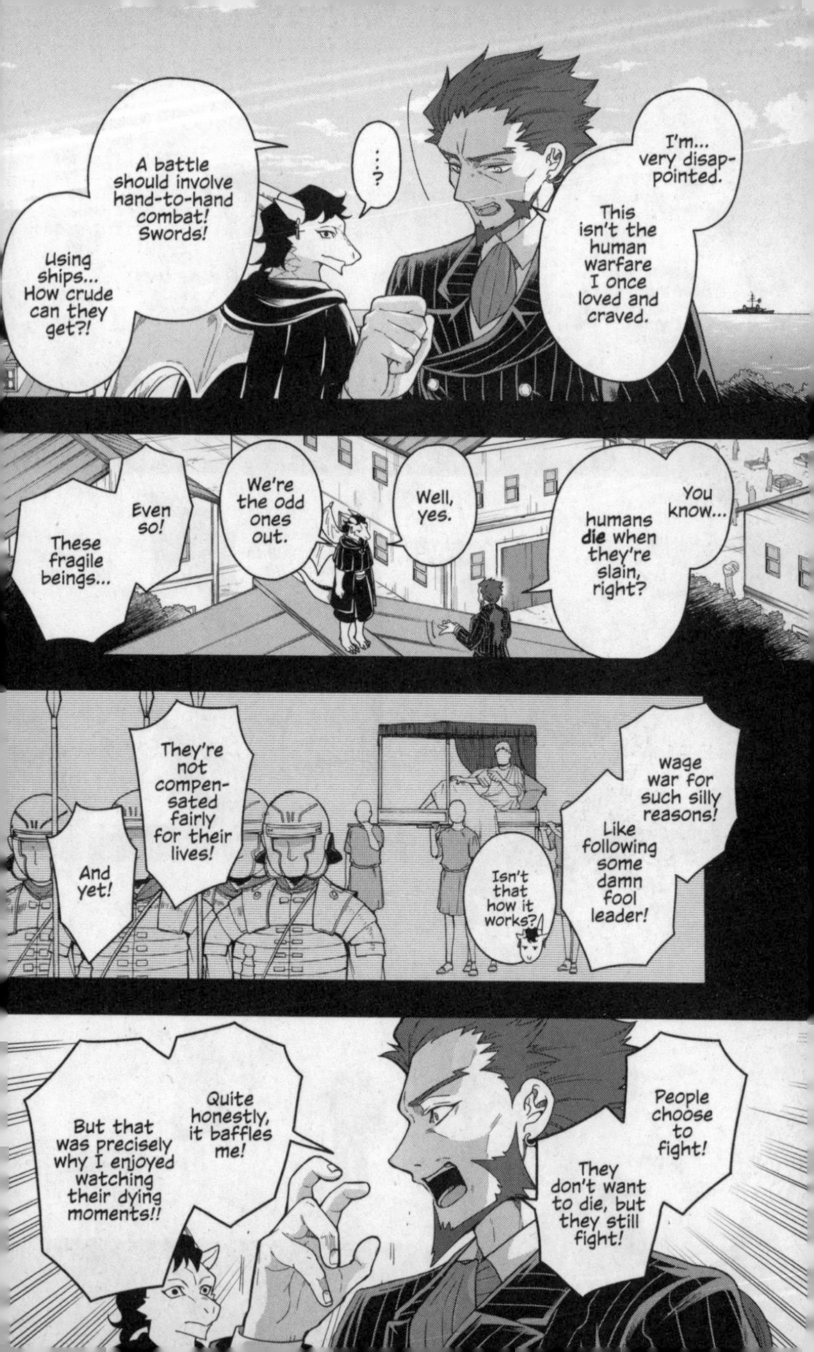
I'm... very disappointed.
This isn't the human warfare I once loved and craved.
...?
A battle should involve hand-to-hand combat! Swords!
Using ships... How crude can they get?!
You know... humans die when they're slain, right?
Well, yes.
We're the odd ones out.
Even so!
These fragile beings...
wage war for such silly reasons!
Like following some damn fool leader!
Isn't that how it works?
They're not compensated fairly for their lives!
And yet!
People choose to fight!
They don't want to die, but they still fight!
Quite honestly, it baffles me!
But that was precisely why I enjoyed watching their dying moments!!

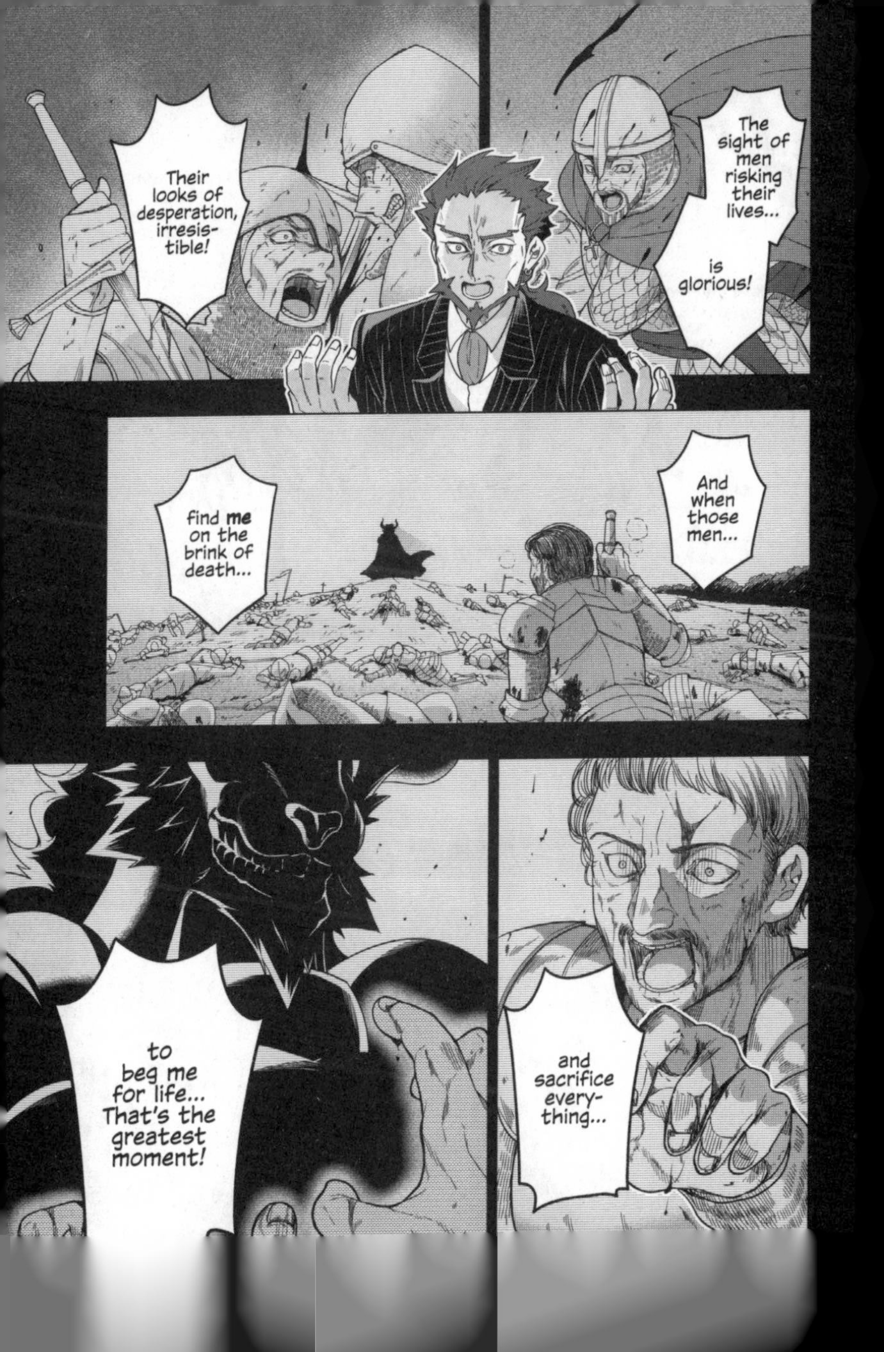
The sight of men risking their lives...
is glorious!
Their looks of desperation, irresistible!
And when those men...
find **me** on the brink of death...
and sacrifice every-thing...
to beg me for life... That's the greatest moment!

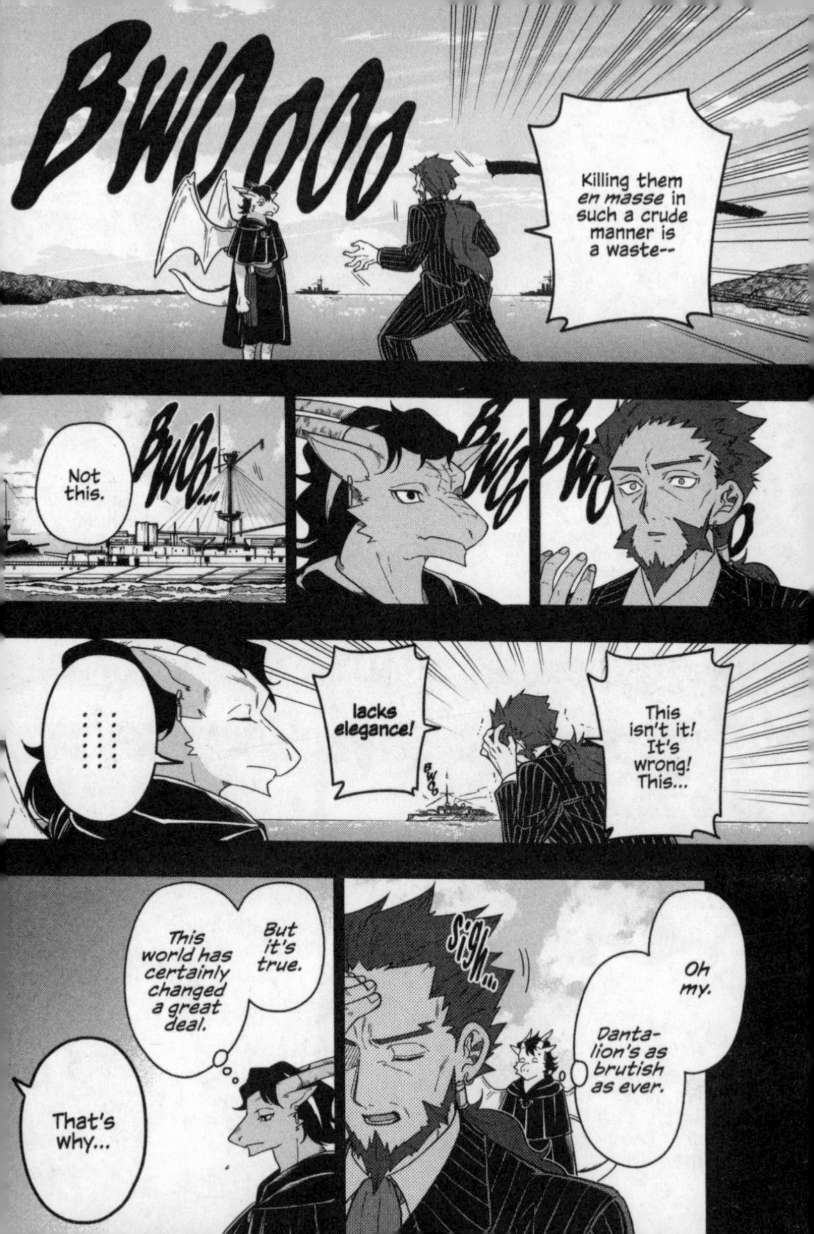
Killing them *en masse* in such a crude manner is a waste--
BWOOOO
BWO
BWO
Not this.
BWO...
This isn't it! It's wrong! This...
lacks elegance!
BWO
......
Oh my.
Dantalion's as brutish as ever.
Sigh...
But it's true.
This world has certainly changed a great deal.
That's why...

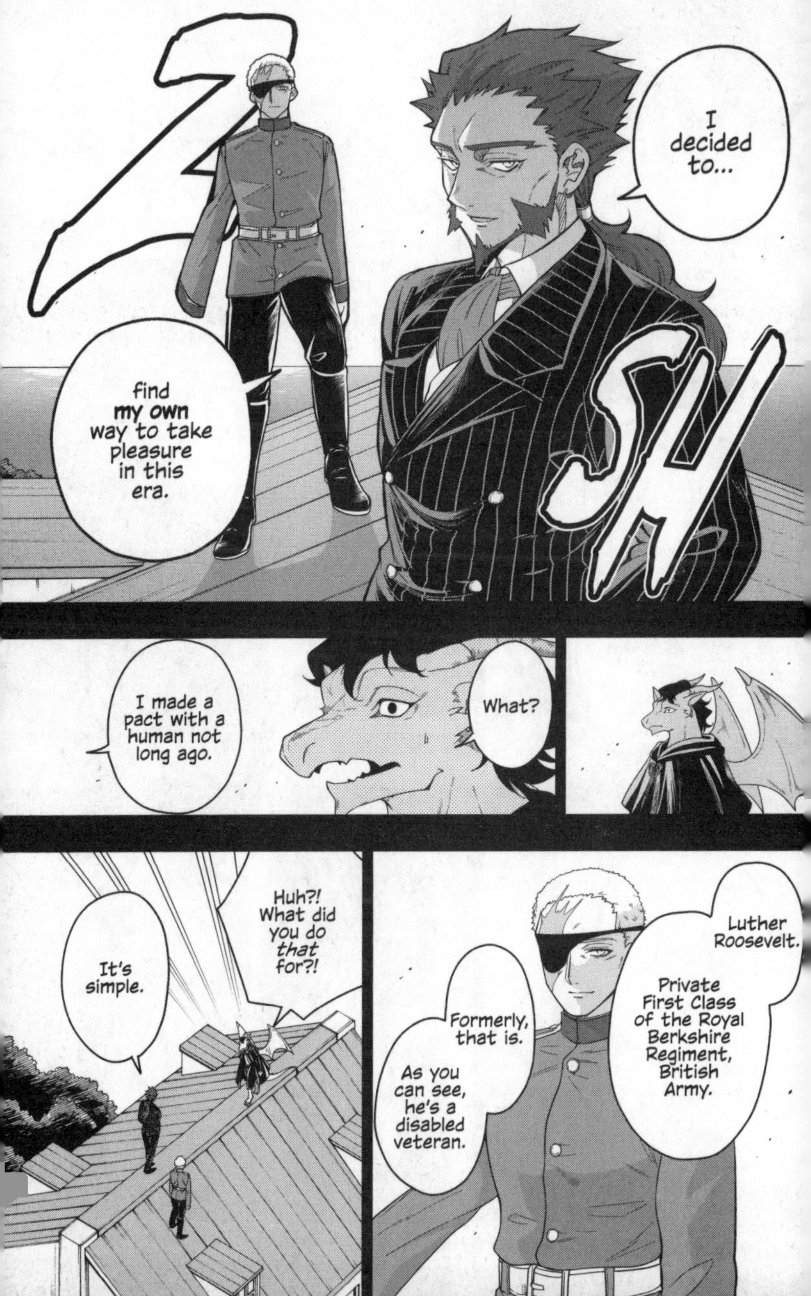
I decided to...
find **my own** way to take pleasure in this era.
SH
What?
I made a pact with a human not long ago.
Luther Roosevelt.
Private First Class of the Royal Berkshire Regiment, British Army.
Formerly, that is.
As you can see, he's a disabled veteran.
Huh?! What did you do *that* for?!
It's simple.

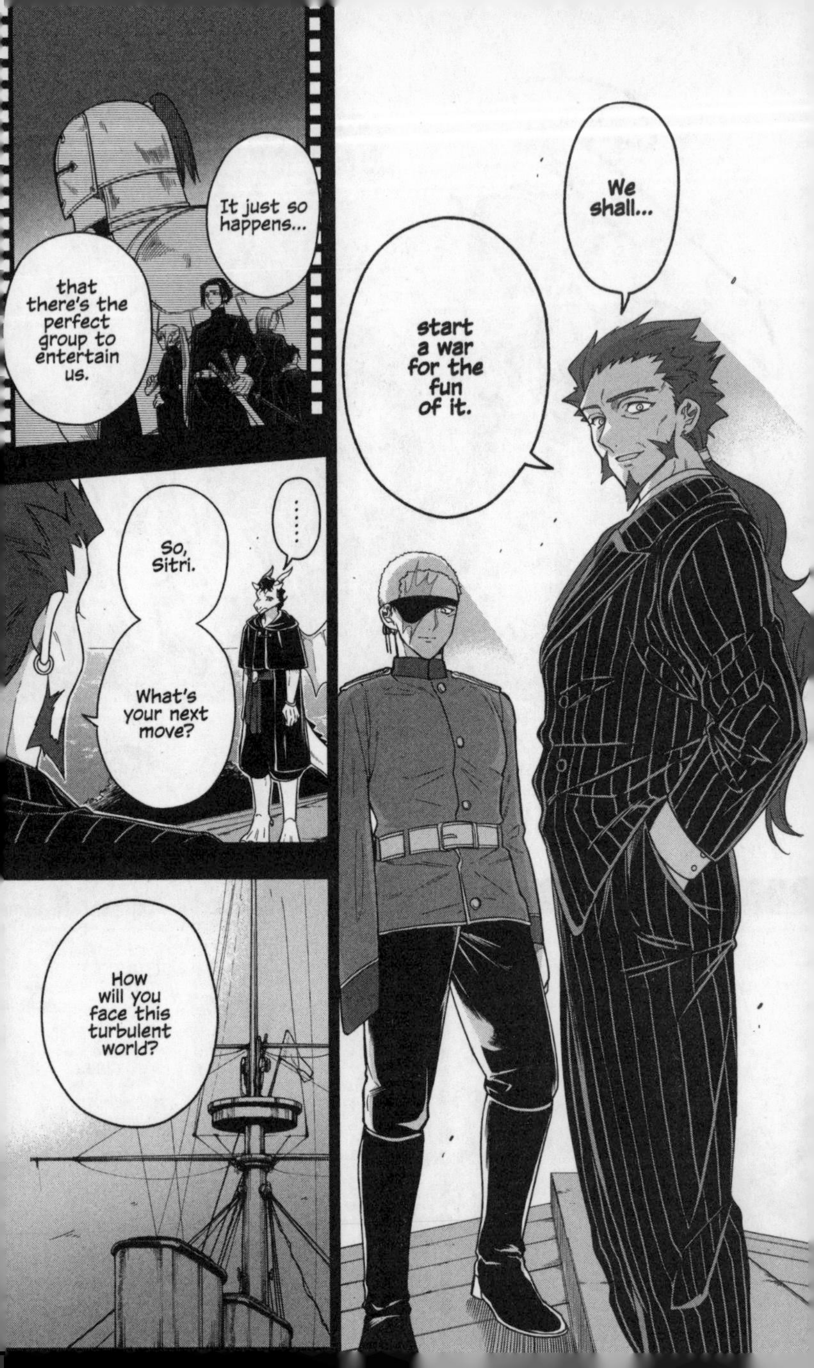
It just so happens...
that there's the perfect group to entertain us.
......
So, Sitri.
What's your next move?
How will you face this turbulent world?
We shall...
start a war for the fun of it.

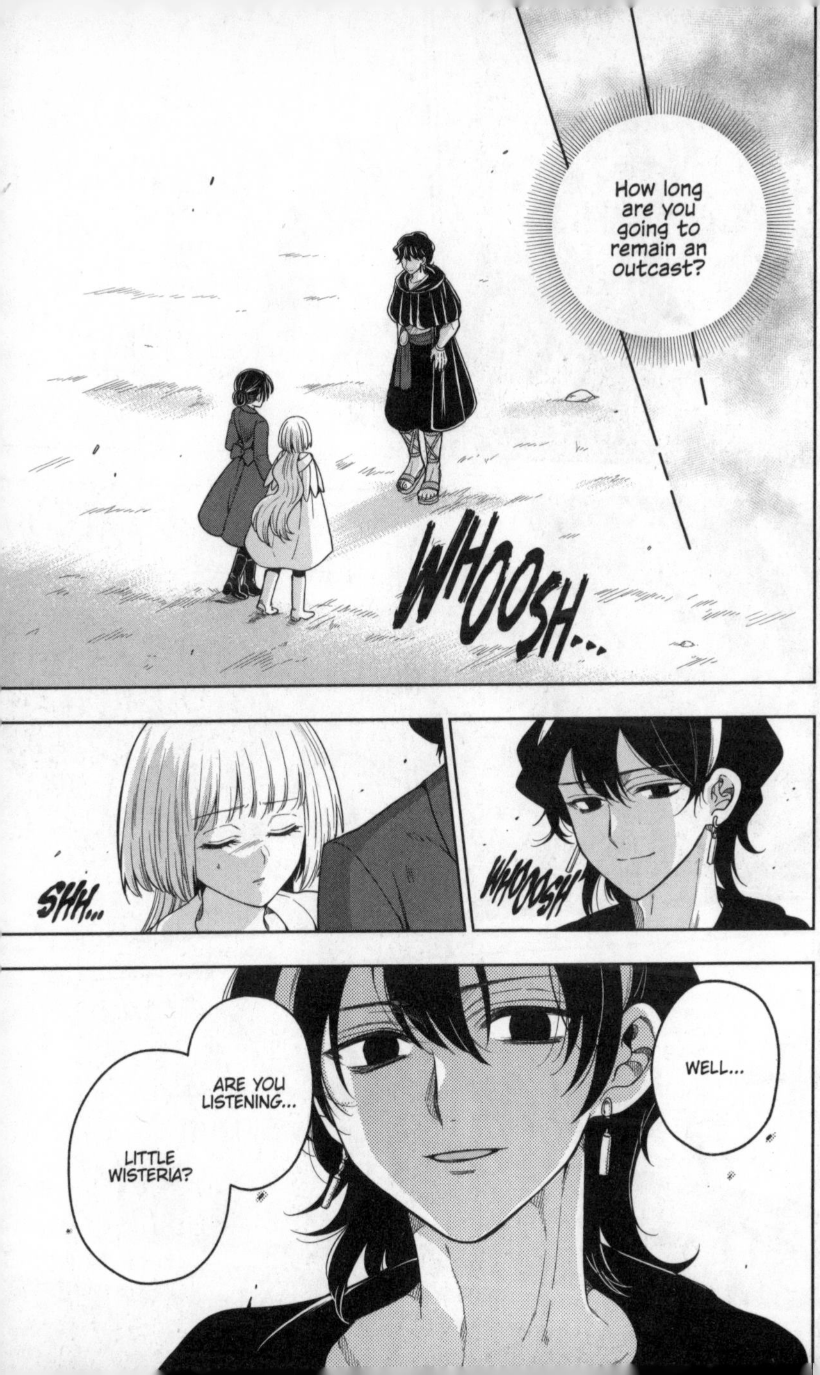
How long are you going to remain an outcast?
WHOOSH...
WHOOOSH
SHH...
WELL...
ARE YOU LISTENING...
LITTLE WISTERIA?

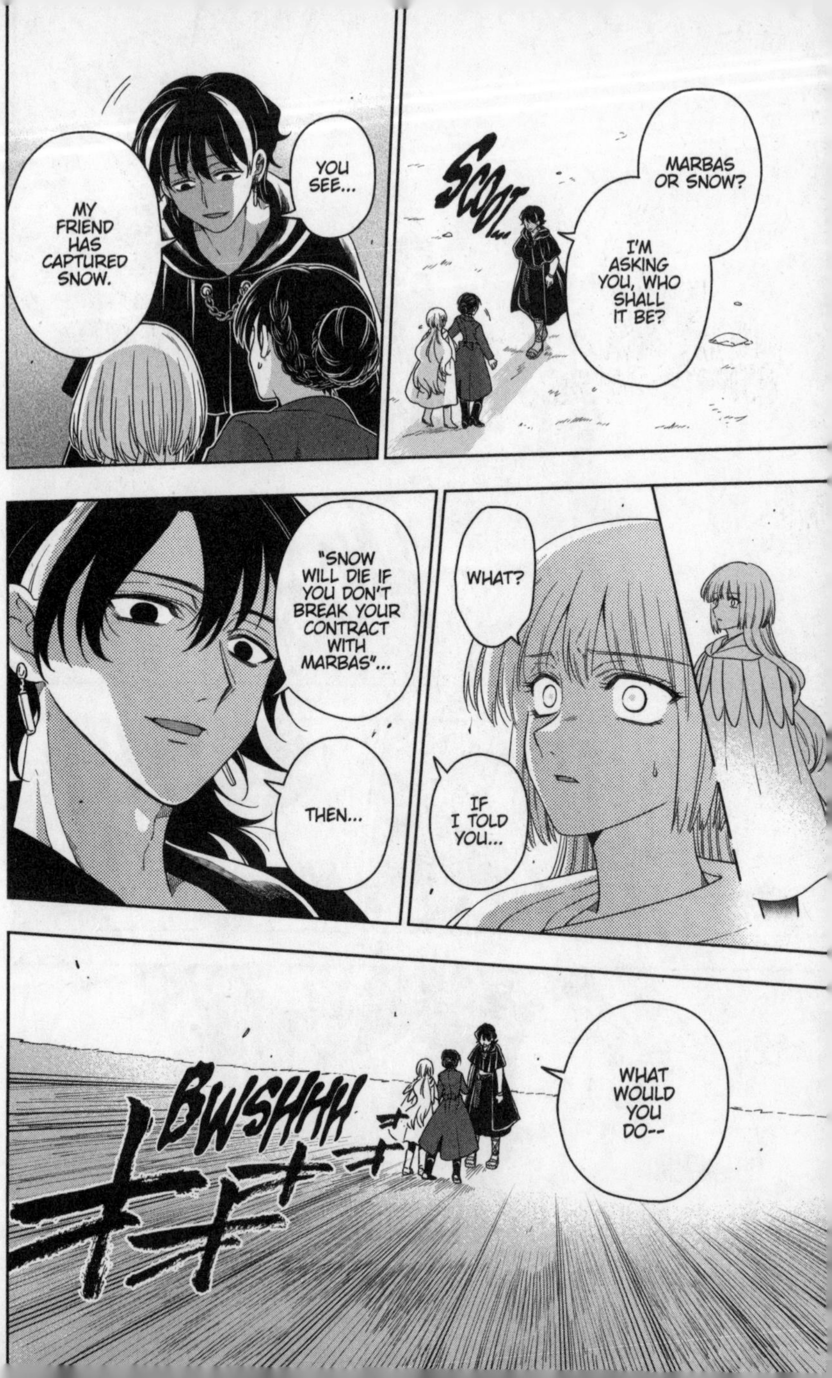
MARBAS OR SNOW?
SCOOT...
I'M ASKING YOU, WHO SHALL IT BE?
YOU SEE...
MY FRIEND HAS CAPTURED SNOW.
WHAT?
IF I TOLD YOU...
"SNOW WILL DIE IF YOU DON'T BREAK YOUR CONTRACT WITH MARBAS"...
THEN...
WHAT WOULD YOU DO--
BWSHHH

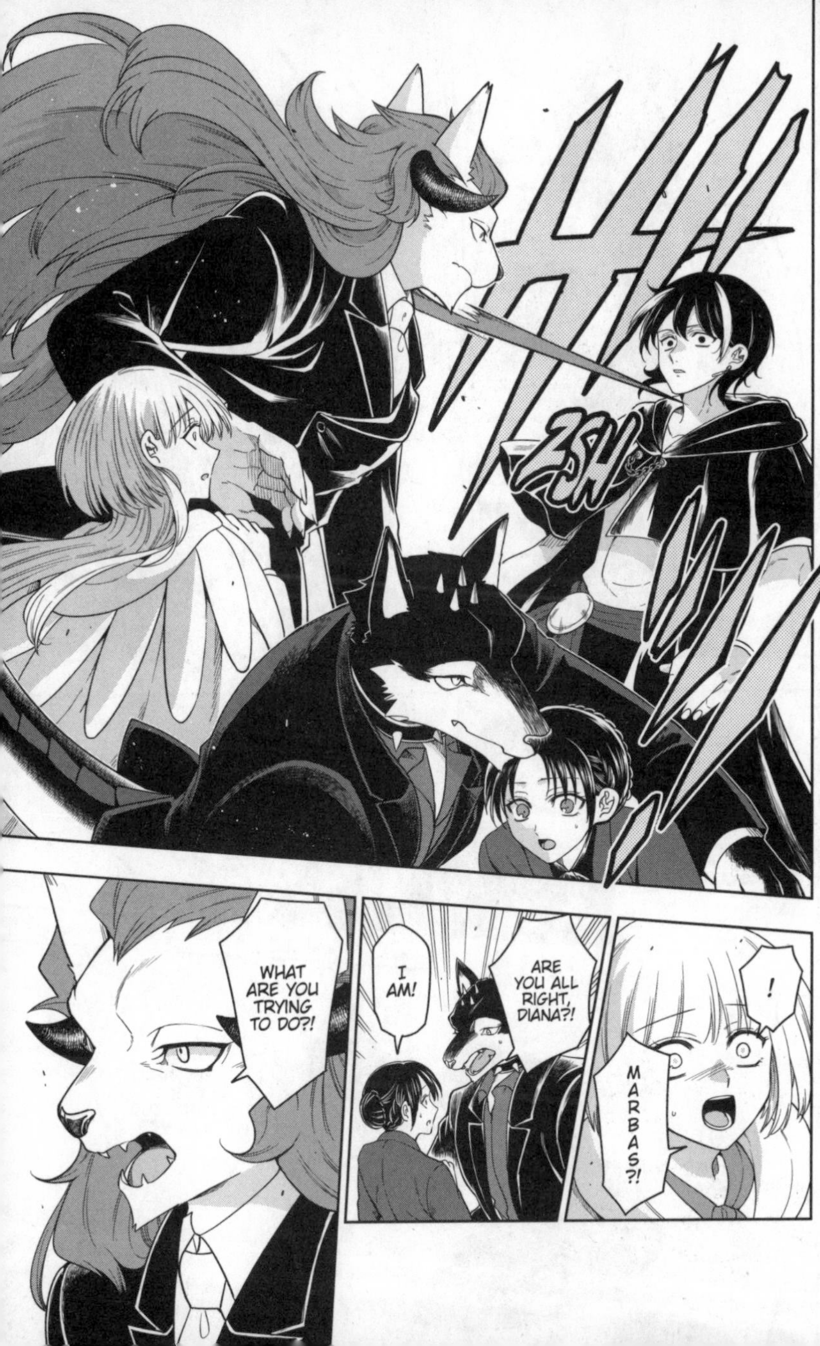
ZSH
!
MARBAS?!
ARE YOU ALL RIGHT, DIANA?!
I AM!
WHAT ARE YOU TRYING TO DO?!

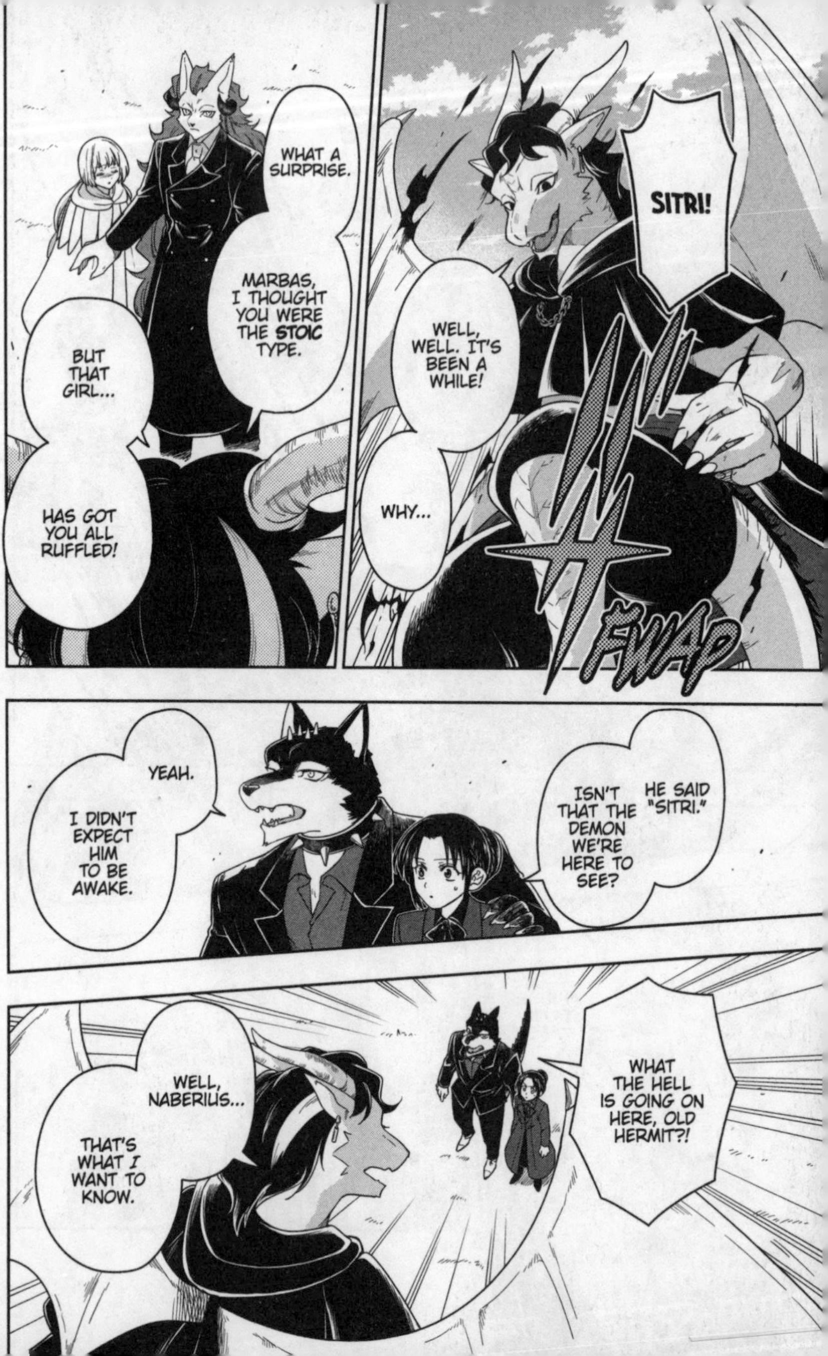
SITRI!
WELL, WELL. IT'S BEEN A WHILE!
WHY...
FWAP
WHAT A SURPRISE.
MARBAS, I THOUGHT YOU WERE THE **STOIC** TYPE.
BUT THAT GIRL...
HAS GOT YOU ALL RUFFLED!
HE SAID "SITRI."
ISN'T THAT THE DEMON WE'RE HERE TO SEE?
YEAH.
I DIDN'T EXPECT HIM TO BE AWAKE.
WHAT THE HELL IS GOING ON HERE, OLD HERMIT?!
WELL, NABERIUS...
THAT'S WHAT I WANT TO KNOW.

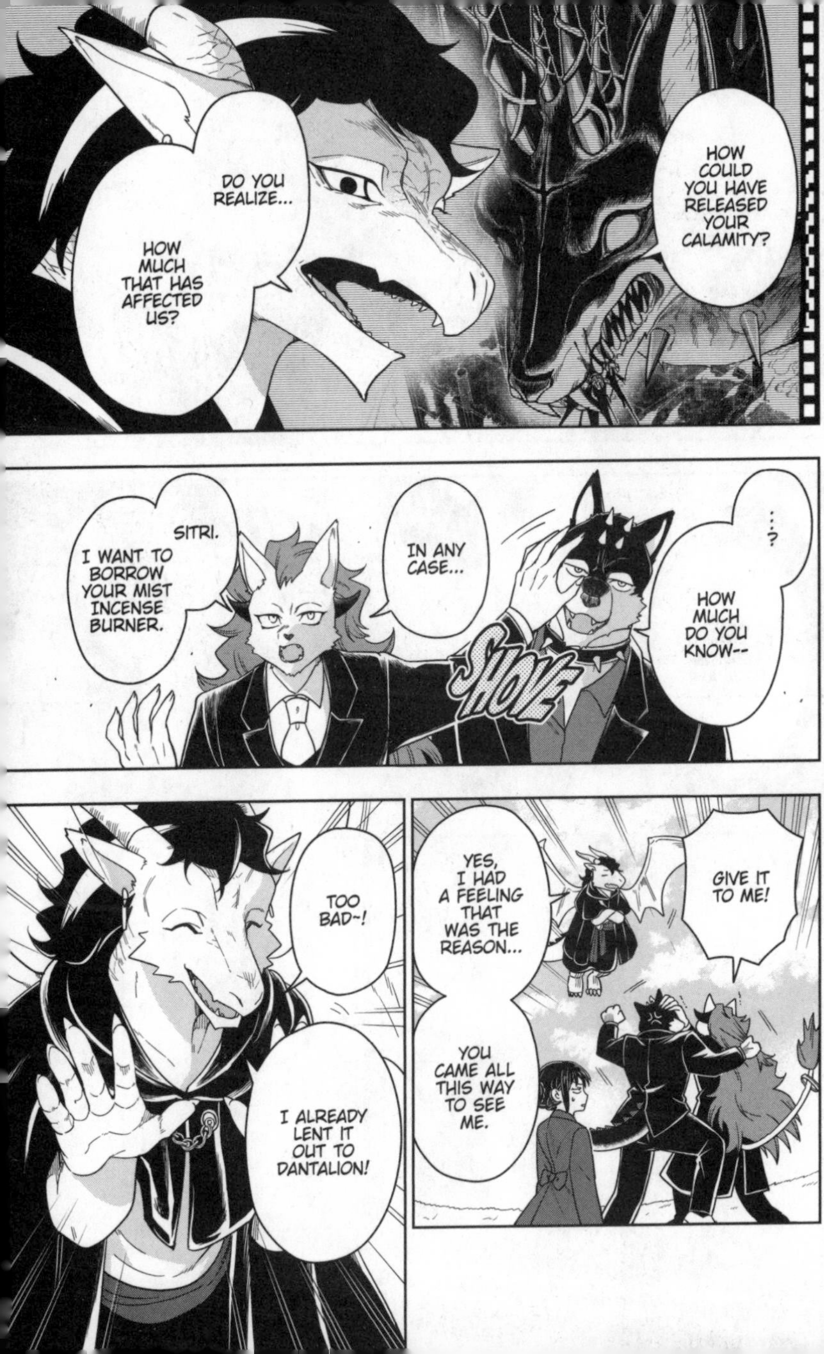
HOW COULD YOU HAVE RELEASED YOUR CALAMITY?
DO YOU REALIZE...
HOW MUCH THAT HAS AFFECTED US?
...?
HOW MUCH DO YOU KNOW--
IN ANY CASE...
SHOVE
SITRI.
I WANT TO BORROW YOUR MIST INCENSE BURNER.
GIVE IT TO ME!
YES, I HAD A FEELING THAT WAS THE REASON...
YOU CAME ALL THIS WAY TO SEE ME.
TOO BAD~!
I ALREADY LENT IT OUT TO DANTALION!

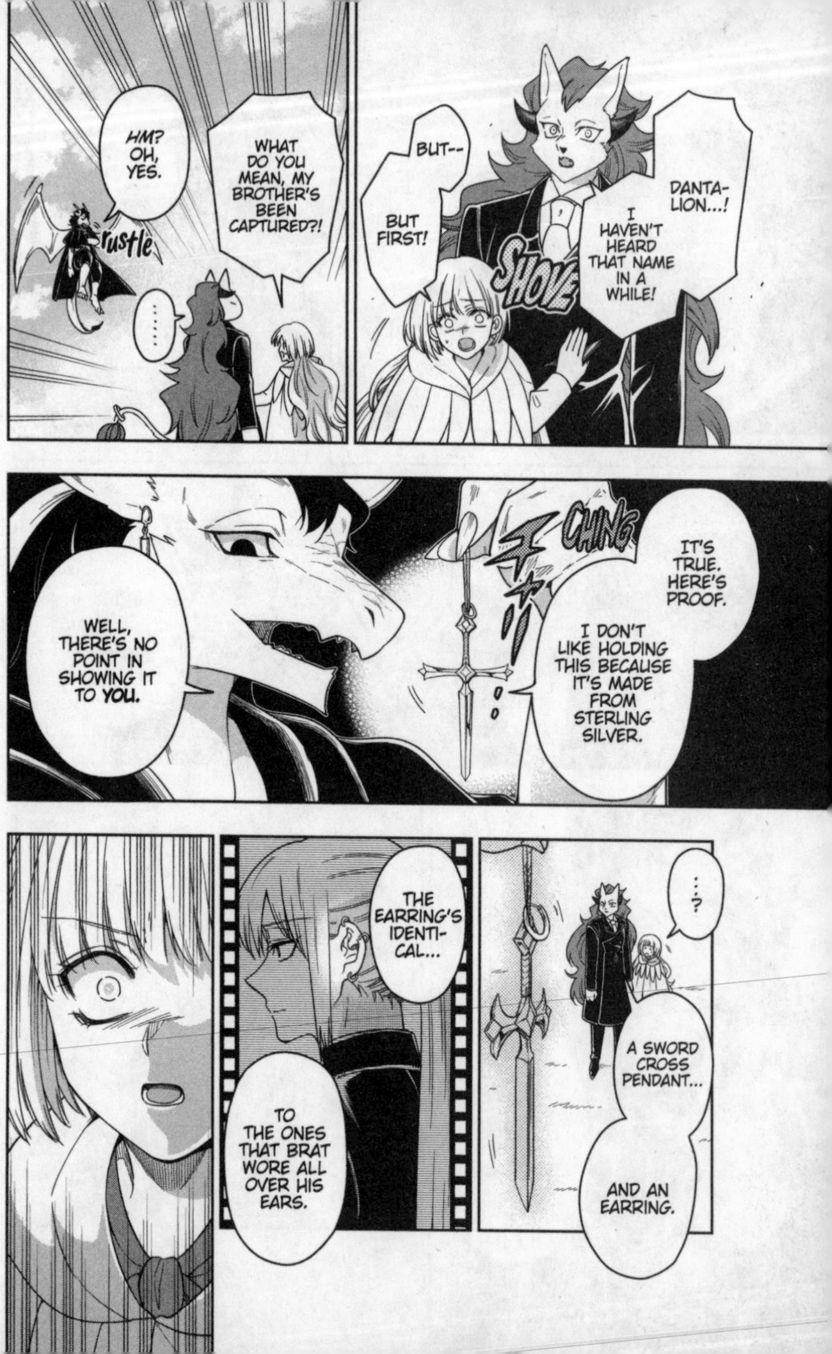
DANTA-LION...!
I HAVEN'T HEARD THAT NAME IN A WHILE!
BUT--
BUT FIRST!
SHOVE
WHAT DO YOU MEAN, MY BROTHER'S BEEN CAPTURED?!
HM? OH, YES.
rustle
......
IT'S TRUE. HERE'S PROOF.
I DON'T LIKE HOLDING THIS BECAUSE IT'S MADE FROM STERLING SILVER.
CHING
WELL, THERE'S NO POINT IN SHOWING IT TO YOU.
...?
A SWORD CROSS PENDANT...
AND AN EARRING.
THE EARRING'S IDENTI-CAL...
TO THE ONES THAT BRAT WORE ALL OVER HIS EARS.

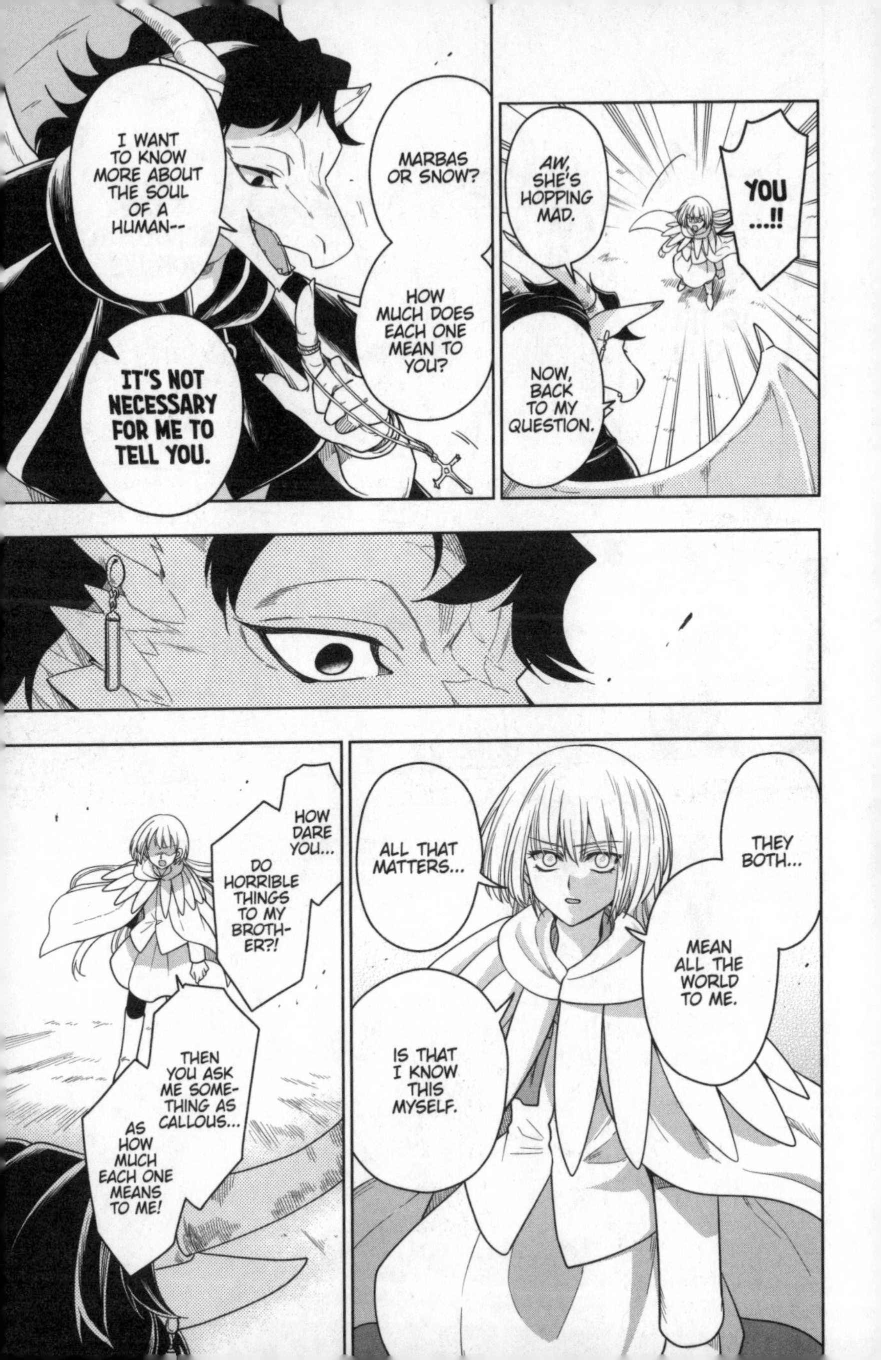
YOU ...!!
AW, SHE'S HOPPING MAD.
NOW, BACK TO MY QUESTION.
MARBAS OR SNOW?
HOW MUCH DOES EACH ONE MEAN TO YOU?
I WANT TO KNOW MORE ABOUT THE SOUL OF A HUMAN--
IT'S NOT NECESSARY FOR ME TO TELL YOU.
THEY BOTH...
MEAN ALL THE WORLD TO ME.
ALL THAT MATTERS...
IS THAT I KNOW THIS MYSELF.
HOW DARE YOU...
DO HORRIBLE THINGS TO MY BROTHER?!
THEN YOU ASK ME SOMETHING AS CALLOUS...
AS HOW MUCH EACH ONE MEANS TO ME!

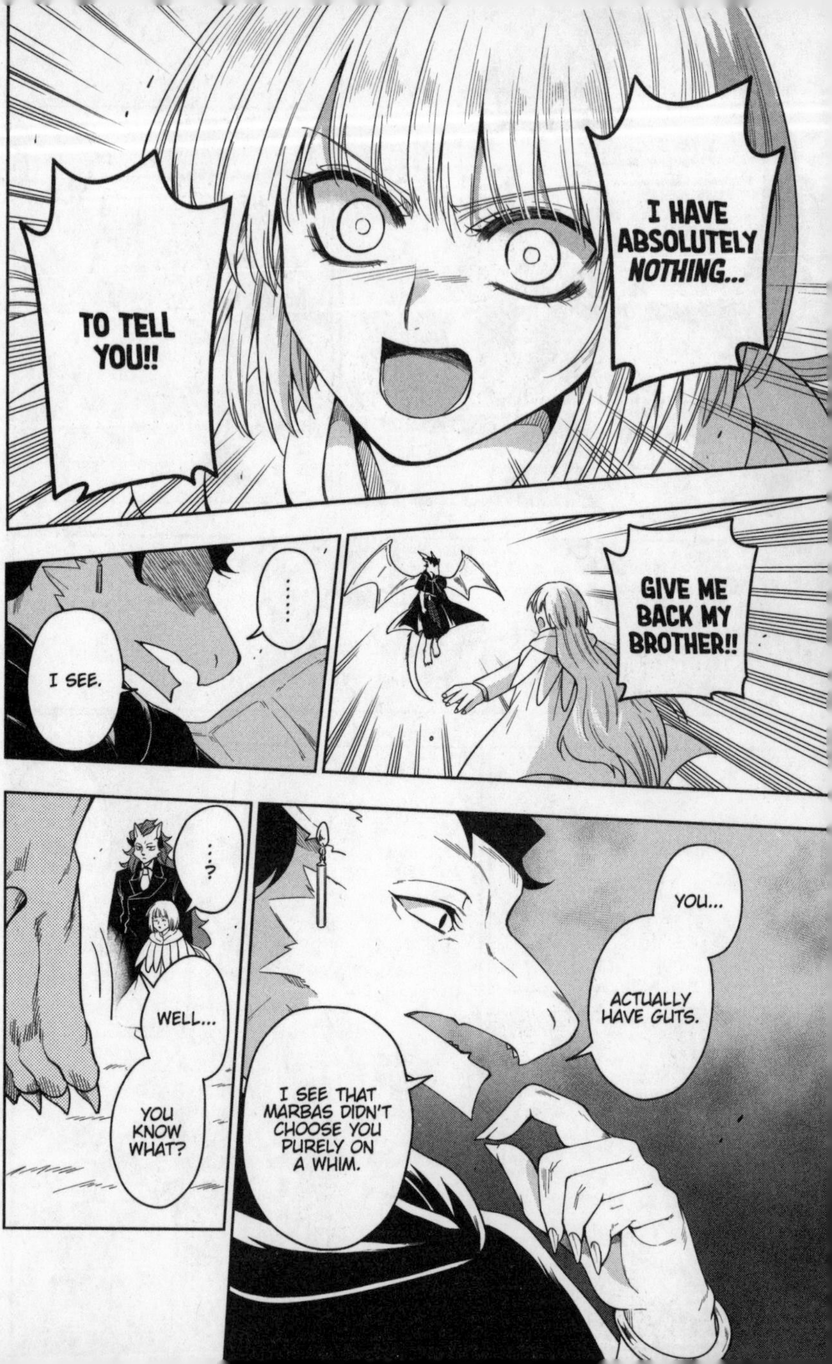
I HAVE ABSOLUTELY *NOTHING*...
TO TELL YOU!!
GIVE ME BACK MY BROTHER!!
......
I SEE.
YOU...
ACTUALLY HAVE GUTS.
I SEE THAT MARBAS DIDN'T CHOOSE YOU PURELY ON A WHIM.
...?
WELL...
YOU KNOW WHAT?

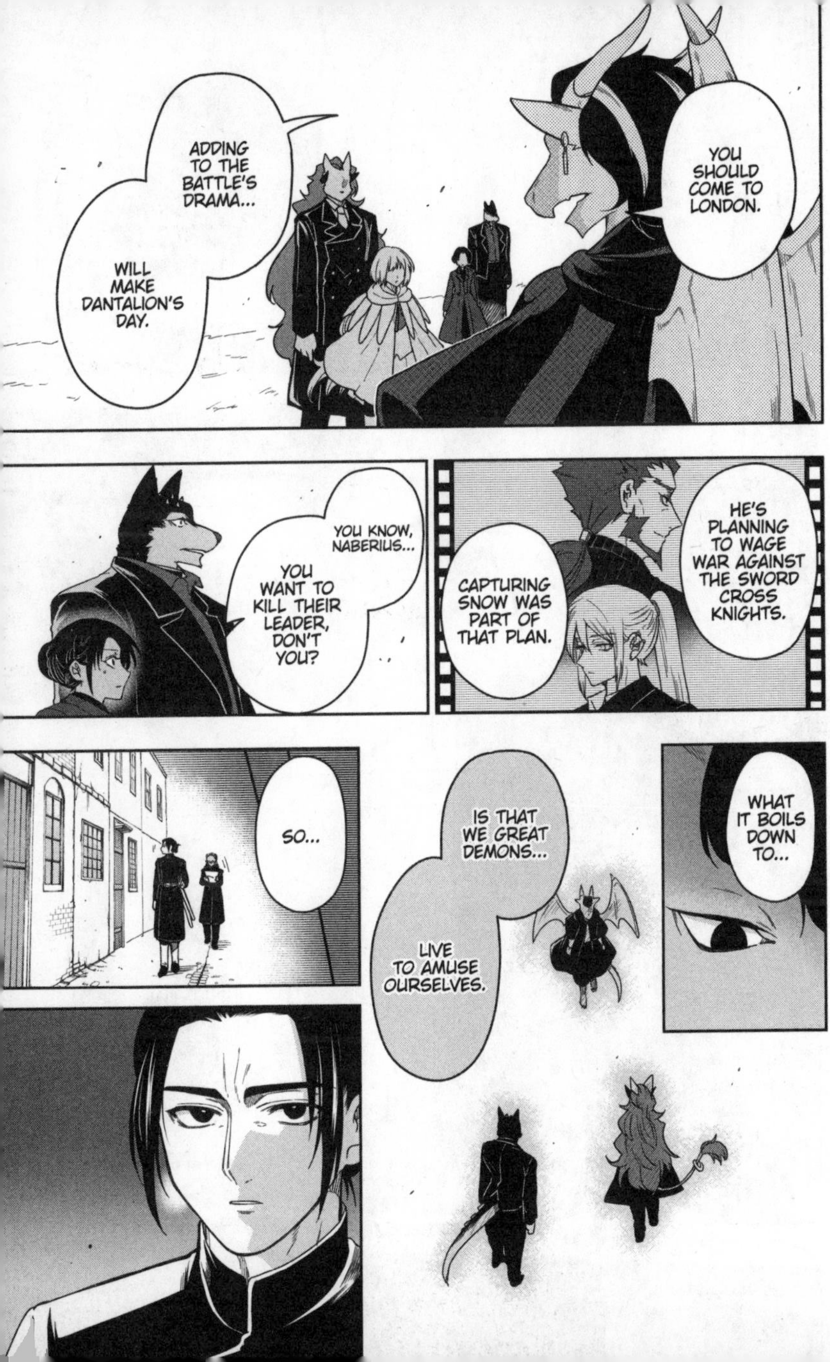
YOU SHOULD COME TO LONDON.
ADDING TO THE BATTLE'S DRAMA...
WILL MAKE DANTALION'S DAY.
HE'S PLANNING TO WAGE WAR AGAINST THE SWORD CROSS KNIGHTS.
CAPTURING SNOW WAS PART OF THAT PLAN.
YOU KNOW, NABERIUS...
YOU WANT TO KILL THEIR LEADER, DON'T YOU?
WHAT IT BOILS DOWN TO...
IS THAT WE GREAT DEMONS...
LIVE TO AMUSE OURSELVES.
SO...

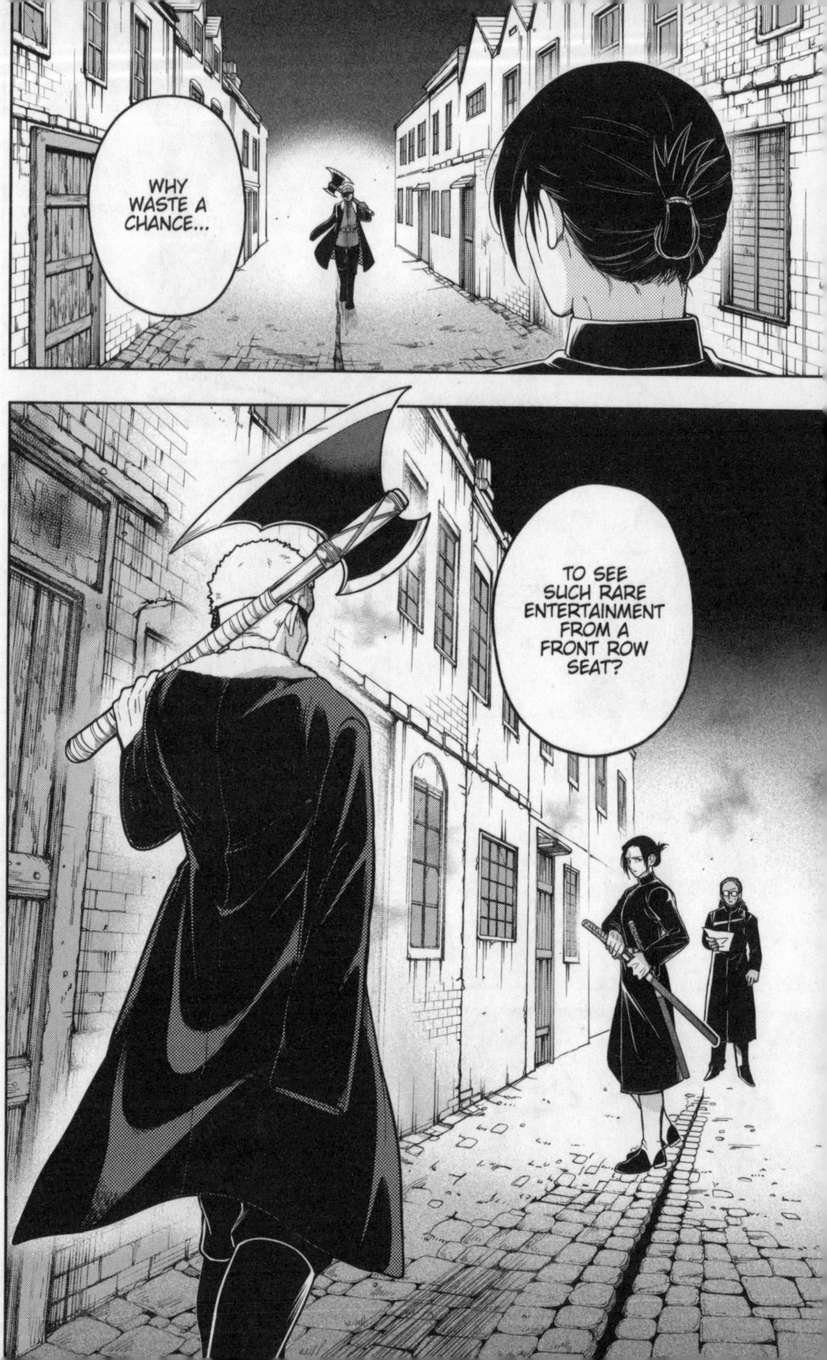
WHY WASTE A CHANCE...
TO SEE SUCH RARE ENTERTAINMENT FROM A FRONT ROW SEAT?

The Tale of the Outcasts

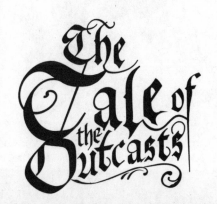

⚜Night 40⚜ Provocation

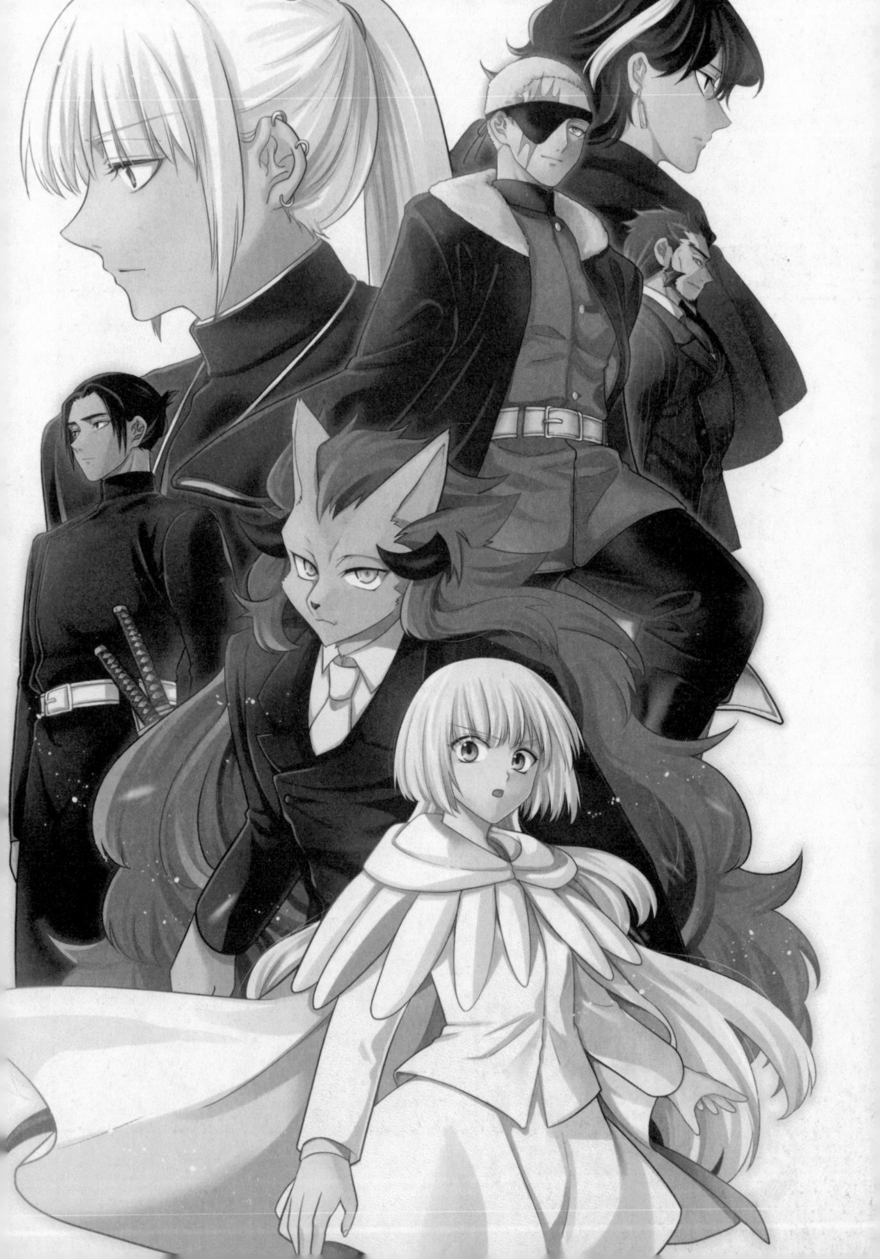

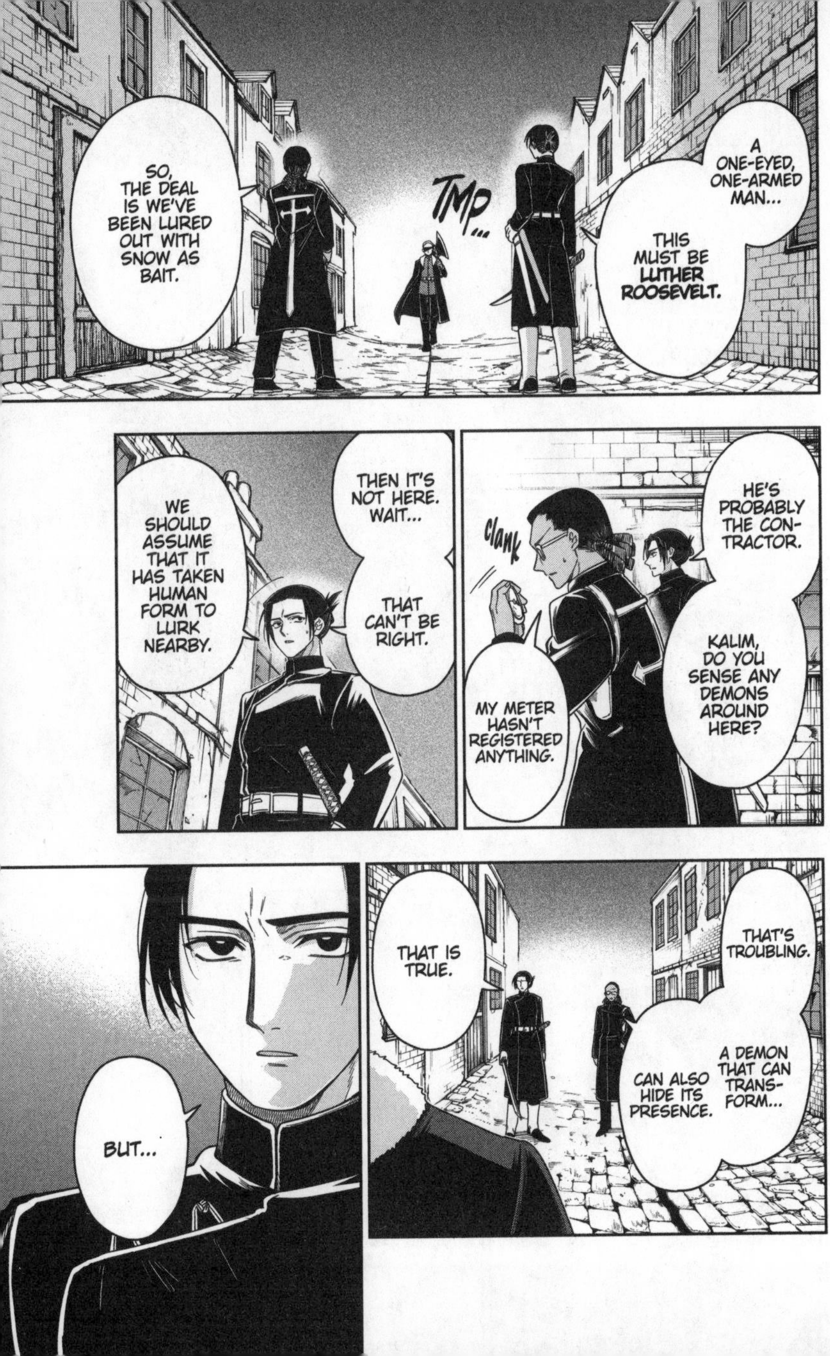
A ONE-EYED, ONE-ARMED MAN...
THIS MUST BE LUTHER ROOSEVELT.
TMP...
SO, THE DEAL IS WE'VE BEEN LURED OUT WITH SNOW AS BAIT.
HE'S PROBABLY THE CONTRACTOR.
KALIM, DO YOU SENSE ANY DEMONS AROUND HERE?
clank
MY METER HASN'T REGISTERED ANYTHING.
THEN IT'S NOT HERE. WAIT...
THAT CAN'T BE RIGHT.
WE SHOULD ASSUME THAT IT HAS TAKEN HUMAN FORM TO LURK NEARBY.
THAT'S TROUBLING.
A DEMON THAT CAN TRANSFORM...
CAN ALSO HIDE ITS PRESENCE.
THAT IS TRUE.
BUT...

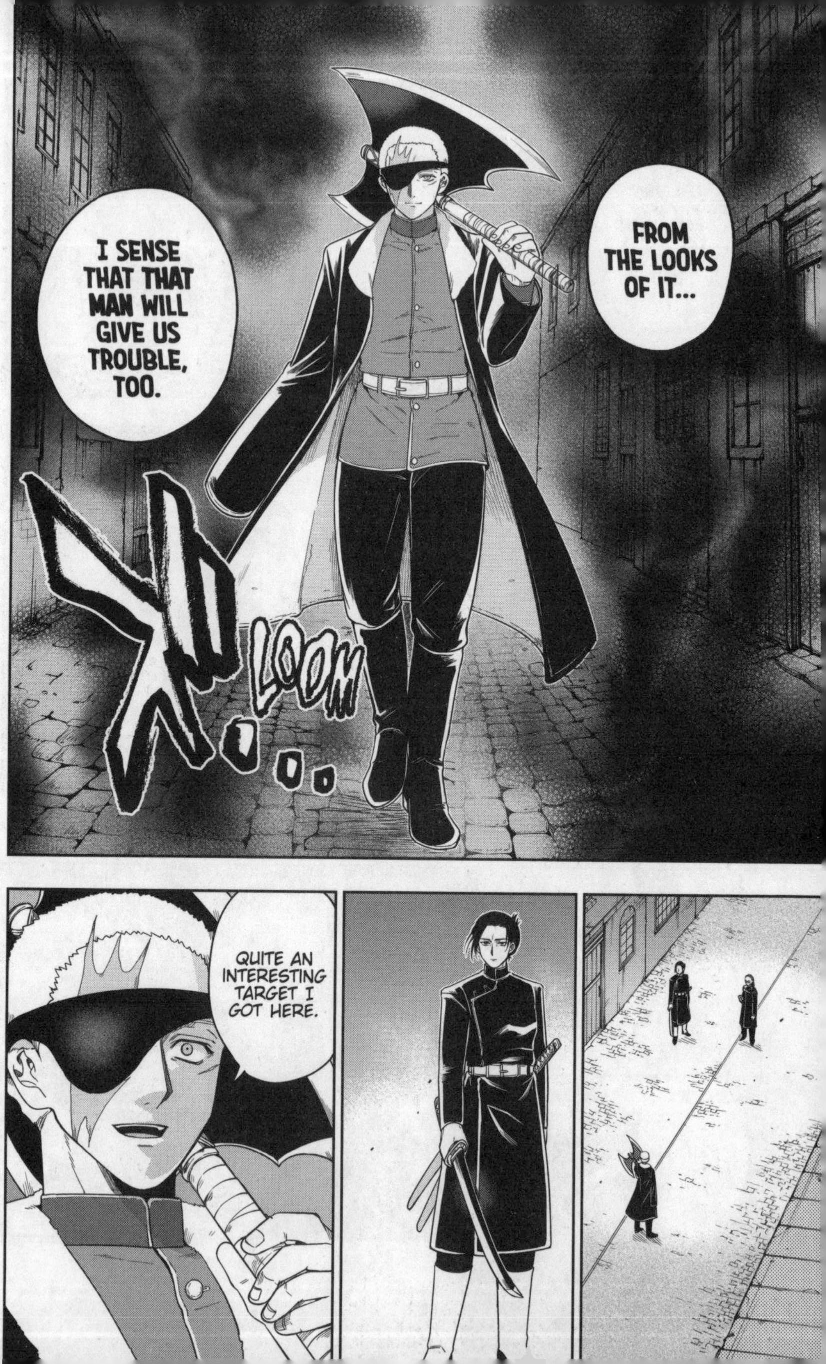
FROM THE LOOKS OF IT...
I SENSE THAT THAT MAN WILL GIVE US TROUBLE, TOO.
LOOM
QUITE AN INTERESTING TARGET I GOT HERE.

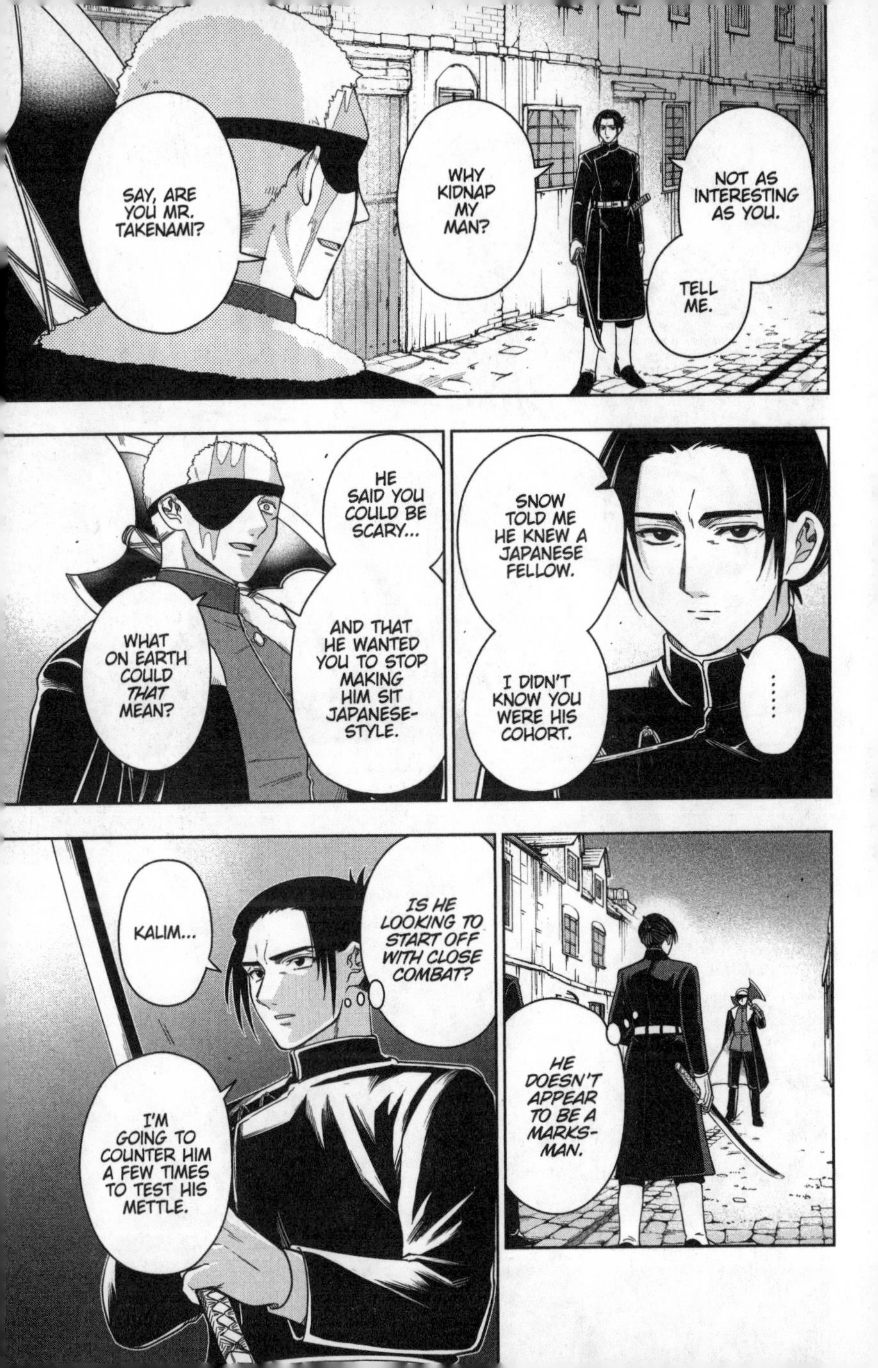
NOT AS INTERESTING AS YOU.
TELL ME.
WHY KIDNAP MY MAN?
SAY, ARE YOU MR. TAKENAMI?
SNOW TOLD ME HE KNEW A JAPANESE FELLOW.
I DIDN'T KNOW YOU WERE HIS COHORT.
......
HE SAID YOU COULD BE SCARY...
AND THAT HE WANTED YOU TO STOP MAKING HIM SIT JAPANESE-STYLE.
WHAT ON EARTH COULD *THAT* MEAN?
HE DOESN'T APPEAR TO BE A MARKS-MAN.
IS HE LOOKING TO START OFF WITH CLOSE COMBAT?
KALIM...
I'M GOING TO COUNTER HIM A FEW TIMES TO TEST HIS METTLE.

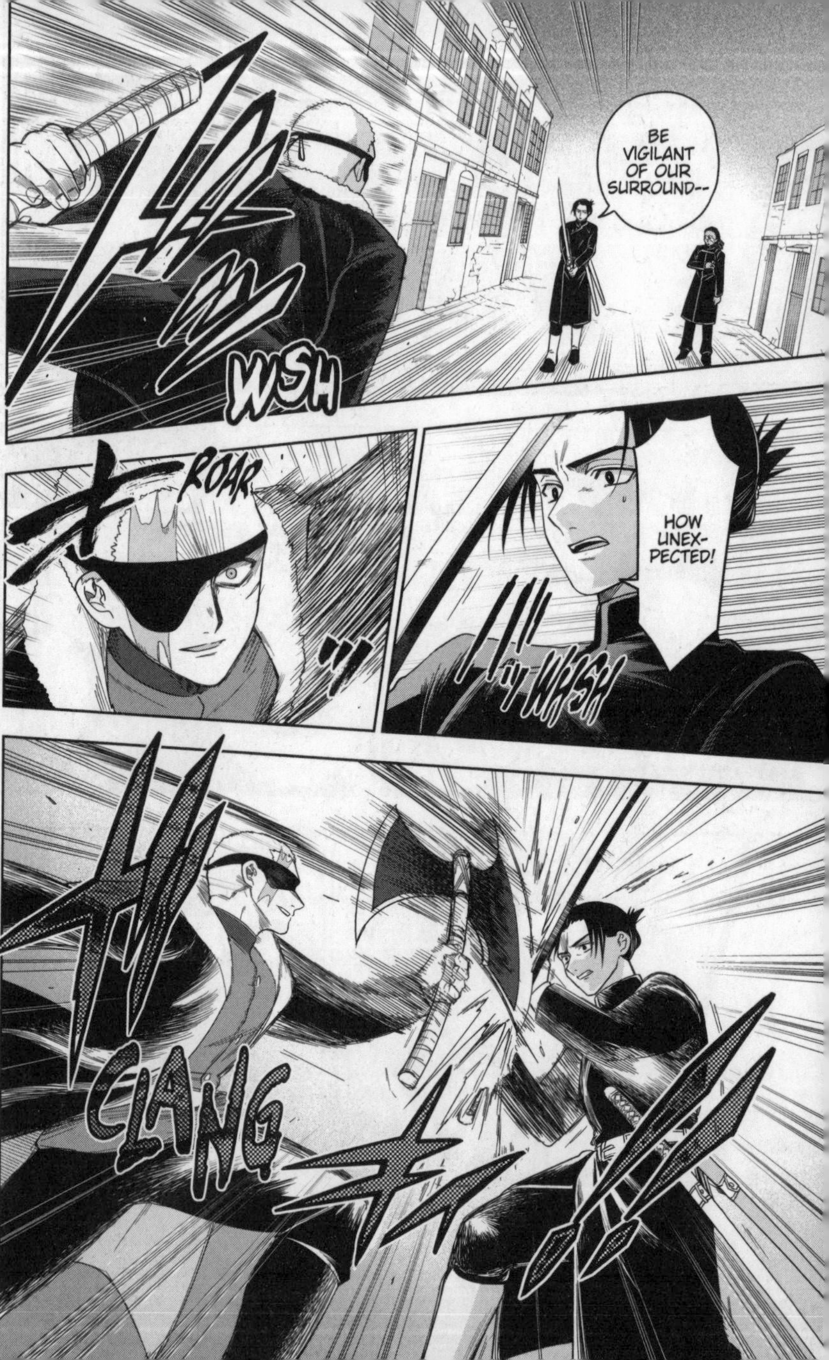
BE VIGILANT OF OUR SURROUND--
WSH
HOW UNEX-PECTED!
WHSH
ROAR
CLANG

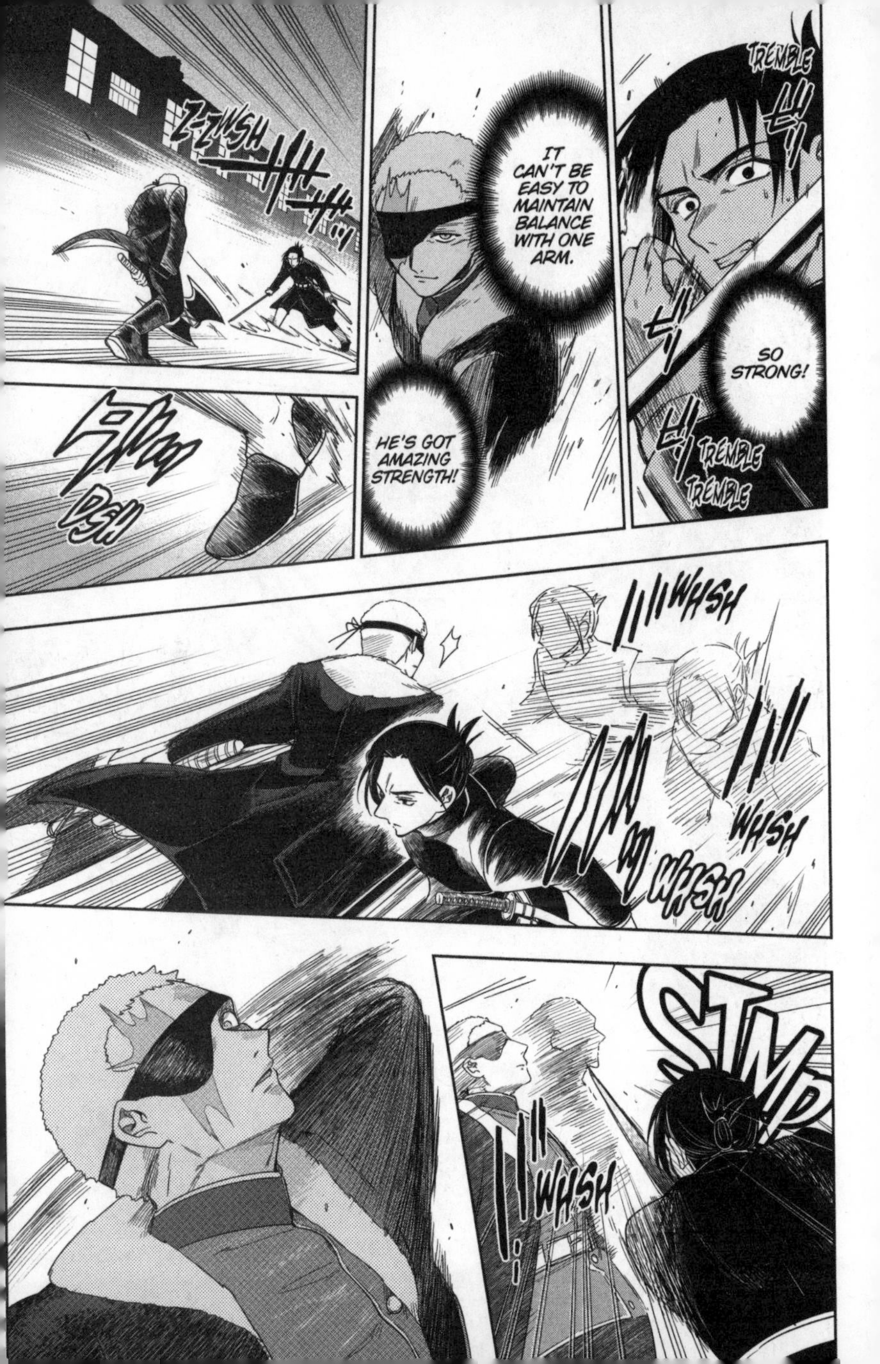
TREMBLE
SO STRONG!
TREMBLE
TREMBLE
IT CAN'T BE EASY TO MAINTAIN BALANCE WITH ONE ARM.
HE'S GOT AMAZING STRENGTH!
Z-ZWSH
DSH
WHSH
WHSH
WHSH
STMP
WHSH

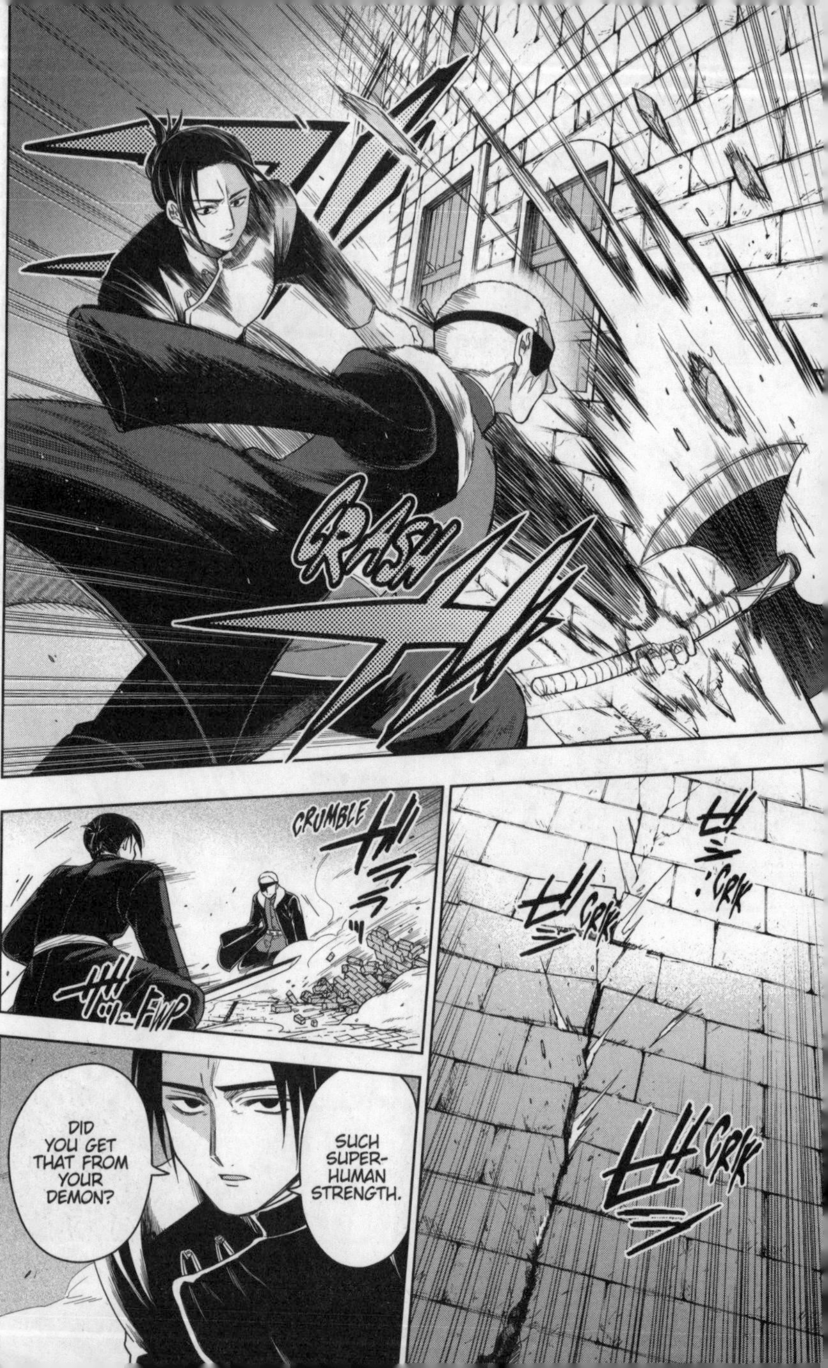
CRASH
CRIK
CRIK
CRIK
CRUMBLE
FWP
SUCH SUPER-HUMAN STRENGTH.
DID YOU GET THAT FROM YOUR DEMON?

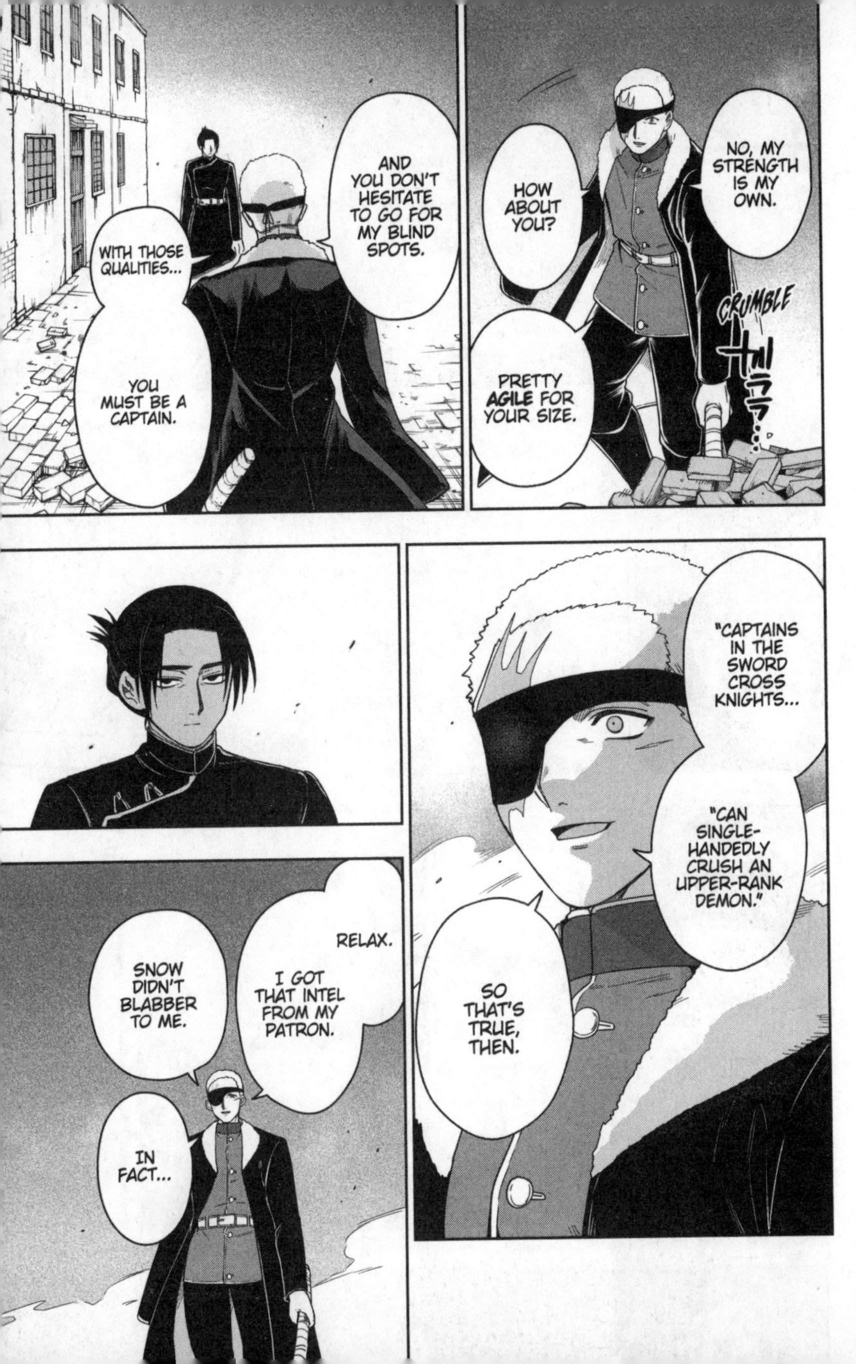
NO, MY STRENGTH IS MY OWN.
HOW ABOUT YOU?
PRETTY AGILE FOR YOUR SIZE.
CRUMBLE
AND YOU DON'T HESITATE TO GO FOR MY BLIND SPOTS.
WITH THOSE QUALITIES...
YOU MUST BE A CAPTAIN.
"CAPTAINS IN THE SWORD CROSS KNIGHTS...
"CAN SINGLE-HANDEDLY CRUSH AN UPPER-RANK DEMON."
SO THAT'S TRUE, THEN.
RELAX.
I GOT THAT INTEL FROM MY PATRON.
SNOW DIDN'T BLABBER TO ME.
IN FACT...

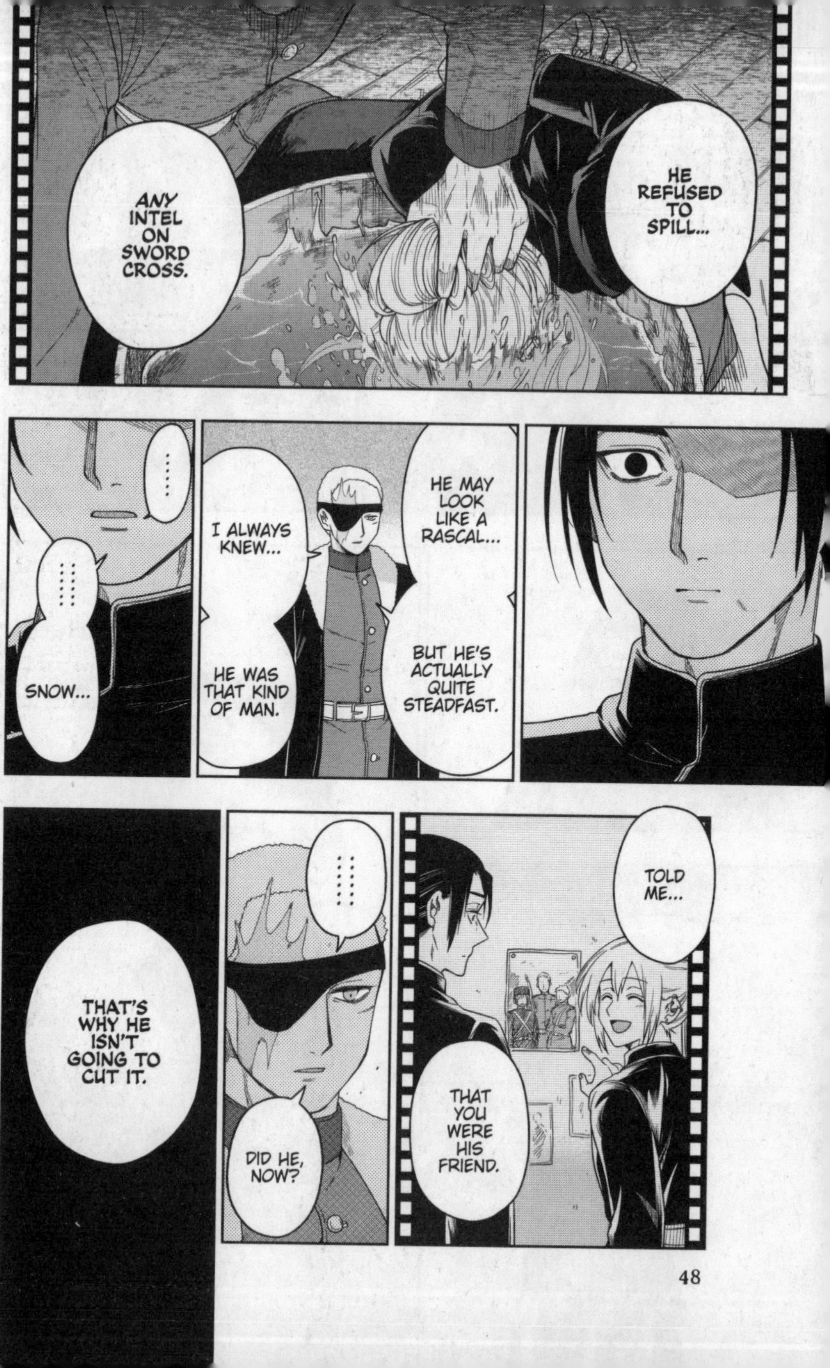
HE REFUSED TO SPILL...
ANY INTEL ON SWORD CROSS.
HE MAY LOOK LIKE A RASCAL...
BUT HE'S ACTUALLY QUITE STEADFAST.
I ALWAYS KNEW...
HE WAS THAT KIND OF MAN.
......
......
SNOW...
TOLD ME...
THAT YOU WERE HIS FRIEND.
...
DID HE, NOW?
THAT'S WHY HE ISN'T GOING TO CUT IT.

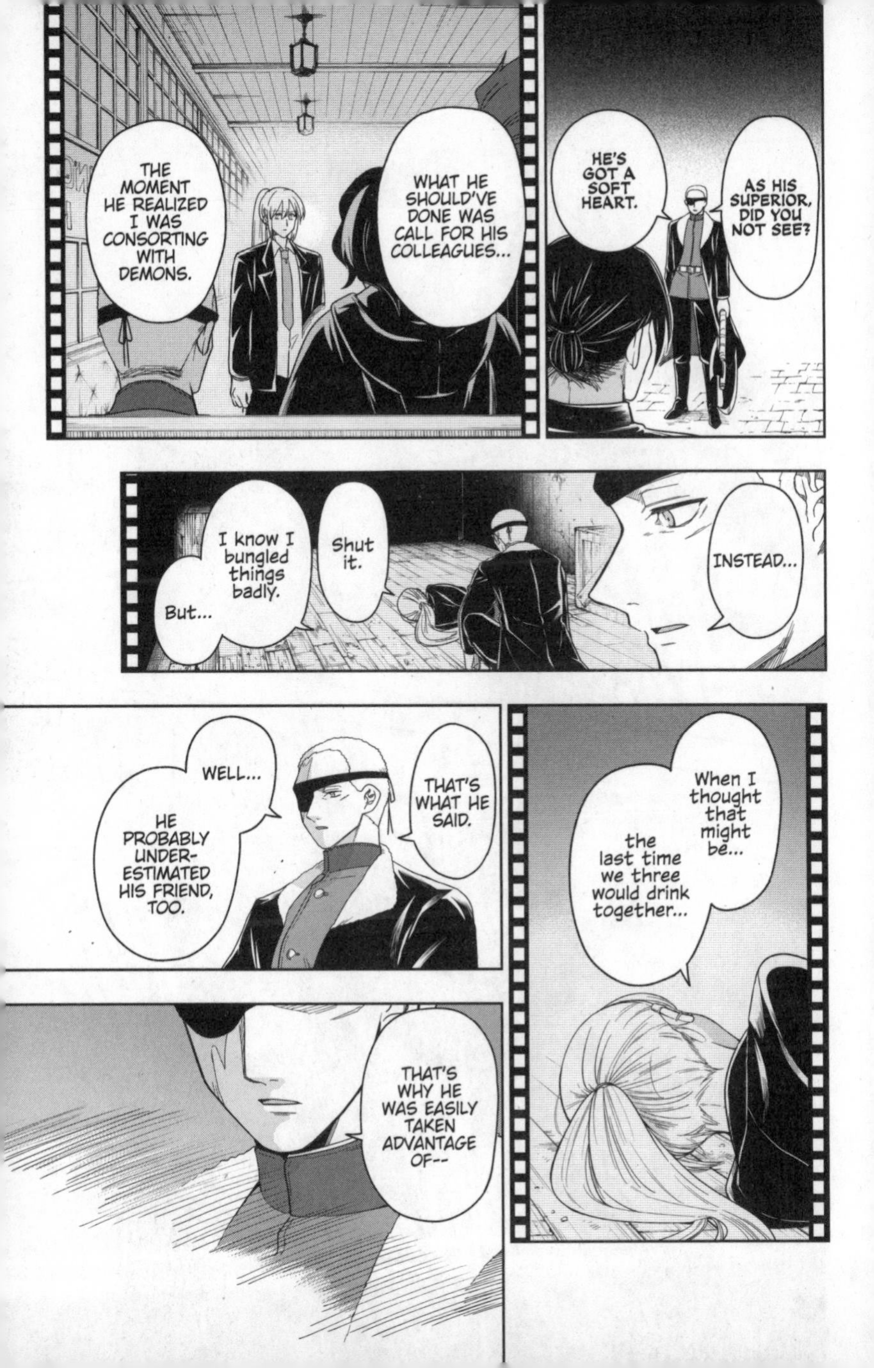
AS HIS SUPERIOR, DID YOU NOT SEE?
HE'S GOT A SOFT HEART.
WHAT HE SHOULD'VE DONE WAS CALL FOR HIS COLLEAGUES...
THE MOMENT HE REALIZED I WAS CONSORTING WITH DEMONS.
INSTEAD...
Shut it.
I know I bungled things badly.
But...
When I thought that might be...
the last time we three would drink together...
THAT'S WHAT HE SAID.
WELL...
HE PROBABLY UNDER-ESTIMATED HIS FRIEND, TOO.
THAT'S WHY HE WAS EASILY TAKEN ADVANTAGE OF--

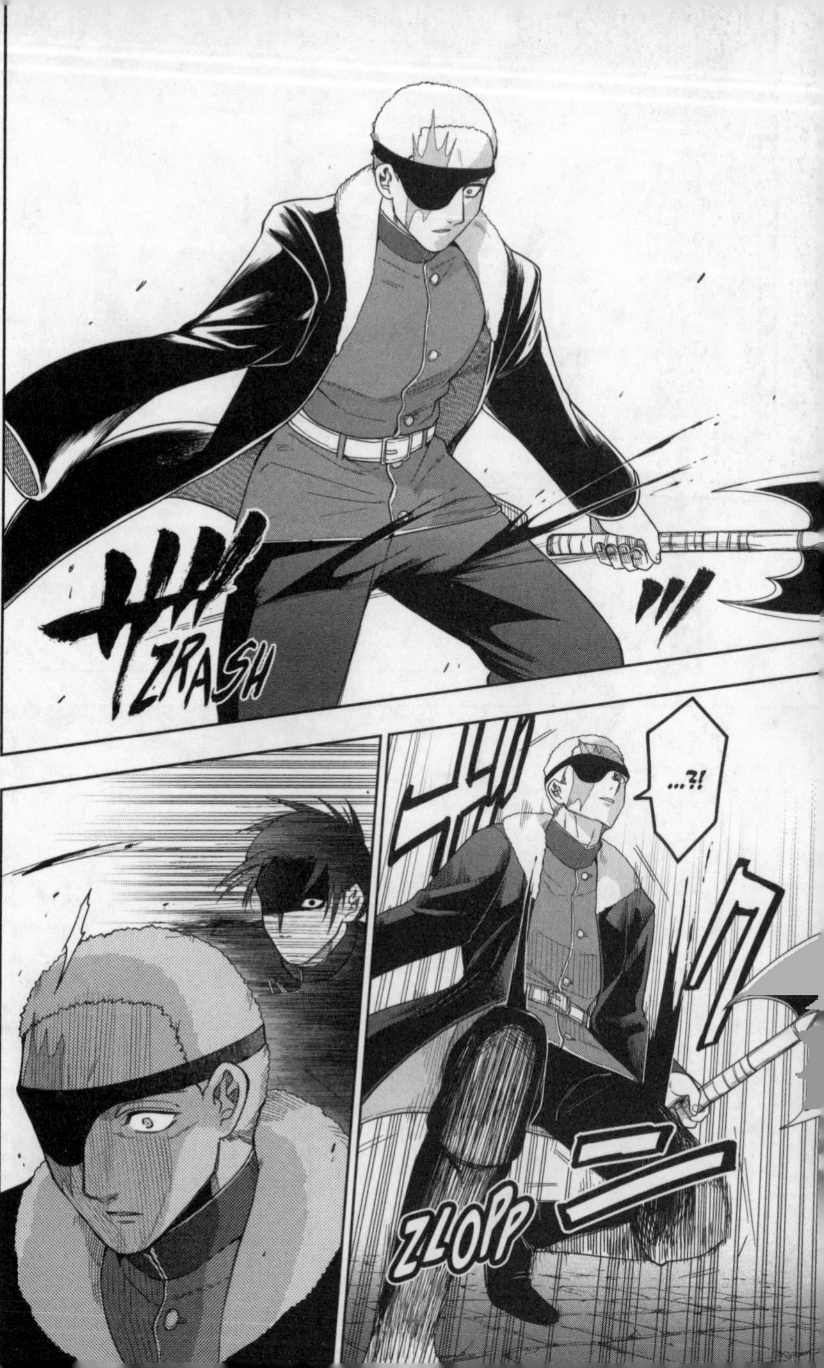
ZRASH
...?!
ZLOPP

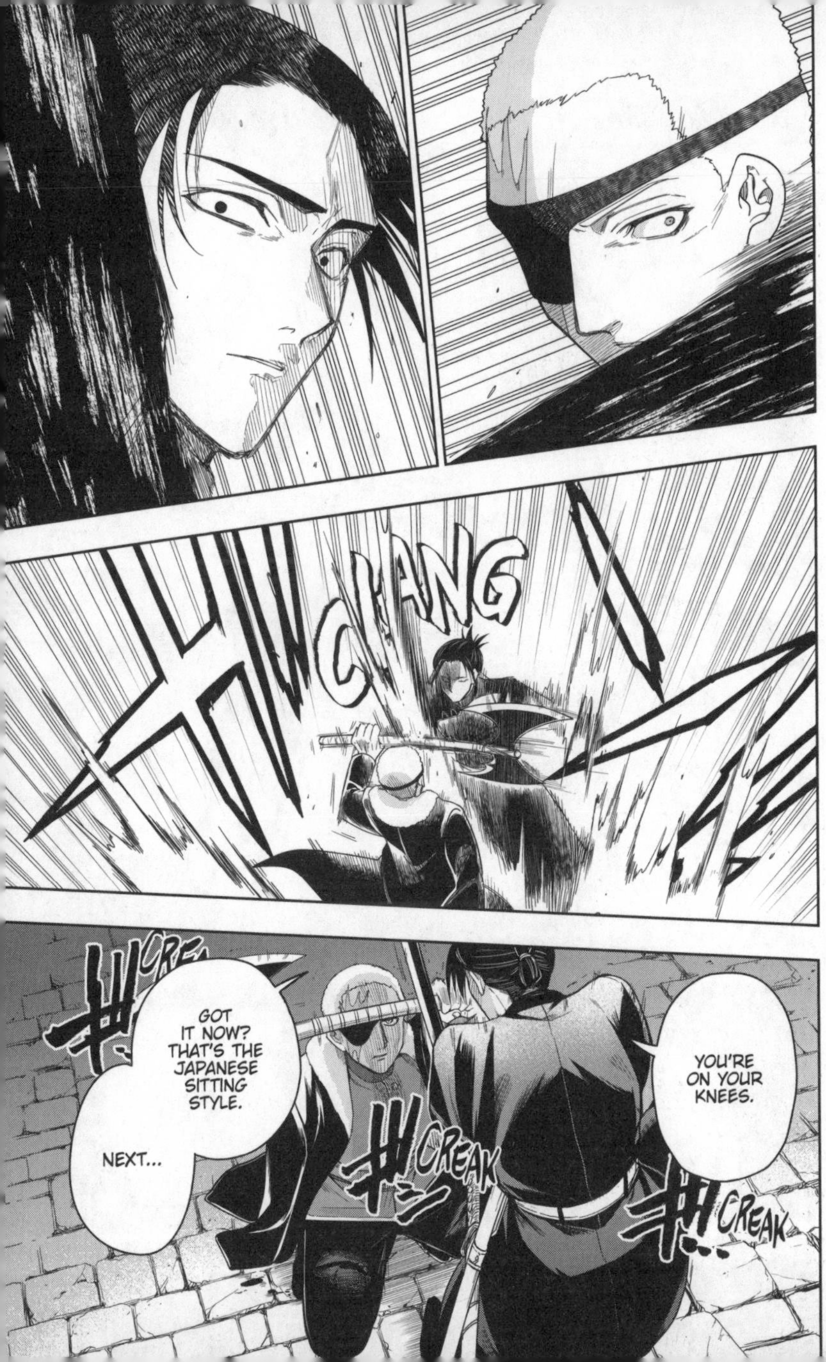
CHANG
YOU'RE ON YOUR KNEES.
CREAK
CREAK
GOT IT NOW? THAT'S THE JAPANESE SITTING STYLE.
NEXT...

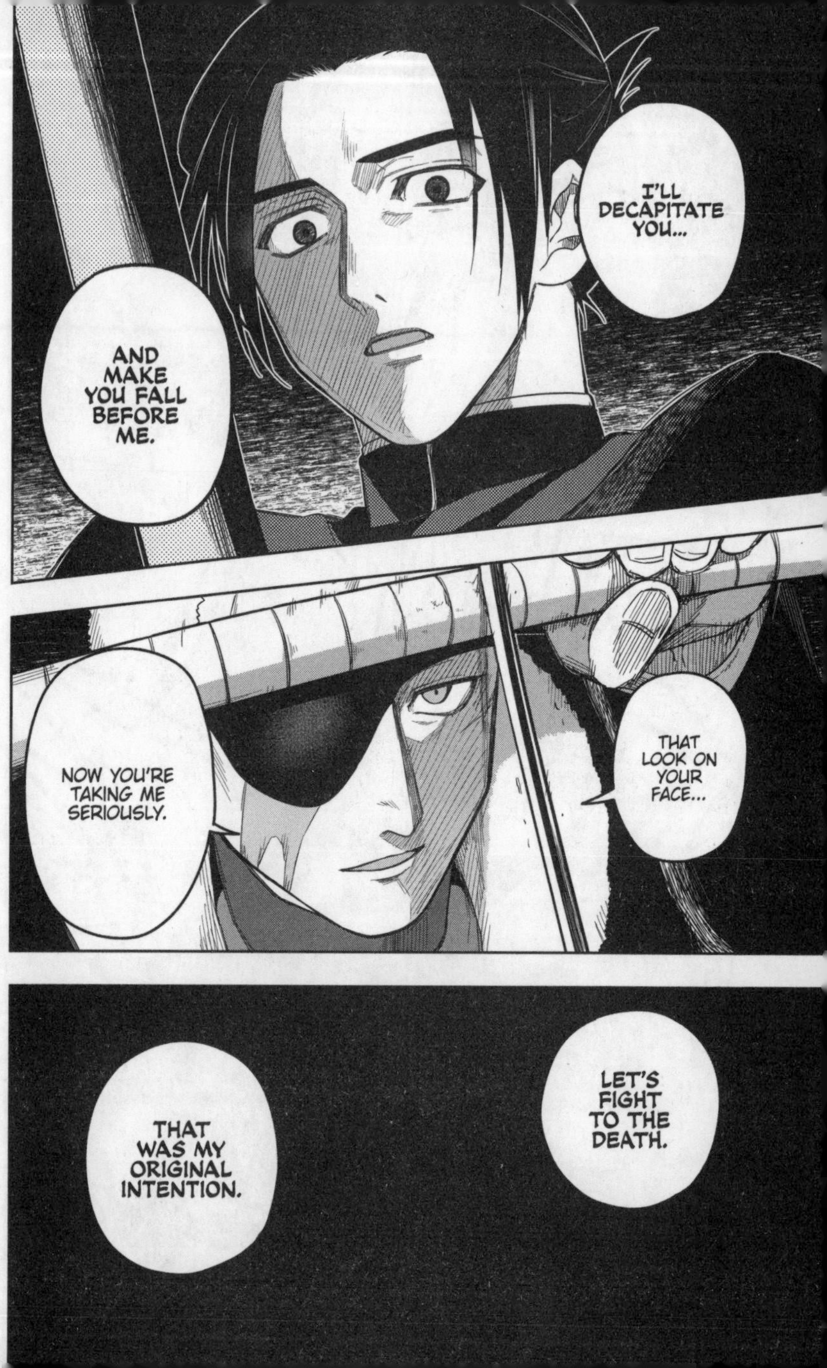
I'LL DECAPITATE YOU...
AND MAKE YOU FALL BEFORE ME.
THAT LOOK ON YOUR FACE...
NOW YOU'RE TAKING ME SERIOUSLY.
LET'S FIGHT TO THE DEATH.
THAT WAS MY ORIGINAL INTENTION.

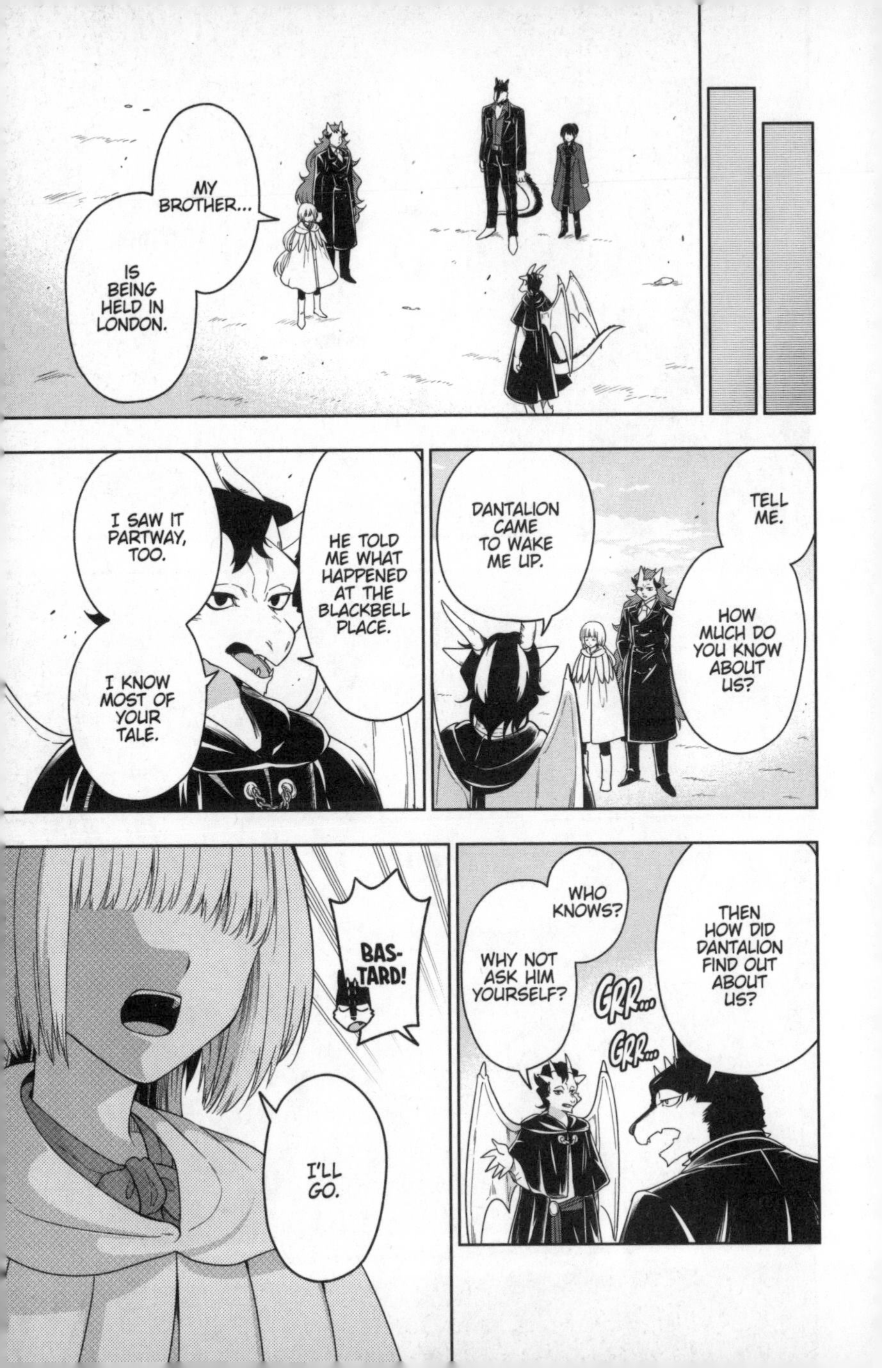
MY BROTHER...
IS BEING HELD IN LONDON.
TELL ME.
HOW MUCH DO YOU KNOW ABOUT US?
DANTALION CAME TO WAKE ME UP.
HE TOLD ME WHAT HAPPENED AT THE BLACKBELL PLACE.
I SAW IT PARTWAY, TOO.
I KNOW MOST OF YOUR TALE.
THEN HOW DID DANTALION FIND OUT ABOUT US?
WHO KNOWS?
WHY NOT ASK HIM YOURSELF?
GRR...
GRR...
BAS-TARD!
I'LL GO.

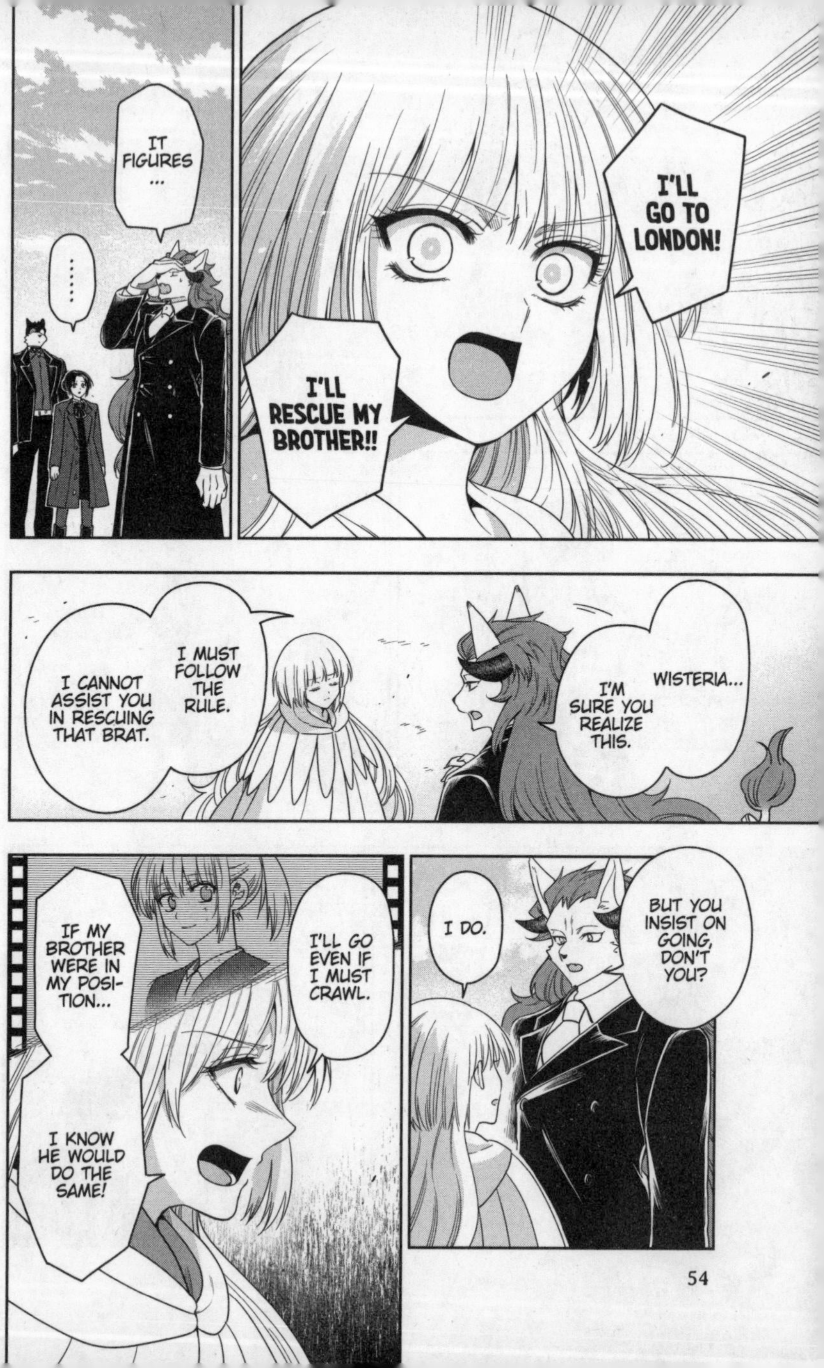
I'LL GO TO LONDON!
I'LL RESCUE MY BROTHER!!
IT FIGURES ...
......
WISTERIA...
I'M SURE YOU REALIZE THIS.
I MUST FOLLOW THE RULE.
I CANNOT ASSIST YOU IN RESCUING THAT BRAT.
BUT YOU INSIST ON GOING, DON'T YOU?
I DO.
I'LL GO EVEN IF I MUST CRAWL.
IF MY BROTHER WERE IN MY POSI-TION...
I KNOW HE WOULD DO THE SAME!

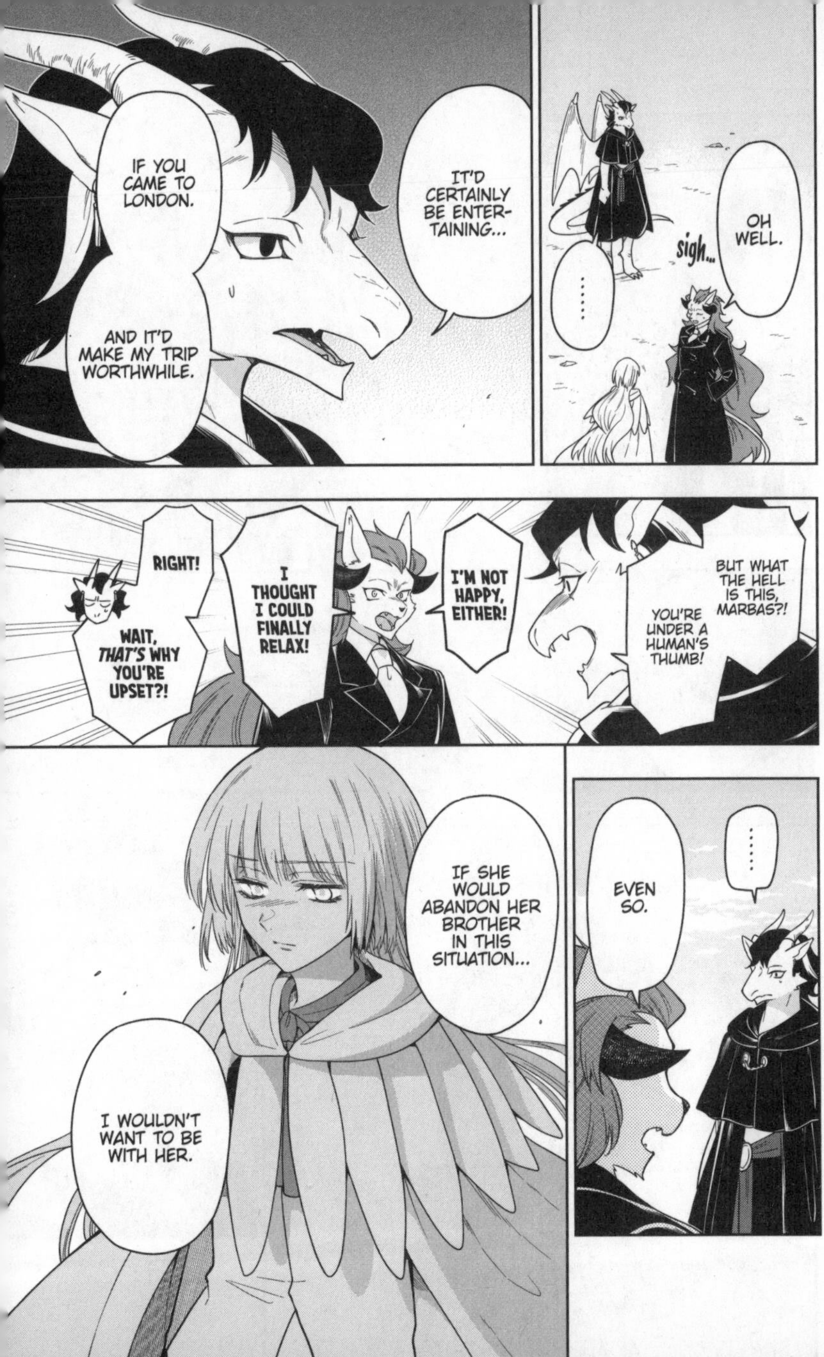
OH WELL.
sigh...
......
IT'D CERTAINLY BE ENTERTAINING...
IF YOU CAME TO LONDON.
AND IT'D MAKE MY TRIP WORTHWHILE.
BUT WHAT THE HELL IS THIS, MARBAS?!
YOU'RE UNDER A HUMAN'S THUMB!
I'M NOT HAPPY, EITHER!
I THOUGHT I COULD FINALLY RELAX!
RIGHT!
WAIT, *THAT'S* WHY YOU'RE UPSET?!
......
EVEN SO.
IF SHE WOULD ABANDON HER BROTHER IN THIS SITUATION...
I WOULDN'T WANT TO BE WITH HER.

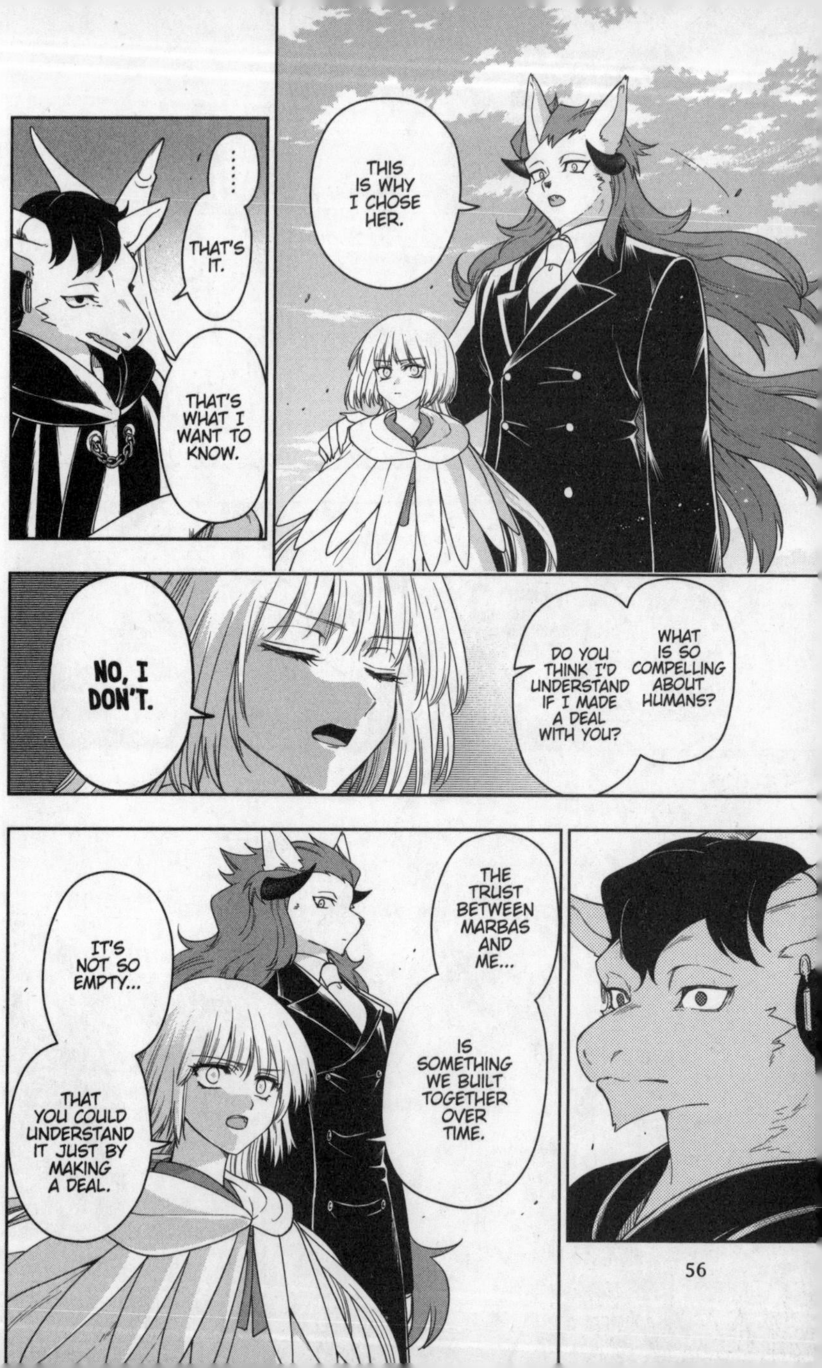
THIS IS WHY I CHOSE HER.
......
THAT'S IT.
THAT'S WHAT I WANT TO KNOW.
WHAT IS SO COMPELLING ABOUT HUMANS?
DO YOU THINK I'D UNDERSTAND IF I MADE A DEAL WITH YOU?
NO, I DON'T.
THE TRUST BETWEEN MARBAS AND ME...
IS SOMETHING WE BUILT TOGETHER OVER TIME.
IT'S NOT SO EMPTY...
THAT YOU COULD UNDERSTAND IT JUST BY MAKING A DEAL.

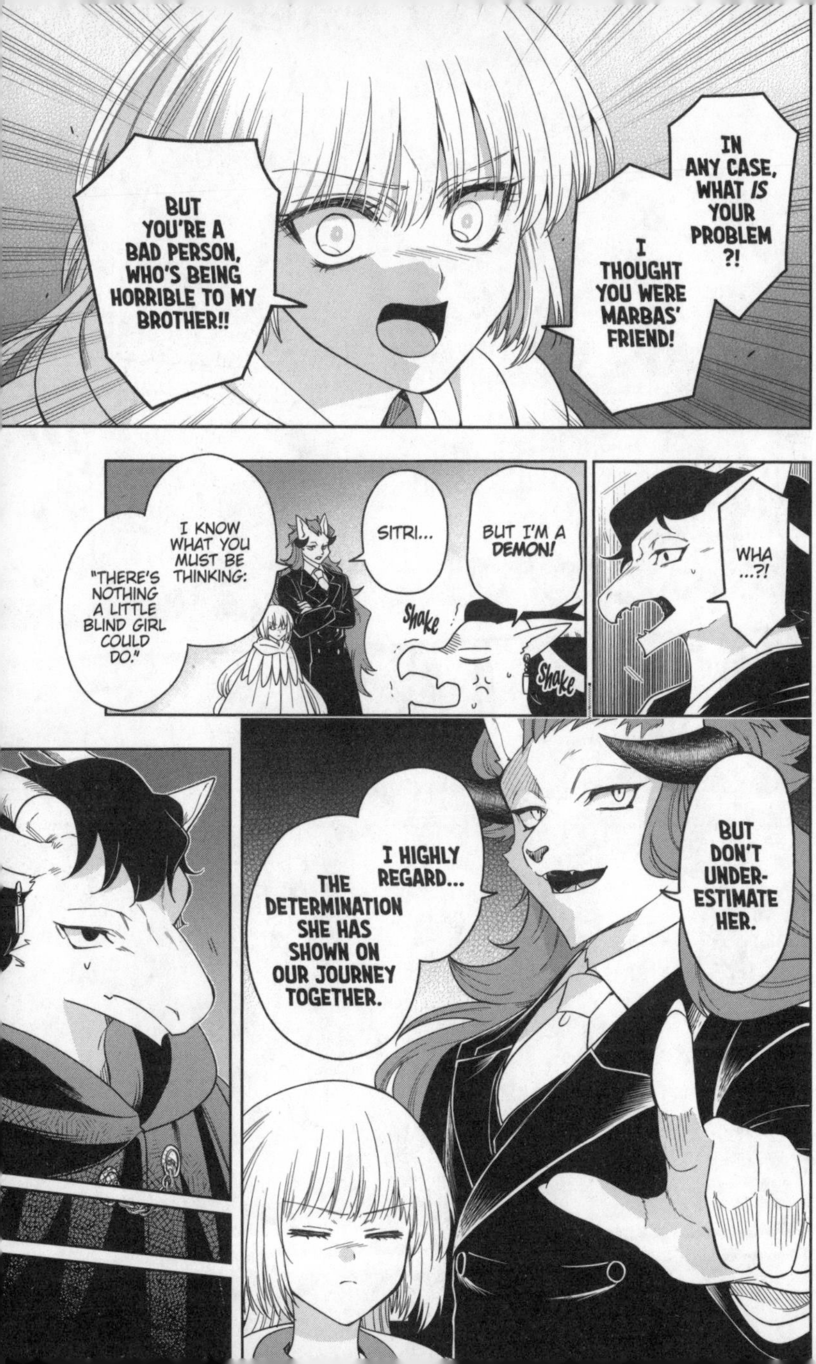
IN ANY CASE, WHAT *IS* YOUR PROBLEM ?!
I THOUGHT YOU WERE MARBAS' FRIEND!
BUT YOU'RE A BAD PERSON, WHO'S BEING HORRIBLE TO MY BROTHER!!
WHA ...?!
BUT I'M A DEMON!
Shake
Shake
SITRI...
I KNOW WHAT YOU MUST BE THINKING:
"THERE'S NOTHING A LITTLE BLIND GIRL COULD DO."
BUT DON'T UNDER-ESTIMATE HER.
I HIGHLY REGARD...
THE DETERMINATION SHE HAS SHOWN ON OUR JOURNEY TOGETHER.

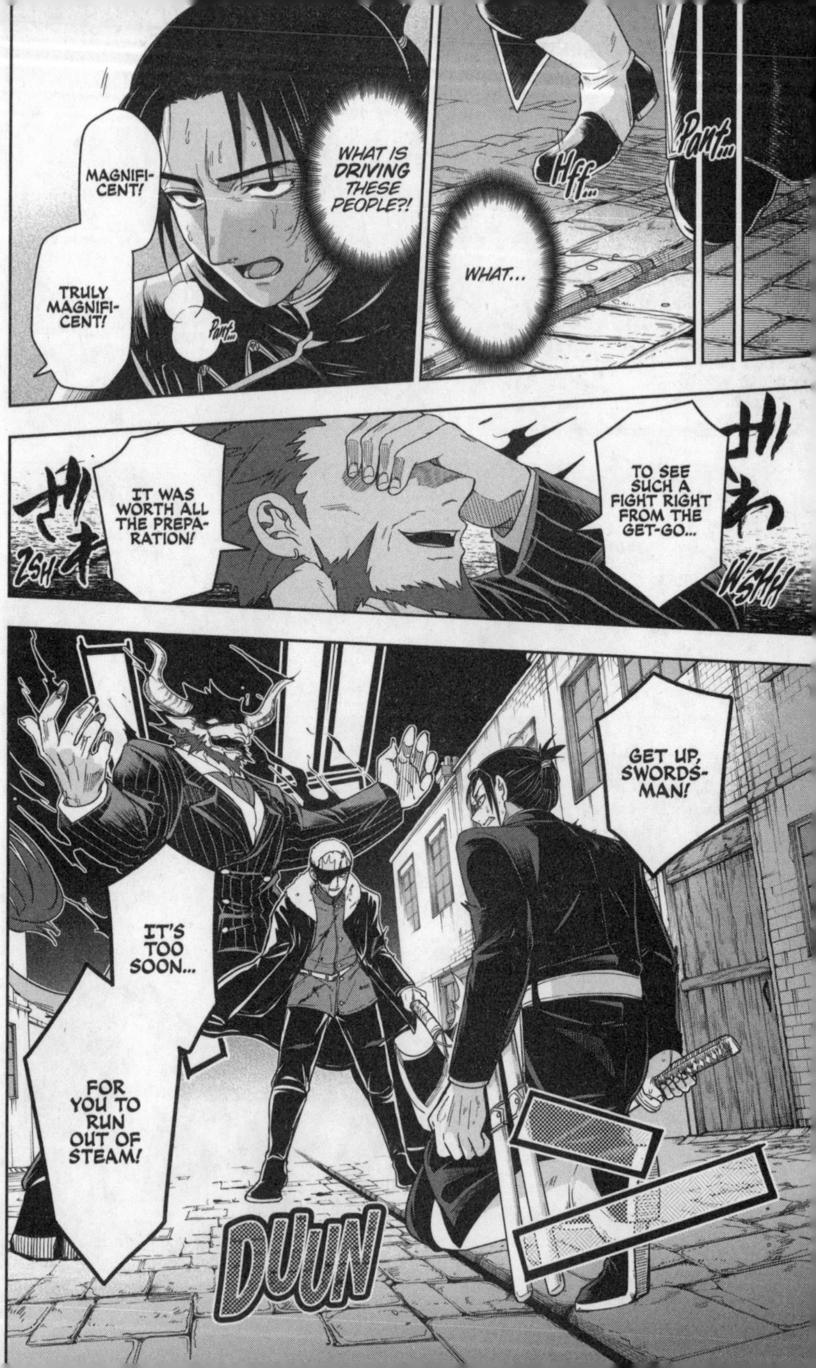
Pant...
Hff...
WHAT...
WHAT IS DRIVING THESE PEOPLE?!
MAGNIFICENT!
TRULY MAGNIFICENT!
Pant...
ざわ
WSHH
TO SEE SUCH A FIGHT RIGHT FROM THE GET-GO...
IT WAS WORTH ALL THE PREPARATION!
ざわ
ZSH
GET UP, SWORDSMAN!
IT'S TOO SOON...
FOR YOU TO RUN OUT OF STEAM!
DUUN

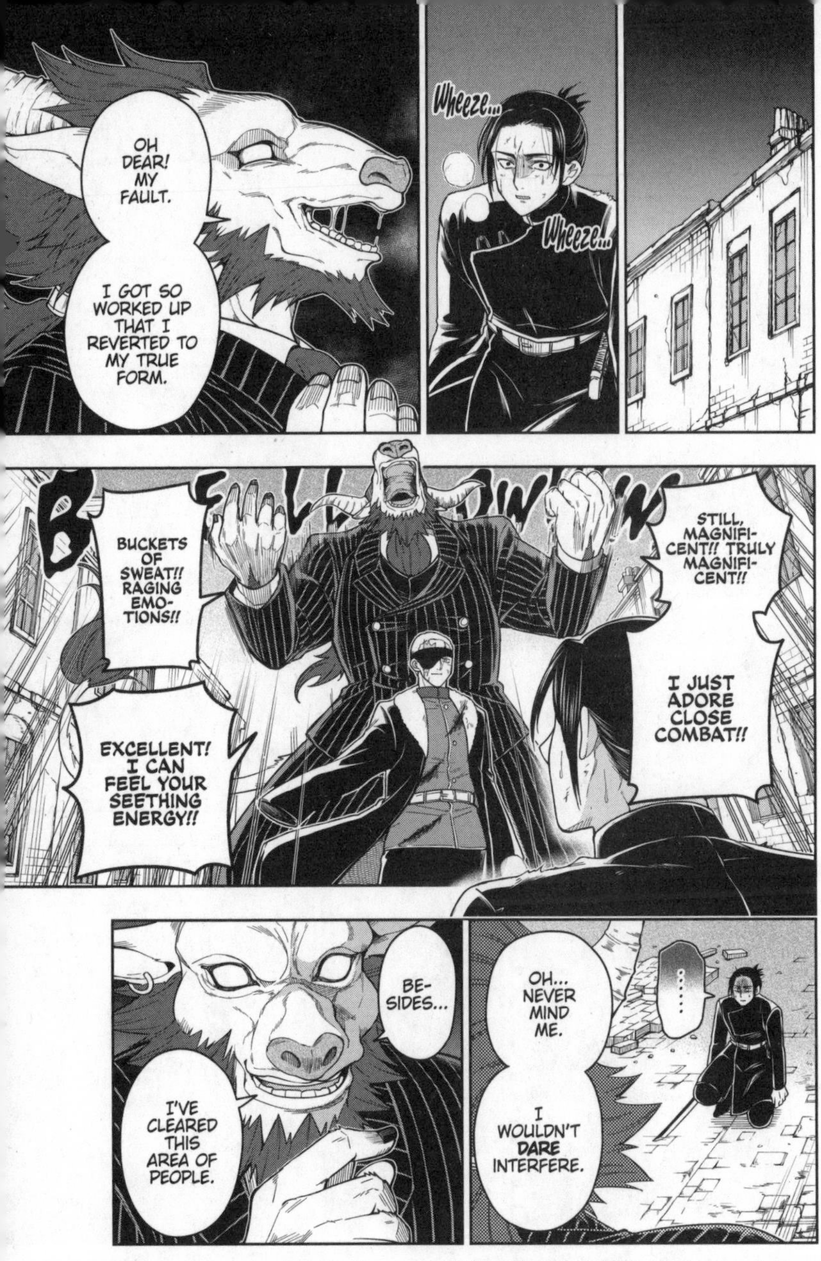
Wheeze...
Wheeze...
OH DEAR! MY FAULT.
I GOT SO WORKED UP THAT I REVERTED TO MY TRUE FORM.
STILL, MAGNIFI-CENT!! TRULY MAGNIFI-CENT!!
I JUST ADORE CLOSE COMBAT!!
BUCKETS OF SWEAT!! RAGING EMO-TIONS!!
EXCELLENT! I CAN FEEL YOUR SEETHING ENERGY!!
......
OH... NEVER MIND ME.
I WOULDN'T DARE INTERFERE.
BE-SIDES...
I'VE CLEARED THIS AREA OF PEOPLE.

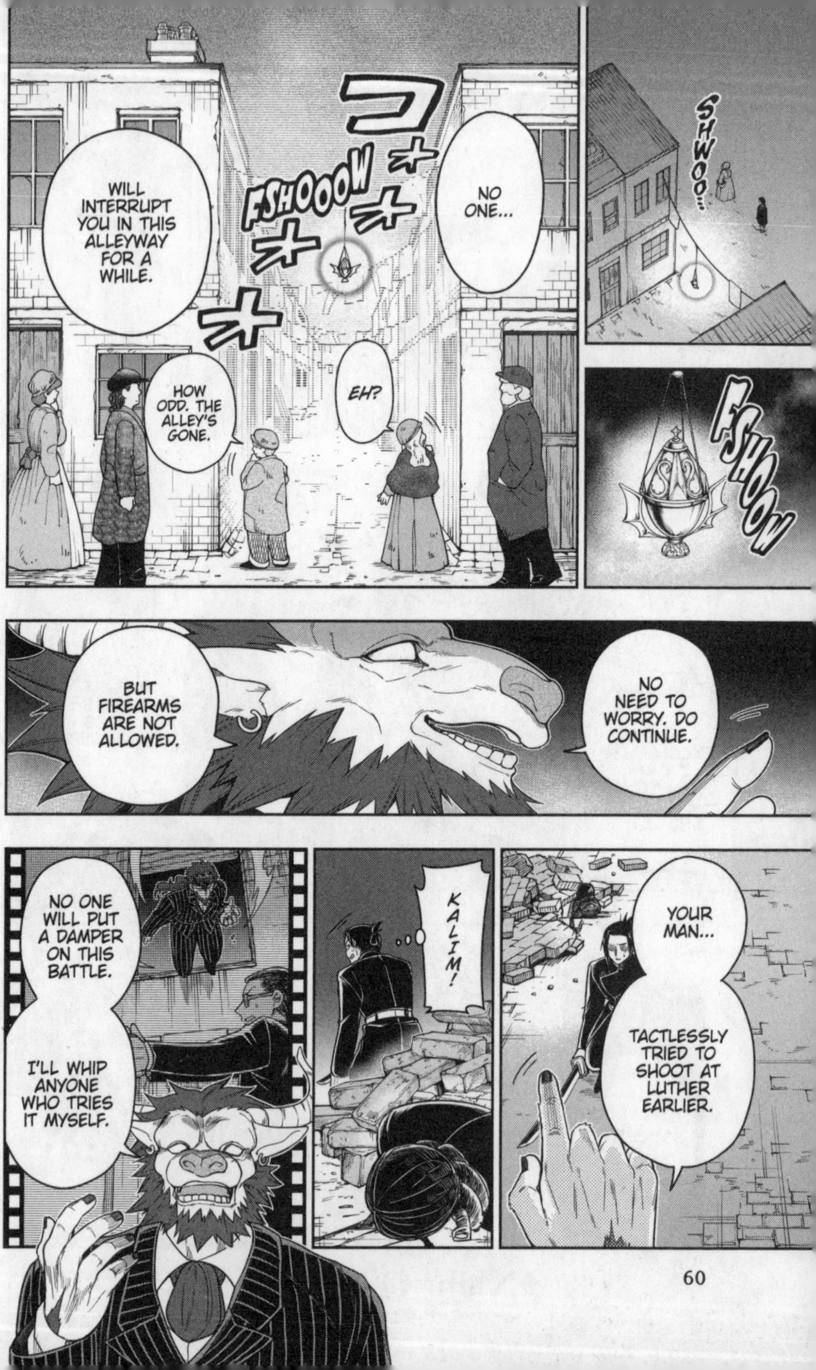
SHWOO...
FSHOOW
NO ONE...
FSHOOOW
WILL INTERRUPT YOU IN THIS ALLEYWAY FOR A WHILE.
EH?
HOW ODD. THE ALLEY'S GONE.
NO NEED TO WORRY. DO CONTINUE.
BUT FIREARMS ARE NOT ALLOWED.
YOUR MAN...
TACTLESSLY TRIED TO SHOOT AT LUTHER EARLIER.
KALIM!
NO ONE WILL PUT A DAMPER ON THIS BATTLE.
I'LL WHIP ANYONE WHO TRIES IT MYSELF.

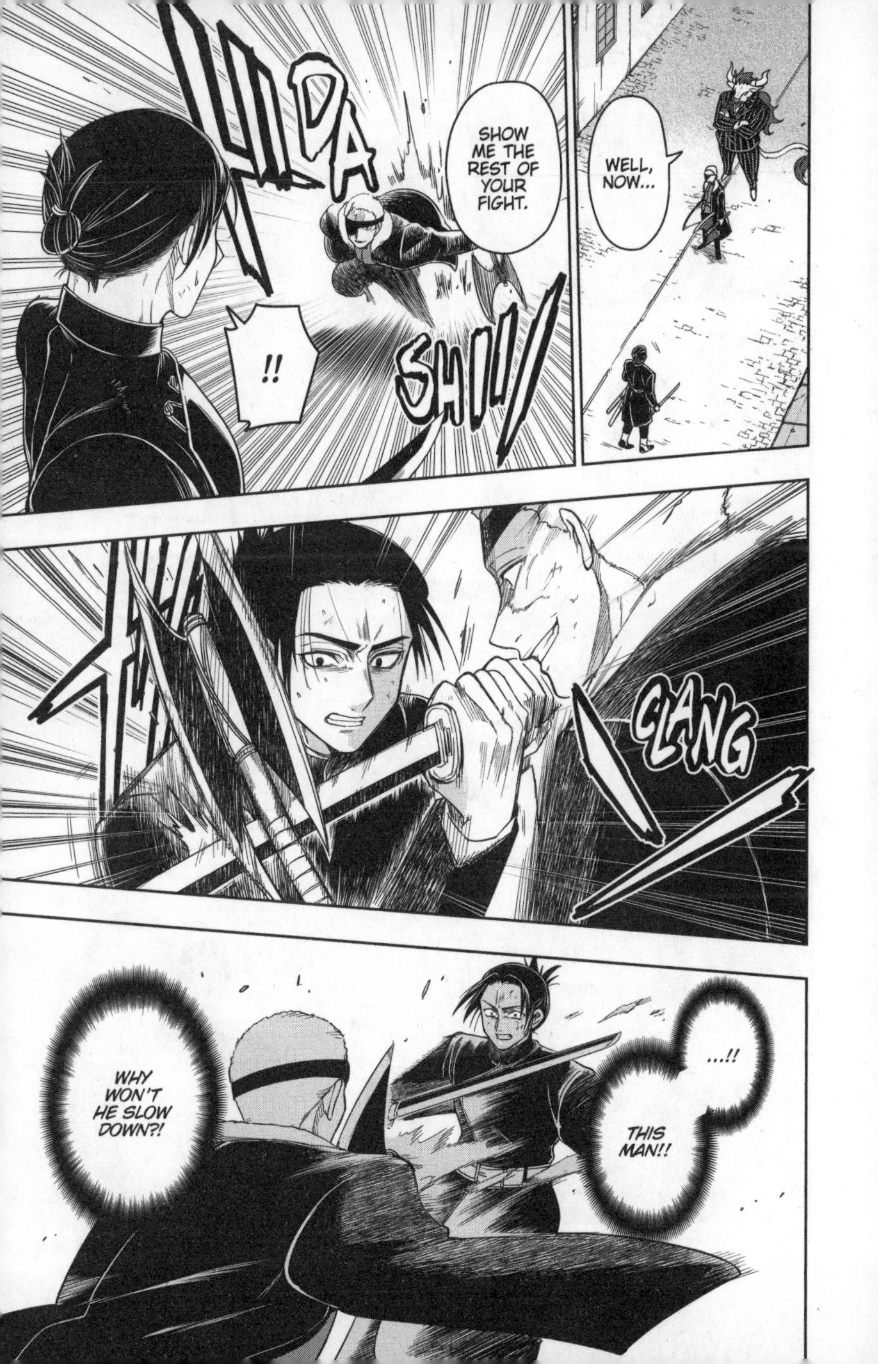
WELL, NOW...
SHOW ME THE REST OF YOUR FIGHT.
DA
SHII
!!
CLANG
...!!
THIS MAN!!
WHY WON'T HE SLOW DOWN?!

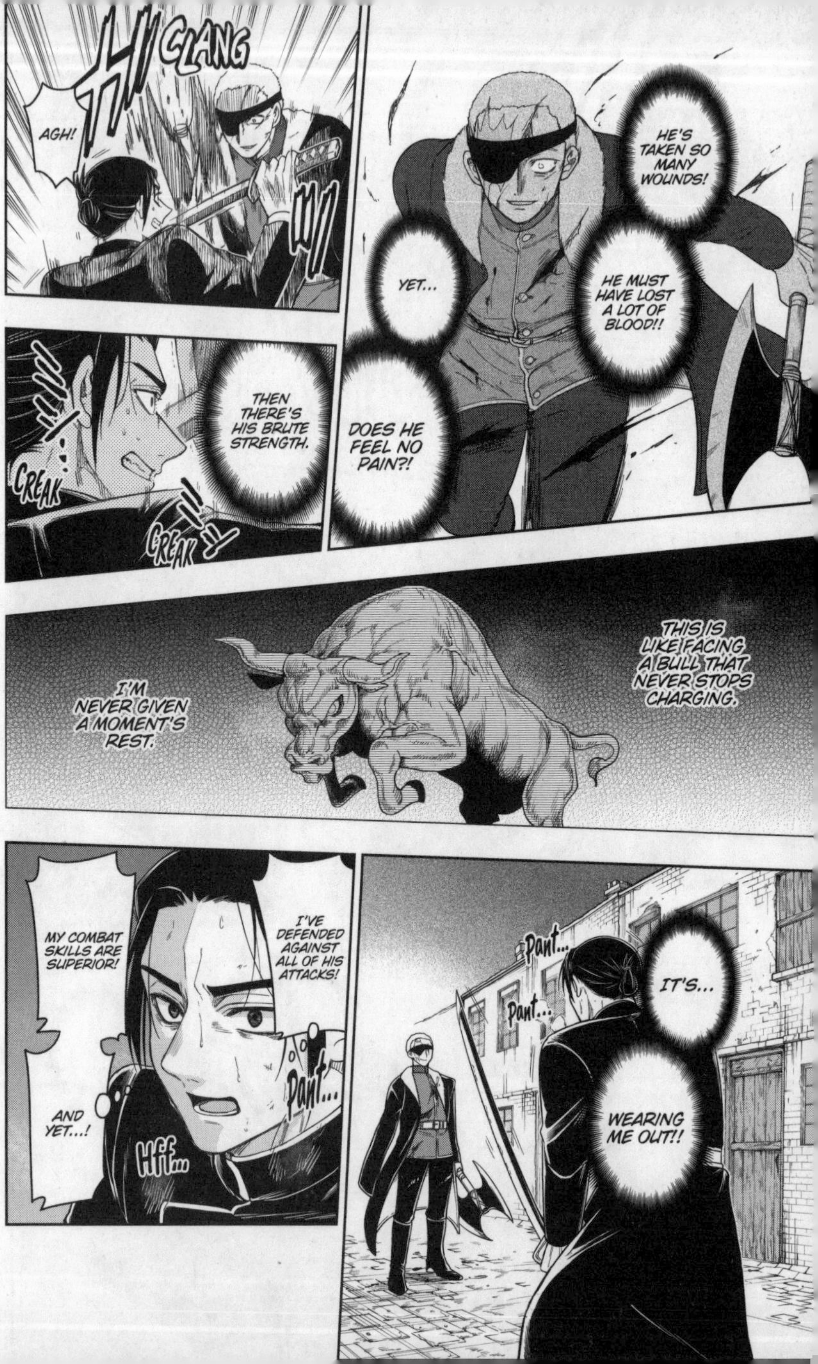
HE'S TAKEN SO MANY WOUNDS!
HE MUST HAVE LOST A LOT OF BLOOD!!
YET...
DOES HE FEEL NO PAIN?!
CLANG
AGH!
THEN THERE'S HIS BRUTE STRENGTH.
CREAK
CREAK
THIS IS LIKE FACING A BULL THAT NEVER STOPS CHARGING.
I'M NEVER GIVEN A MOMENT'S REST.
IT'S...
Pant...
Pant...
WEARING ME OUT!!
I'VE DEFENDED AGAINST ALL OF HIS ATTACKS!
MY COMBAT SKILLS ARE SUPERIOR!
Pant...
AND YET...!
Hff...

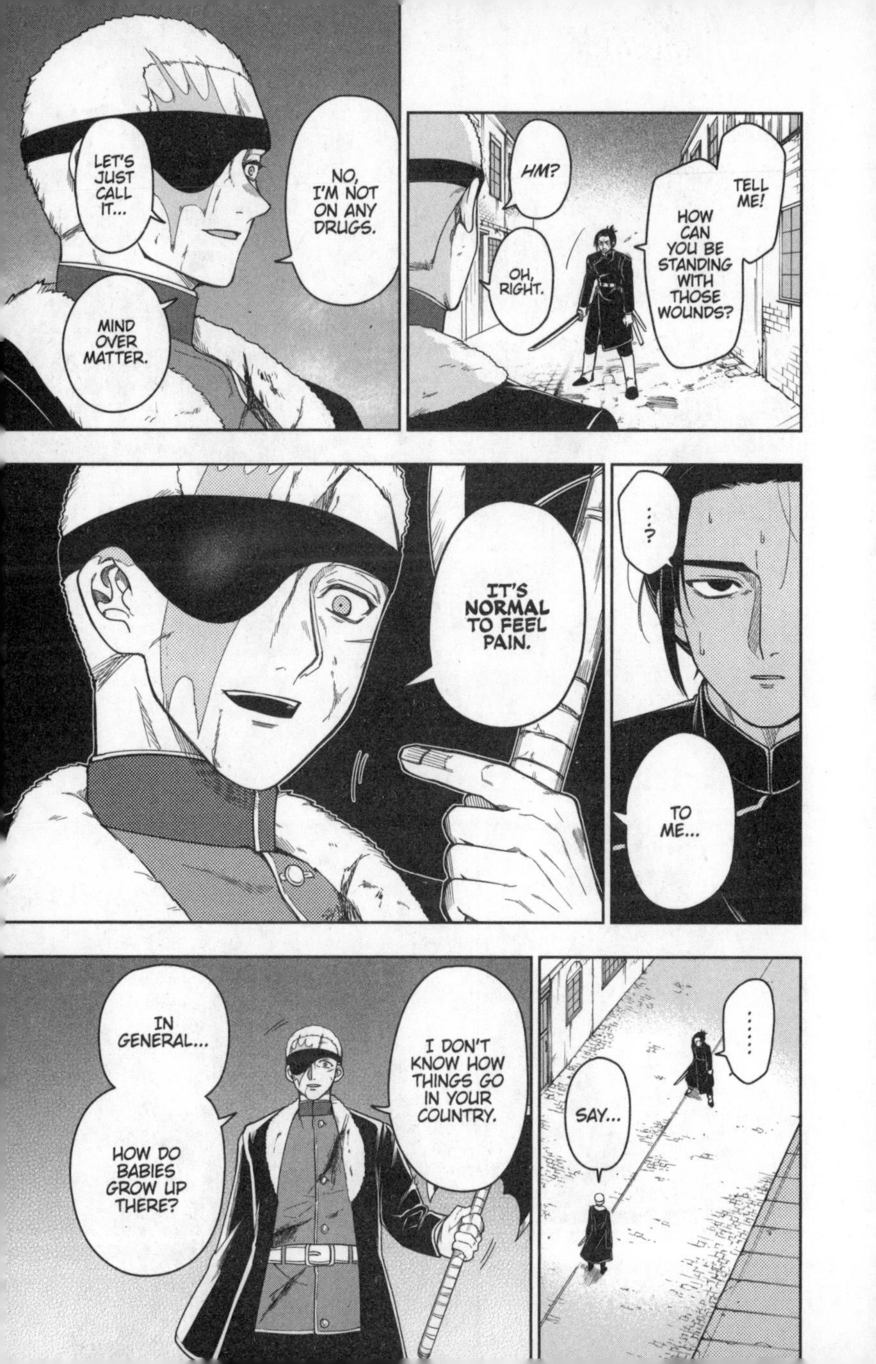
TELL ME! HOW CAN YOU BE STANDING WITH THOSE WOUNDS?
HM?
OH, RIGHT.
NO, I'M NOT ON ANY DRUGS.
LET'S JUST CALL IT...
MIND OVER MATTER.
...?
TO ME...
IT'S NORMAL TO FEEL PAIN.
......
SAY...
I DON'T KNOW HOW THINGS GO IN YOUR COUNTRY.
IN GENERAL...
HOW DO BABIES GROW UP THERE?

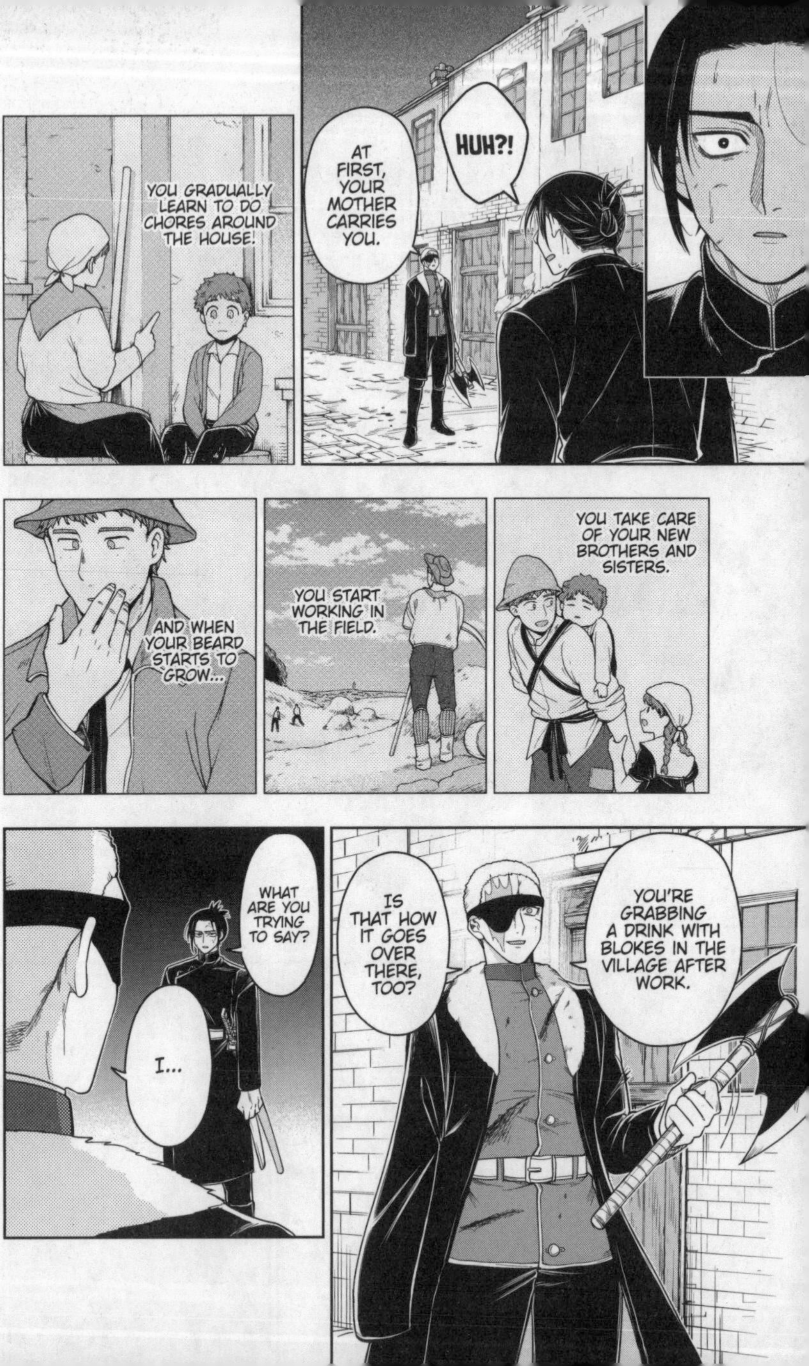
HUH?!
AT FIRST, YOUR MOTHER CARRIES YOU.
YOU GRADUALLY LEARN TO DO CHORES AROUND THE HOUSE!
YOU TAKE CARE OF YOUR NEW BROTHERS AND SISTERS.
YOU START WORKING IN THE FIELD.
AND WHEN YOUR BEARD STARTS TO GROW...
YOU'RE GRABBING A DRINK WITH BLOKES IN THE VILLAGE AFTER WORK.
IS THAT HOW IT GOES OVER THERE, TOO?
WHAT ARE YOU TRYING TO SAY?
I...

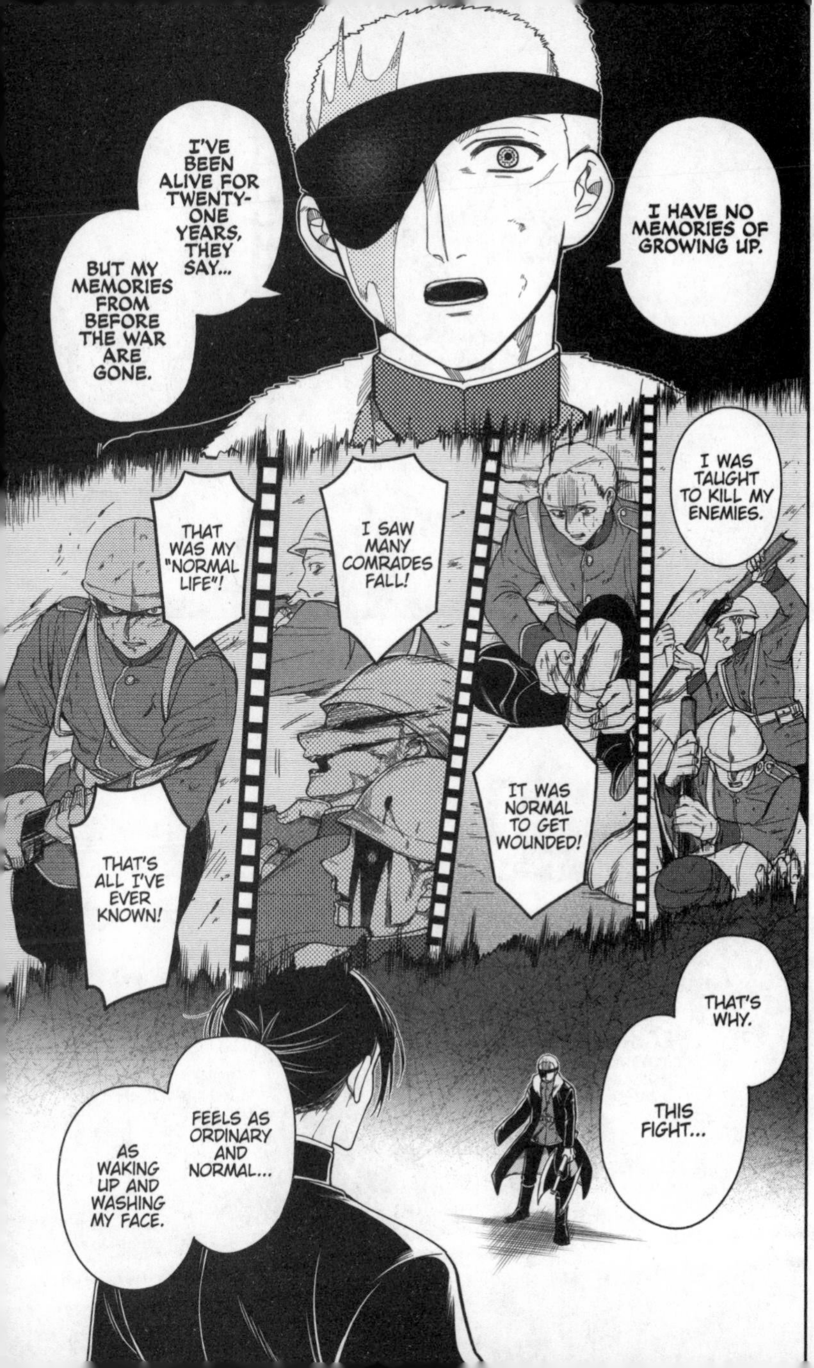
I HAVE NO MEMORIES OF GROWING UP.
I'VE BEEN ALIVE FOR TWENTY-ONE YEARS, THEY SAY...
BUT MY MEMORIES FROM BEFORE THE WAR ARE GONE.
I WAS TAUGHT TO KILL MY ENEMIES.
IT WAS NORMAL TO GET WOUNDED!
I SAW MANY COMRADES FALL!
THAT WAS MY "NORMAL LIFE"!
THAT'S ALL I'VE EVER KNOWN!
THAT'S WHY.
THIS FIGHT...
FEELS AS ORDINARY AND NORMAL...
AS WAKING UP AND WASHING MY FACE.

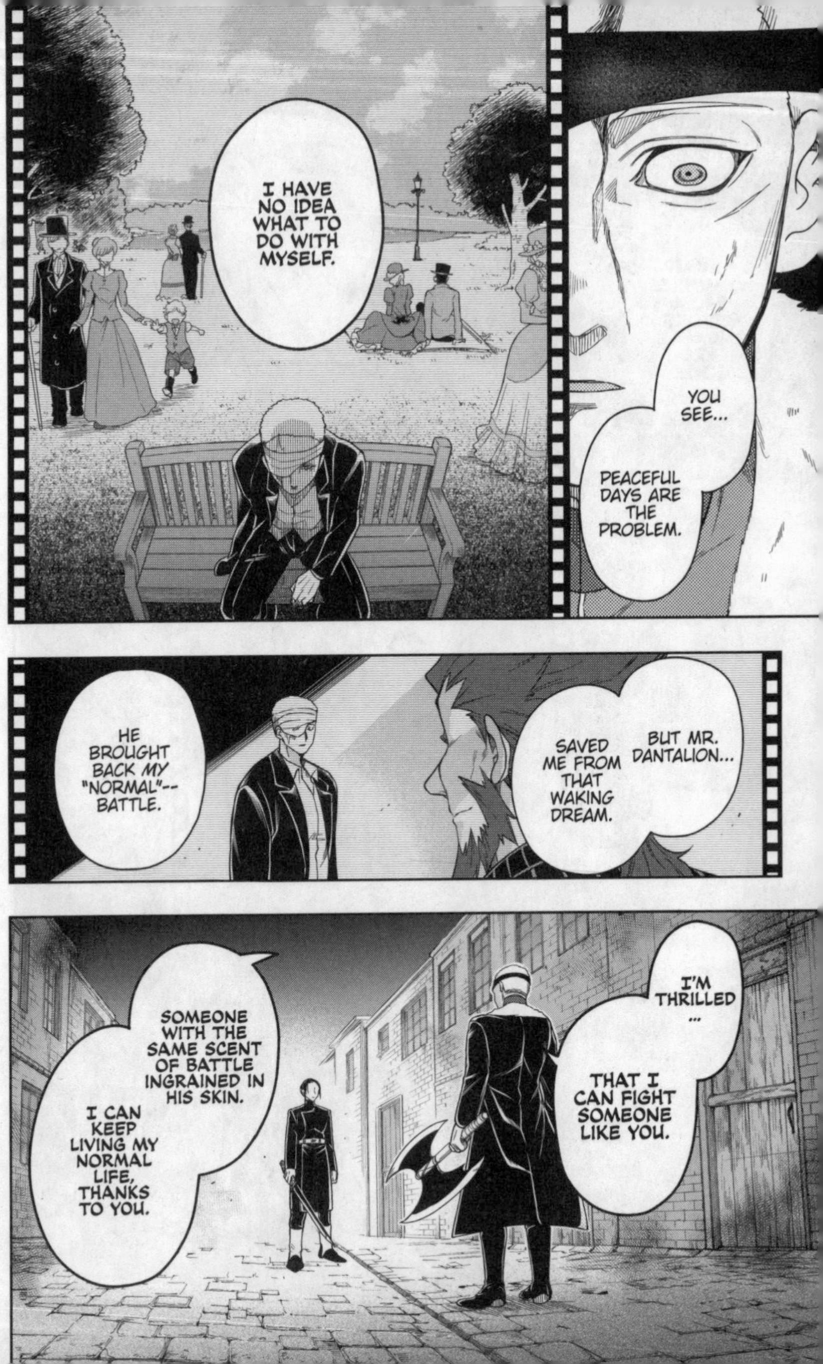
YOU SEE...
PEACEFUL DAYS ARE THE PROBLEM.
I HAVE NO IDEA WHAT TO DO WITH MYSELF.
BUT MR. DANTALION...
SAVED ME FROM THAT WAKING DREAM.
HE BROUGHT BACK MY "NORMAL"-- BATTLE.
I'M THRILLED ...
THAT I CAN FIGHT SOMEONE LIKE YOU.
SOMEONE WITH THE SAME SCENT OF BATTLE INGRAINED IN HIS SKIN.
I CAN KEEP LIVING MY NORMAL LIFE, THANKS TO YOU.

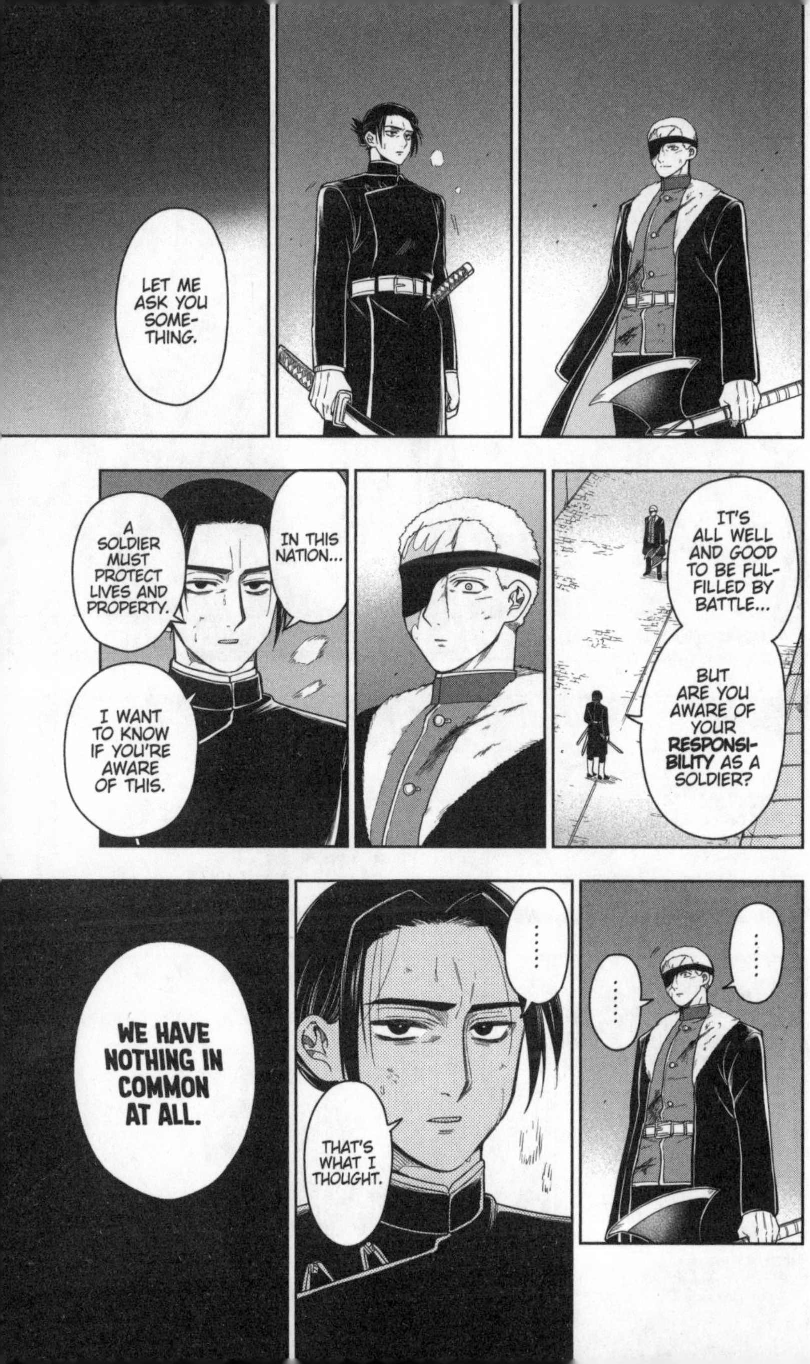
LET ME ASK YOU SOME-THING.
IT'S ALL WELL AND GOOD TO BE FUL-FILLED BY BATTLE...
BUT ARE YOU AWARE OF YOUR **RESPONSI-BILITY** AS A SOLDIER?
IN THIS NATION...
A SOLDIER MUST PROTECT LIVES AND PROPERTY.
I WANT TO KNOW IF YOU'RE AWARE OF THIS.
......
......
......
THAT'S WHAT I THOUGHT.
WE HAVE NOTHING IN COMMON AT ALL.

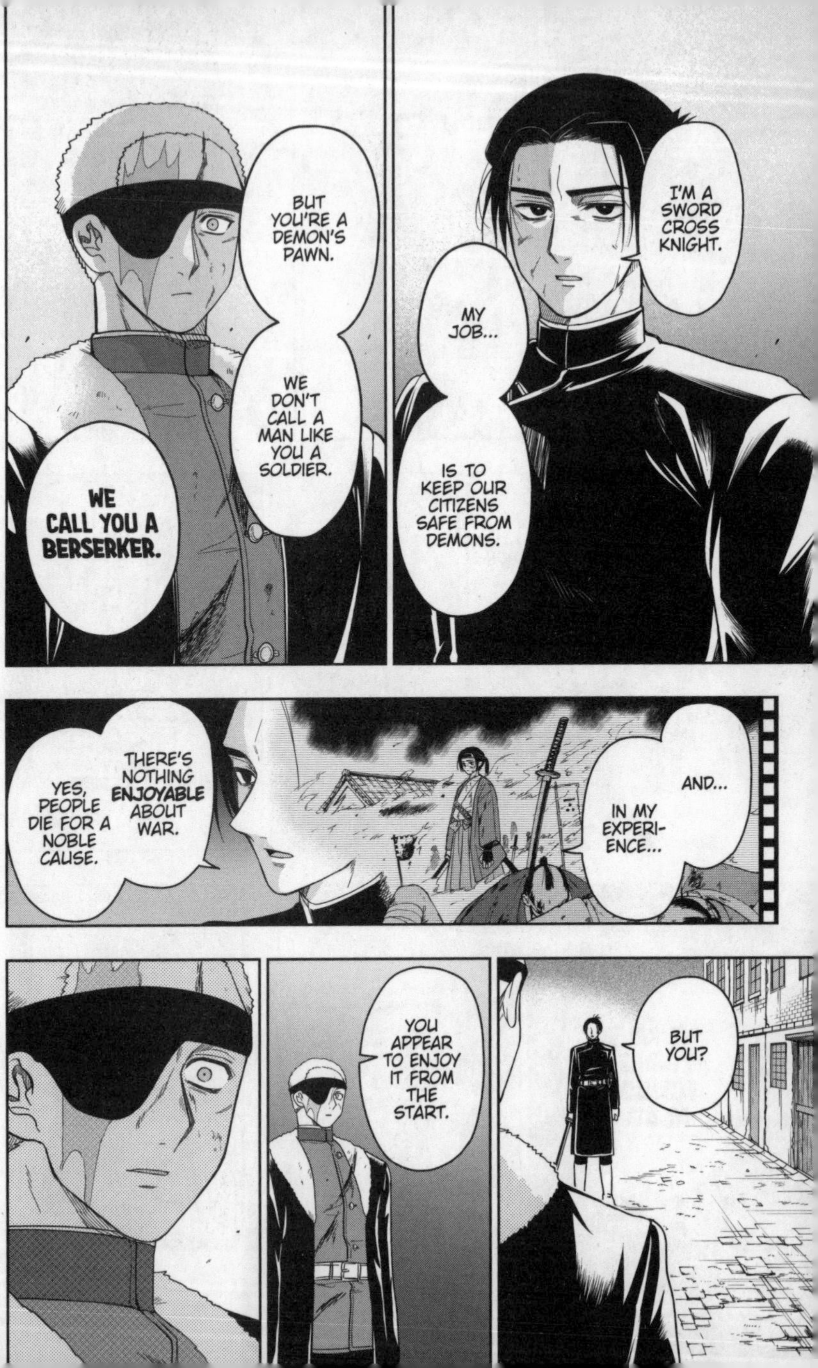
I'M A SWORD CROSS KNIGHT.
MY JOB...
IS TO KEEP OUR CITIZENS SAFE FROM DEMONS.
BUT YOU'RE A DEMON'S PAWN.
WE DON'T CALL A MAN LIKE YOU A SOLDIER.
WE CALL YOU A BERSERKER.
AND...
IN MY EXPERIENCE...
THERE'S NOTHING ENJOYABLE ABOUT WAR.
YES, PEOPLE DIE FOR A NOBLE CAUSE.
BUT YOU?
YOU APPEAR TO ENJOY IT FROM THE START.

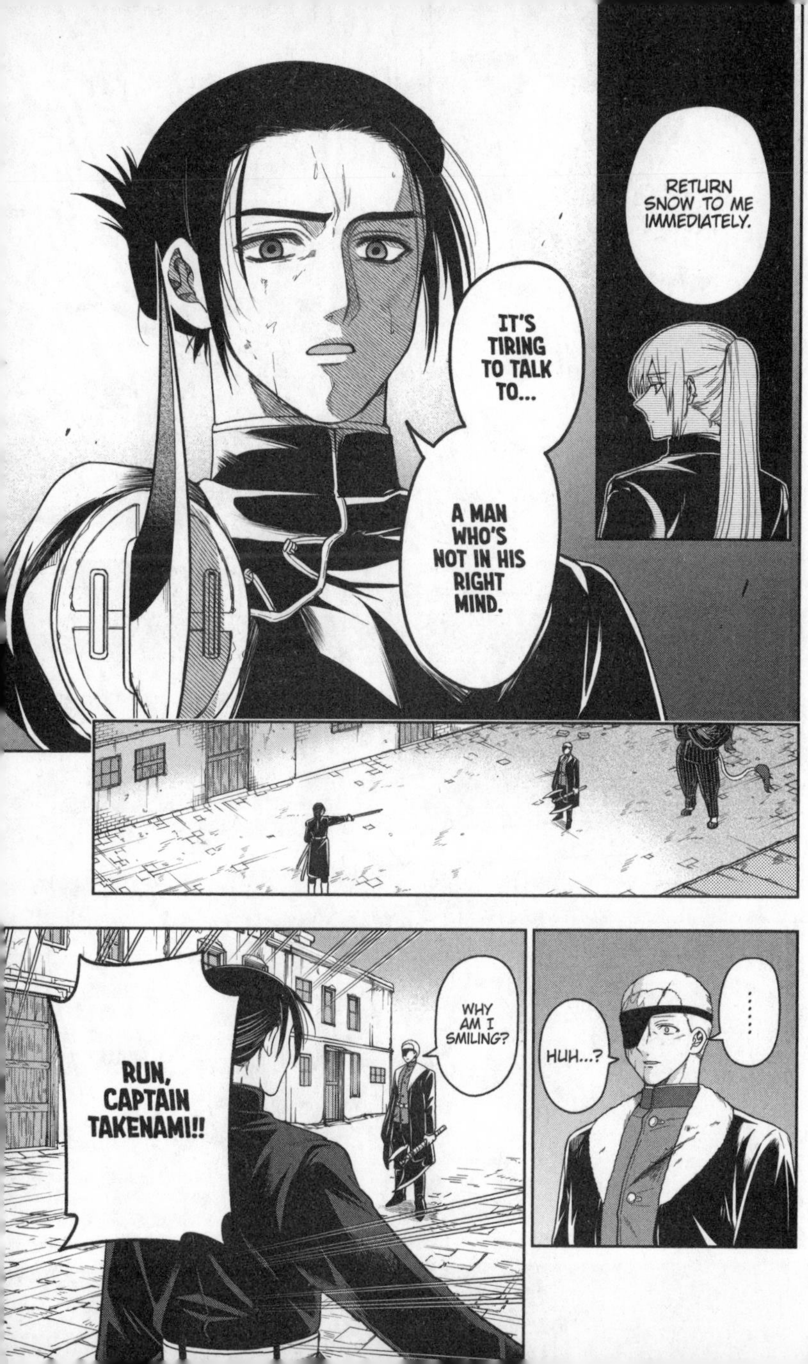
RETURN SNOW TO ME IMMEDIATELY.
IT'S TIRING TO TALK TO...
A MAN WHO'S NOT IN HIS RIGHT MIND.
......
HUH...?
WHY AM I SMILING?
RUN, CAPTAIN TAKENAMI!!

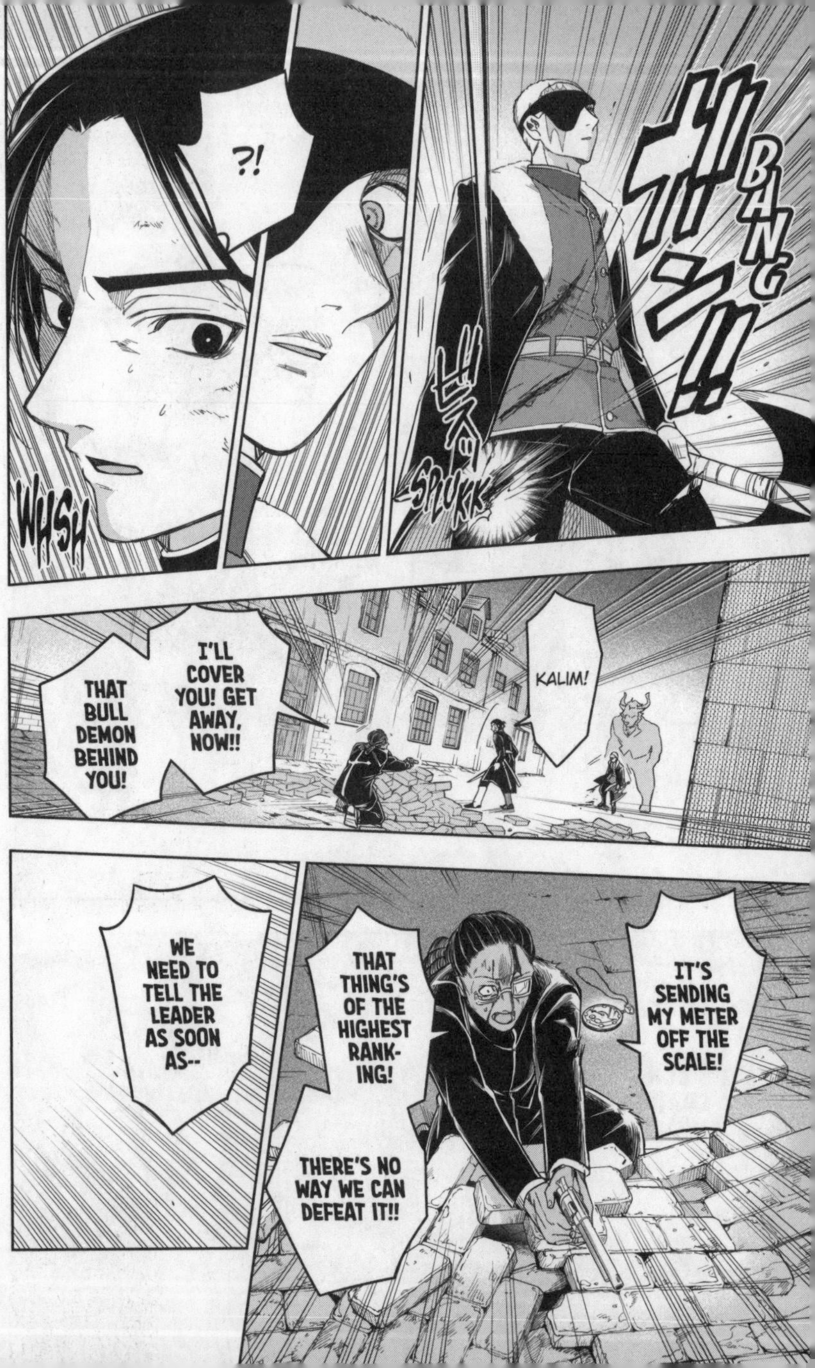
BANG
SPLUKK
?!
WHSH
KALIM!
I'LL COVER YOU! GET AWAY, NOW!!
THAT BULL DEMON BEHIND YOU!
IT'S SENDING MY METER OFF THE SCALE!
THAT THING'S OF THE HIGHEST RANK-ING!
THERE'S NO WAY WE CAN DEFEAT IT!!
WE NEED TO TELL THE LEADER AS SOON AS--

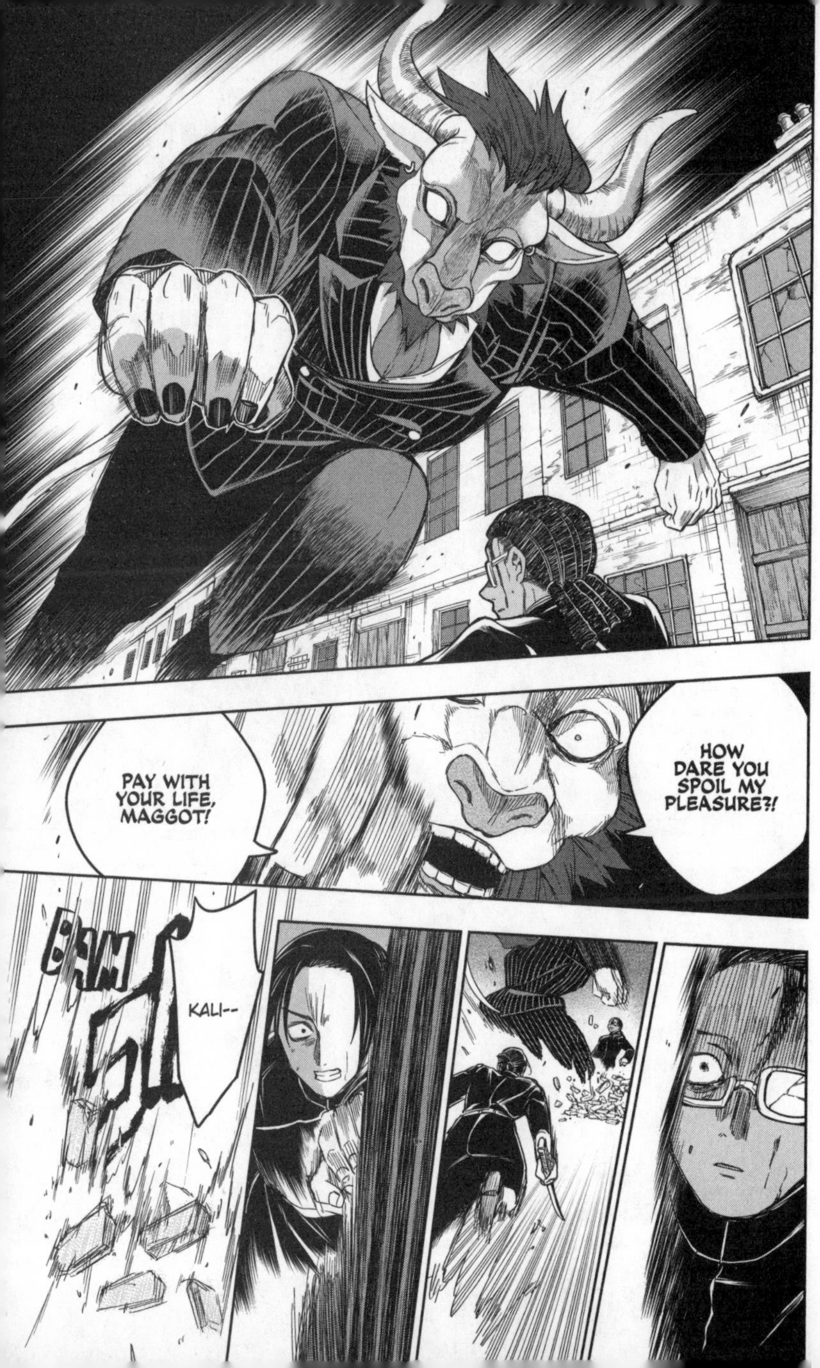
HOW DARE YOU SPOIL MY PLEASURE?!
PAY WITH YOUR LIFE, MAGGOT!
KALI--

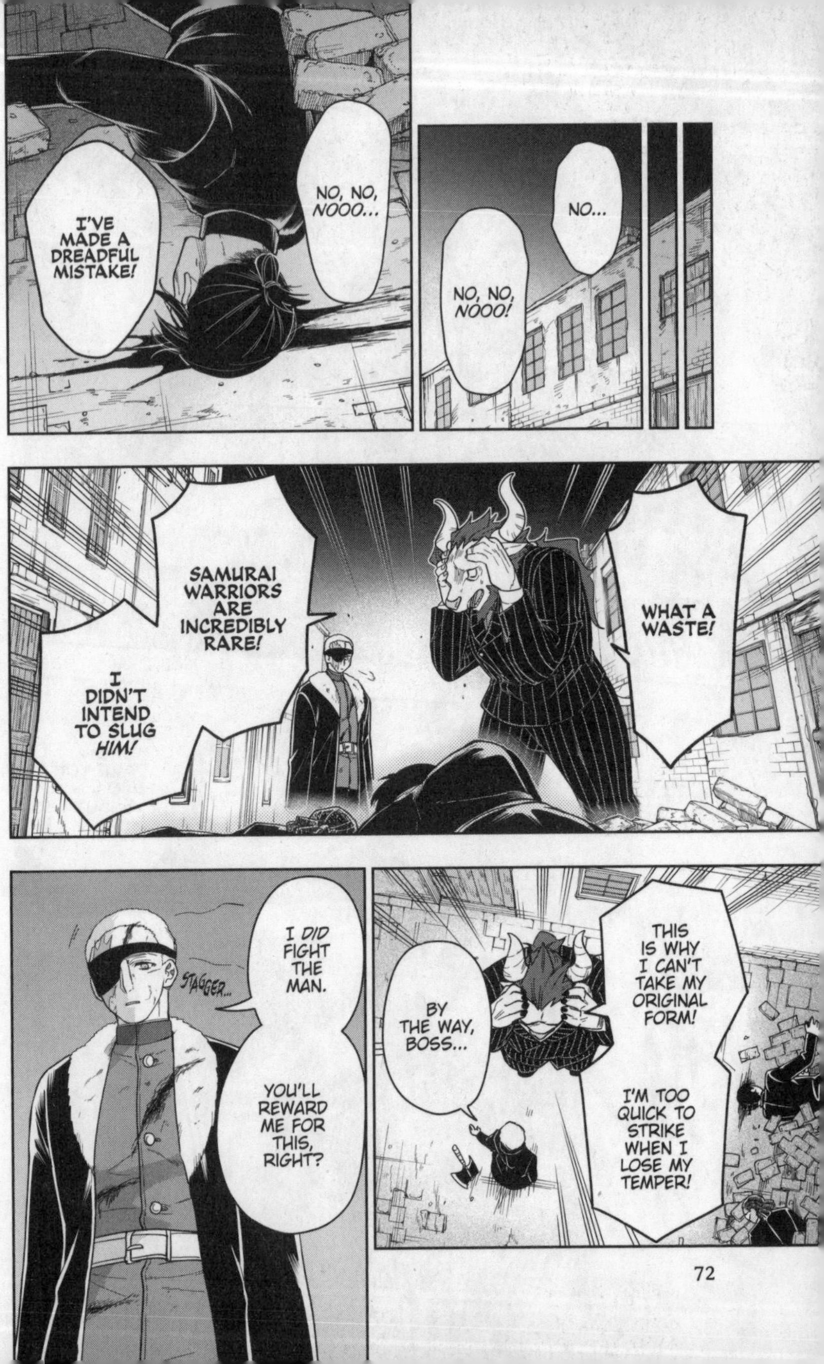
NO...
NO, NO, NOOO!
NO, NO, NOOO...
I'VE MADE A DREADFUL MISTAKE!
WHAT A WASTE!
SAMURAI WARRIORS ARE INCREDIBLY RARE!
I DIDN'T INTEND TO SLUG HIM!
THIS IS WHY I CAN'T TAKE MY ORIGINAL FORM!
I'M TOO QUICK TO STRIKE WHEN I LOSE MY TEMPER!
BY THE WAY, BOSS...
I DID FIGHT THE MAN.
STAGGER...
YOU'LL REWARD ME FOR THIS, RIGHT?

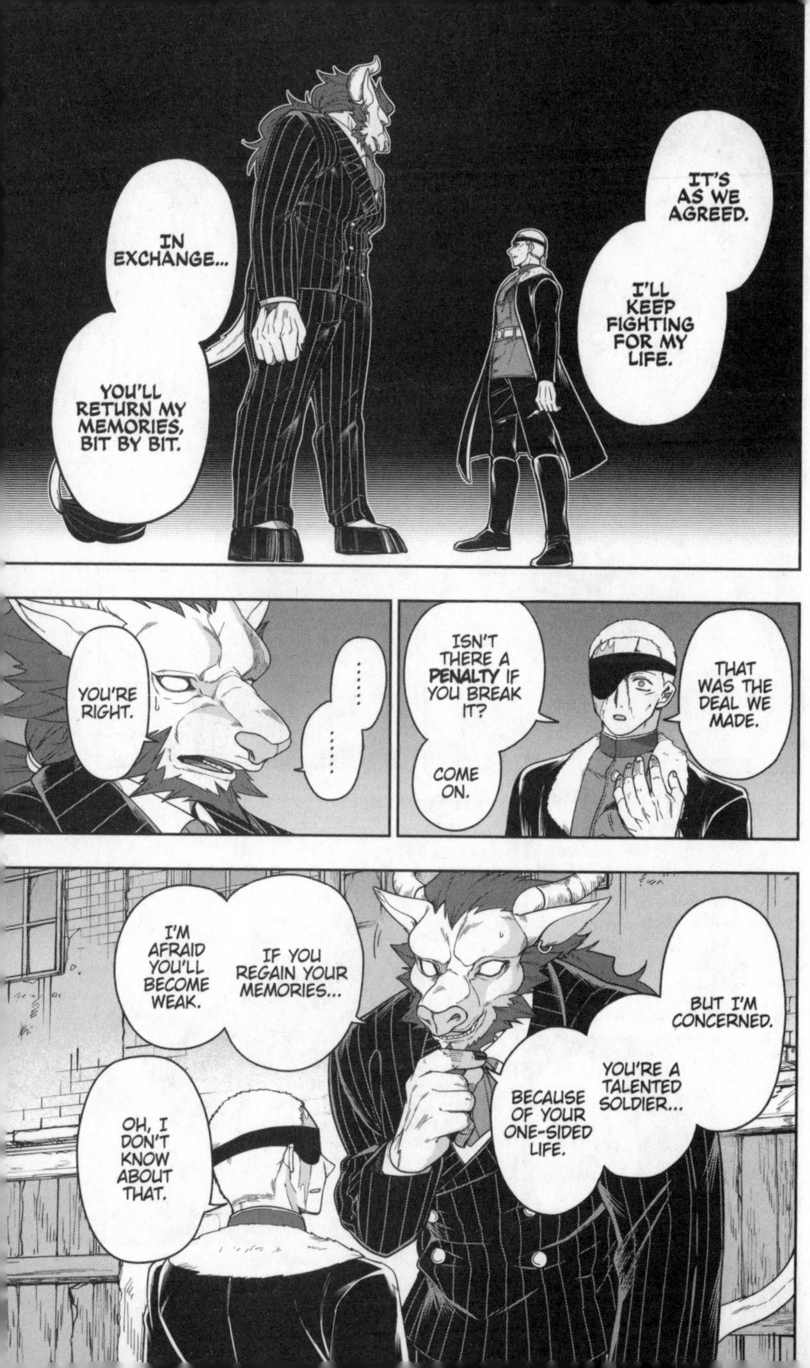
IT'S AS WE AGREED.
I'LL KEEP FIGHTING FOR MY LIFE.
IN EXCHANGE...
YOU'LL RETURN MY MEMORIES, BIT BY BIT.
THAT WAS THE DEAL WE MADE.
ISN'T THERE A **PENALTY** IF YOU BREAK IT?
COME ON.
......
YOU'RE RIGHT.
BUT I'M CONCERNED.
YOU'RE A TALENTED SOLDIER...
BECAUSE OF YOUR ONE-SIDED LIFE.
IF YOU REGAIN YOUR MEMORIES...
I'M AFRAID YOU'LL BECOME WEAK.
OH, I DON'T KNOW ABOUT THAT.

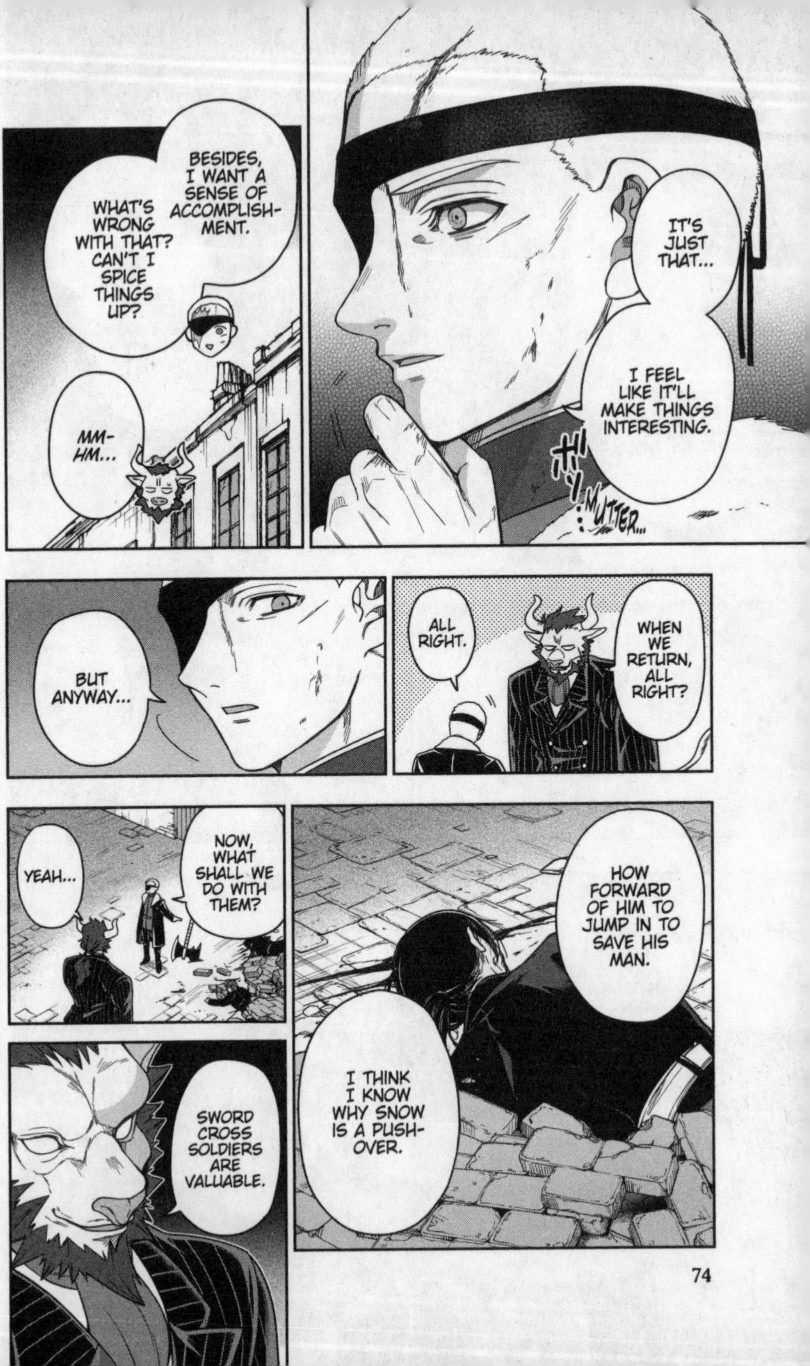
IT'S JUST THAT...
I FEEL LIKE IT'LL MAKE THINGS INTERESTING.
MUTTER...
BESIDES, I WANT A SENSE OF ACCOMPLISHMENT.
WHAT'S WRONG WITH THAT? CAN'T I SPICE THINGS UP?
MM-HM...
WHEN WE RETURN, ALL RIGHT?
ALL RIGHT.
BUT ANYWAY...
HOW FORWARD OF HIM TO JUMP IN TO SAVE HIS MAN.
I THINK I KNOW WHY SNOW IS A PUSH-OVER.
NOW, WHAT SHALL WE DO WITH THEM?
YEAH...
SWORD CROSS SOLDIERS ARE VALUABLE.

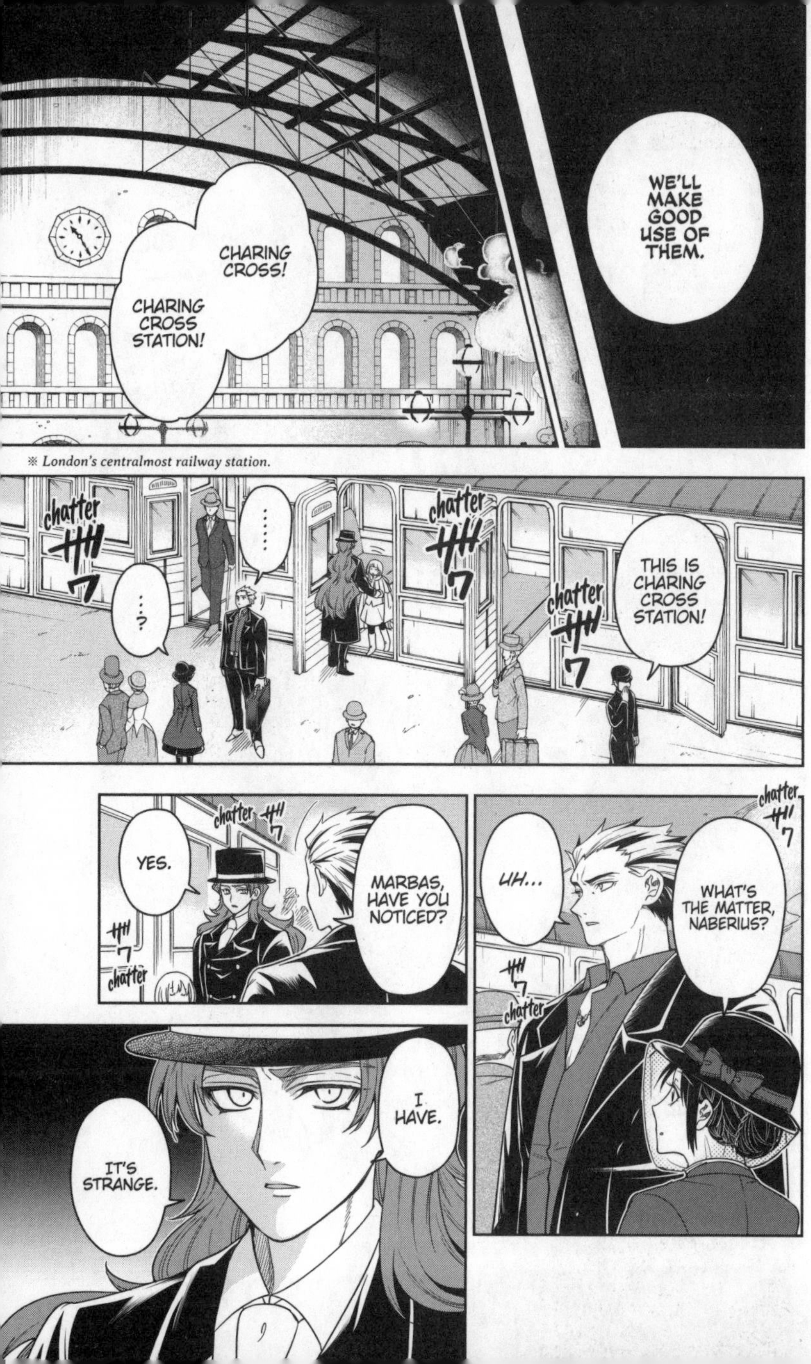
WE'LL MAKE GOOD USE OF THEM.
CHARING CROSS!
CHARING CROSS STATION!
chatter
THIS IS CHARING CROSS STATION!
chatter
chatter
......
...?
chatter
WHAT'S THE MATTER, NABERIUS?
UH...
chatter
MARBAS, HAVE YOU NOTICED?
chatter
YES.
chatter
I HAVE.
IT'S STRANGE.

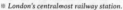

※ *London's centralmost railway station.*

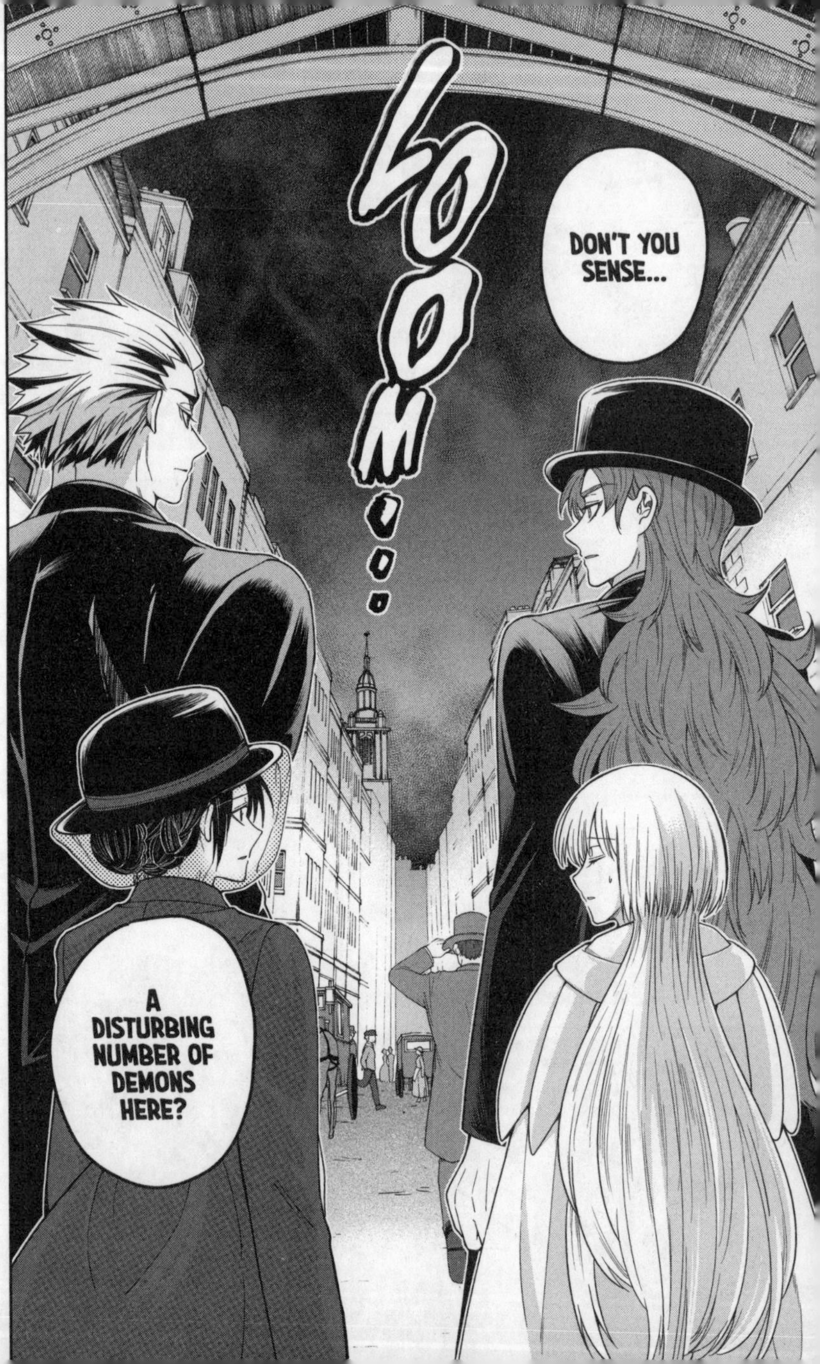
DON'T YOU SENSE...
LOOOM...
A DISTURBING NUMBER OF DEMONS HERE?

The Tale of the Outcasts

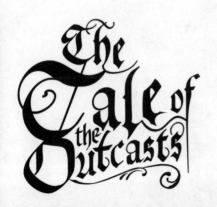

Night 42 Three-Sided Struggle

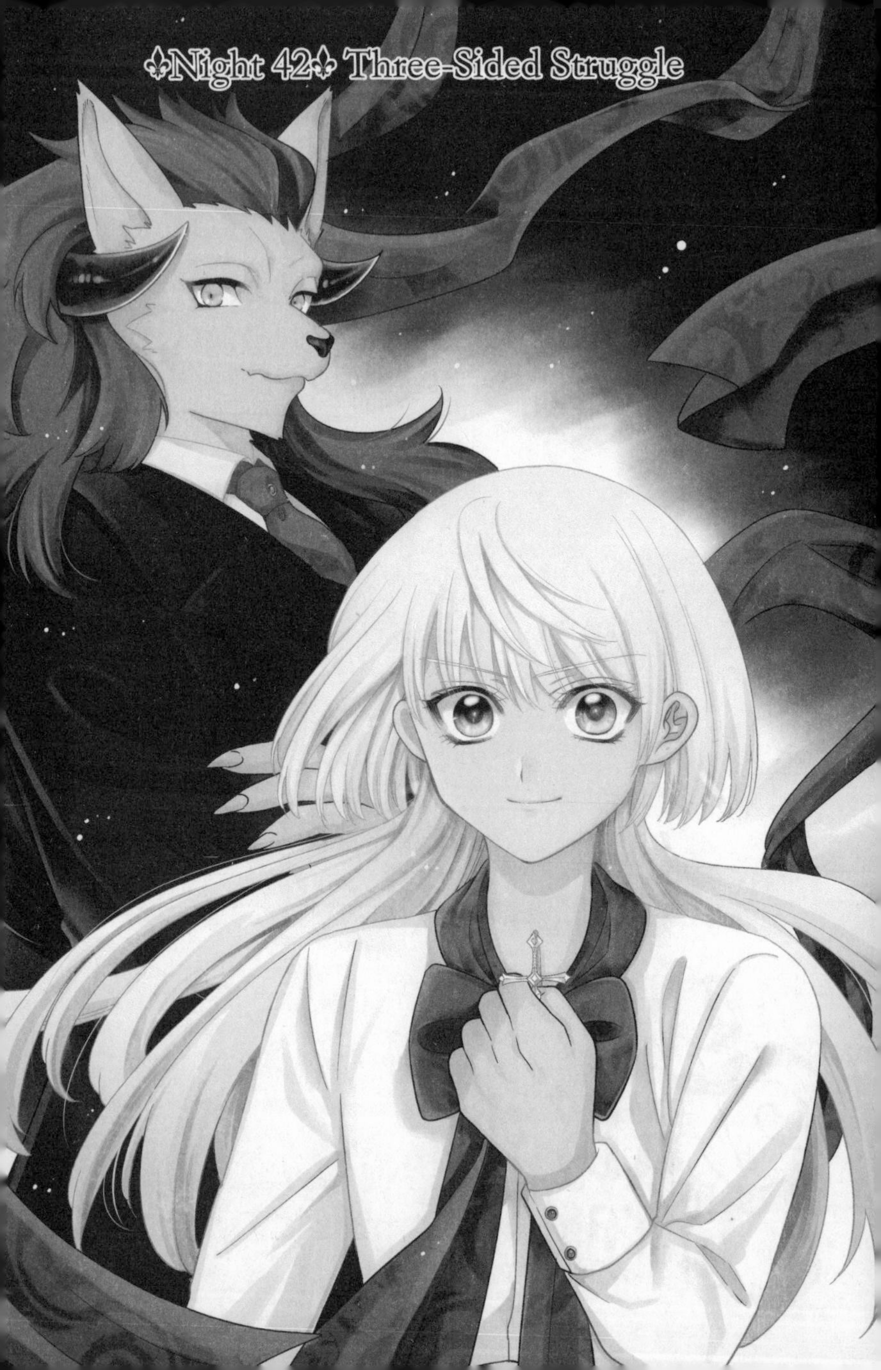

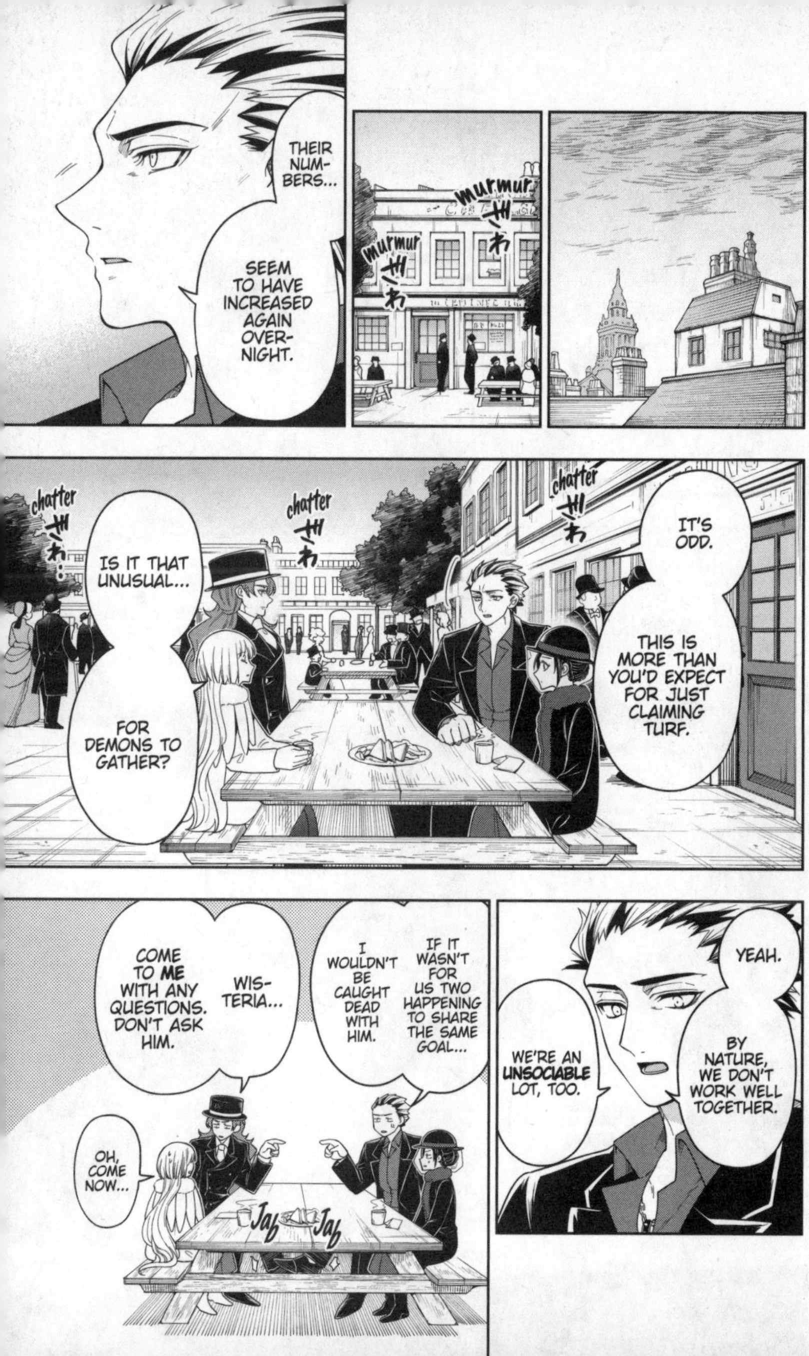
murmur ざわ
murmur ざわ
THEIR NUMBERS...
SEEM TO HAVE INCREASED AGAIN OVERNIGHT.
chatter ざわ
IT'S ODD.
THIS IS MORE THAN YOU'D EXPECT FOR JUST CLAIMING TURF.
chatter ざわ
IS IT THAT UNUSUAL...
FOR DEMONS TO GATHER?
chatter ざわ...
YEAH.
BY NATURE, WE DON'T WORK WELL TOGETHER.
WE'RE AN UNSOCIABLE LOT, TOO.
IF IT WASN'T FOR US TWO HAPPENING TO SHARE THE SAME GOAL...
I WOULDN'T BE CAUGHT DEAD WITH HIM.
WISTERIA...
COME TO ME WITH ANY QUESTIONS. DON'T ASK HIM.
OH, COME NOW...
Jab Jab

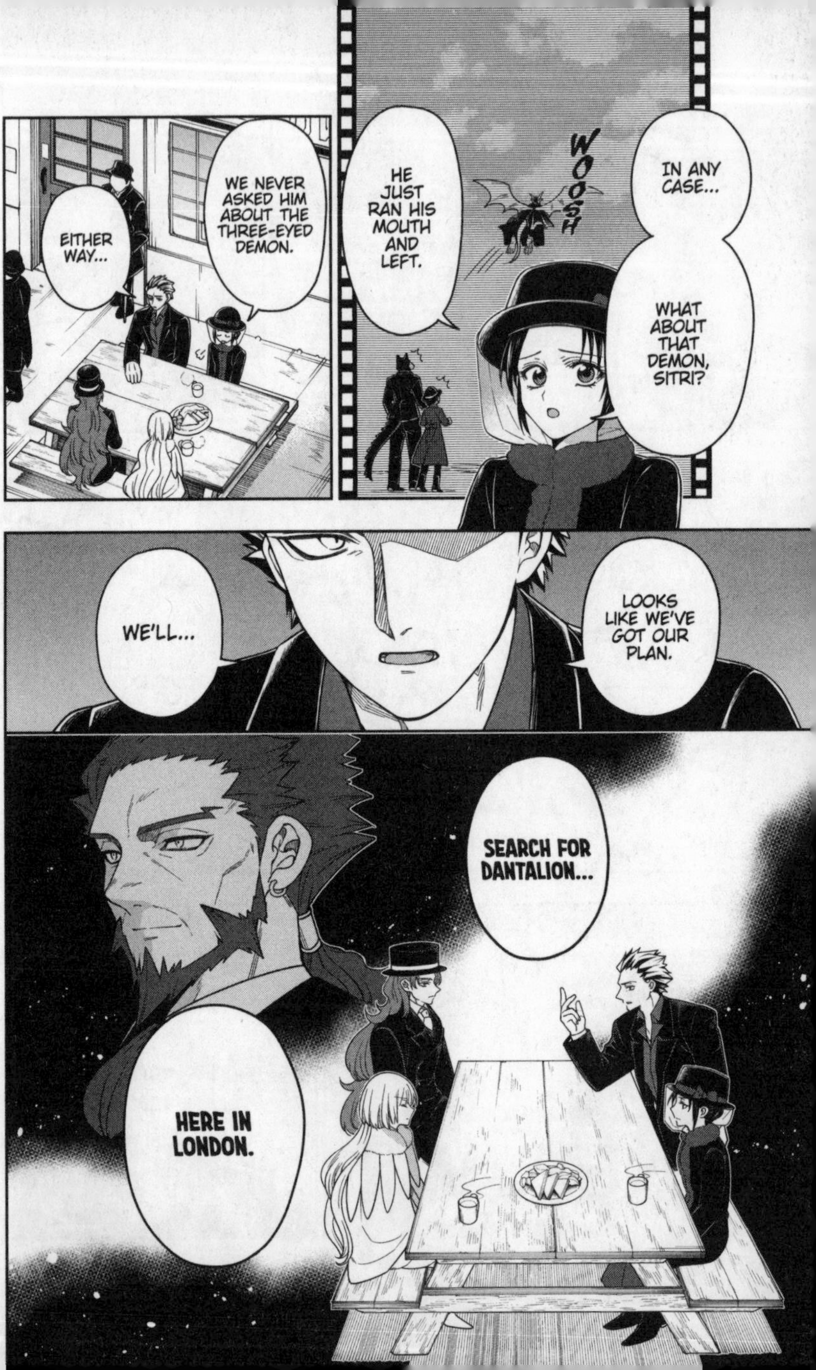
IN ANY CASE...
WHAT ABOUT THAT DEMON, SITRI?
WOOOSH
HE JUST RAN HIS MOUTH AND LEFT.
WE NEVER ASKED HIM ABOUT THE THREE-EYED DEMON.
EITHER WAY...
LOOKS LIKE WE'VE GOT OUR PLAN.
WE'LL...
SEARCH FOR DANTALION...
HERE IN LONDON.

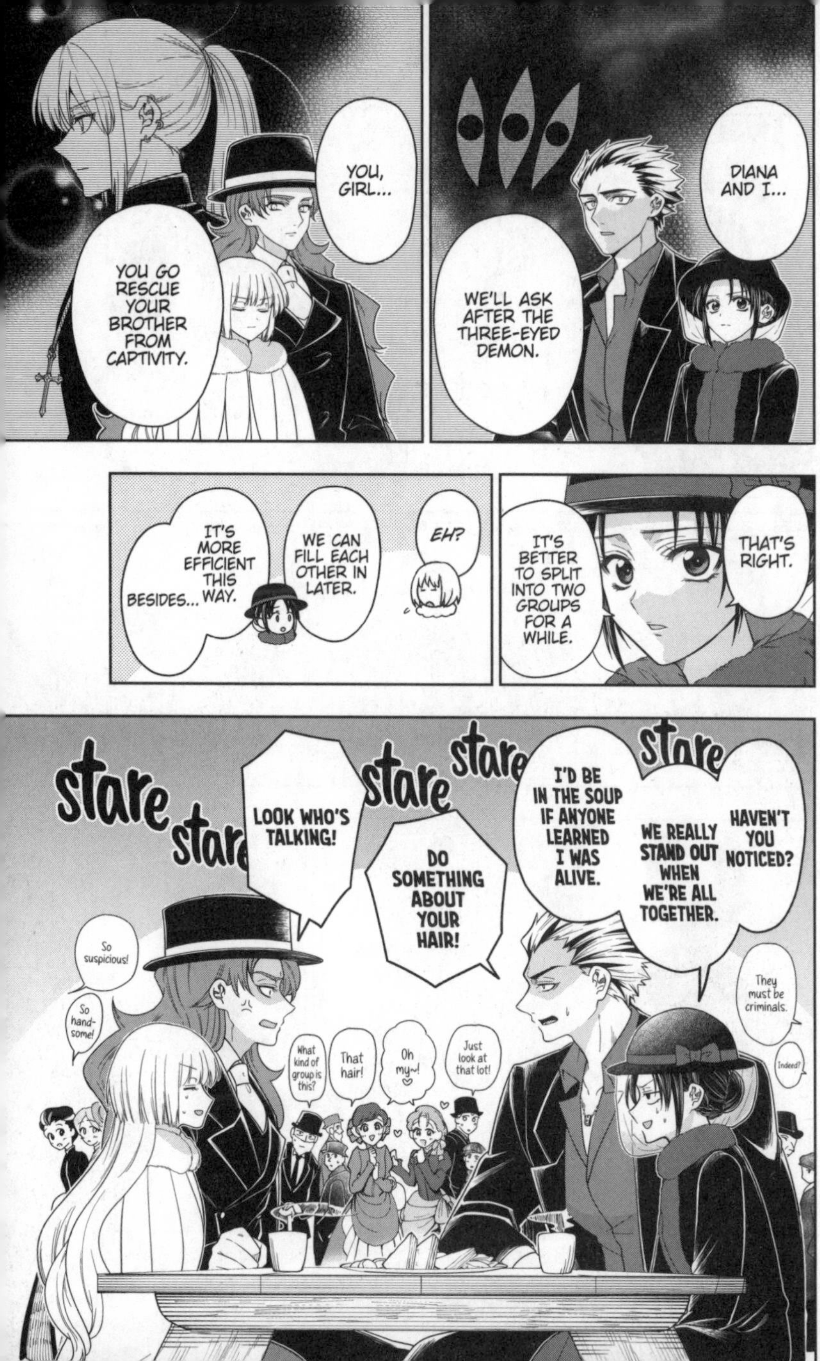
DIANA AND I...
WE'LL ASK AFTER THE THREE-EYED DEMON.
YOU, GIRL...
YOU GO RESCUE YOUR BROTHER FROM CAPTIVITY.
THAT'S RIGHT.
IT'S BETTER TO SPLIT INTO TWO GROUPS FOR A WHILE.
EH?
WE CAN FILL EACH OTHER IN LATER.
IT'S MORE EFFICIENT THIS WAY.
BESIDES...
stare
stare
stare
stare
stare
HAVEN'T YOU NOTICED?
WE REALLY STAND OUT WHEN WE'RE ALL TOGETHER.
I'D BE IN THE SOUP IF ANYONE LEARNED I WAS ALIVE.
DO SOMETHING ABOUT YOUR HAIR!
LOOK WHO'S TALKING!
They must be criminals.
Indeed?
Just look at that lot!
Oh my~!
That hair!
What kind of group is this?
So suspicious!
So handsome!

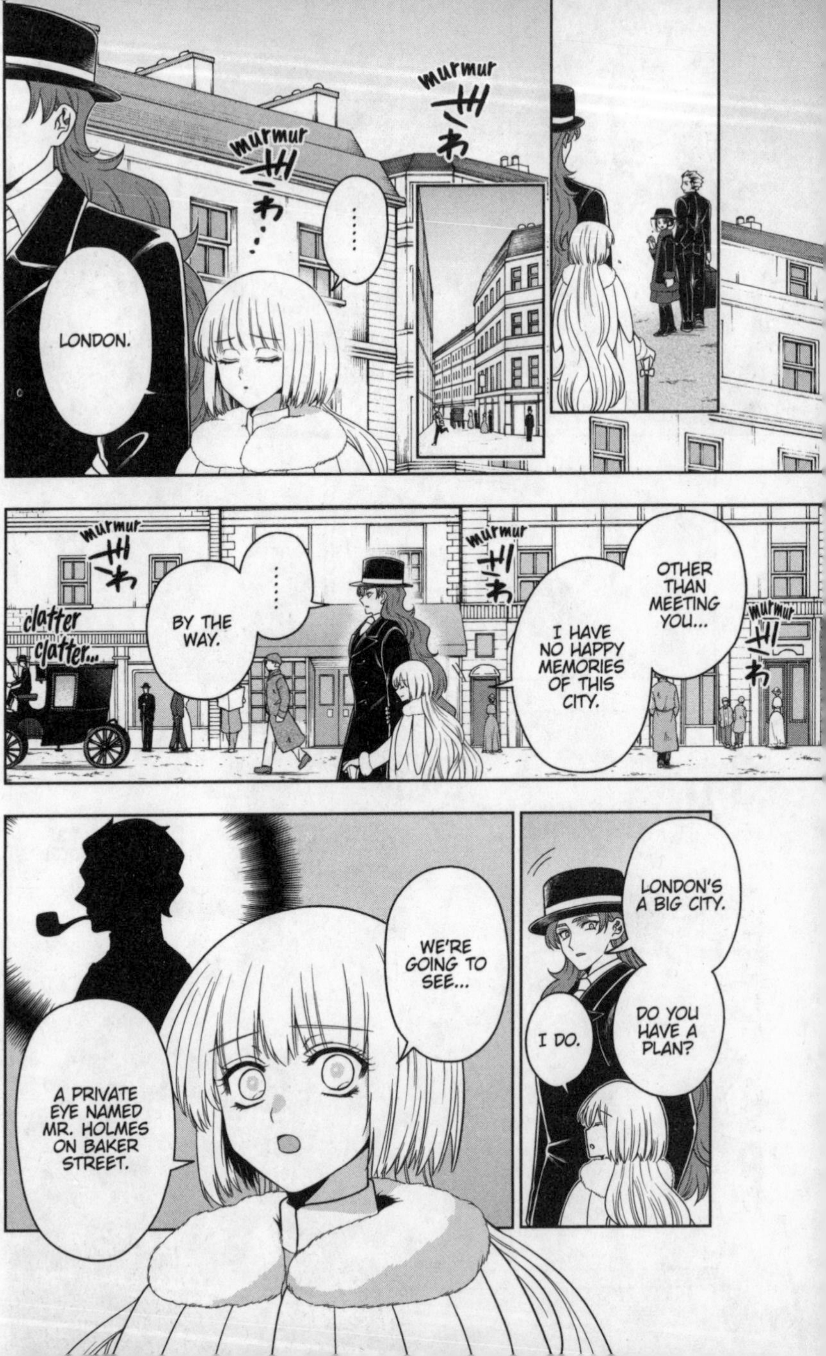
murmur
ざわ
murmur
ざわ
......
LONDON.
murmur
ざわ
OTHER THAN MEETING YOU...
I HAVE NO HAPPY MEMORIES OF THIS CITY.
murmur
ざわ
......
BY THE WAY.
murmur
ざわ
clatter clatter...
LONDON'S A BIG CITY.
DO YOU HAVE A PLAN?
I DO.
WE'RE GOING TO SEE...
A PRIVATE EYE NAMED MR. HOLMES ON BAKER STREET.

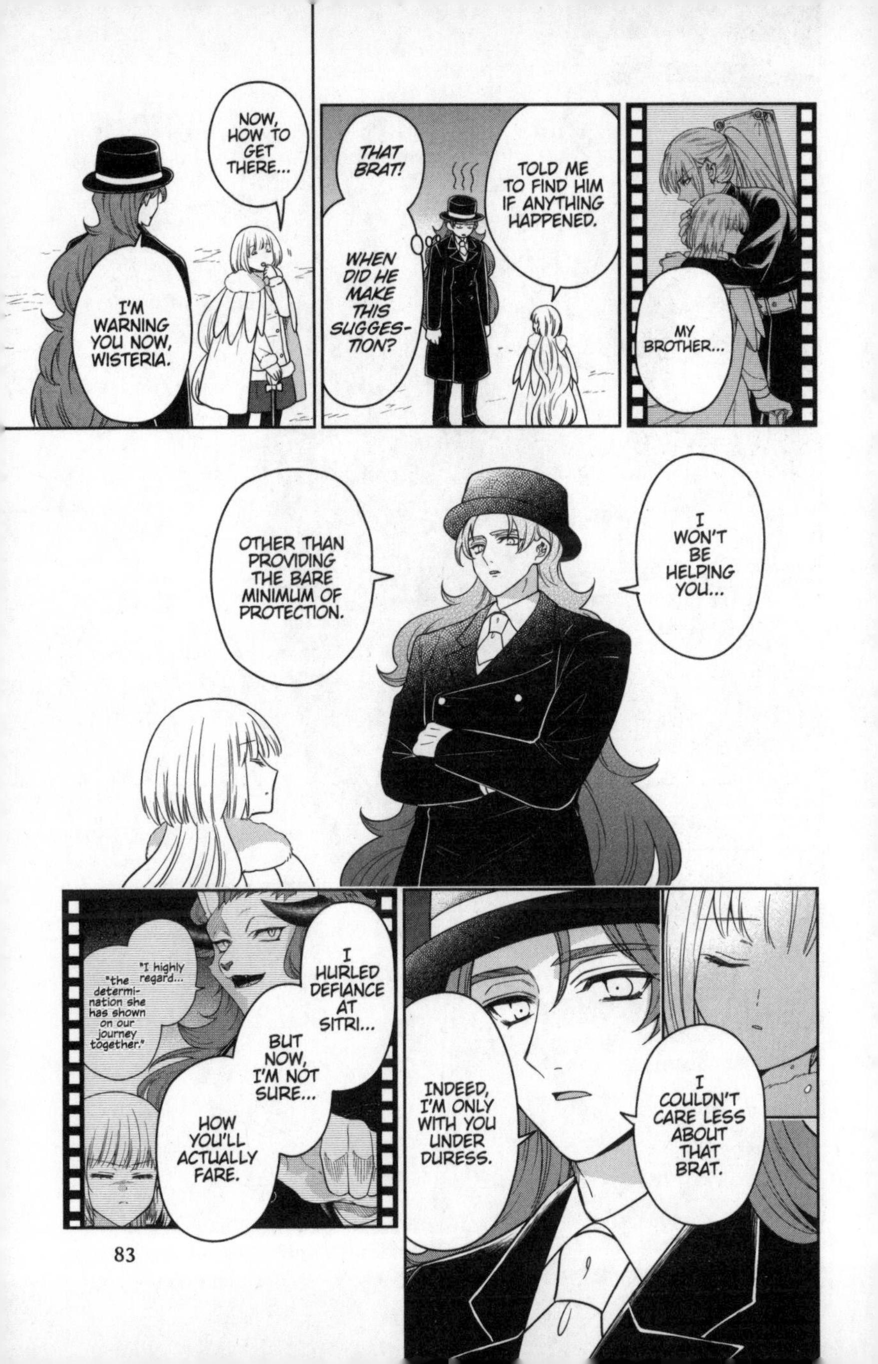
MY BROTHER...
TOLD ME TO FIND HIM IF ANYTHING HAPPENED.
THAT BRAT!
WHEN DID HE MAKE THIS SUGGES-TION?
NOW, HOW TO GET THERE...
I'M WARNING YOU NOW, WISTERIA.
I WON'T BE HELPING YOU...
OTHER THAN PROVIDING THE BARE MINIMUM OF PROTECTION.
I COULDN'T CARE LESS ABOUT THAT BRAT.
INDEED, I'M ONLY WITH YOU UNDER DURESS.
I HURLED DEFIANCE AT SITRI...
"I highly regard...
"the determi-nation she has shown on our journey together."
BUT NOW, I'M NOT SURE...
HOW YOU'LL ACTUALLY FARE.

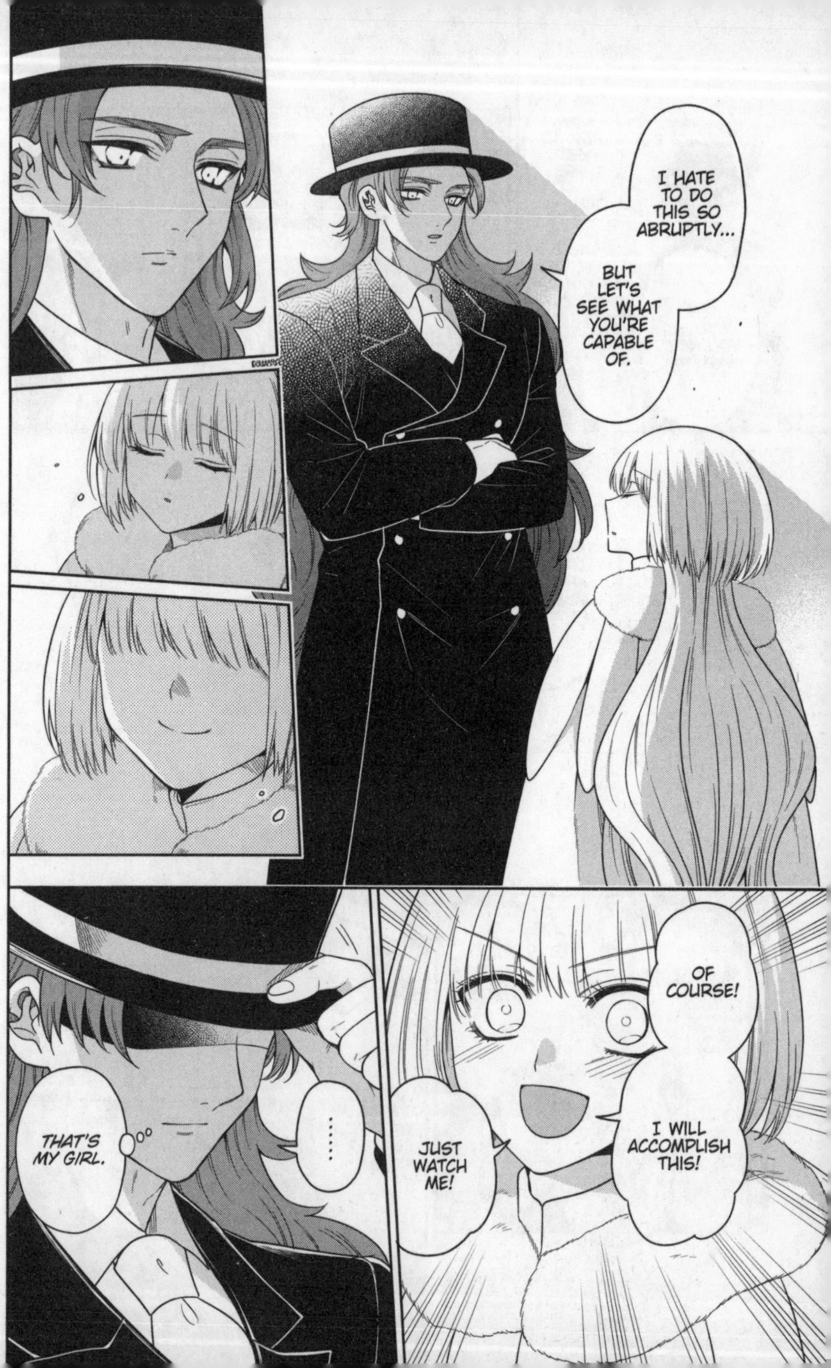
I HATE TO DO THIS SO ABRUPTLY...
BUT LET'S SEE WHAT YOU'RE CAPABLE OF.
OF COURSE!
I WILL ACCOMPLISH THIS!
JUST WATCH ME!
......
THAT'S MY GIRL.

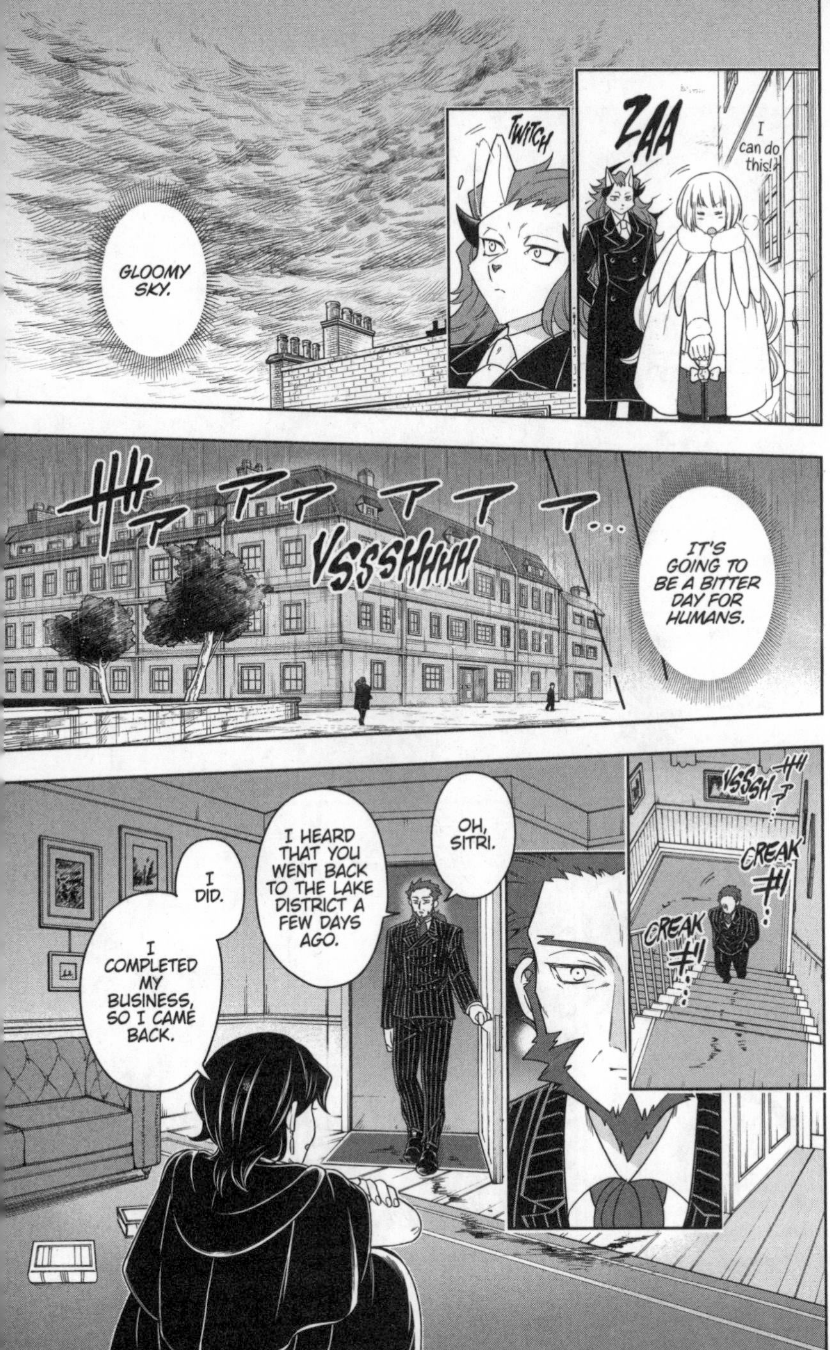
ZAA
I can do this!?
TWITCH
GLOOMY SKY.
ザアアアア…
VSSSHHHH
IT'S GOING TO BE A BITTER DAY FOR HUMANS.
VSSSH ザァ…
CREAK ギィ…
CREAK ギィ…
OH, SITRI.
I HEARD THAT YOU WENT BACK TO THE LAKE DISTRICT A FEW DAYS AGO.
I DID.
I COMPLETED MY BUSINESS, SO I CAME BACK.

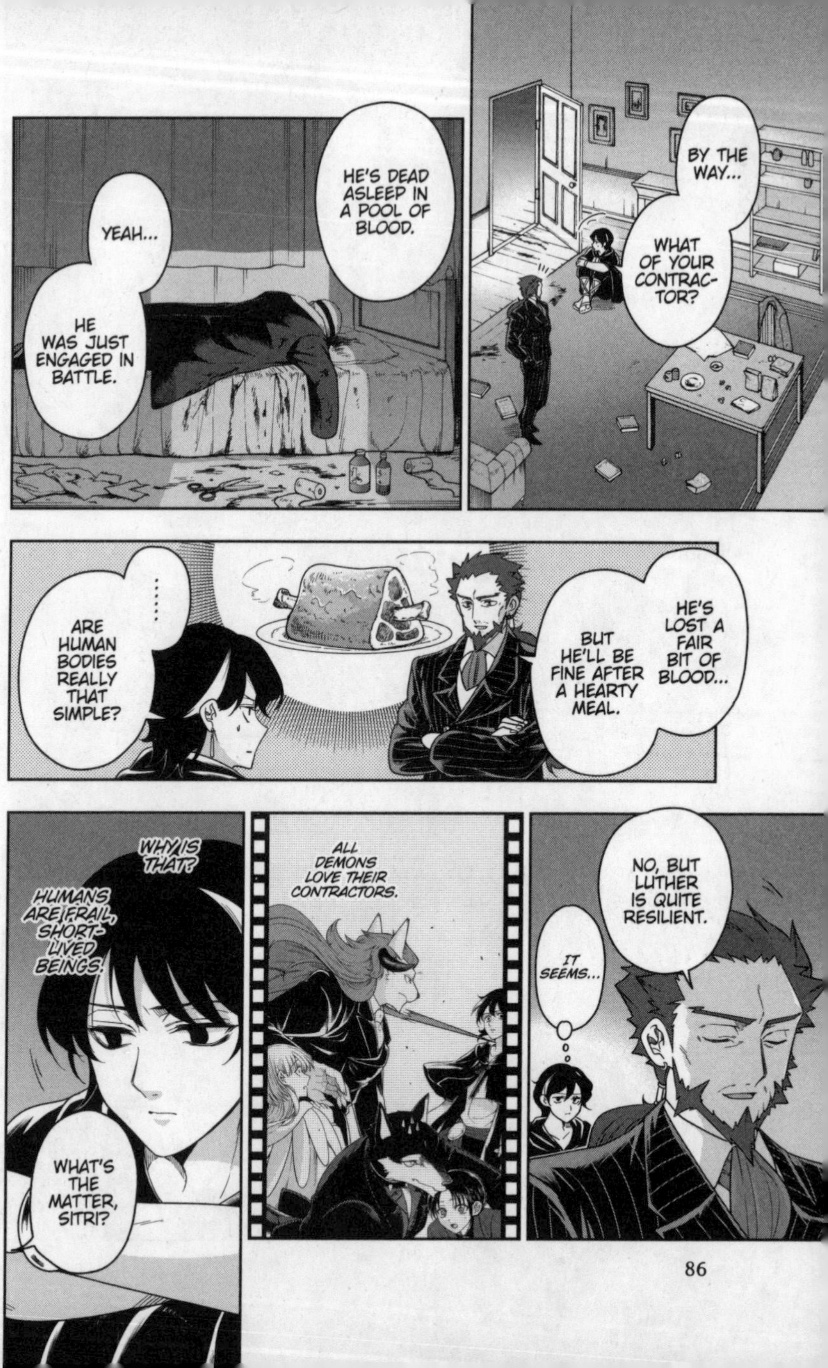
BY THE WAY...
WHAT OF YOUR CONTRACTOR?
HE'S DEAD ASLEEP IN A POOL OF BLOOD.
YEAH...
HE WAS JUST ENGAGED IN BATTLE.
HE'S LOST A FAIR BIT OF BLOOD...
BUT HE'LL BE FINE AFTER A HEARTY MEAL.
......
ARE HUMAN BODIES REALLY THAT SIMPLE?
NO, BUT LUTHER IS QUITE RESILIENT.
IT SEEMS...
ALL DEMONS LOVE THEIR CONTRACTORS.
WHY IS THAT?
HUMANS ARE FRAIL, SHORT-LIVED BEINGS.
WHAT'S THE MATTER, SITRI?

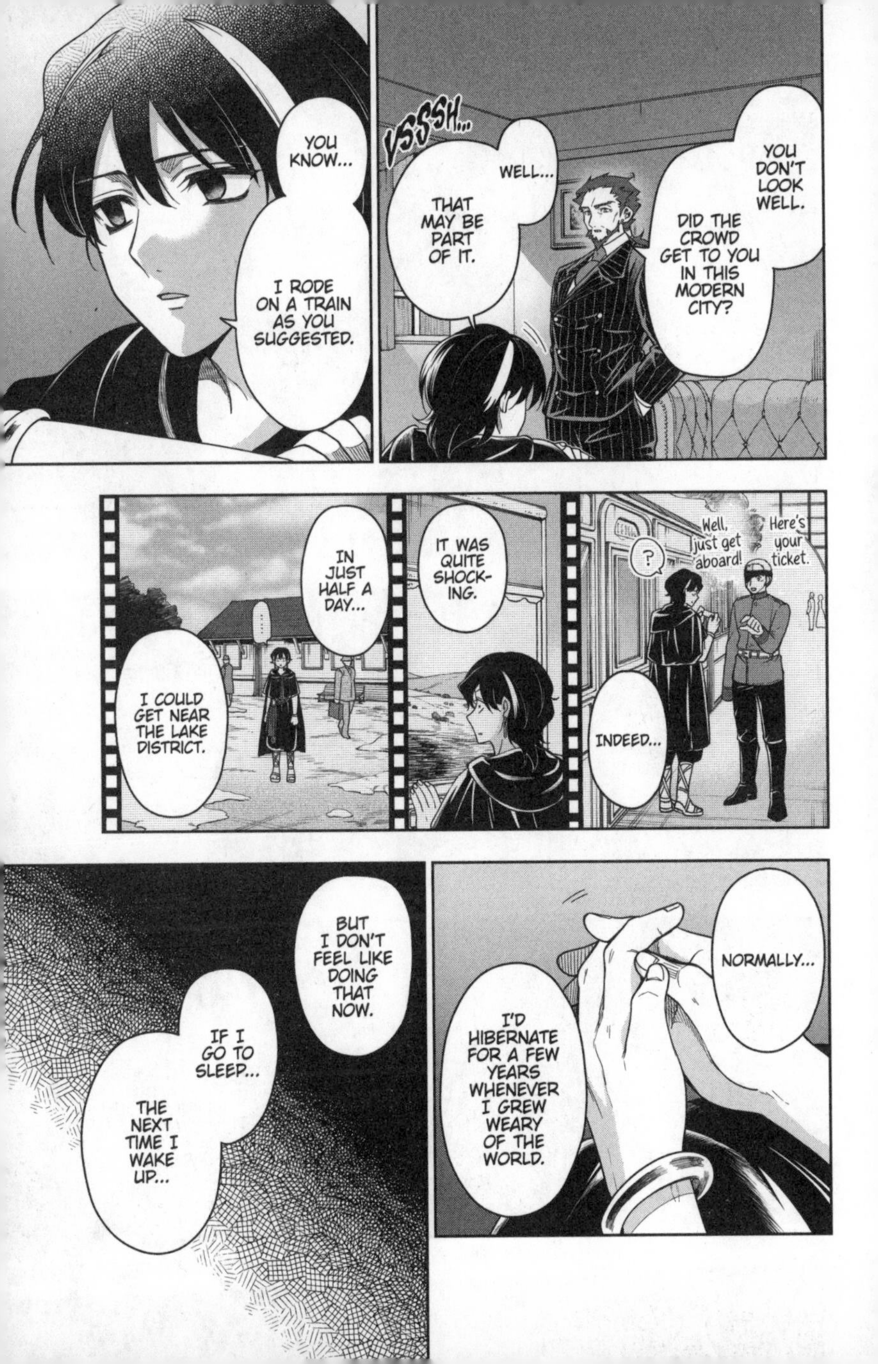

YOU DON'T LOOK WELL.
DID THE CROWD GET TO YOU IN THIS MODERN CITY?
VSSSH...
WELL...
THAT MAY BE PART OF IT.
YOU KNOW...
I RODE ON A TRAIN AS YOU SUGGESTED.
Here's your ticket.
Well, just get aboard!
?
INDEED...
IT WAS QUITE SHOCK-ING.
IN JUST HALF A DAY...
...
I COULD GET NEAR THE LAKE DISTRICT.
NORMALLY...
I'D HIBERNATE FOR A FEW YEARS WHENEVER I GREW WEARY OF THE WORLD.
BUT I DON'T FEEL LIKE DOING THAT NOW.
IF I GO TO SLEEP...
THE NEXT TIME I WAKE UP...

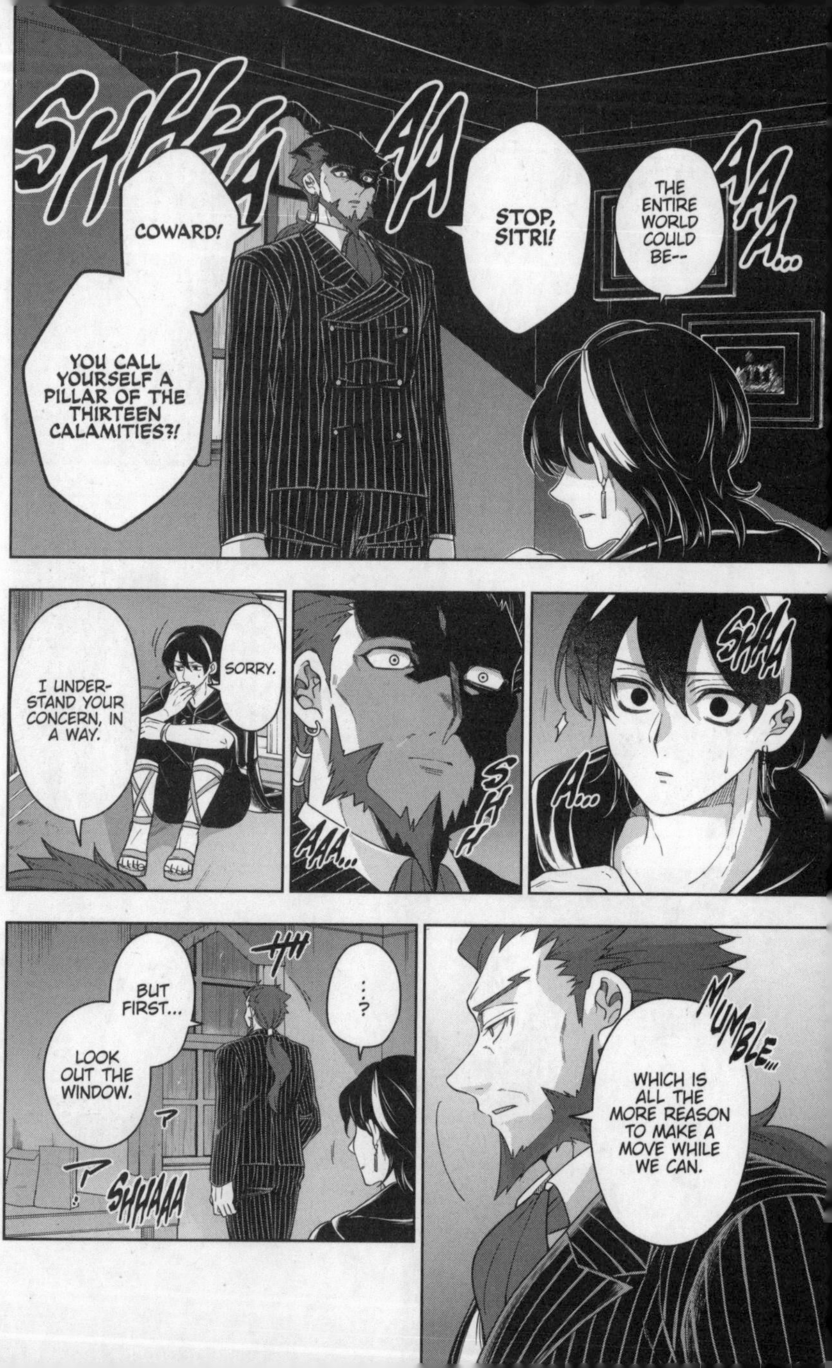
THE ENTIRE WORLD COULD BE--
STOP, SITRI!
SHHAA AA AAA...
COWARD!
YOU CALL YOURSELF A PILLAR OF THE THIRTEEN CALAMITIES?!
SHAA
A...
SHH
AAA...
SORRY.
I UNDER-STAND YOUR CONCERN, IN A WAY.
MUMBLE...
WHICH IS ALL THE MORE REASON TO MAKE A MOVE WHILE WE CAN.
HH
...?
BUT FIRST...
LOOK OUT THE WINDOW.
SHHAAA

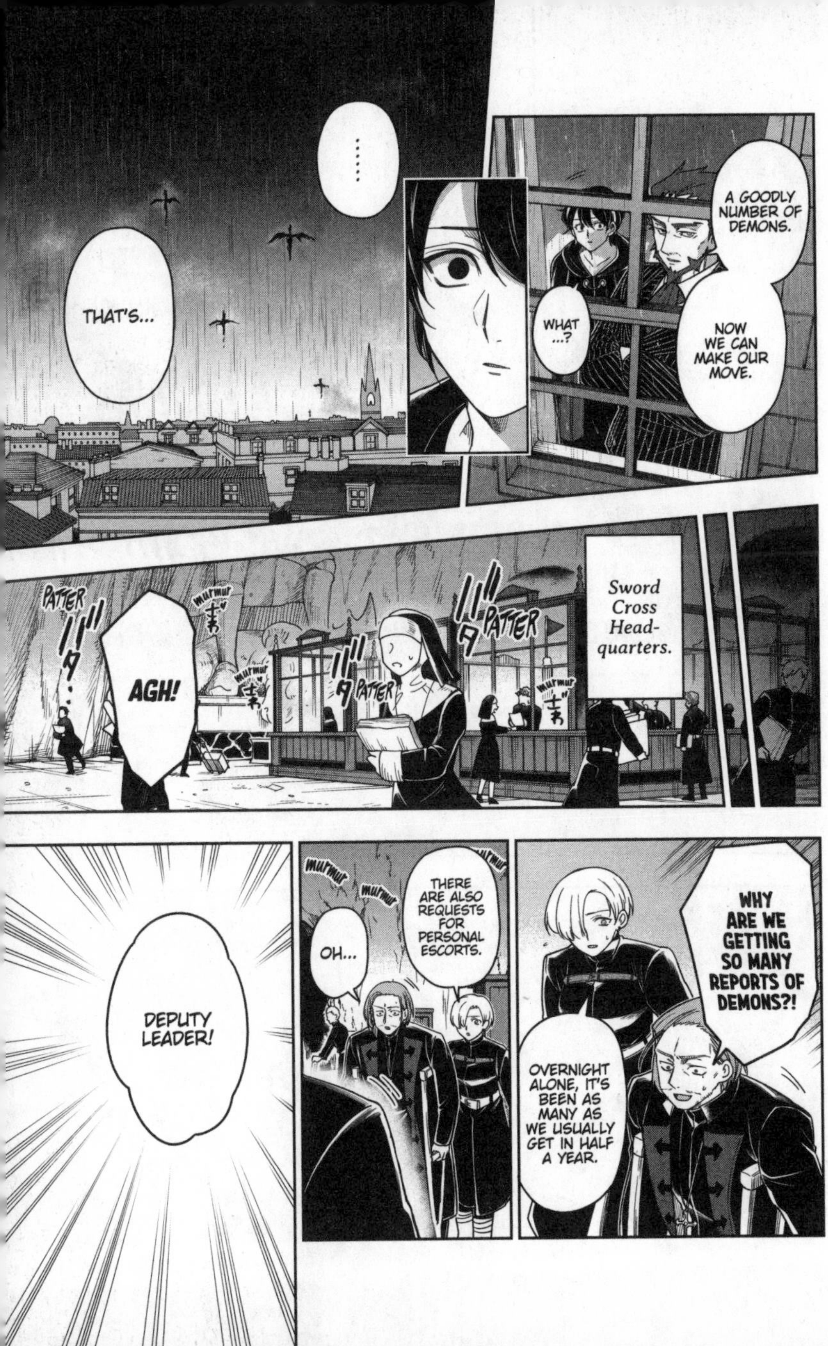
A GOODLY NUMBER OF DEMONS.
NOW WE CAN MAKE OUR MOVE.
WHAT ...?
......
THAT'S...
Sword Cross Head-quarters.
PATTER
murmur
PATTER
PATTER
murmur
murmur
AGH!
PATTER
WHY ARE WE GETTING SO MANY REPORTS OF DEMONS?!
OVERNIGHT ALONE, IT'S BEEN AS MANY AS WE USUALLY GET IN HALF A YEAR.
murmur
THERE ARE ALSO REQUESTS FOR PERSONAL ESCORTS.
OH...
murmur
murmur
DEPUTY LEADER!

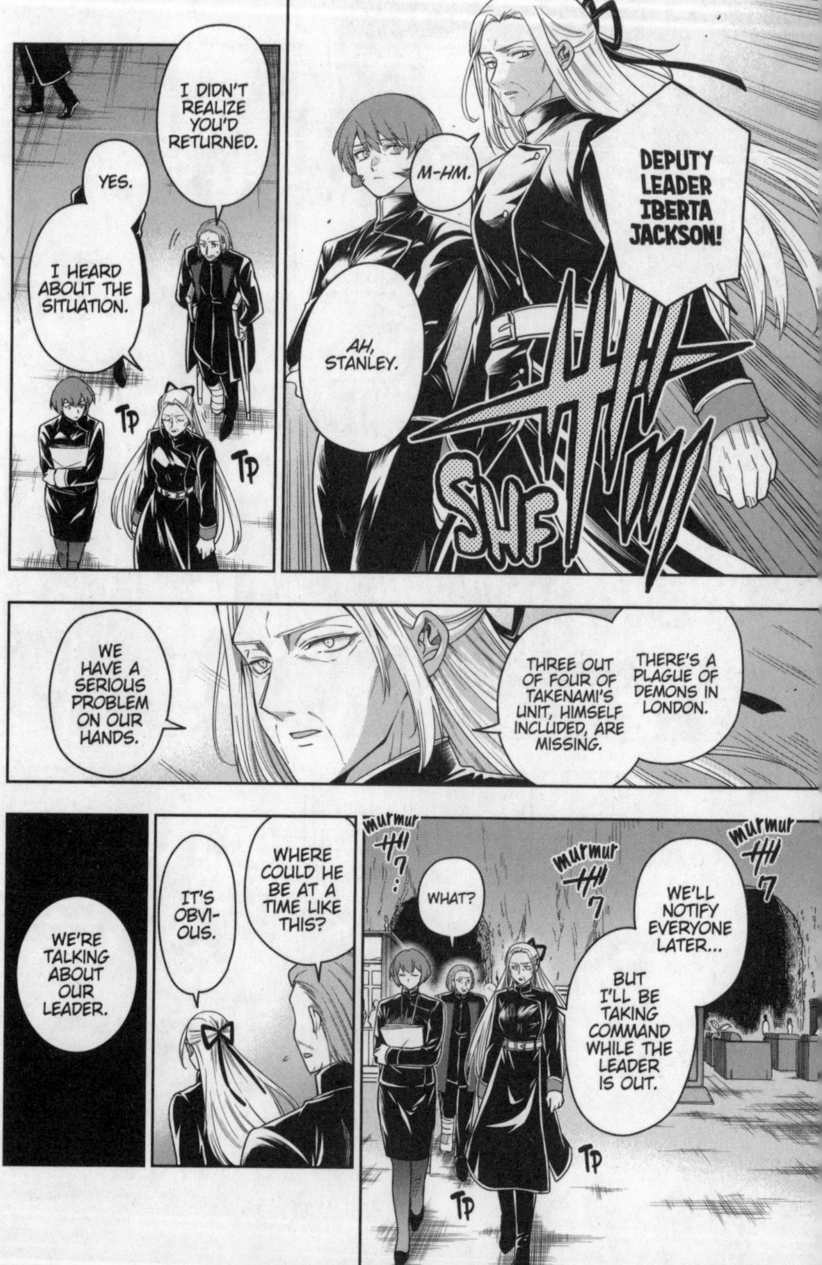
DEPUTY LEADER IBERTA JACKSON!
M-HM.
AH, STANLEY.
SHF
I DIDN'T REALIZE YOU'D RETURNED.
YES.
I HEARD ABOUT THE SITUATION.
Tp
Tp
THERE'S A PLAGUE OF DEMONS IN LONDON.
THREE OUT OF FOUR OF TAKENAMI'S UNIT, HIMSELF INCLUDED, ARE MISSING.
WE HAVE A SERIOUS PROBLEM ON OUR HANDS.
murmur
murmur
WE'LL NOTIFY EVERYONE LATER...
BUT I'LL BE TAKING COMMAND WHILE THE LEADER IS OUT.
WHAT?
murmur
Tp
Tp
WHERE COULD HE BE AT A TIME LIKE THIS?
IT'S OBVIOUS.
WE'RE TALKING ABOUT OUR LEADER.

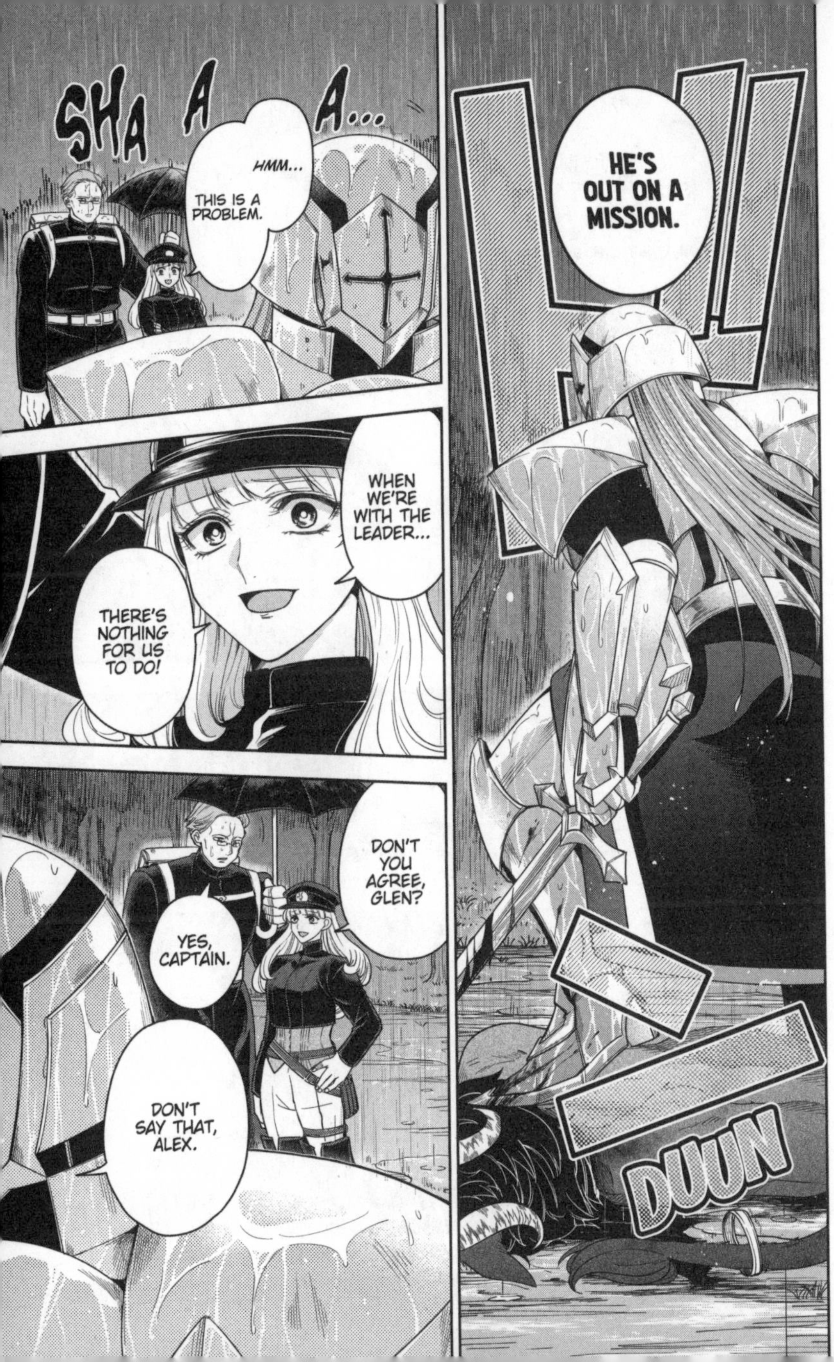
HE'S OUT ON A MISSION.
DUUN
SHA A A...
HMM...
THIS IS A PROBLEM.
WHEN WE'RE WITH THE LEADER...
THERE'S NOTHING FOR US TO DO!
DON'T YOU AGREE, GLEN?
YES, CAPTAIN.
DON'T SAY THAT, ALEX.

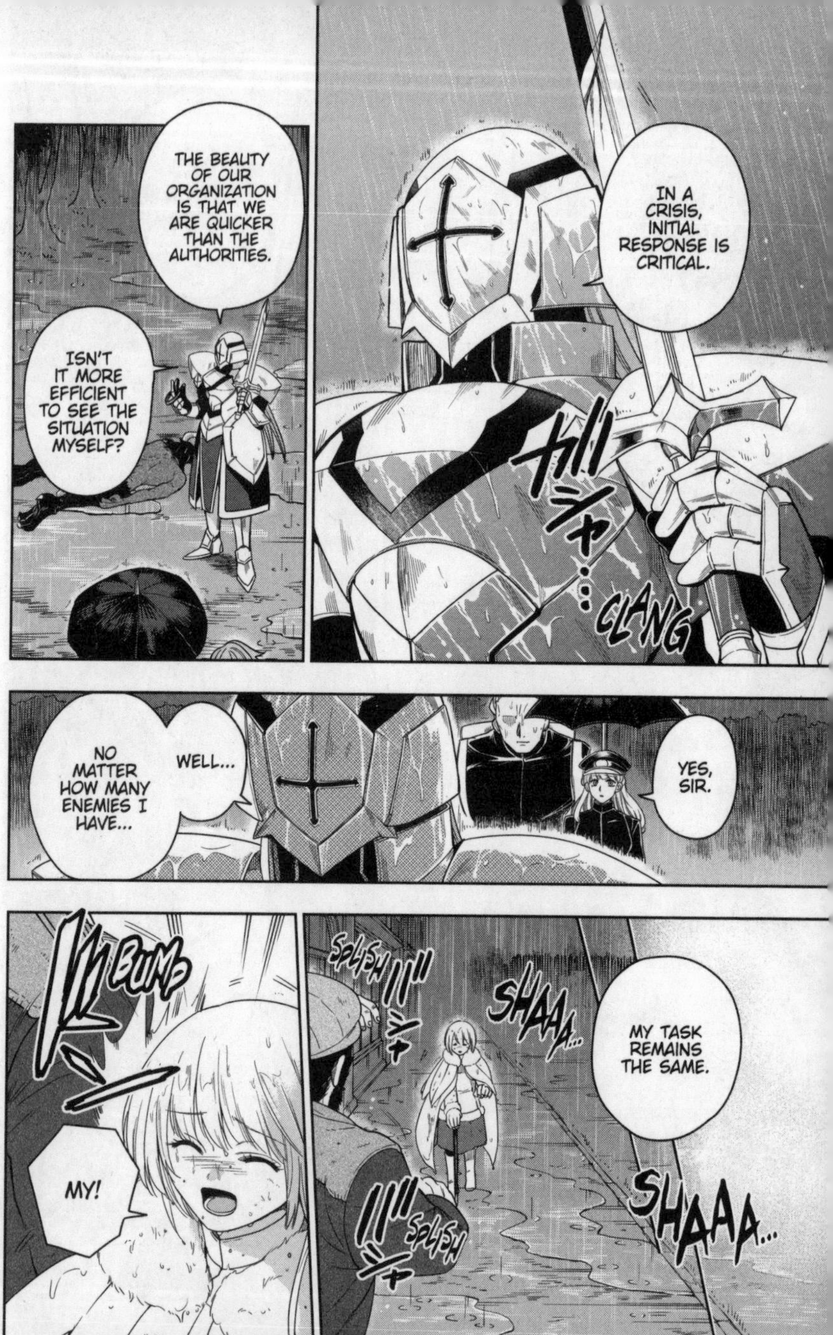
IN A CRISIS, INITIAL RESPONSE IS CRITICAL.
CLANG
THE BEAUTY OF OUR ORGANIZATION IS THAT WE ARE QUICKER THAN THE AUTHORITIES.
ISN'T IT MORE EFFICIENT TO SEE THE SITUATION MYSELF?
YES, SIR.
WELL...
NO MATTER HOW MANY ENEMIES I HAVE...
SPLISH
SHAAA...
MY TASK REMAINS THE SAME.
SHAAA...
SPLISH
BUMP
MY!

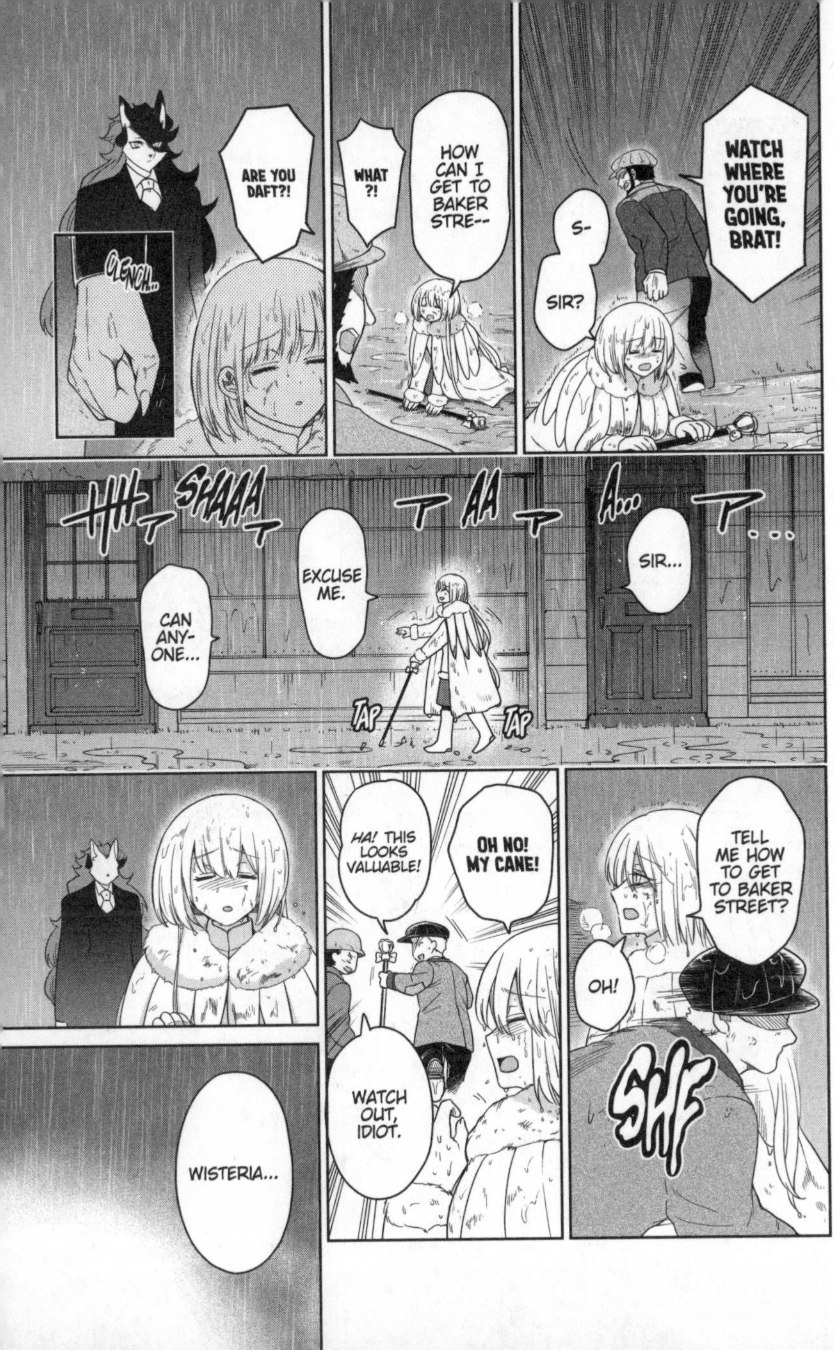
WATCH WHERE YOU'RE GOING, BRAT!
S-
SIR?
HOW CAN I GET TO BAKER STRE--
WHAT ?!
ARE YOU DAFT?!
CLENCH...
A...
SIR...
AA
EXCUSE ME.
SHAAAA
HHH
CAN ANYONE...
TAP
TAP
TELL ME HOW TO GET TO BAKER STREET?
OH!
SHF
OH NO! MY CANE!
HA! THIS LOOKS VALUABLE!
WATCH OUT, IDIOT.
WISTERIA...

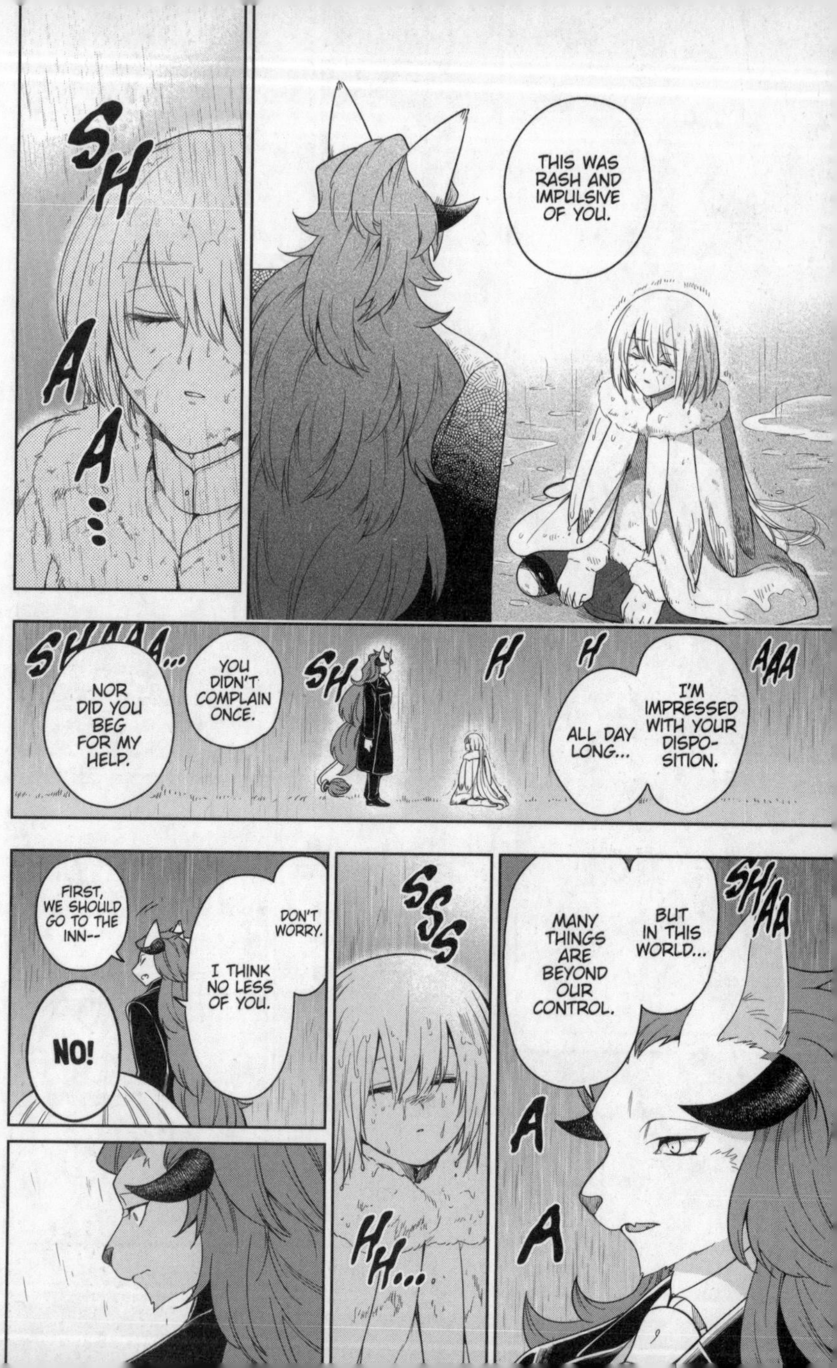
THIS WAS RASH AND IMPULSIVE OF YOU.
SHAAA...
AAA
H
H
I'M IMPRESSED WITH YOUR DISPO-SITION.
ALL DAY LONG...
SH
YOU DIDN'T COMPLAIN ONCE.
NOR DID YOU BEG FOR MY HELP.
SHAAAA...
SHAA
BUT IN THIS WORLD...
MANY THINGS ARE BEYOND OUR CONTROL.
AA
SSS
HH...
DON'T WORRY.
I THINK NO LESS OF YOU.
FIRST, WE SHOULD GO TO THE INN--
NO!

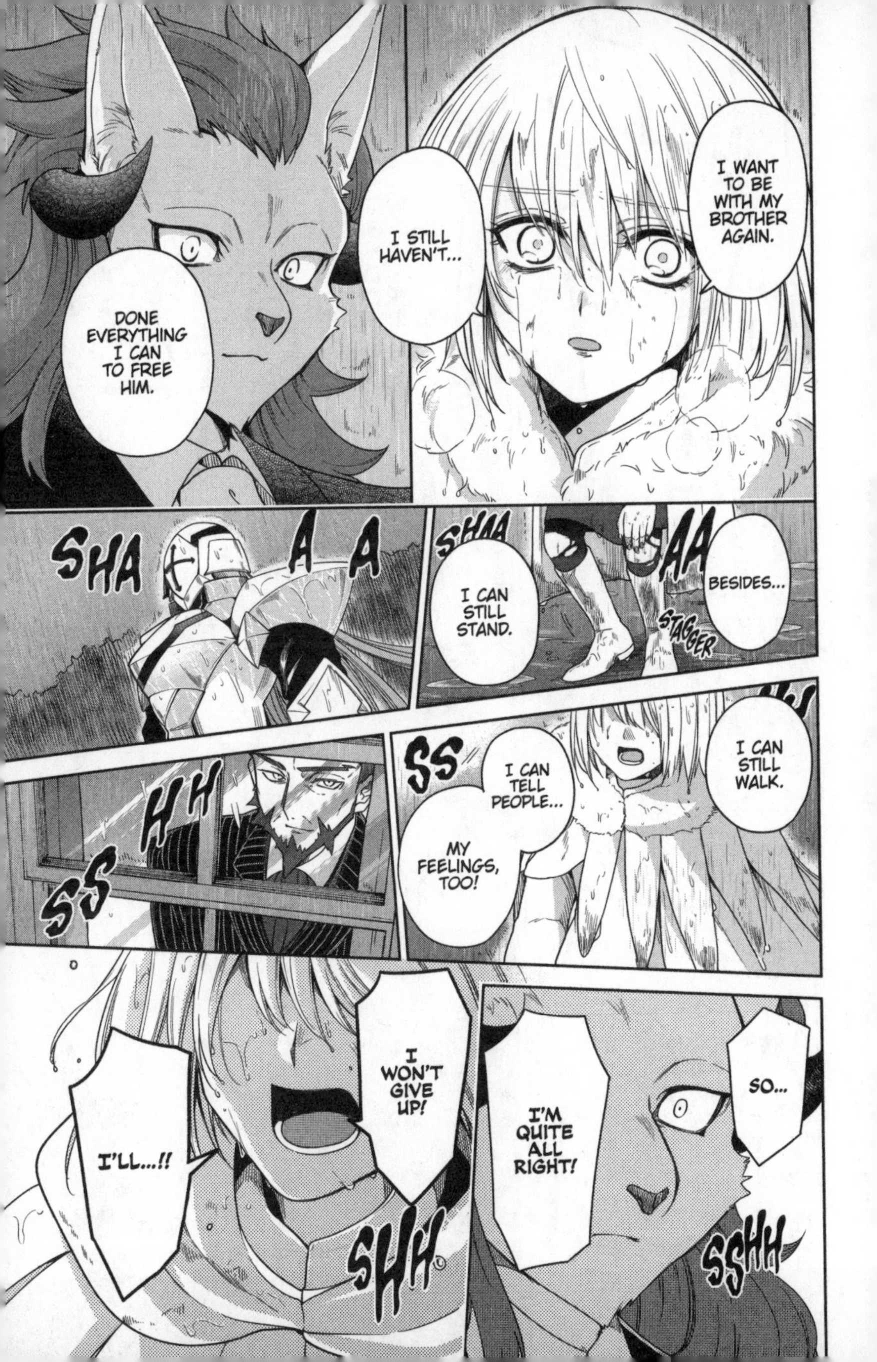
I WANT TO BE WITH MY BROTHER AGAIN.
I STILL HAVEN'T...
DONE EVERYTHING I CAN TO FREE HIM.
BESIDES...
SHAA
AA
STAGGER
I CAN STILL STAND.
SHA
A
A
I CAN STILL WALK.
I CAN TELL PEOPLE...
MY FEELINGS, TOO!
SS
SS
H
H
SO...
I'M QUITE ALL RIGHT!
SSHH
I WON'T GIVE UP!
I'LL...!!
SHH

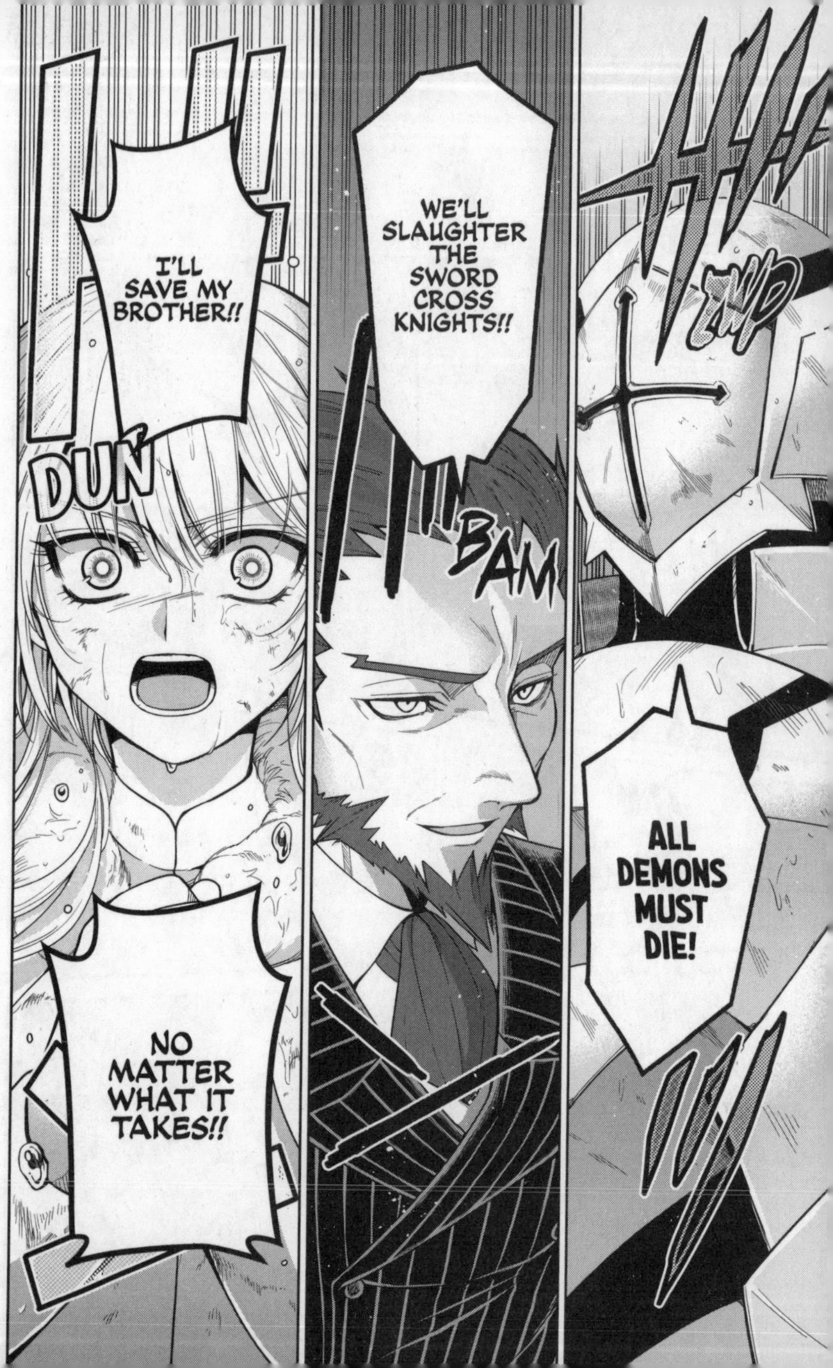
ALL DEMONS MUST DIE!
WE'LL SLAUGHTER THE SWORD CROSS KNIGHTS!!
BAM
I'LL SAVE MY BROTHER!!
DUN
NO MATTER WHAT IT TAKES!!

The Tale of the Outcasts

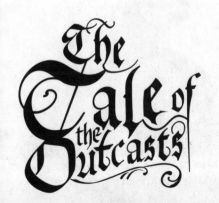

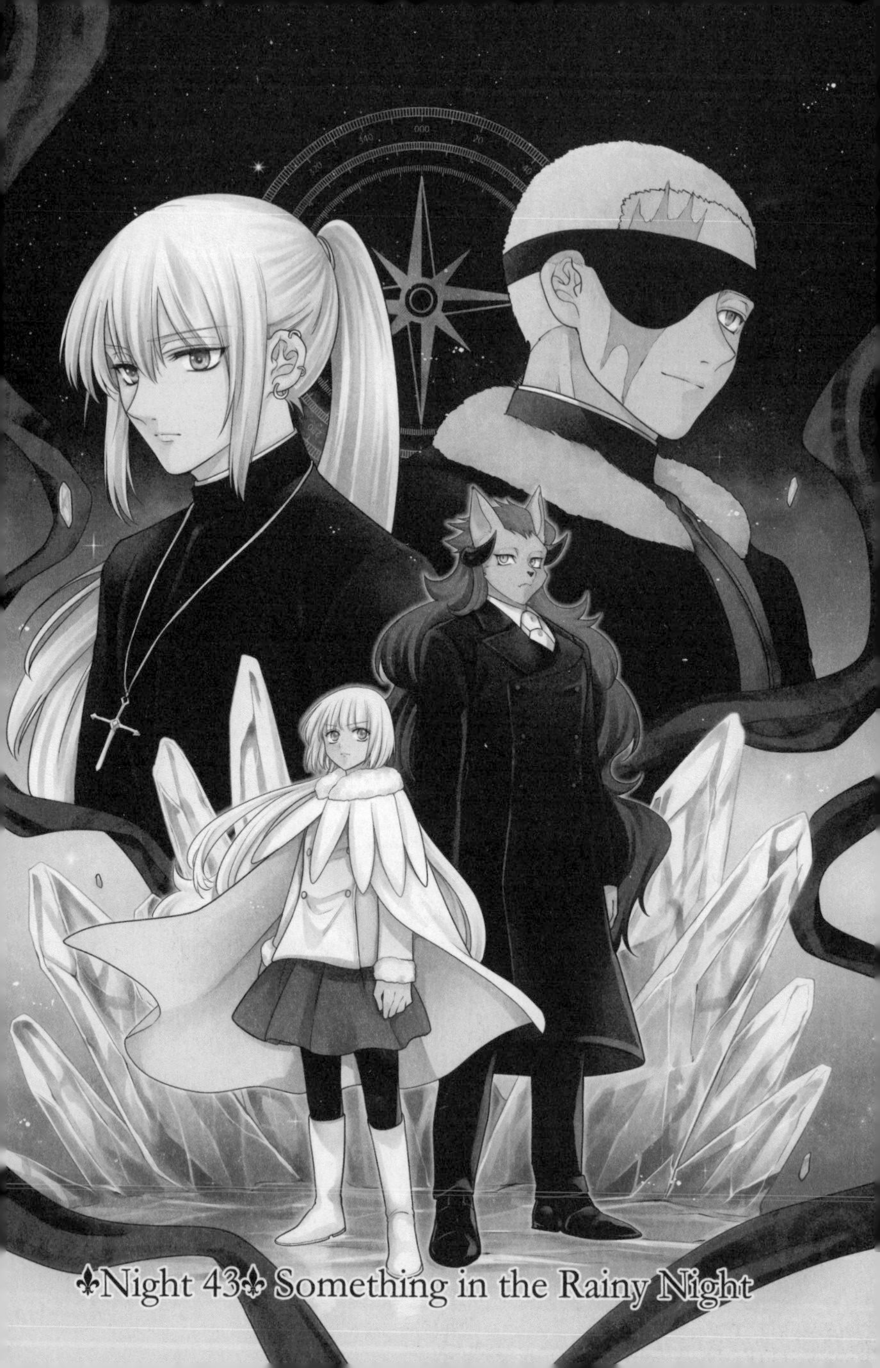

Night 43 Something in the Rainy Night

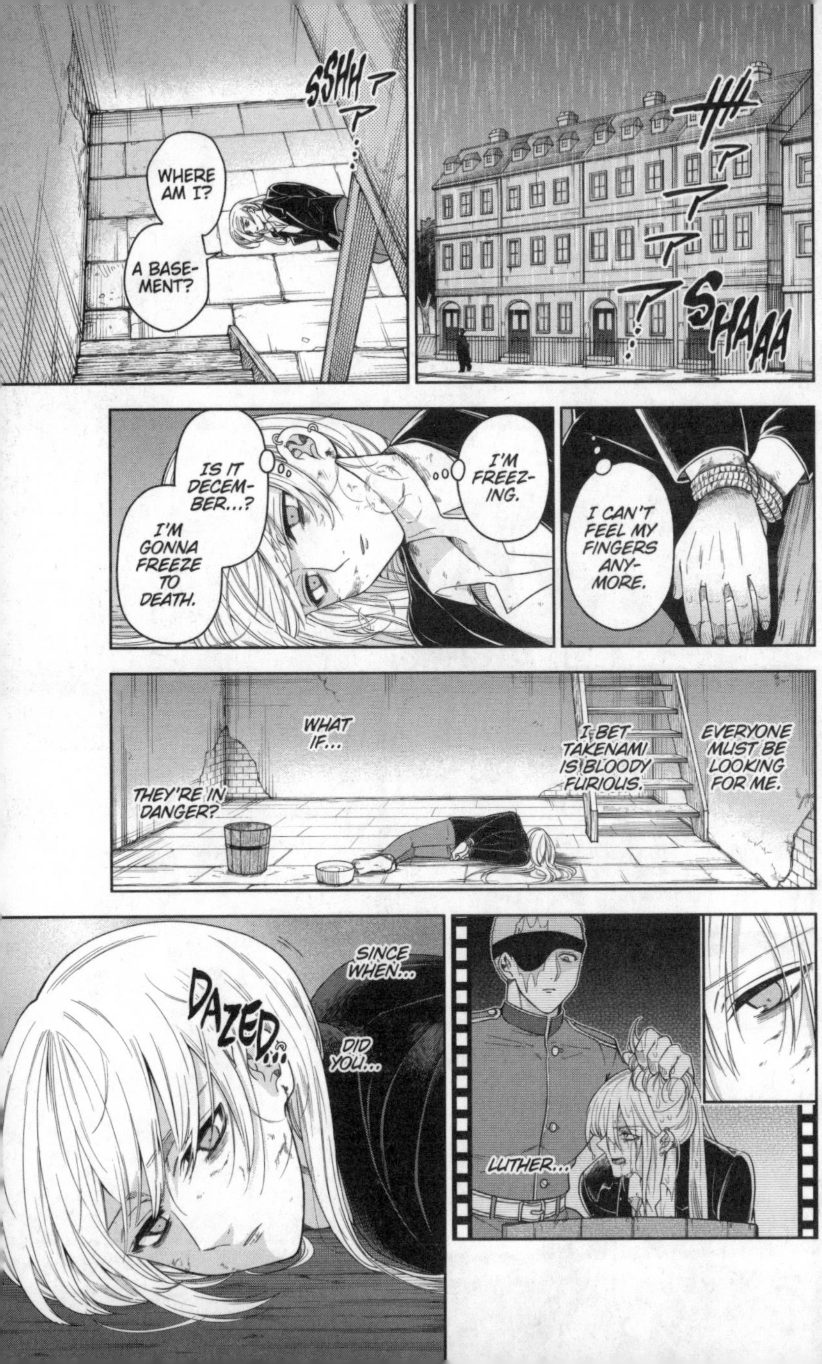
SHAAA
SSHH
WHERE AM I?
A BASEMENT?
I CAN'T FEEL MY FINGERS ANYMORE.
I'M FREEZING.
IS IT DECEMBER...?
I'M GONNA FREEZE TO DEATH.
EVERYONE MUST BE LOOKING FOR ME.
I BET TAKENAMI IS BLOODY FURIOUS.
WHAT IF...
THEY'RE IN DANGER?
LUTHER...
DAZED...
SINCE WHEN...
DID YOU...

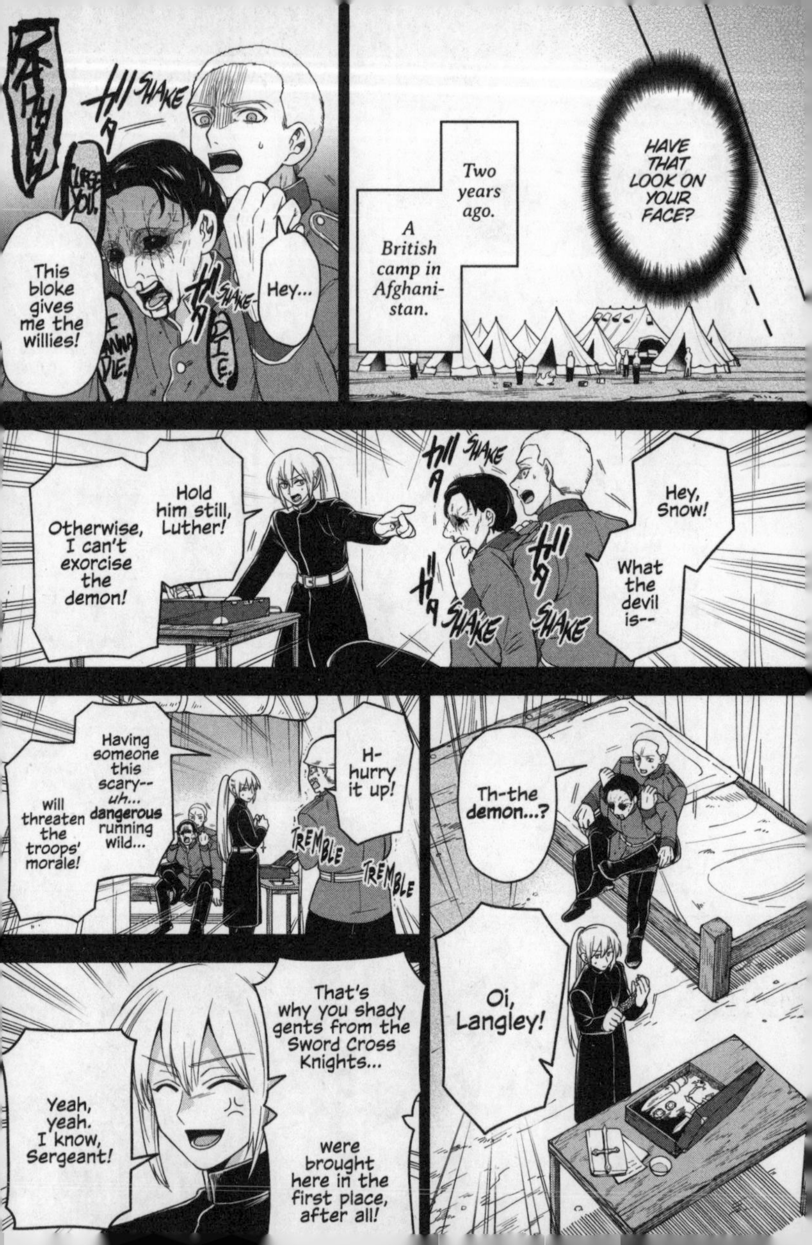
HAVE THAT LOOK ON YOUR FACE?
Two years ago.
A British camp in Afghanistan.
SHAKE
CURSE YOU.
Hey...
SHAKE
DIE.
I WANNA DIE.
This bloke gives me the willies!
Hey, Snow!
What the devil is--
SHAKE
SHAKE
SHAKE
Hold him still, Luther!
Otherwise, I can't exorcise the demon!
Th-the demon...?
Oi, Langley!
H-hurry it up!
TREMBLE
TREMBLE
Having someone this scary--uh... dangerous running wild...
will threaten the troops' morale!
That's why you shady gents from the Sword Cross Knights...
were brought here in the first place, after all!
Yeah, yeah. I know, Sergeant!

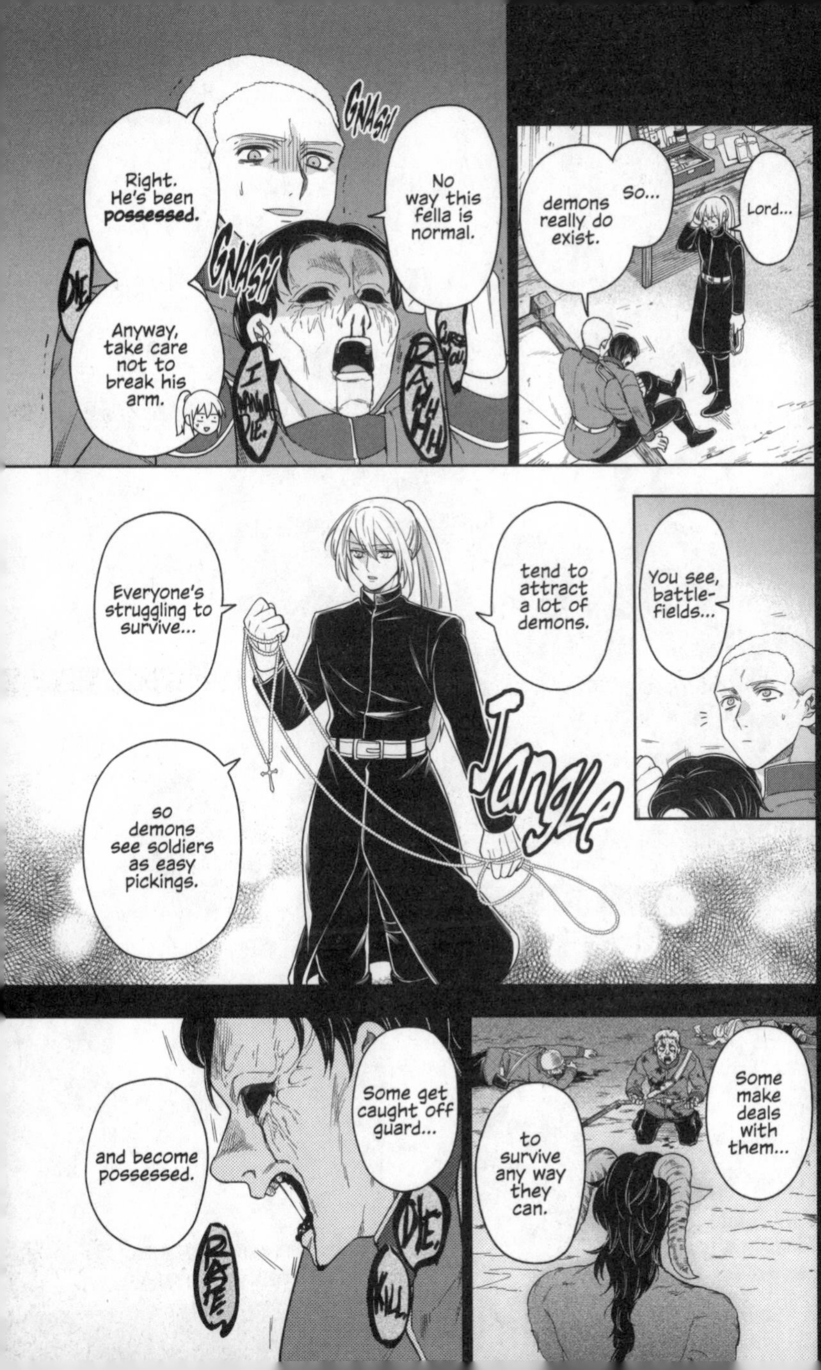
Lord...
So...
demons really do exist.
No way this fella is normal.
GNASH
Right. He's been **possessed.**
GNASH
Anyway, take care not to break his arm.
You see, battle-fields...
tend to attract a lot of demons.
Everyone's struggling to survive...
so demons see soldiers as easy pickings.
JANGLE
Some make deals with them...
to survive any way they can.
Some get caught off guard...
and become possessed.
DIE,
KILL

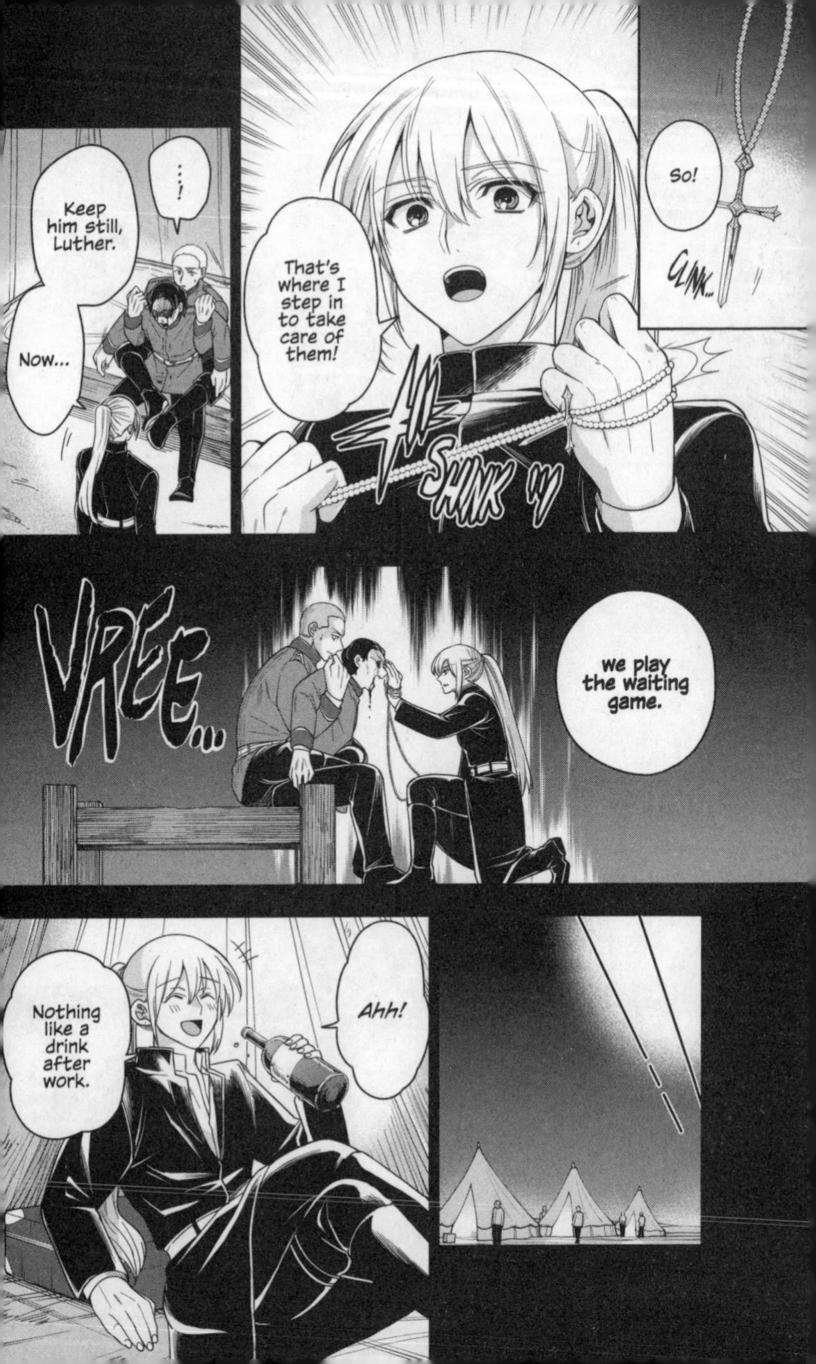
So!
CLINK...
That's where I step in to take care of them!
SHINK
...!
Keep him still, Luther.
Now...
we play the waiting game.
VREE...
Ahh!
Nothing like a drink after work.

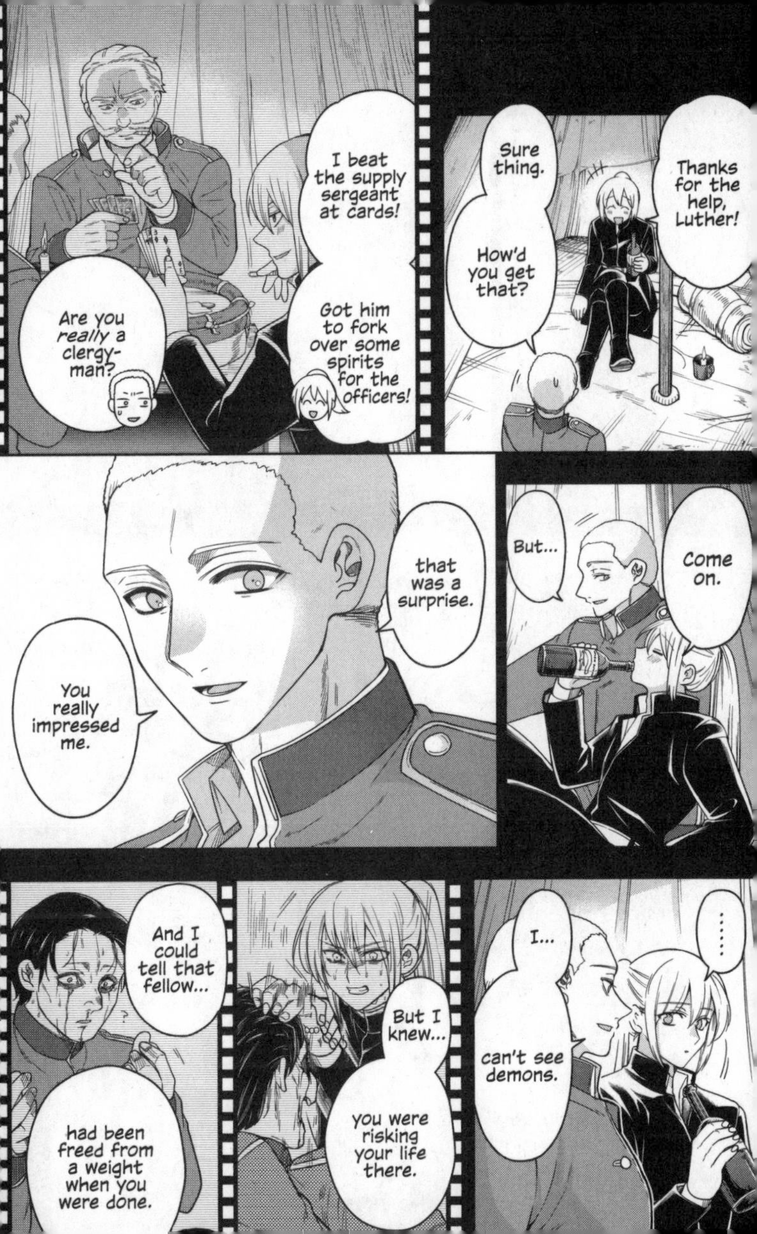
Thanks for the help, Luther!
Sure thing.
How'd you get that?
I beat the supply sergeant at cards!
Got him to fork over some spirits for the officers!
Are you *really* a clergyman?
Come on.
But...
that was a surprise.
You really impressed me.
......
I...
can't see demons.
But I knew...
you were risking your life there.
And I could tell that fellow...
had been freed from a weight when you were done.

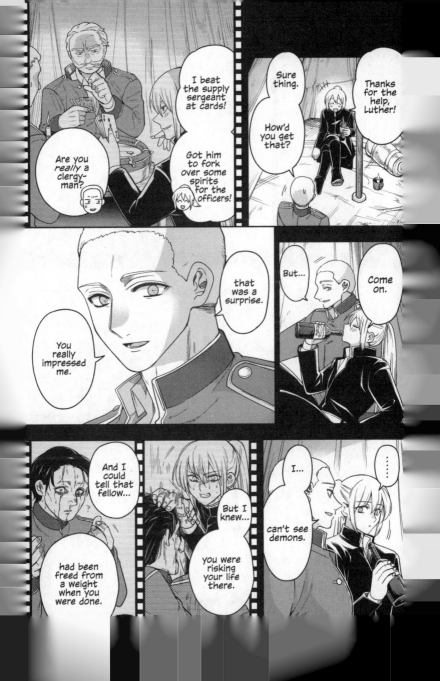

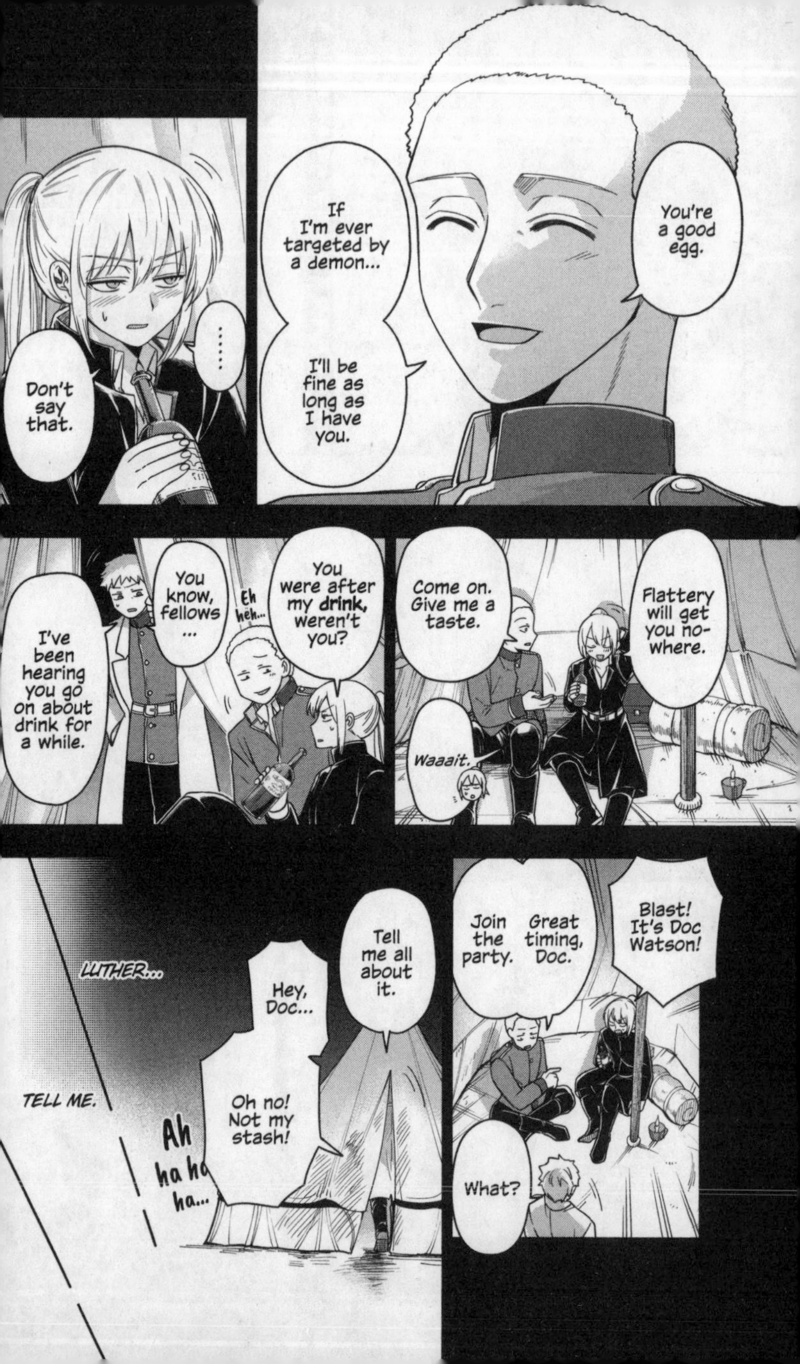
You're a good egg.
If I'm ever targeted by a demon...
I'll be fine as long as I have you.
......
Don't say that.
Flattery will get you no-where.
Come on. Give me a taste.
Waaait.
You were after my **drink,** weren't you?
Eh heh...
You know, fellows...
I've been hearing you go on about drink for a while.
Blast! It's Doc Watson!
Great timing, Doc.
Join the party.
...
What?
Tell me all about it.
Hey, Doc...
LUTHER...
Oh no! Not my stash!
TELL ME.
Ah ha ha ha...

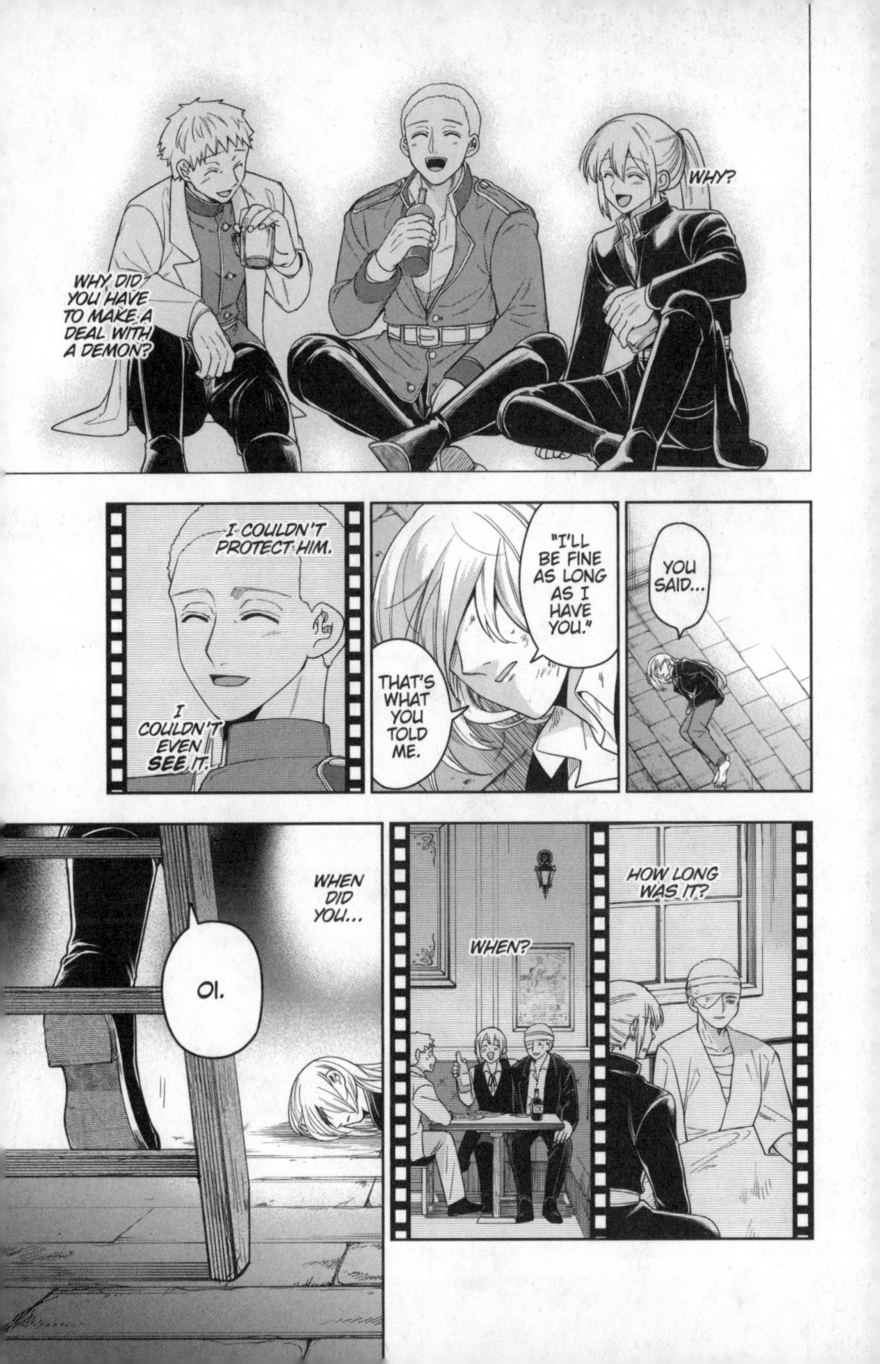
WHY?
WHY DID YOU HAVE TO MAKE A DEAL WITH A DEMON?
YOU SAID...
"I'LL BE FINE AS LONG AS I HAVE YOU."
THAT'S WHAT YOU TOLD ME.
I COULDN'T PROTECT HIM.
I COULDN'T EVEN SEE IT.
HOW LONG WAS IT?
WHEN?
WHEN DID YOU...
OI.

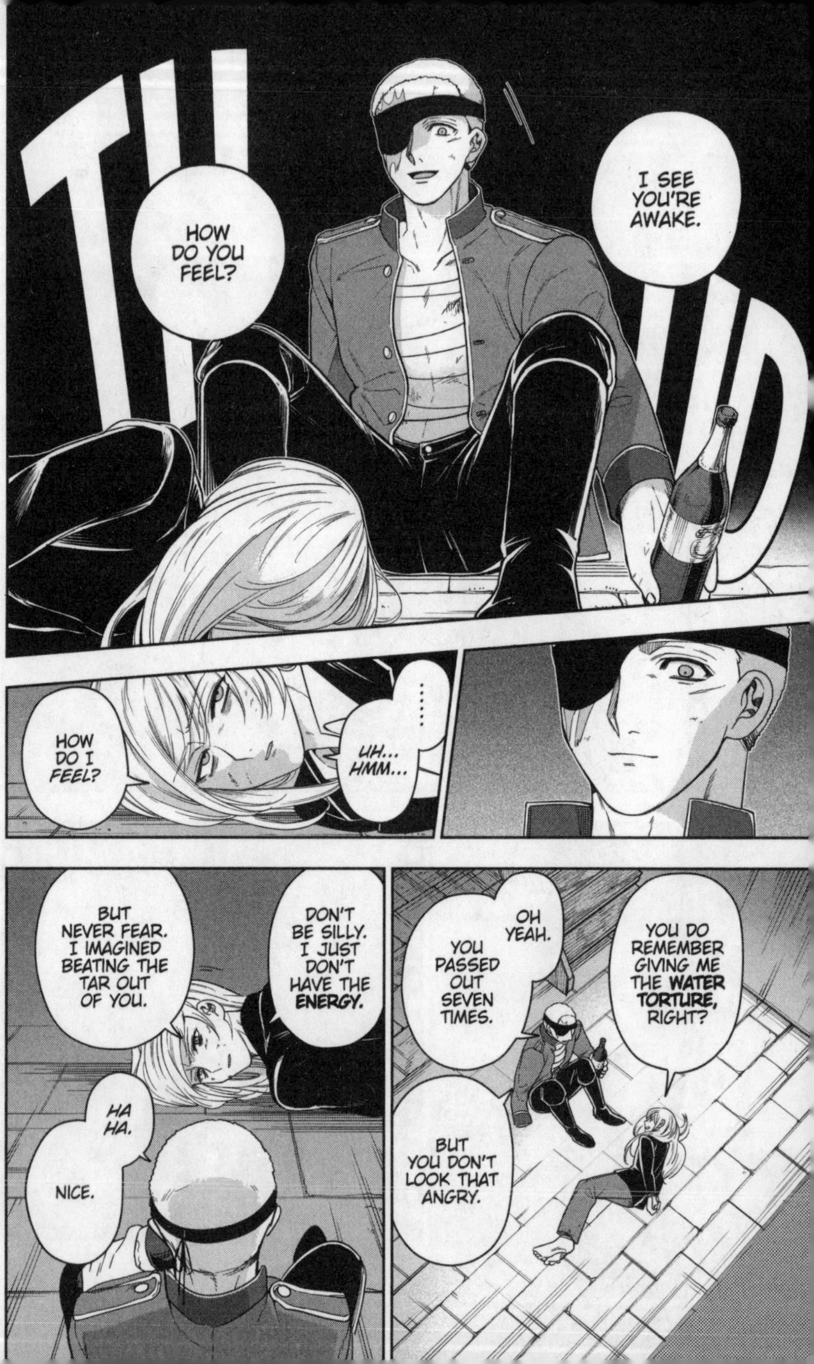
THUD
I SEE YOU'RE AWAKE.
HOW DO YOU FEEL?
......
UH... HMM...
HOW DO I FEEL?
YOU DO REMEMBER GIVING ME THE **WATER TORTURE,** RIGHT?
OH YEAH.
YOU PASSED OUT SEVEN TIMES.
BUT YOU DON'T LOOK THAT ANGRY.
DON'T BE SILLY. I JUST DON'T HAVE THE **ENERGY.**
BUT NEVER FEAR. I IMAGINED BEATING THE TAR OUT OF YOU.
HA HA.
NICE.

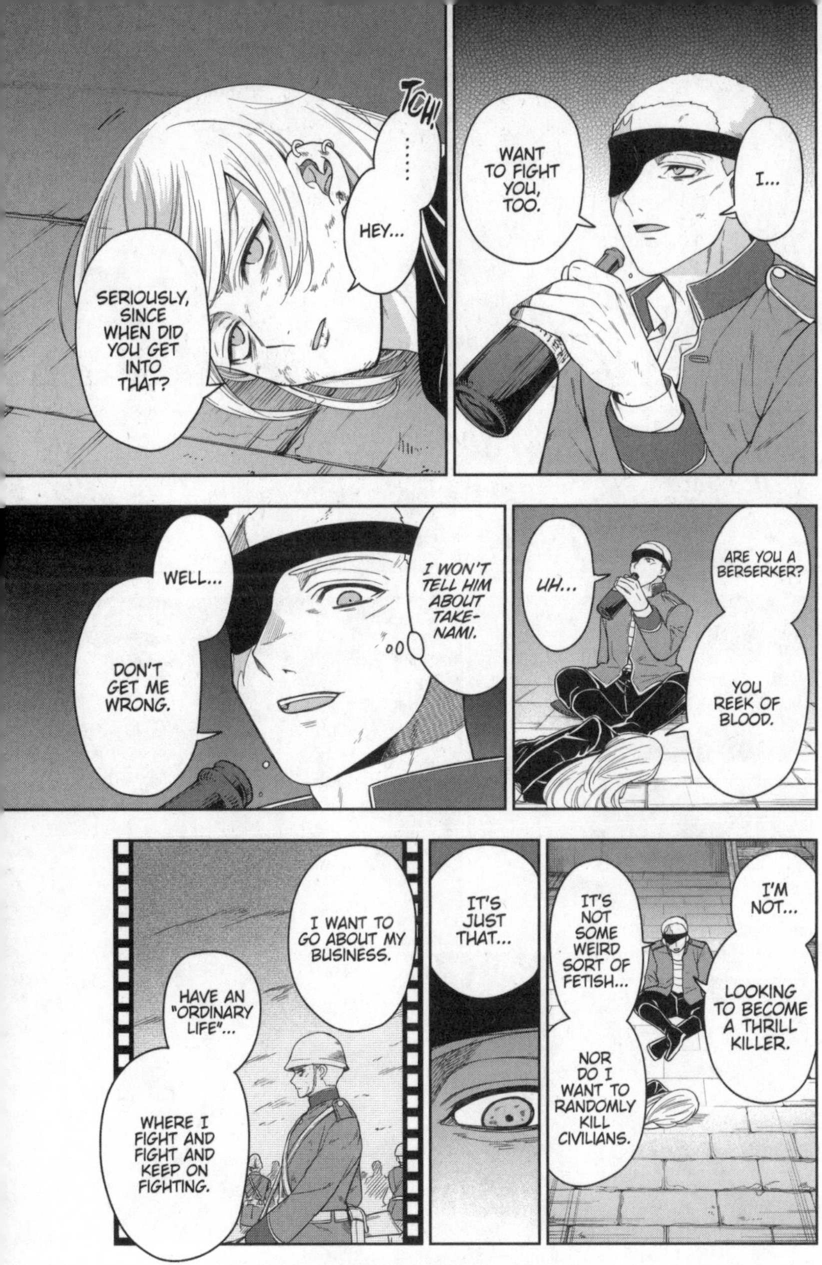
I...
WANT TO FIGHT YOU, TOO.
TCH!
......
HEY...
SERIOUSLY, SINCE WHEN DID YOU GET INTO THAT?
ARE YOU A BERSERKER?
YOU REEK OF BLOOD.
UH...
I WON'T TELL HIM ABOUT TAKE-NAMI.
WELL...
DON'T GET ME WRONG.
I'M NOT...
LOOKING TO BECOME A THRILL KILLER.
IT'S NOT SOME WEIRD SORT OF FETISH...
NOR DO I WANT TO RANDOMLY KILL CIVILIANS.
IT'S JUST THAT...
I WANT TO GO ABOUT MY BUSINESS.
HAVE AN "ORDINARY LIFE"...
WHERE I FIGHT AND FIGHT AND KEEP ON FIGHTING.

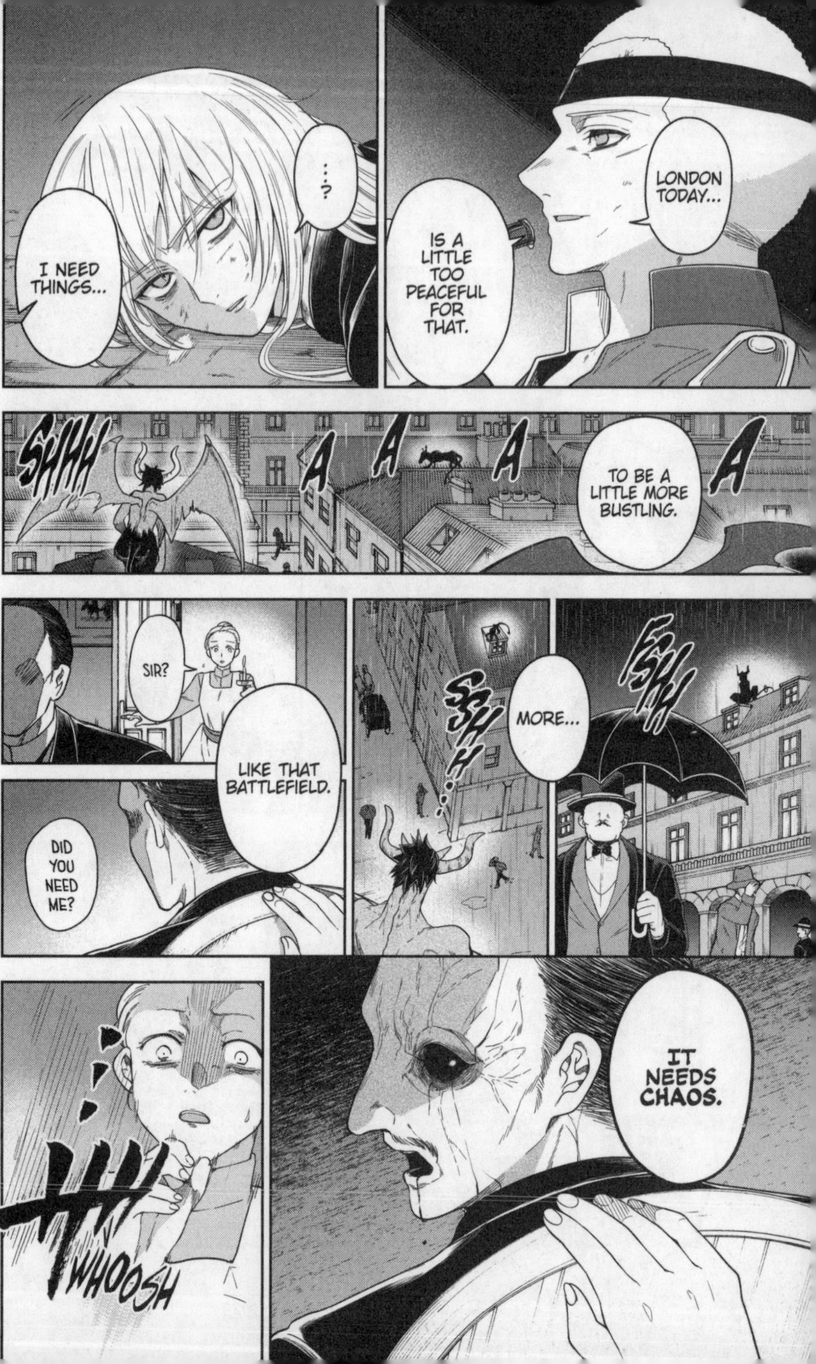
LONDON TODAY...
IS A LITTLE TOO PEACEFUL FOR THAT.
...?
I NEED THINGS...
TO BE A LITTLE MORE BUSTLING.
A
A
A
A
SHHH
FSHH
MORE...
SSHH...
LIKE THAT BATTLEFIELD.
SIR?
DID YOU NEED ME?
IT NEEDS CHAOS.
HH
WHOOSH

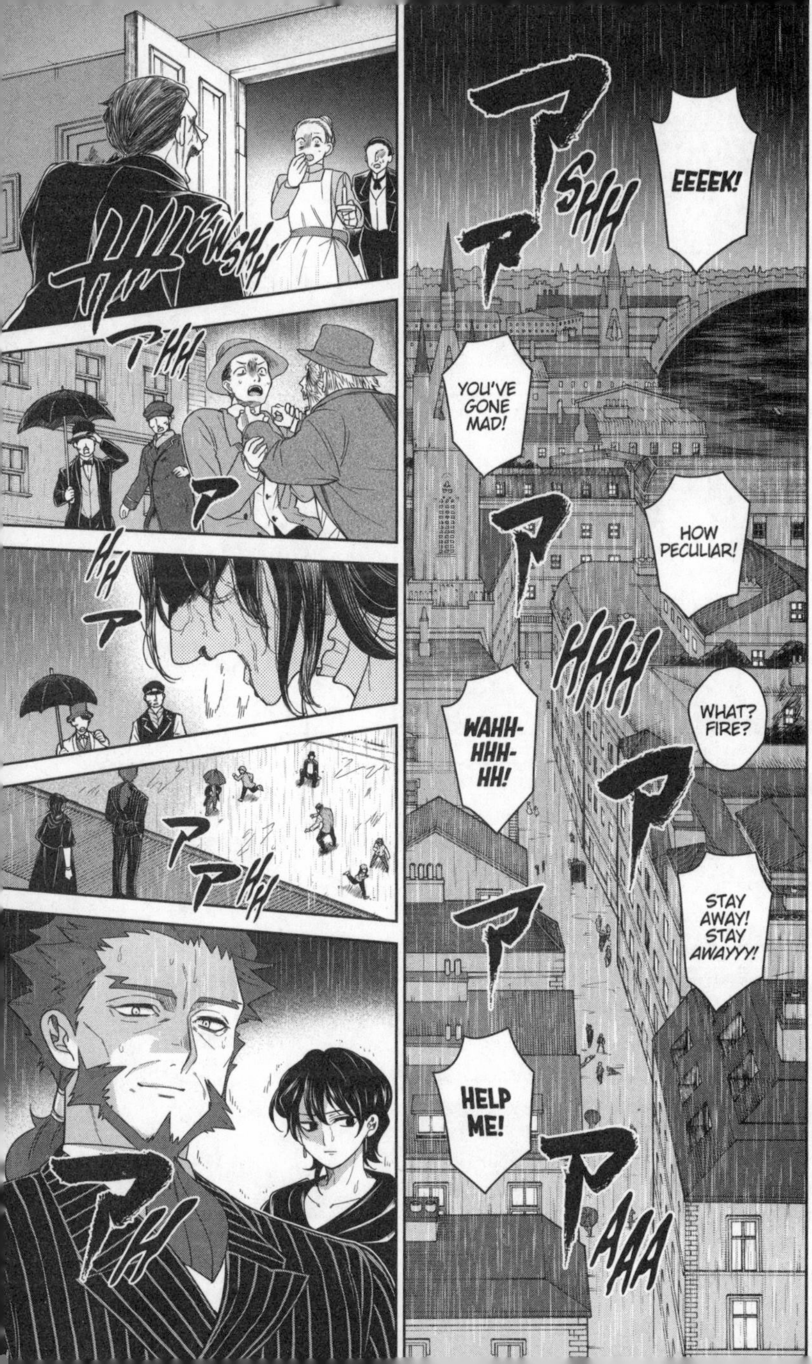
アSHH
EEEEK!
YOU'VE GONE MAD!
HOW PECULIAR!
アアHHH
WHAT? FIRE?
WAHH-HHH-HH!
STAY AWAY! STAY AWAYYY!
アア
HELP ME!
アAAA
アHH
ア
HH
ア
アアHH
アH

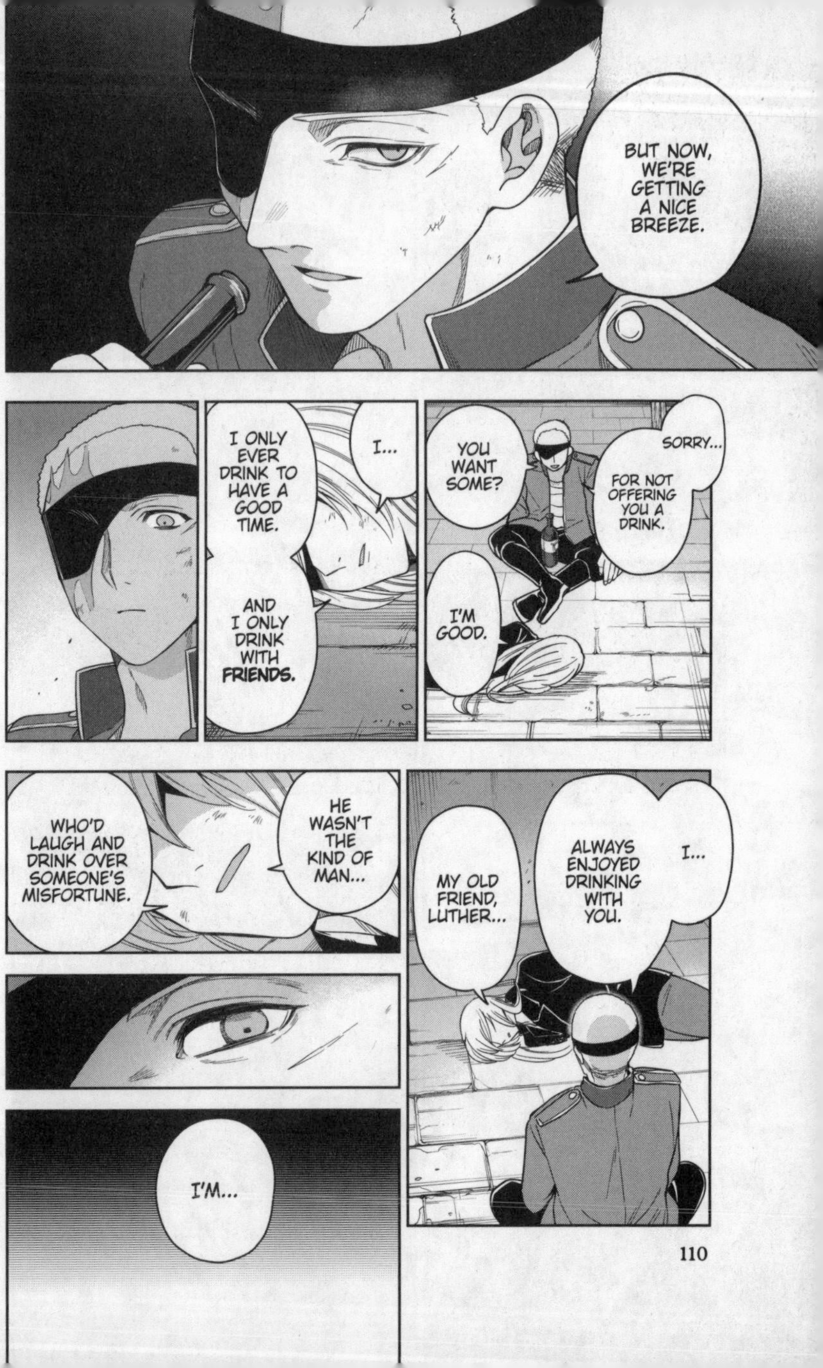
BUT NOW, WE'RE GETTING A NICE BREEZE.
SORRY...
FOR NOT OFFERING YOU A DRINK.
YOU WANT SOME?
I'M GOOD.
I...
I ONLY EVER DRINK TO HAVE A GOOD TIME.
AND I ONLY DRINK WITH **FRIENDS.**
I...
ALWAYS ENJOYED DRINKING WITH YOU.
MY OLD FRIEND, LUTHER...
HE WASN'T THE KIND OF MAN...
WHO'D LAUGH AND DRINK OVER SOMEONE'S MISFORTUNE.
I'M...

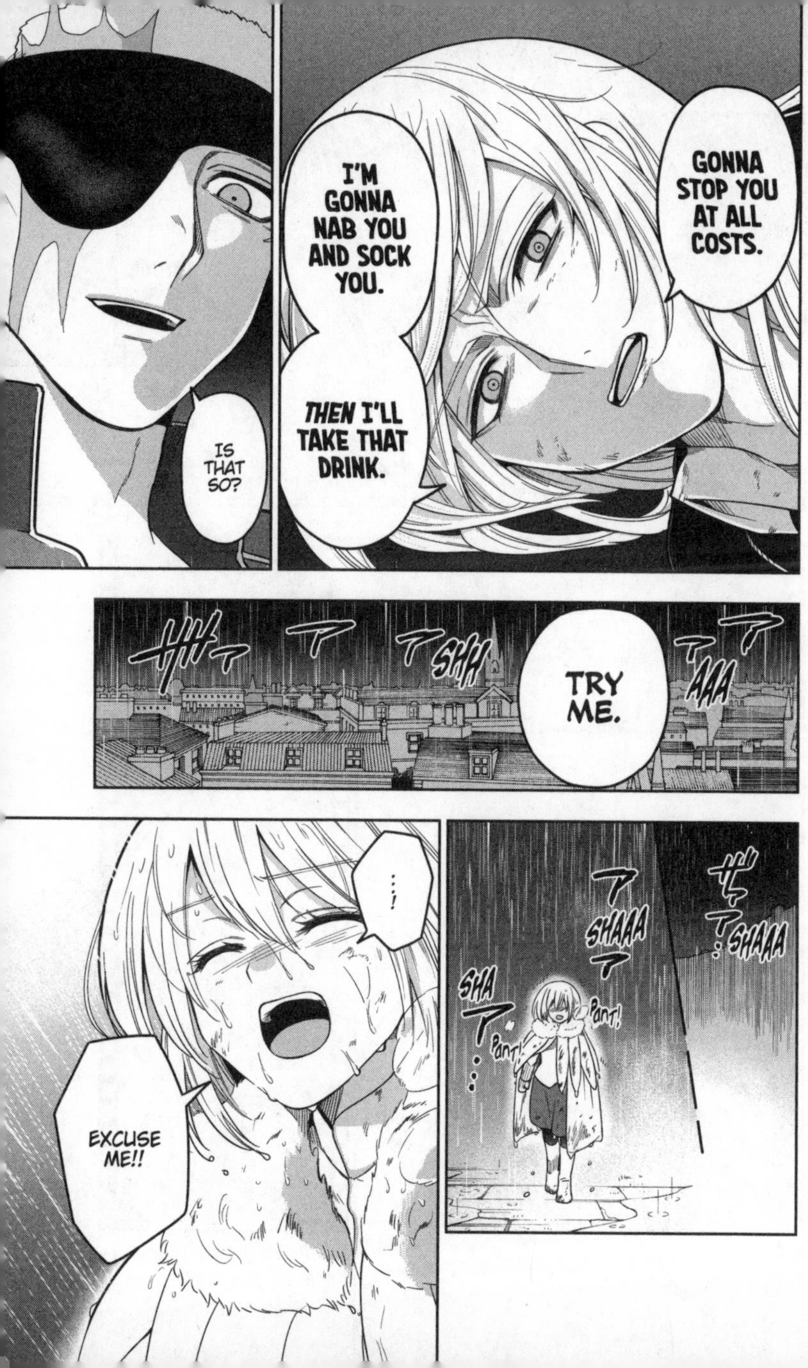
GONNA STOP YOU AT ALL COSTS.
I'M GONNA NAB YOU AND SOCK YOU.
THEN I'LL TAKE THAT DRINK.
IS THAT SO?
AAA
TRY ME.
SHH
HH
SHAAA
SHAAA
Pant!
SHA
Pant!
...!
EXCUSE ME!!

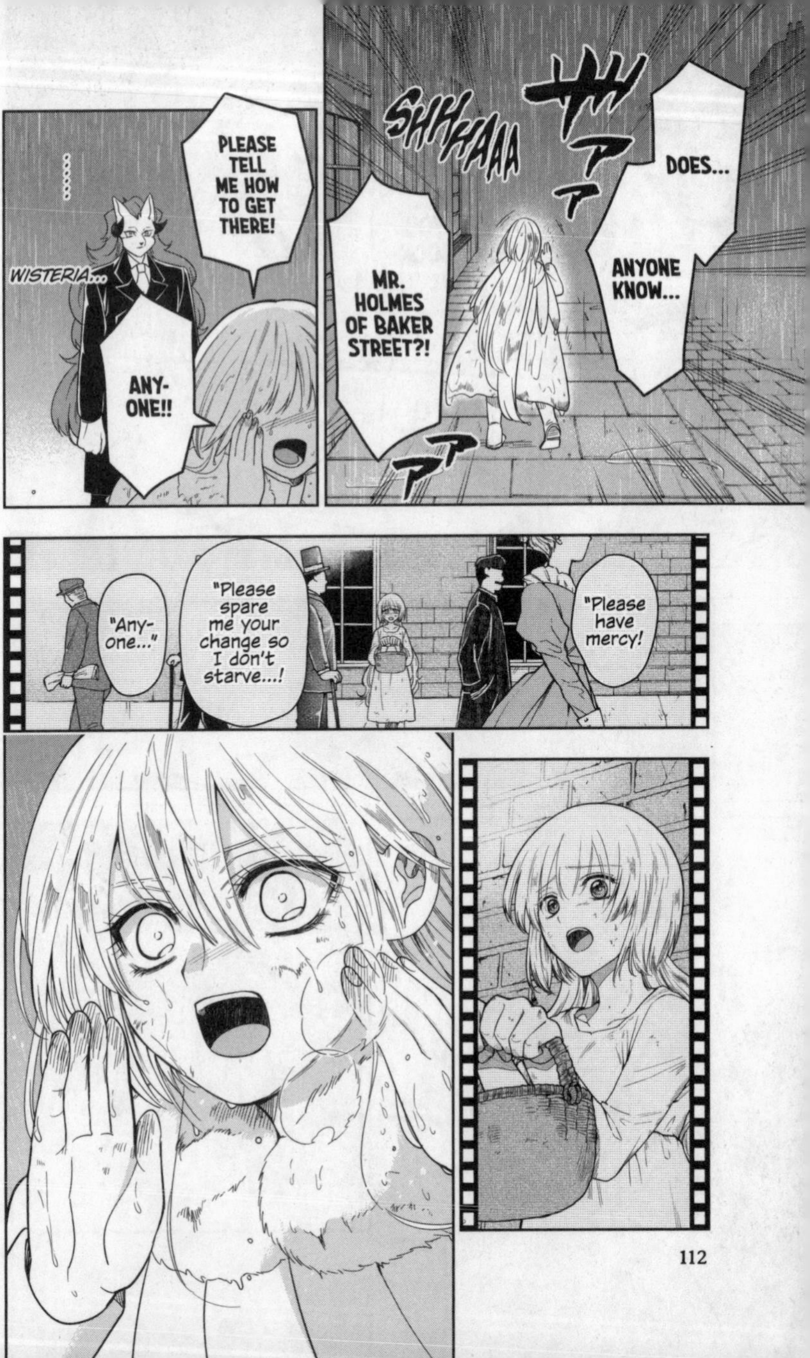
DOES...
ANYONE KNOW...
MR. HOLMES OF BAKER STREET?!
SHHAAA
PLEASE TELL ME HOW TO GET THERE!
......
WISTERIA...
ANY-ONE!!
"Please have mercy!
"Please spare me your change so I don't starve...!
"Any-one..."

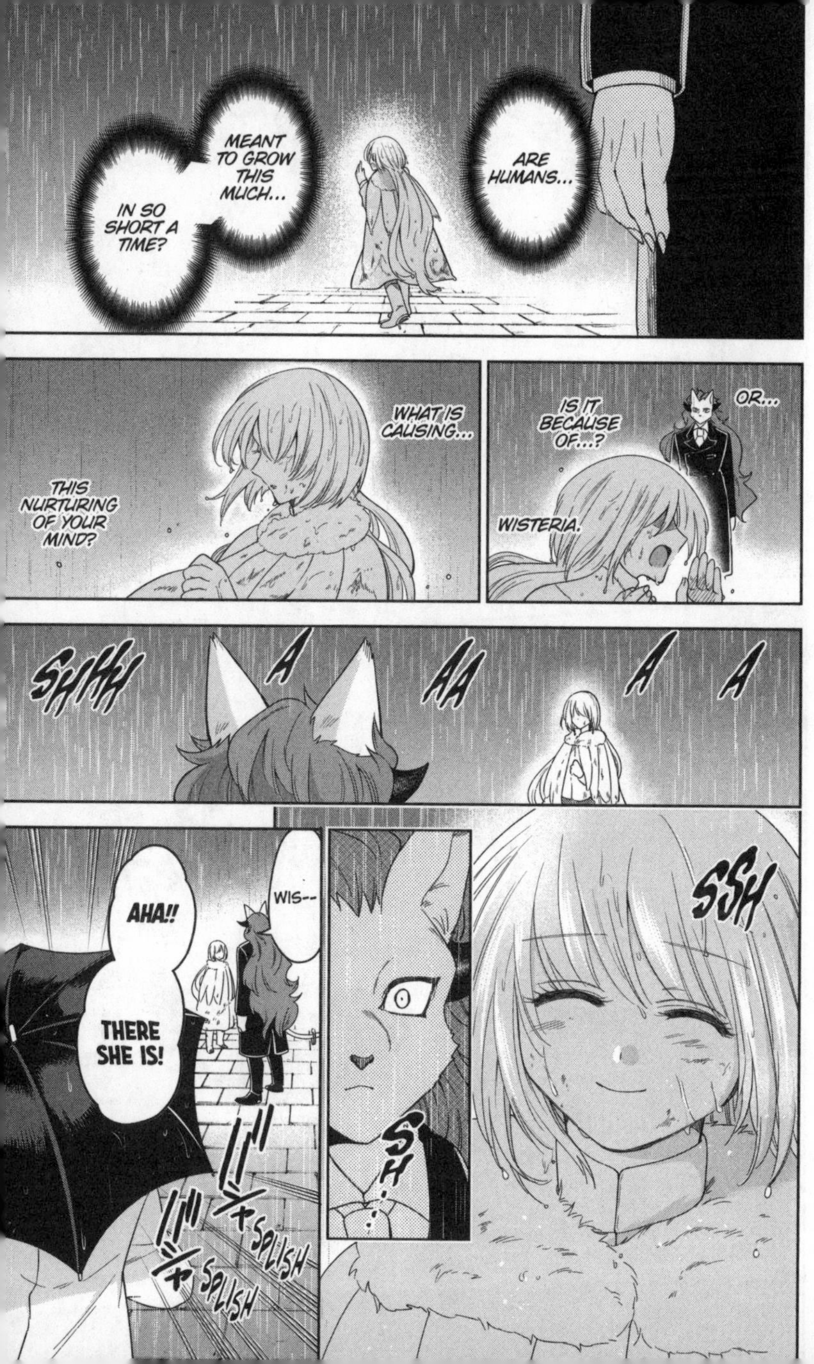
ARE HUMANS...
MEANT TO GROW THIS MUCH...
IN SO SHORT A TIME?
OR...
IS IT BECAUSE OF...?
WISTERIA.
WHAT IS CAUSING...
THIS NURTURING OF YOUR MIND?
SHKK A AA A A
SSH
WIS--
SH...
AHA!!
THERE SHE IS!
SPLISH
SPLISH

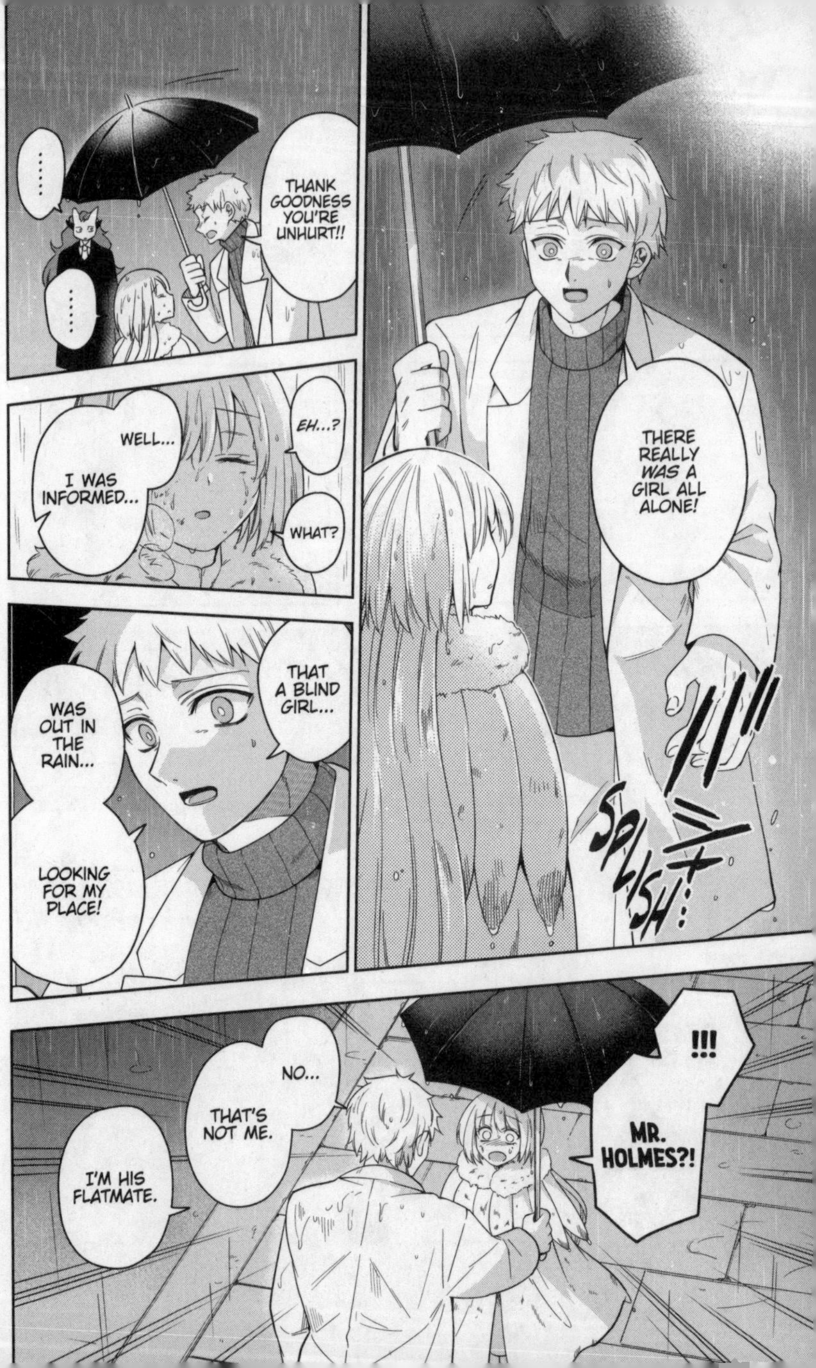
THERE REALLY *WAS* A GIRL ALL ALONE!
SPLISH…
THANK GOODNESS YOU'RE UNHURT!!
……
……
EH…?
WHAT?
WELL…
I WAS INFORMED…
THAT A BLIND GIRL…
WAS OUT IN THE RAIN…
LOOKING FOR MY PLACE!
!!!
MR. HOLMES?!
NO…
THAT'S NOT ME.
I'M HIS FLATMATE.

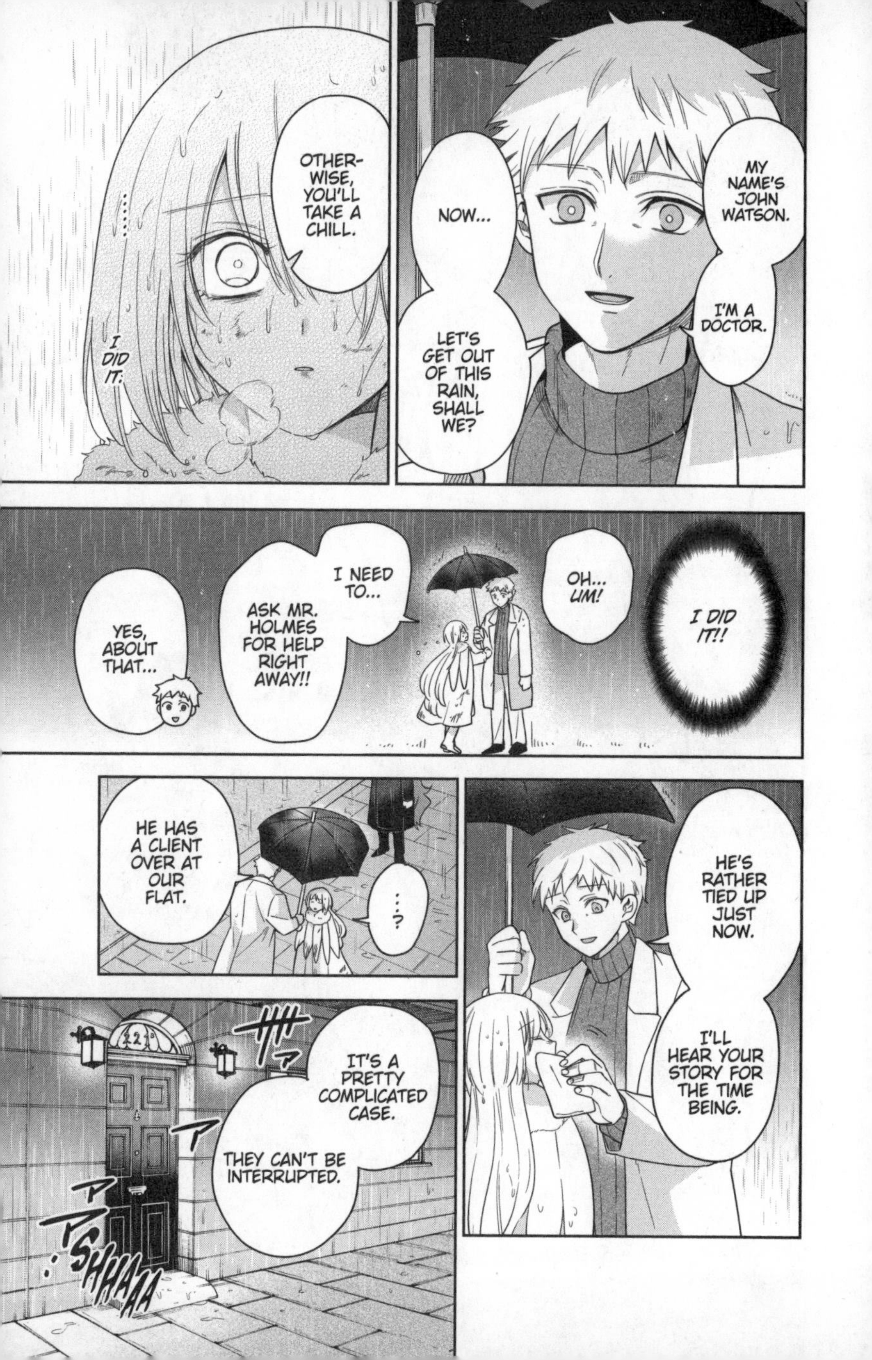

MY NAME'S JOHN WATSON.
I'M A DOCTOR.
NOW...
LET'S GET OUT OF THIS RAIN, SHALL WE?
OTHER-WISE, YOU'LL TAKE A CHILL.
......
I DID IT.
I DID IT!!
OH... UM!
I NEED TO...
ASK MR. HOLMES FOR HELP RIGHT AWAY!!
YES, ABOUT THAT...
HE'S RATHER TIED UP JUST NOW.
I'LL HEAR YOUR STORY FOR THE TIME BEING.
HE HAS A CLIENT OVER AT OUR FLAT.
...?
IT'S A PRETTY COMPLICATED CASE.
THEY CAN'T BE INTERRUPTED.
PSHHAAA

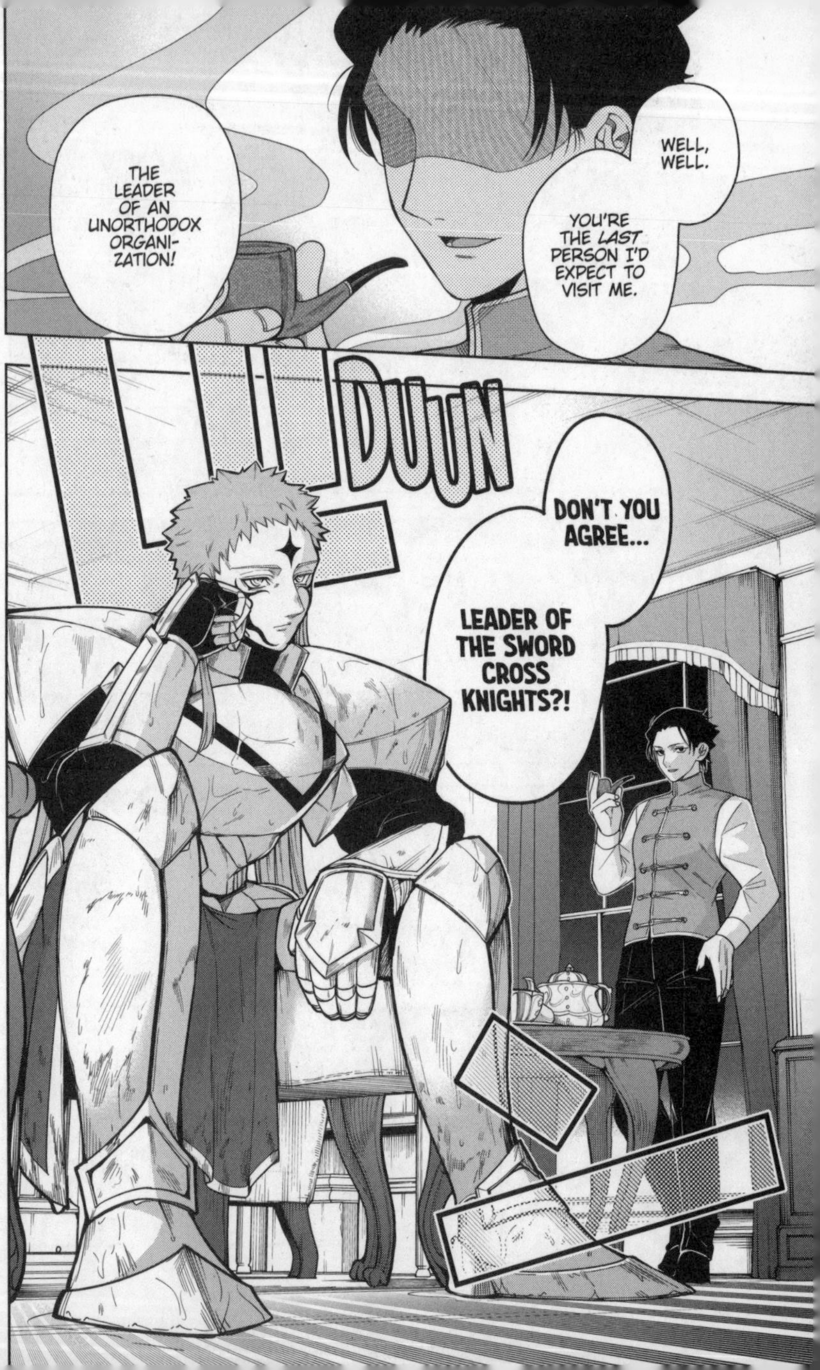
WELL, WELL.
YOU'RE THE *LAST* PERSON I'D EXPECT TO VISIT ME.
THE LEADER OF AN UNORTHODOX ORGANI-ZATION!
DUUN
DON'T YOU AGREE...
LEADER OF THE SWORD CROSS KNIGHTS?!

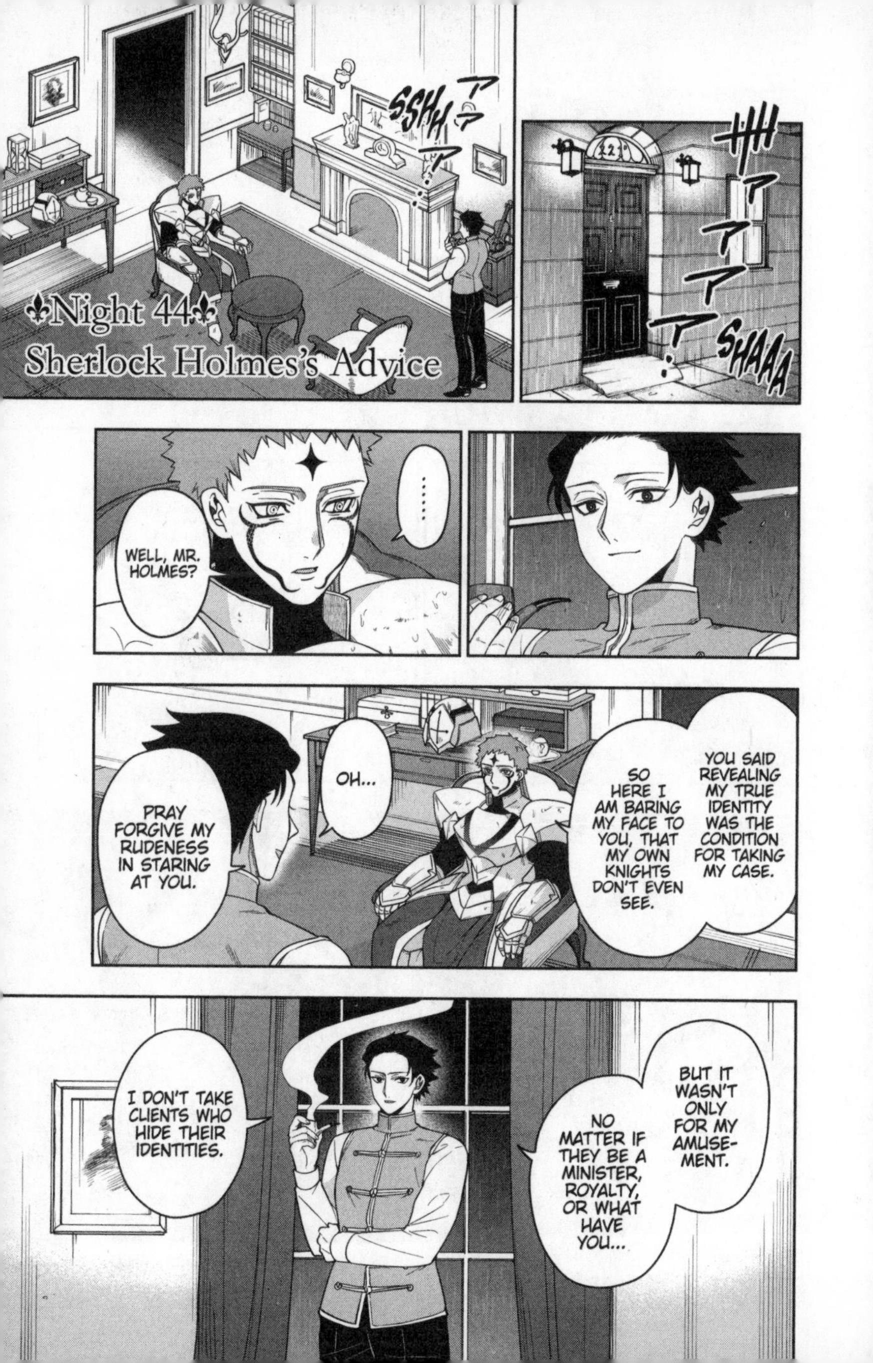
SHAAA
SSHH
Night 44
Sherlock Holmes's Advice
......
WELL, MR. HOLMES?
YOU SAID REVEALING MY TRUE IDENTITY WAS THE CONDITION FOR TAKING MY CASE.
SO HERE I AM BARING MY FACE TO YOU, THAT MY OWN KNIGHTS DON'T EVEN SEE.
OH...
PRAY FORGIVE MY RUDENESS IN STARING AT YOU.
BUT IT WASN'T ONLY FOR MY AMUSE-MENT.
NO MATTER IF THEY BE A MINISTER, ROYALTY, OR WHAT HAVE YOU...
I DON'T TAKE CLIENTS WHO HIDE THEIR IDENTITIES.

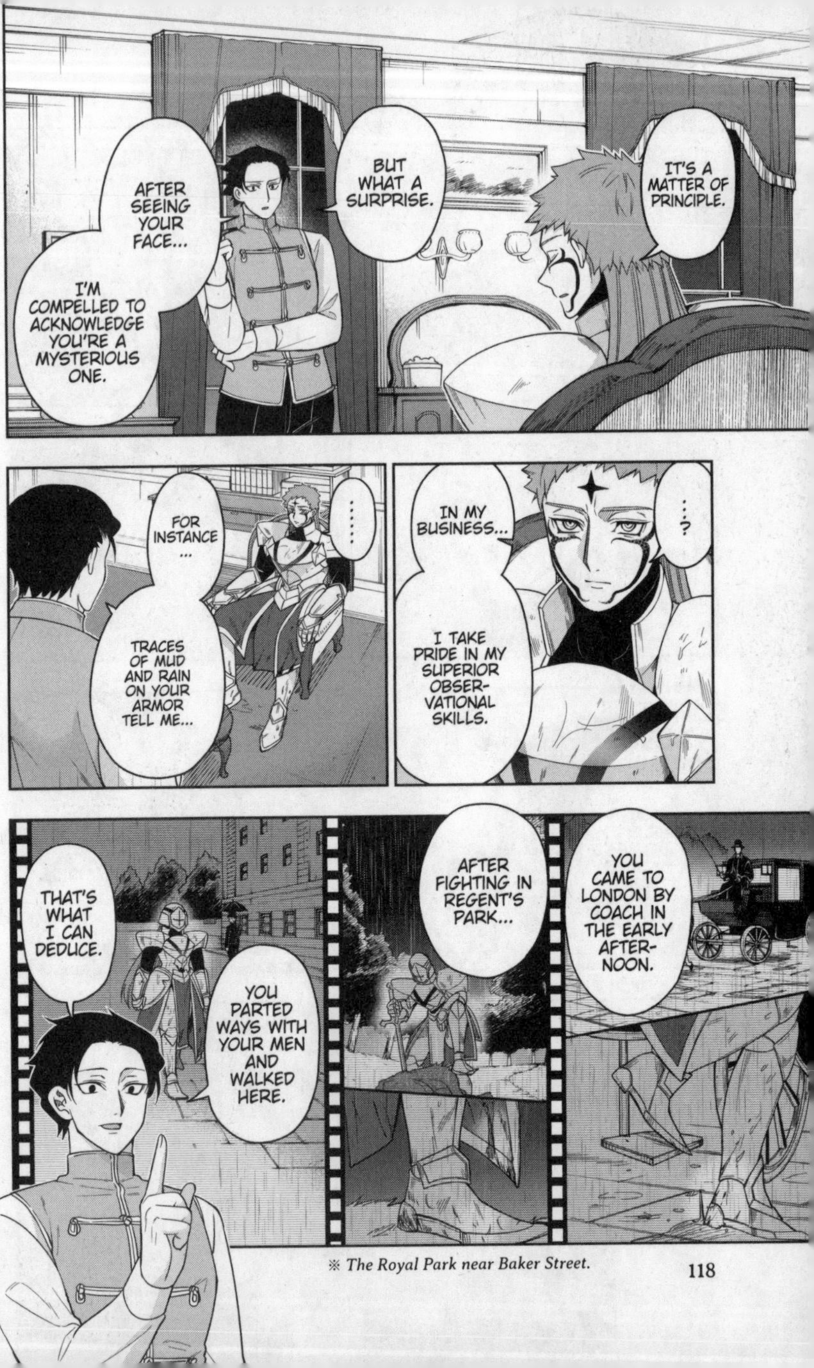
IT'S A MATTER OF PRINCIPLE.
BUT WHAT A SURPRISE.
AFTER SEEING YOUR FACE...
I'M COMPELLED TO ACKNOWLEDGE YOU'RE A MYSTERIOUS ONE.
...?
IN MY BUSINESS...
I TAKE PRIDE IN MY SUPERIOR OBSERVATIONAL SKILLS.
......
FOR INSTANCE ...
TRACES OF MUD AND RAIN ON YOUR ARMOR TELL ME...
YOU CAME TO LONDON BY COACH IN THE EARLY AFTERNOON.
AFTER FIGHTING IN REGENT'S PARK...
YOU PARTED WAYS WITH YOUR MEN AND WALKED HERE.
THAT'S WHAT I CAN DEDUCE.

※ *The Royal Park near Baker Street.*

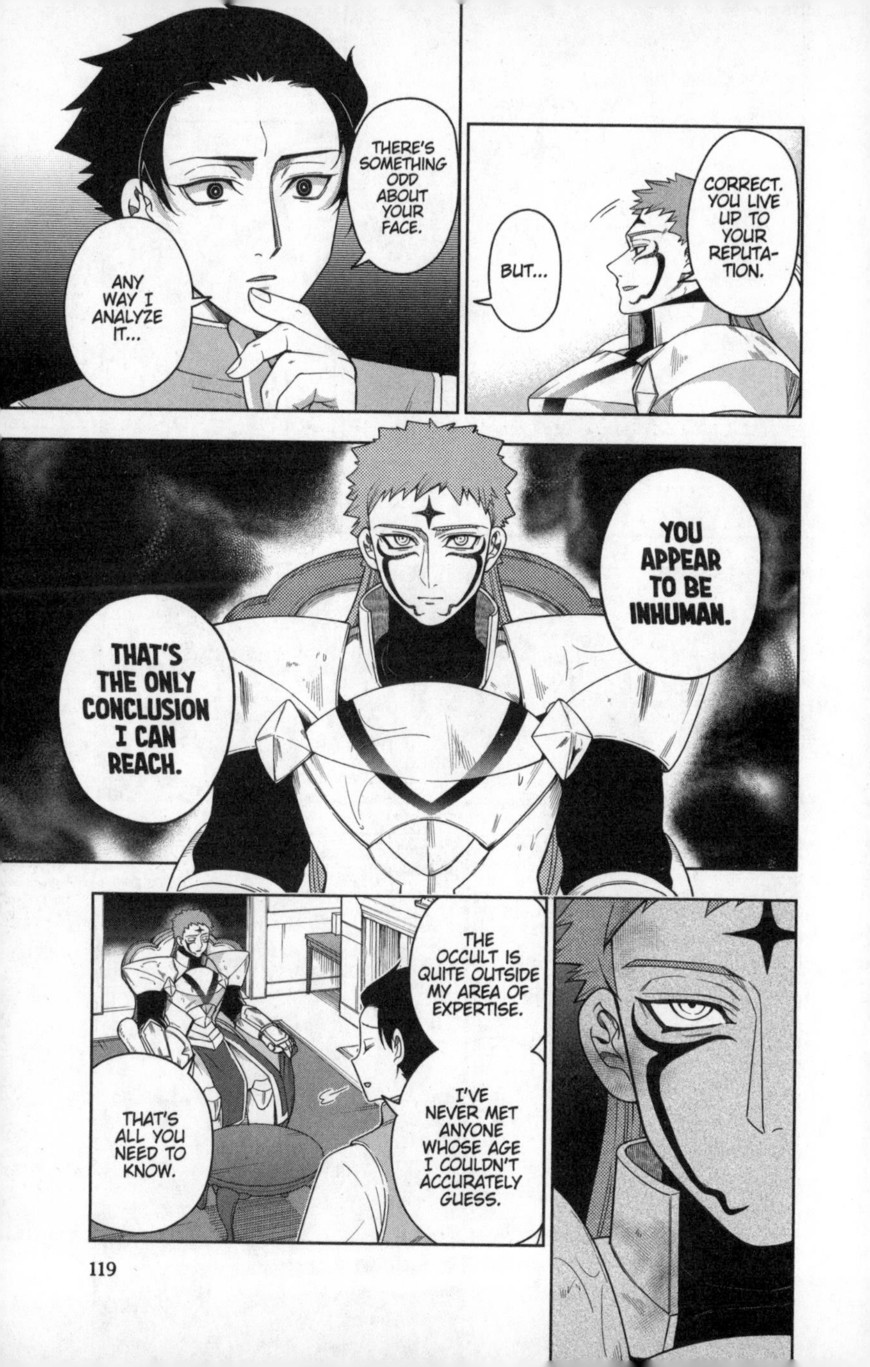
CORRECT. YOU LIVE UP TO YOUR REPUTATION.
BUT...
THERE'S SOMETHING ODD ABOUT YOUR FACE.
ANY WAY I ANALYZE IT...
YOU APPEAR TO BE INHUMAN.
THAT'S THE ONLY CONCLUSION I CAN REACH.
THE OCCULT IS QUITE OUTSIDE MY AREA OF EXPERTISE.
I'VE NEVER MET ANYONE WHOSE AGE I COULDN'T ACCURATELY GUESS.
THAT'S ALL YOU NEED TO KNOW.

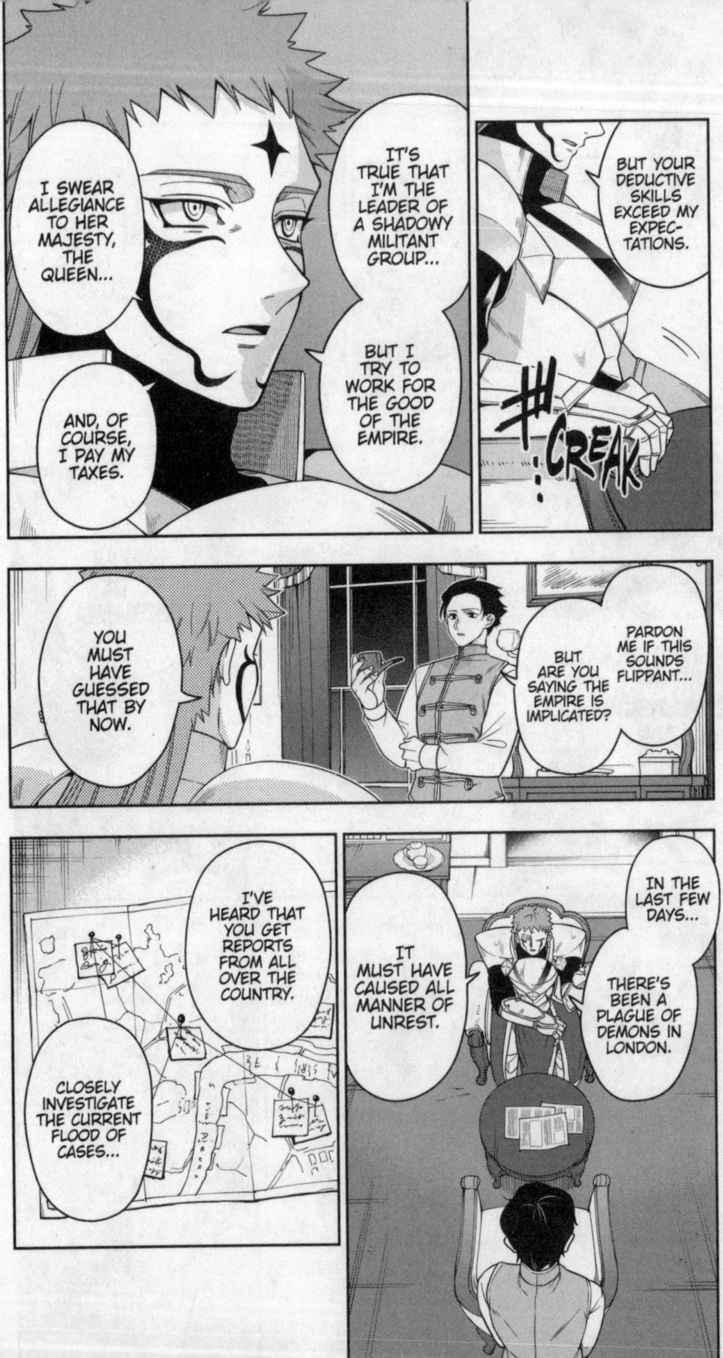
BUT YOUR DEDUCTIVE SKILLS EXCEED MY EXPEC-TATIONS.
CREAK
IT'S TRUE THAT I'M THE LEADER OF A SHADOWY MILITANT GROUP...
BUT I TRY TO WORK FOR THE GOOD OF THE EMPIRE.
I SWEAR ALLEGIANCE TO HER MAJESTY, THE QUEEN...
AND, OF COURSE, I PAY MY TAXES.
PARDON ME IF THIS SOUNDS FLIPPANT...
BUT ARE YOU SAYING THE EMPIRE IS IMPLICATED?
YOU MUST HAVE GUESSED THAT BY NOW.
IN THE LAST FEW DAYS...
THERE'S BEEN A PLAGUE OF DEMONS IN LONDON.
IT MUST HAVE CAUSED ALL MANNER OF UNREST.
I'VE HEARD THAT YOU GET REPORTS FROM ALL OVER THE COUNTRY.
CLOSELY INVESTIGATE THE CURRENT FLOOD OF CASES...

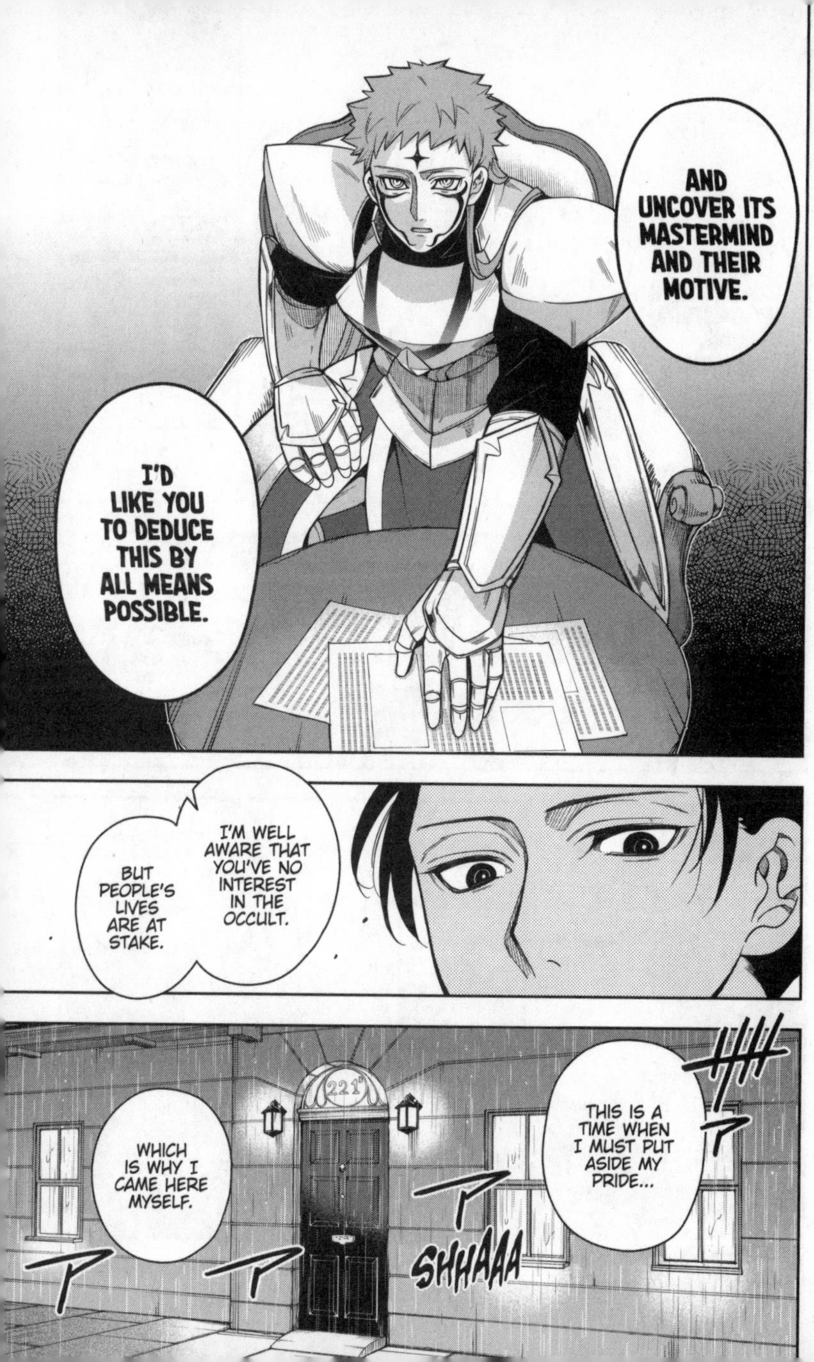
AND UNCOVER ITS MASTERMIND AND THEIR MOTIVE.
I'D LIKE YOU TO DEDUCE THIS BY ALL MEANS POSSIBLE.
I'M WELL AWARE THAT YOU'VE NO INTEREST IN THE OCCULT.
BUT PEOPLE'S LIVES ARE AT STAKE.
THIS IS A TIME WHEN I MUST PUT ASIDE MY PRIDE...
SHHAAA
WHICH IS WHY I CAME HERE MYSELF.

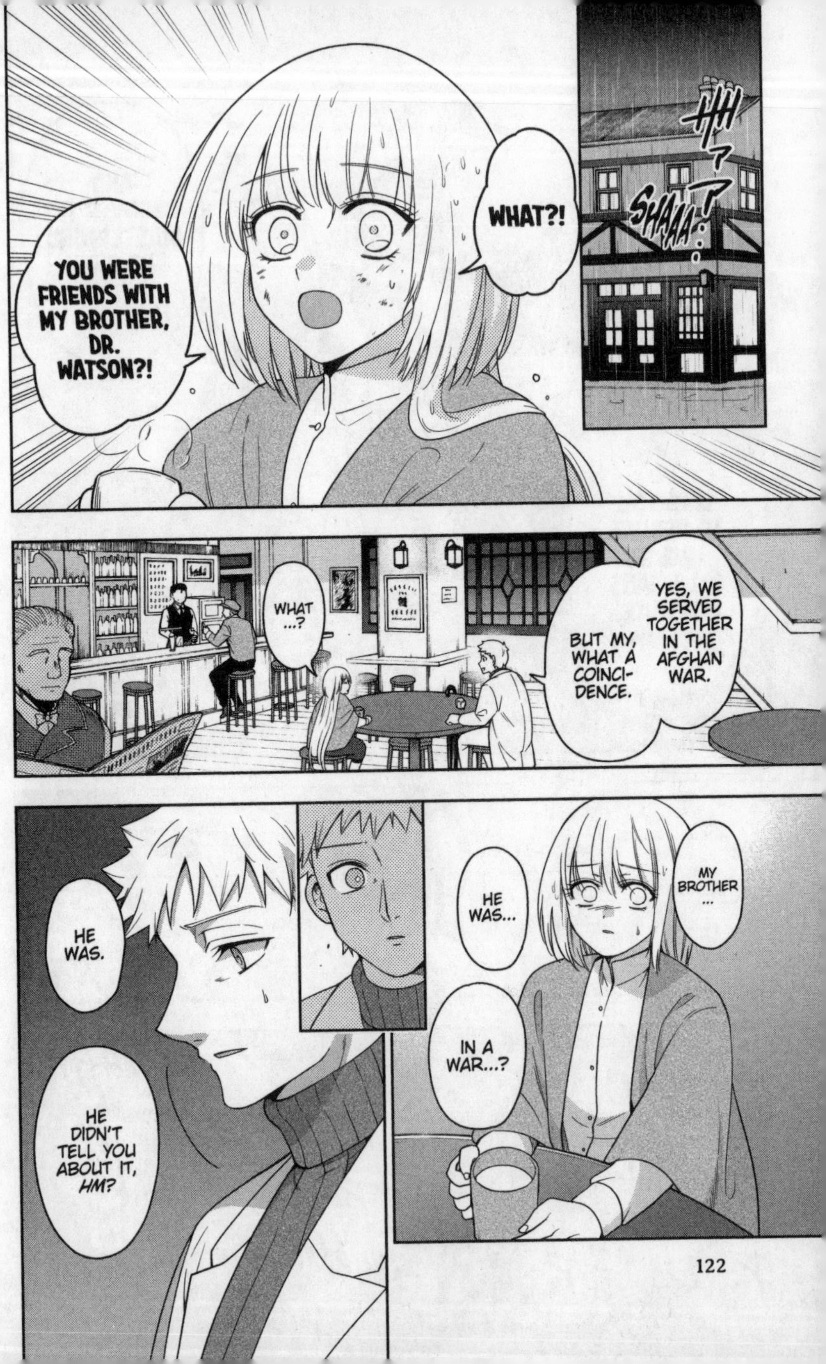
SHAAA
WHAT?!
YOU WERE FRIENDS WITH MY BROTHER, DR. WATSON?!
YES, WE SERVED TOGETHER IN THE AFGHAN WAR.
BUT MY, WHAT A COINCI- DENCE.
WHAT ...?
MY BROTHER ...
HE WAS...
IN A WAR...?
HE WAS.
HE DIDN'T TELL YOU ABOUT IT, *HM?*

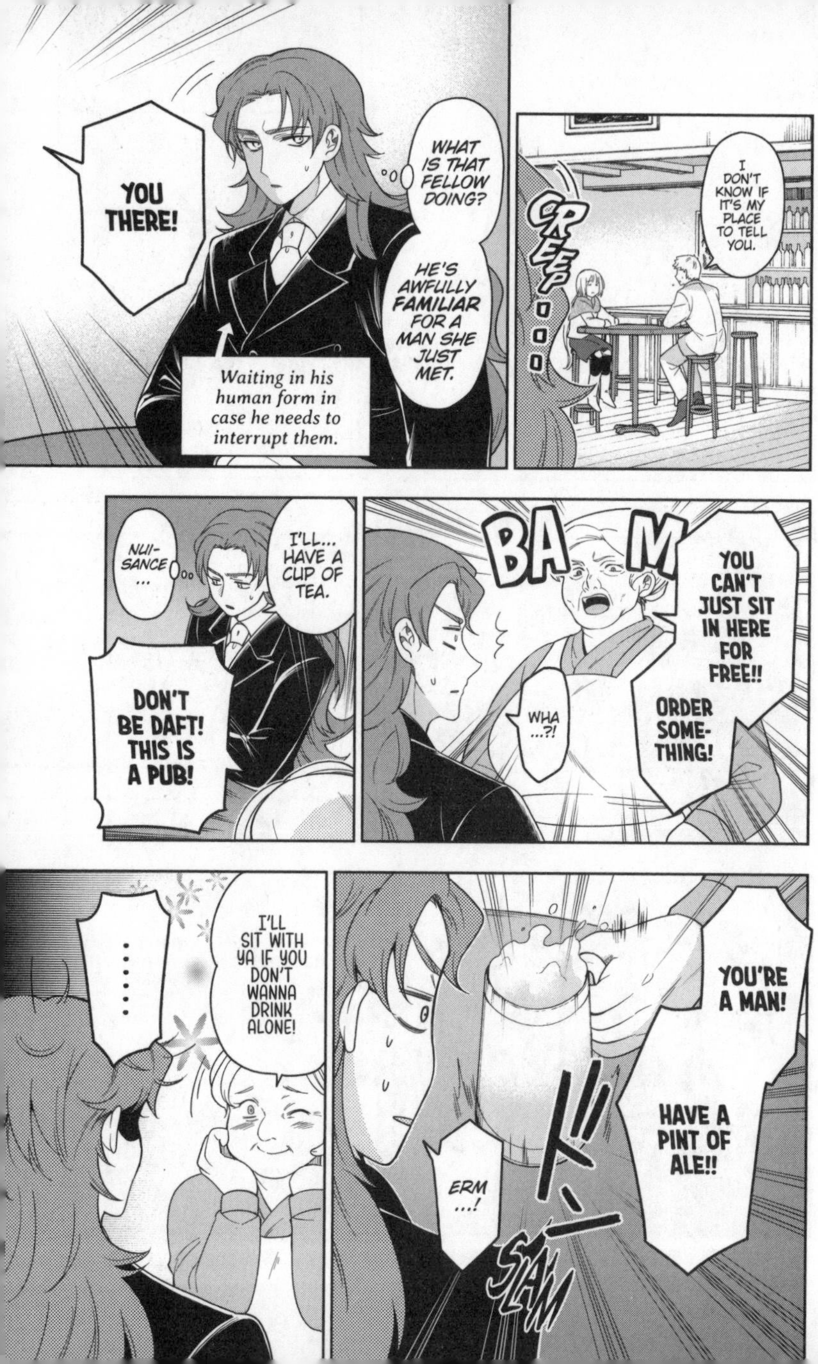
I DON'T KNOW IF IT'S MY PLACE TO TELL YOU.
CREEP...
WHAT IS THAT FELLOW DOING?
HE'S AWFULLY FAMILIAR FOR A MAN SHE JUST MET.
YOU THERE!
Waiting in his human form in case he needs to interrupt them.
BAM
YOU CAN'T JUST SIT IN HERE FOR FREE!!
ORDER SOME-THING!
WHA ...?!
I'LL... HAVE A CUP OF TEA.
NUI-SANCE ...
DON'T BE DAFT! THIS IS A PUB!
YOU'RE A MAN!
HAVE A PINT OF ALE!!
ERM ...!
SLAM
I'LL SIT WITH YA IF YOU DON'T WANNA DRINK ALONE!
......

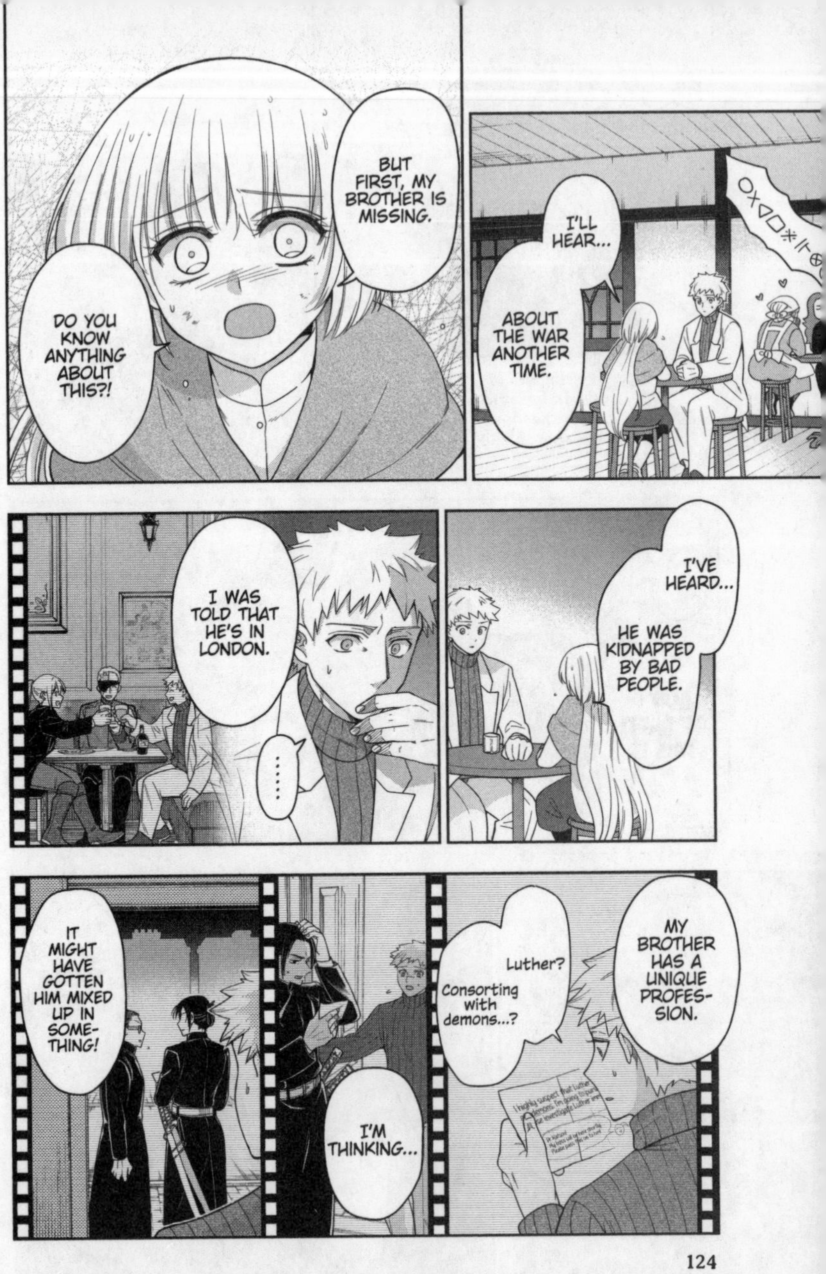
I'LL HEAR...
ABOUT THE WAR ANOTHER TIME.
BUT FIRST, MY BROTHER IS MISSING.
DO YOU KNOW ANYTHING ABOUT THIS?!
I'VE HEARD...
HE WAS KIDNAPPED BY BAD PEOPLE.
I WAS TOLD THAT HE'S IN LONDON.
......
MY BROTHER HAS A UNIQUE PROFES-SION.
Luther?
Consorting with demons...?
I'M THINKING...
IT MIGHT HAVE GOTTEN HIM MIXED UP IN SOME-THING!

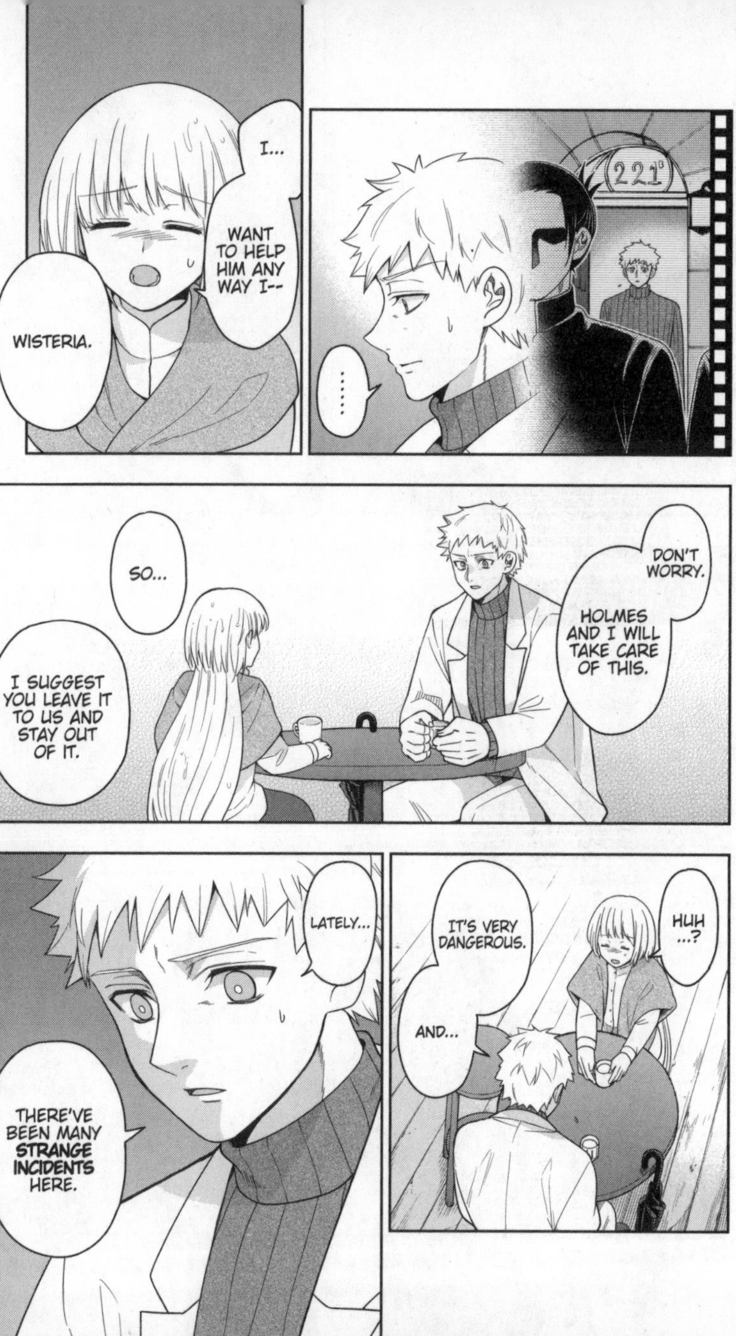
221B
......
I...
WANT TO HELP HIM ANY WAY I--
WISTERIA.
DON'T WORRY.
HOLMES AND I WILL TAKE CARE OF THIS.
SO...
I SUGGEST YOU LEAVE IT TO US AND STAY OUT OF IT.
HUH ...?
IT'S VERY DANGEROUS.
AND...
LATELY...
THERE'VE BEEN MANY **STRANGE INCIDENTS** HERE.

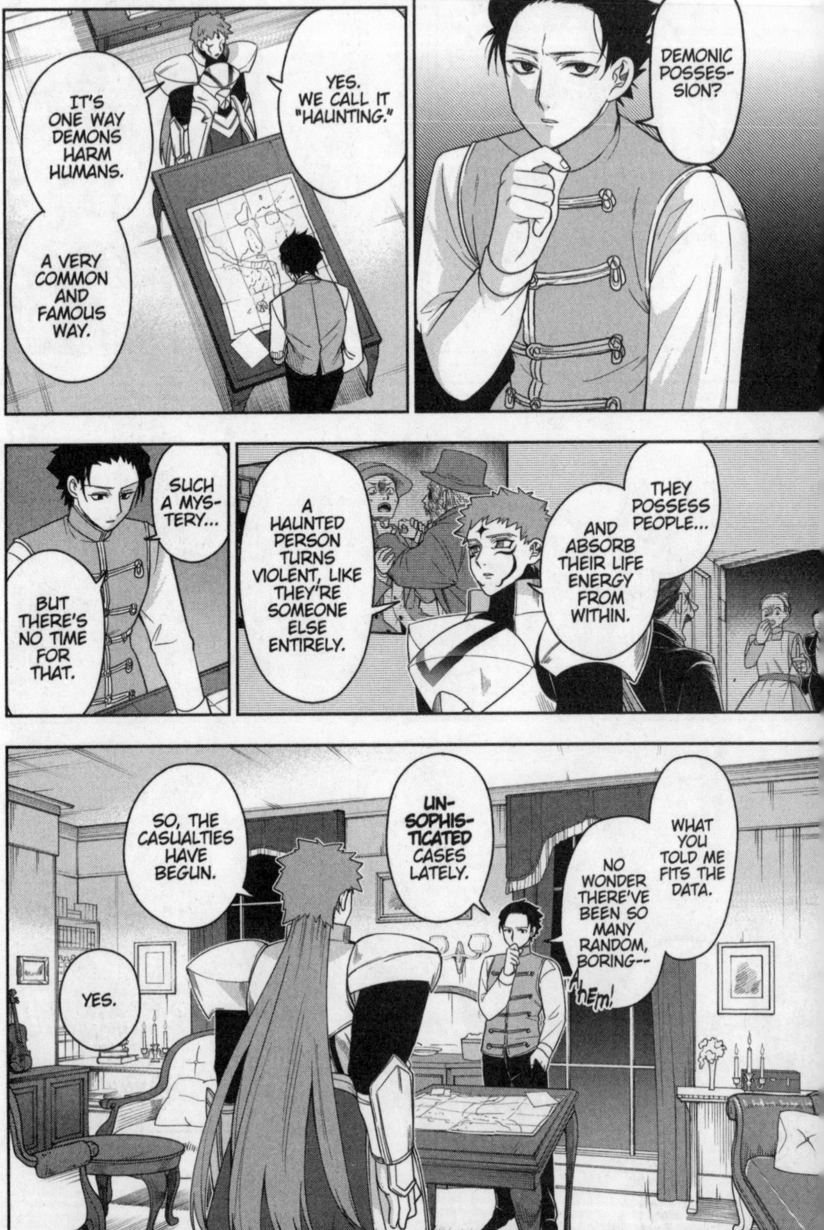
DEMONIC POSSES-SION?
YES. WE CALL IT "HAUNTING."
IT'S ONE WAY DEMONS HARM HUMANS.
A VERY COMMON AND FAMOUS WAY.
THEY POSSESS PEOPLE...
AND ABSORB THEIR LIFE ENERGY FROM WITHIN.
A HAUNTED PERSON TURNS VIOLENT, LIKE THEY'RE SOMEONE ELSE ENTIRELY.
SUCH A MYS-TERY...
BUT THERE'S NO TIME FOR THAT.
WHAT YOU TOLD ME FITS THE DATA.
NO WONDER THERE'VE BEEN SO MANY RANDOM, BORING--
AHEM!
UN-SOPHIS-TICATED CASES LATELY.
SO, THE CASUALTIES HAVE BEGUN.
YES.

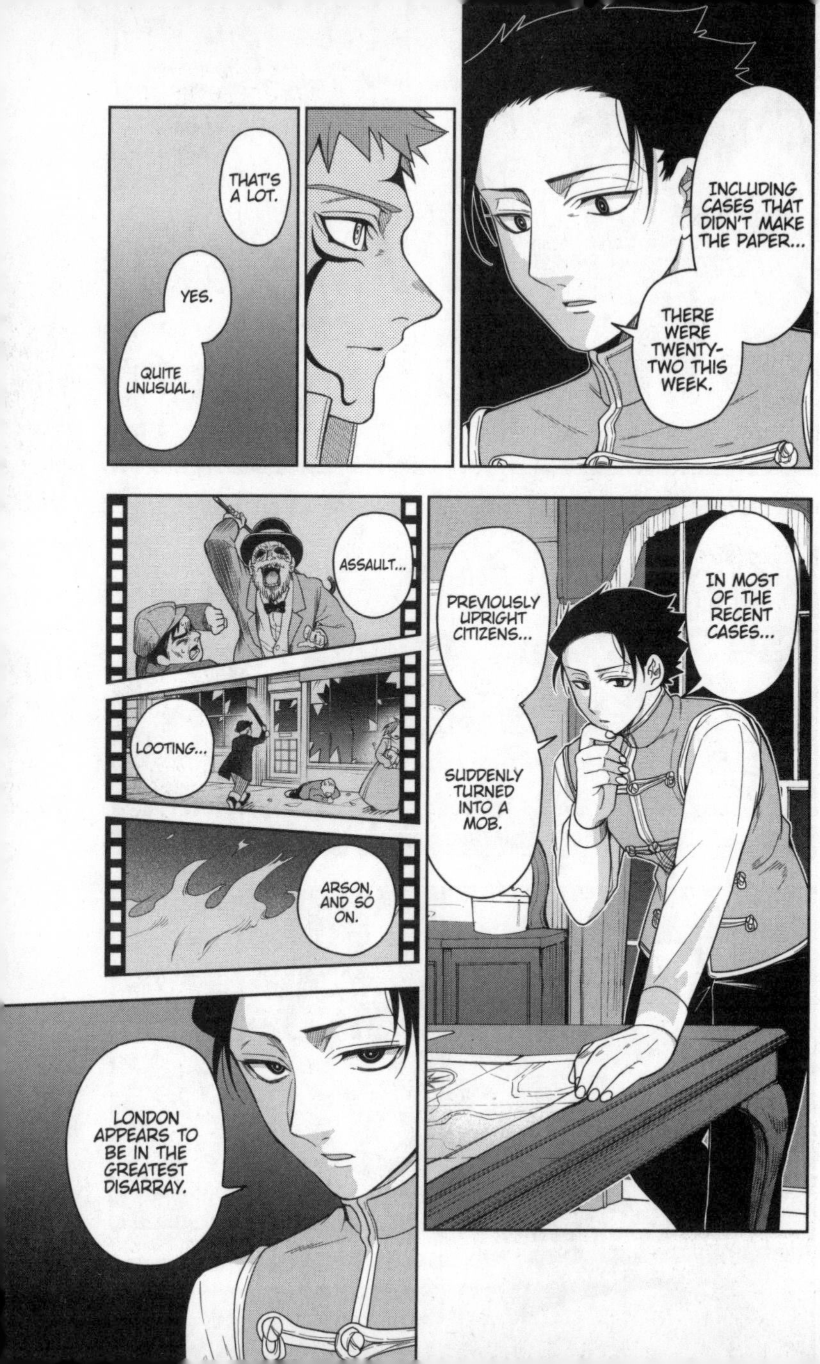
INCLUDING CASES THAT DIDN'T MAKE THE PAPER...
THERE WERE TWENTY-TWO THIS WEEK.
THAT'S A LOT.
YES.
QUITE UNUSUAL.
IN MOST OF THE RECENT CASES...
PREVIOUSLY UPRIGHT CITIZENS...
SUDDENLY TURNED INTO A MOB.
ASSAULT...
LOOTING...
ARSON, AND SO ON.
LONDON APPEARS TO BE IN THE GREATEST DISARRAY.

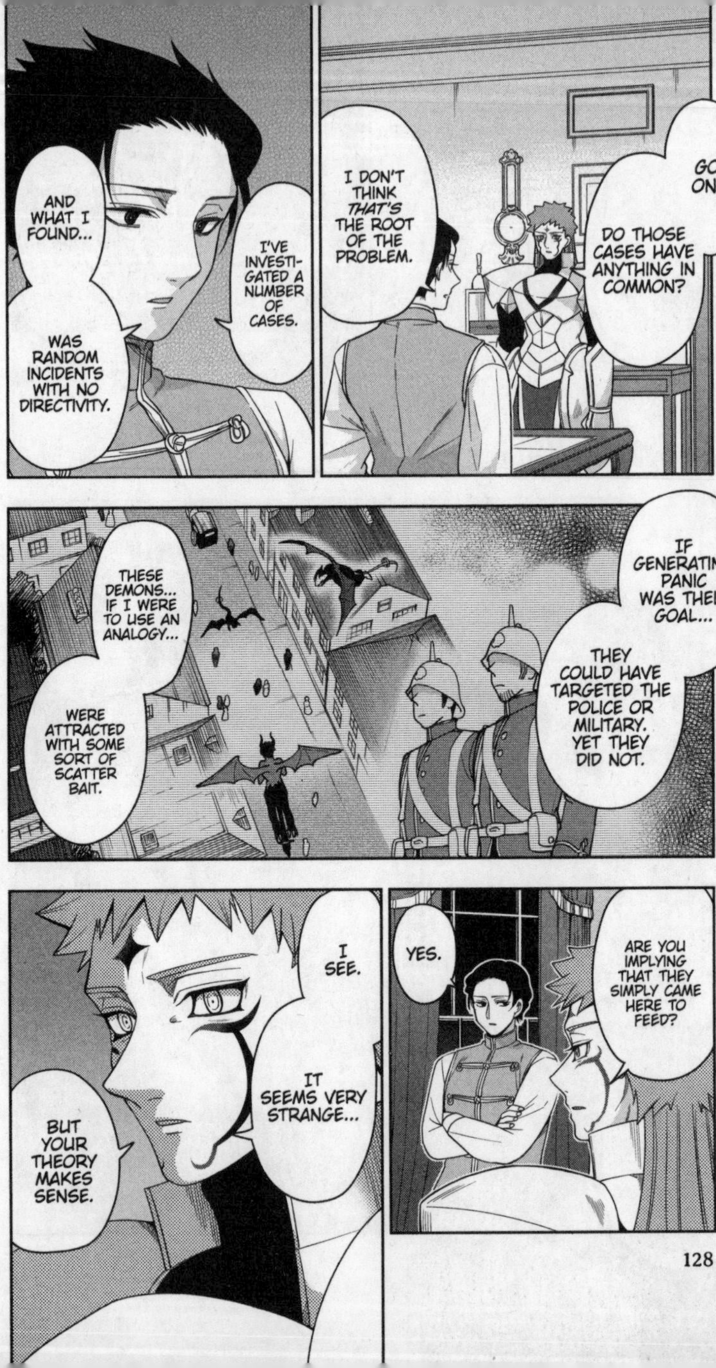
GO ON.
DO THOSE CASES HAVE ANYTHING IN COMMON?
I DON'T THINK *THAT'S* THE ROOT OF THE PROBLEM.
I'VE INVESTI-GATED A NUMBER OF CASES.
AND WHAT I FOUND...
WAS RANDOM INCIDENTS WITH NO DIRECTIVITY.
IF GENERATING PANIC WAS THEIR GOAL...
THEY COULD HAVE TARGETED THE POLICE OR MILITARY. YET THEY DID NOT.
THESE DEMONS... IF I WERE TO USE AN ANALOGY...
WERE ATTRACTED WITH SOME SORT OF SCATTER BAIT.
ARE YOU IMPLYING THAT THEY SIMPLY CAME HERE TO FEED?
YES.
I SEE.
IT SEEMS VERY STRANGE...
BUT YOUR THEORY MAKES SENSE.

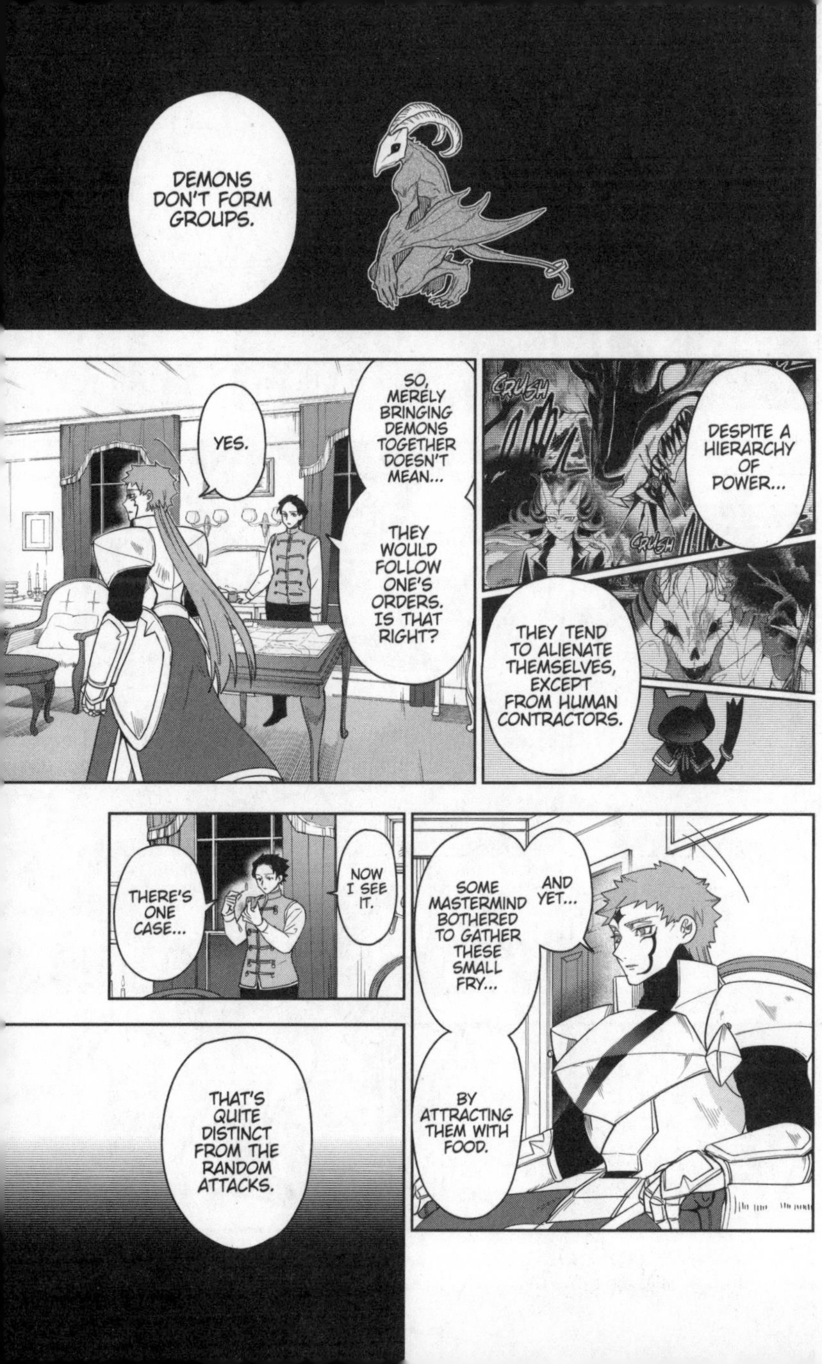
DEMONS DON'T FORM GROUPS.
CRUSH
DESPITE A HIERARCHY OF POWER...
CRUSH
THEY TEND TO ALIENATE THEMSELVES, EXCEPT FROM HUMAN CONTRACTORS.
SO, MERELY BRINGING DEMONS TOGETHER DOESN'T MEAN...
THEY WOULD FOLLOW ONE'S ORDERS. IS THAT RIGHT?
YES.
AND YET...
SOME MASTERMIND BOTHERED TO GATHER THESE SMALL FRY...
BY ATTRACTING THEM WITH FOOD.
NOW I SEE IT.
THERE'S ONE CASE...
THAT'S QUITE DISTINCT FROM THE RANDOM ATTACKS.

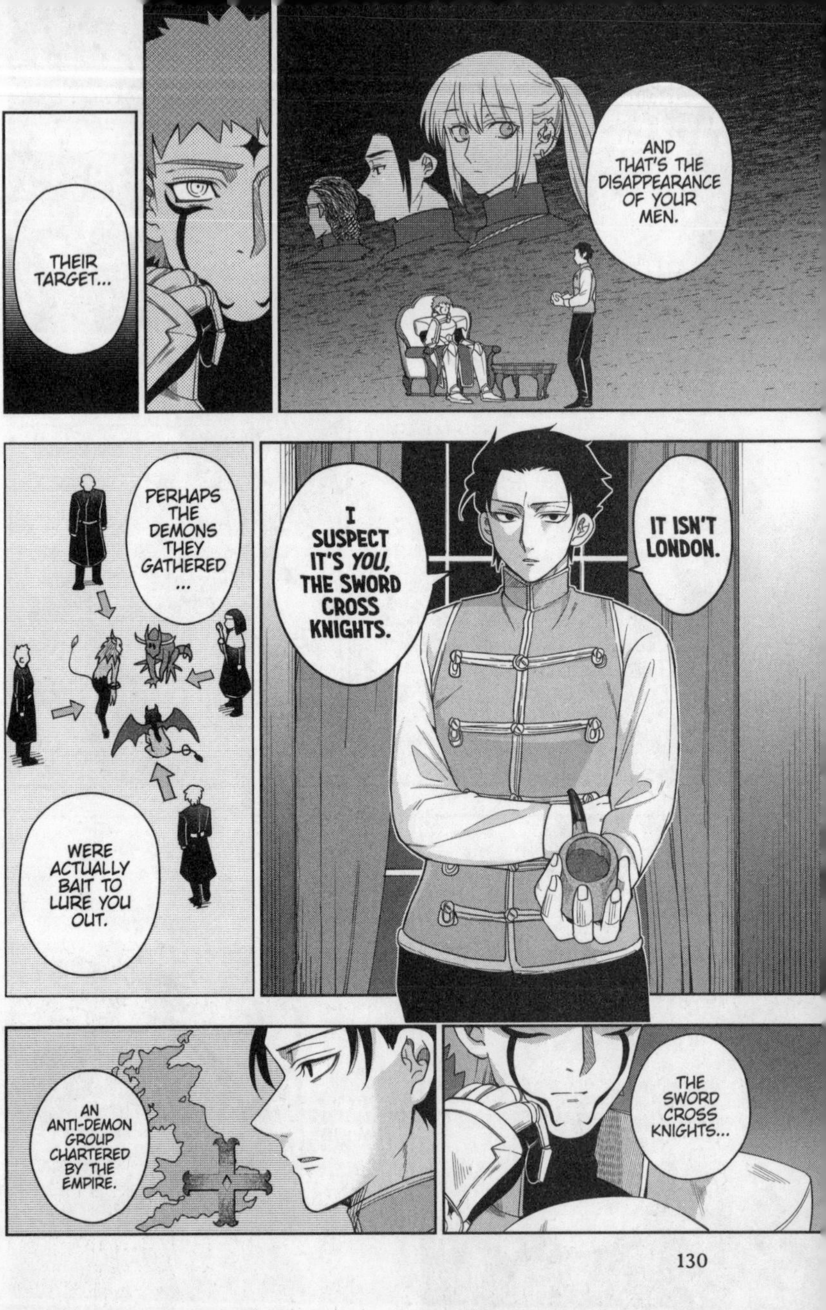

AND THAT'S THE DISAPPEARANCE OF YOUR MEN.
THEIR TARGET...
IT ISN'T LONDON.
I SUSPECT IT'S *YOU*, THE SWORD CROSS KNIGHTS.
PERHAPS THE DEMONS THEY GATHERED ...
WERE ACTUALLY BAIT TO LURE YOU OUT.
THE SWORD CROSS KNIGHTS...
AN ANTI-DEMON GROUP CHARTERED BY THE EMPIRE.

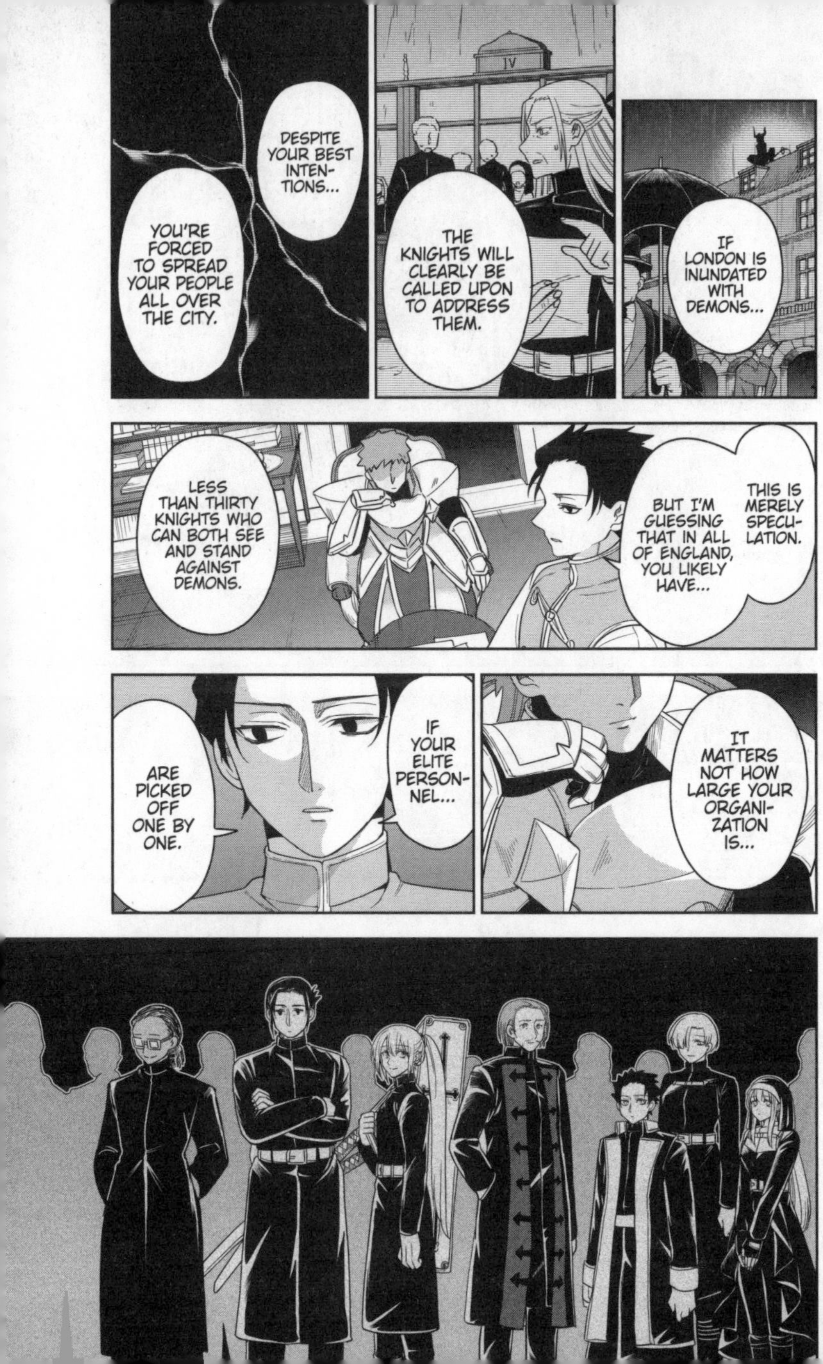
IF LONDON IS INUNDATED WITH DEMONS...
THE KNIGHTS WILL CLEARLY BE CALLED UPON TO ADDRESS THEM.
DESPITE YOUR BEST INTEN- TIONS...
YOU'RE FORCED TO SPREAD YOUR PEOPLE ALL OVER THE CITY.
THIS IS MERELY SPECU- LATION.
BUT I'M GUESSING THAT IN ALL OF ENGLAND, YOU LIKELY HAVE...
LESS THAN THIRTY KNIGHTS WHO CAN BOTH SEE AND STAND AGAINST DEMONS.
IT MATTERS NOT HOW LARGE YOUR ORGANI- ZATION IS...
IF YOUR ELITE PERSON- NEL...
ARE PICKED OFF ONE BY ONE.

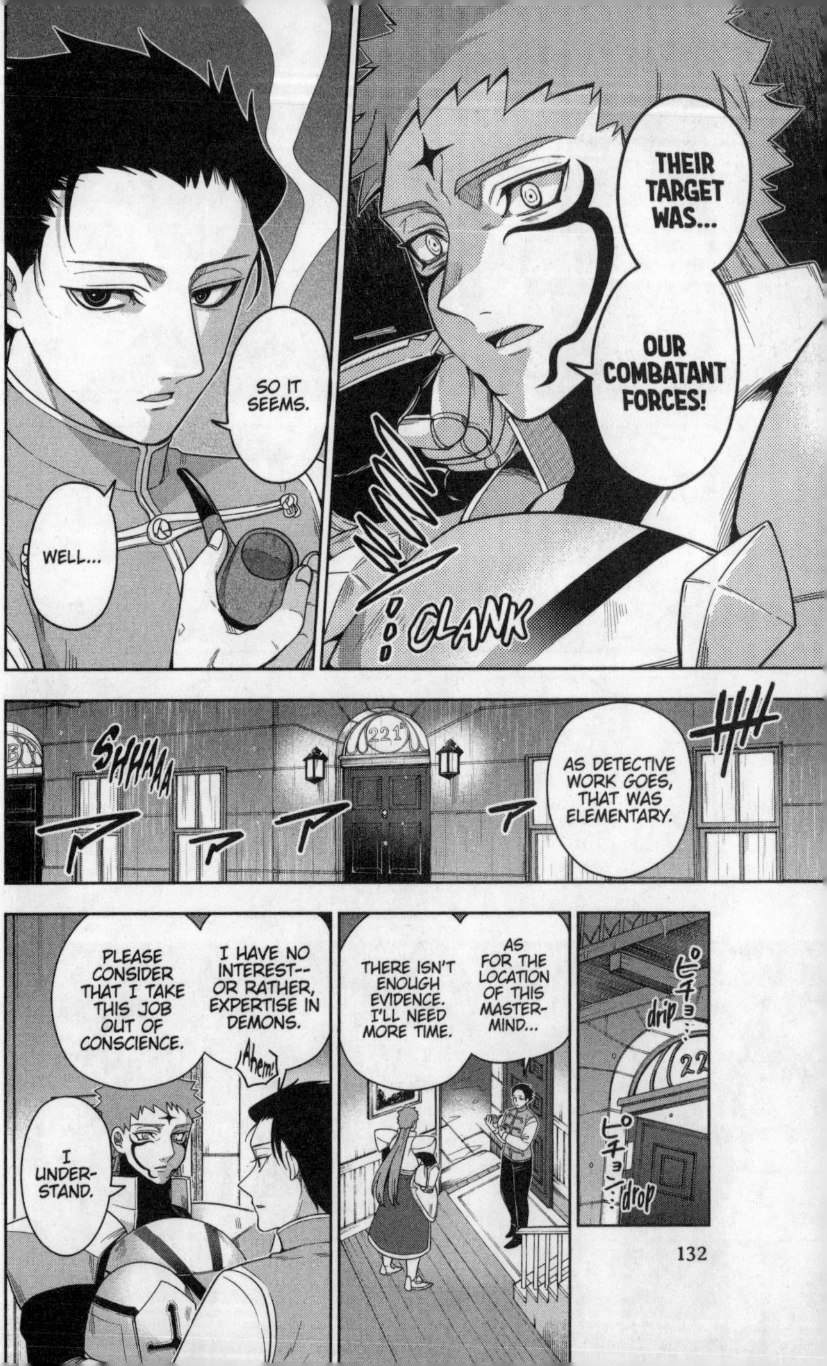
THEIR TARGET WAS...
OUR COMBATANT FORCES!
CLANK
SO IT SEEMS.
WELL...
AS DETECTIVE WORK GOES, THAT WAS ELEMENTARY.
221B
SHHAAA
ピチョ
drip
ピチョン
drop
AS FOR THE LOCATION OF THIS MASTER-MIND...
THERE ISN'T ENOUGH EVIDENCE. I'LL NEED MORE TIME.
I HAVE NO INTEREST-- OR RATHER, EXPERTISE IN DEMONS.
PLEASE CONSIDER THAT I TAKE THIS JOB OUT OF CONSCIENCE.
Ahem!
I UNDER-STAND.

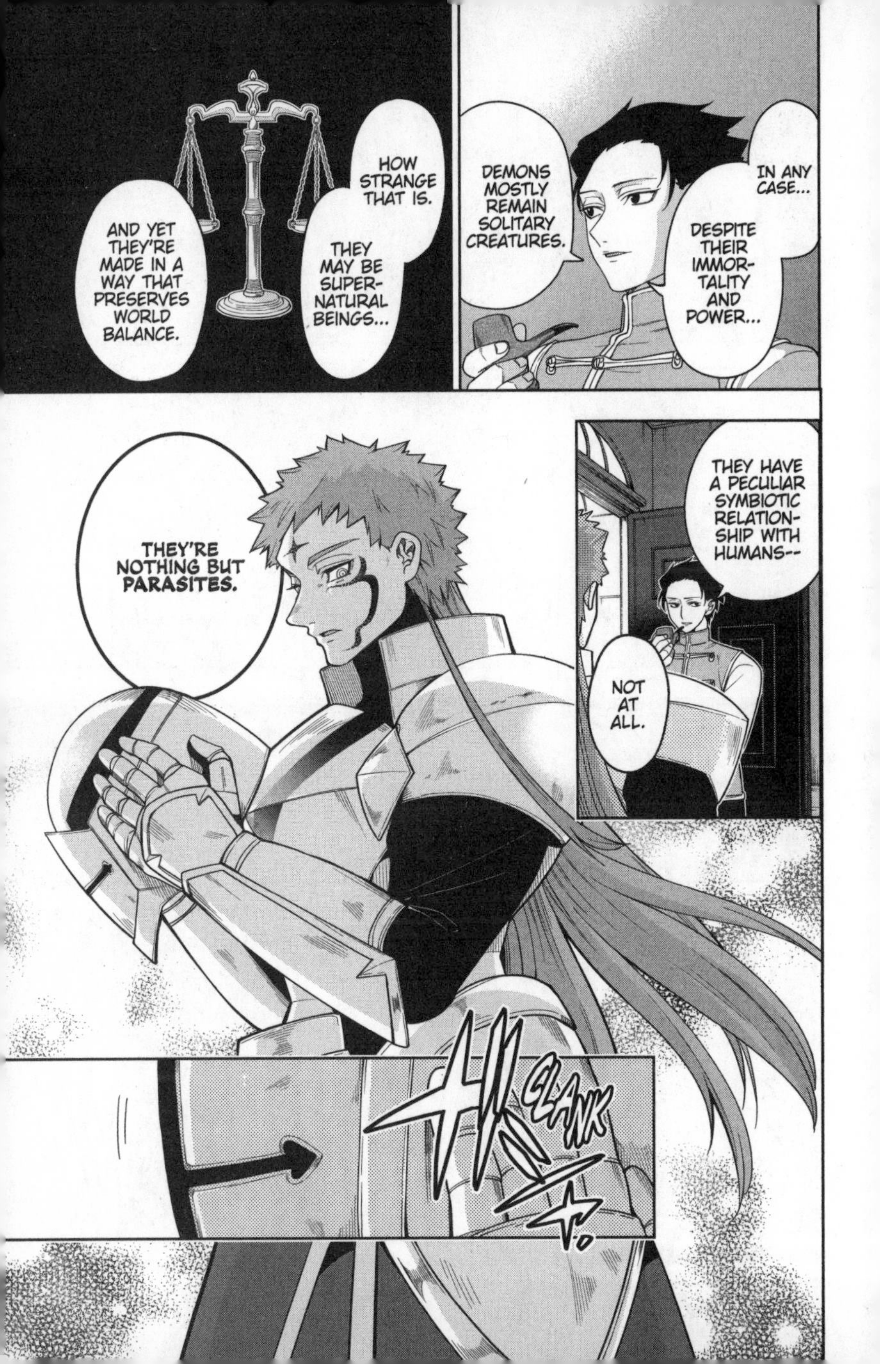
IN ANY CASE...
DESPITE THEIR IMMORTALITY AND POWER...
DEMONS MOSTLY REMAIN SOLITARY CREATURES.
HOW STRANGE THAT IS.
THEY MAY BE SUPERNATURAL BEINGS...
AND YET THEY'RE MADE IN A WAY THAT PRESERVES WORLD BALANCE.
THEY HAVE A PECULIAR SYMBIOTIC RELATIONSHIP WITH HUMANS--
NOT AT ALL.
THEY'RE NOTHING BUT **PARASITES.**
CLANK

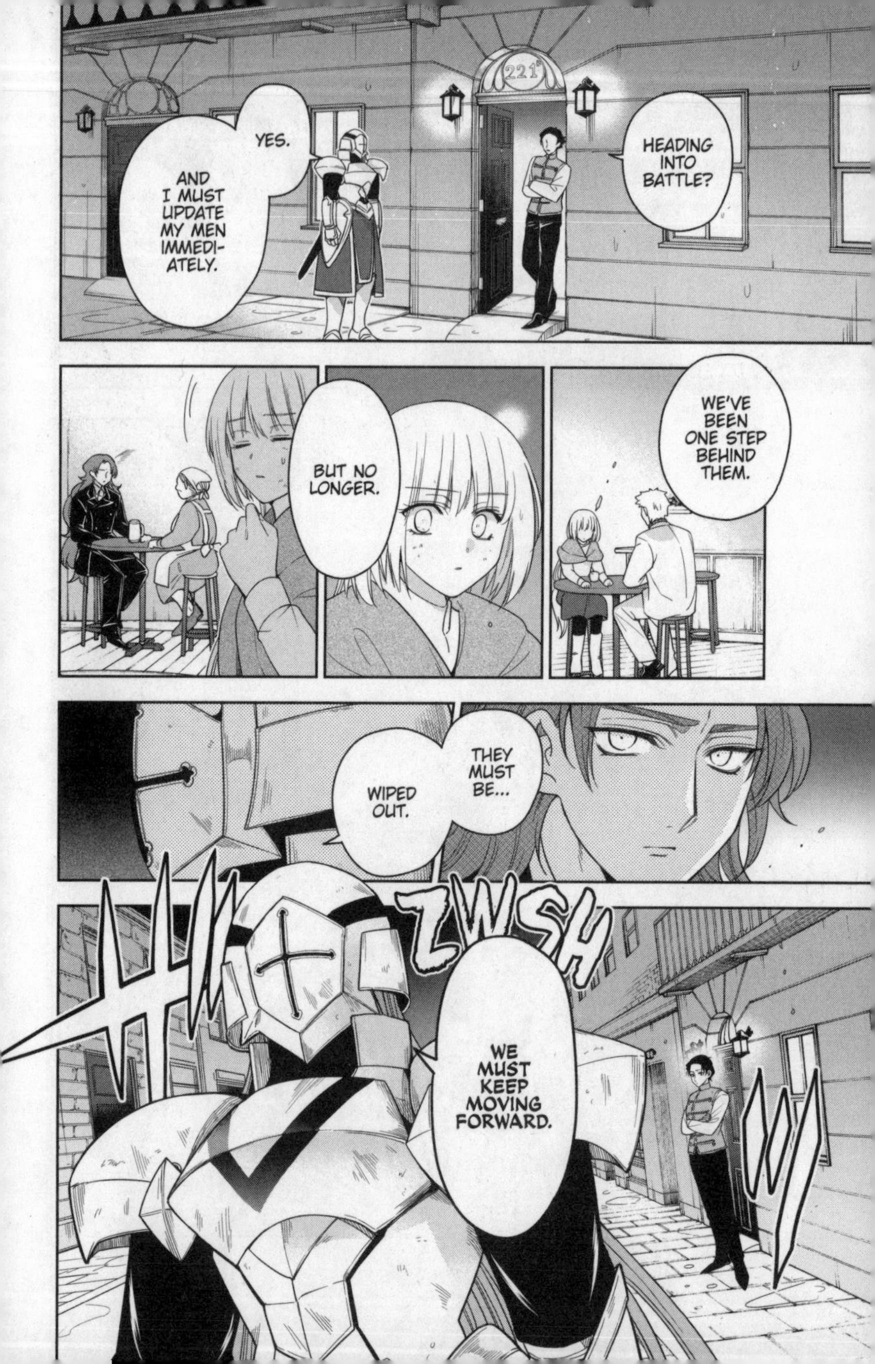
HEADING INTO BATTLE?
YES.
AND I MUST UPDATE MY MEN IMMEDIATELY.
WE'VE BEEN ONE STEP BEHIND THEM.
BUT NO LONGER.
THEY MUST BE...
WIPED OUT.
ZWSH
WE MUST KEEP MOVING FORWARD.

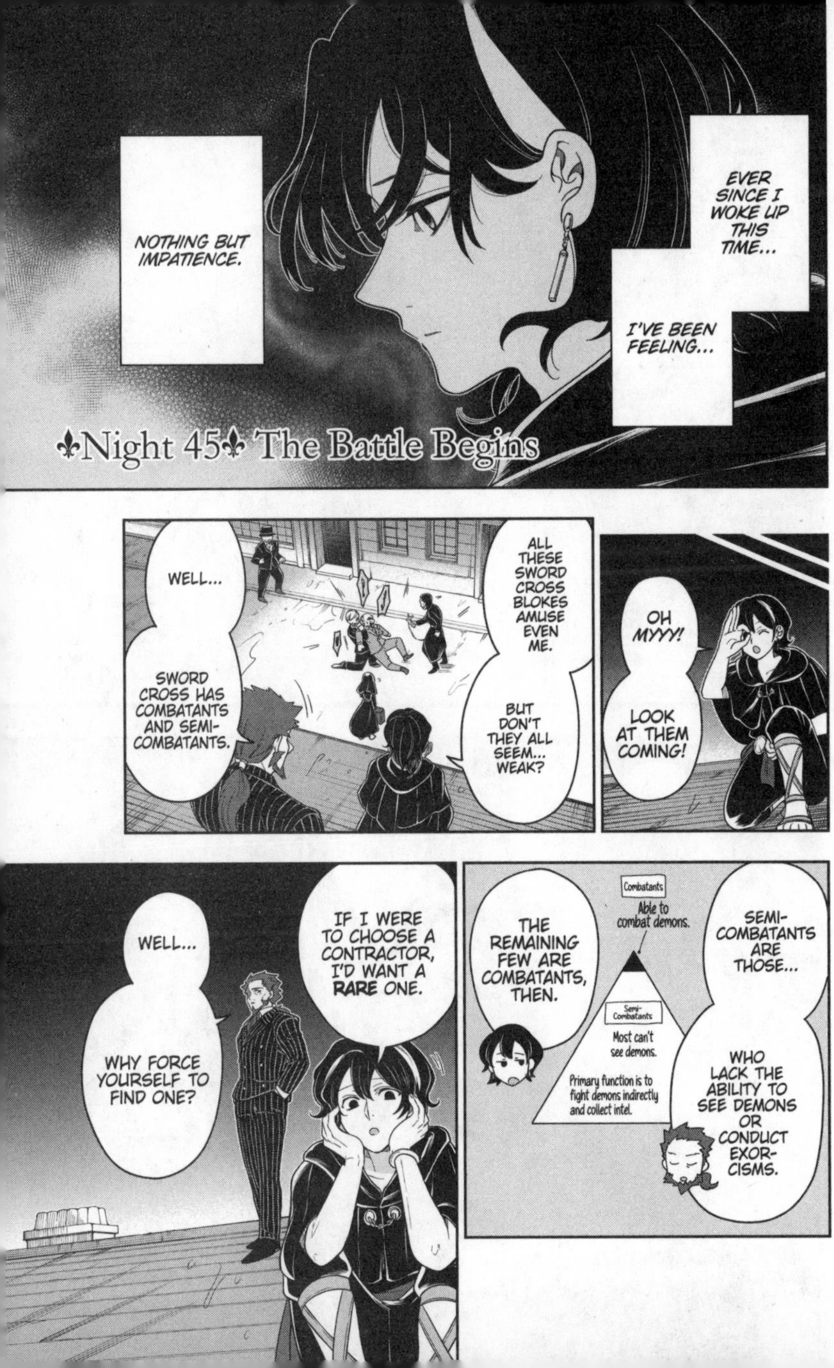
EVER SINCE I WOKE UP THIS TIME...
I'VE BEEN FEELING...
NOTHING BUT IMPATIENCE.
Night 45 The Battle Begins
OH MYYY!
LOOK AT THEM COMING!
ALL THESE SWORD CROSS BLOKES AMUSE EVEN ME.
BUT DON'T THEY ALL SEEM... WEAK?
WELL...
SWORD CROSS HAS COMBATANTS AND SEMI-COMBATANTS.
SEMI-COMBATANTS ARE THOSE...
WHO LACK THE ABILITY TO SEE DEMONS OR CONDUCT EXORCISMS.
Combatants
Able to combat demons.
Semi-Combatants
Most can't see demons.
Primary function is to fight demons indirectly and collect intel.
THE REMAINING FEW ARE COMBATANTS, THEN.
IF I WERE TO CHOOSE A CONTRACTOR, I'D WANT A RARE ONE.
WELL...
WHY FORCE YOURSELF TO FIND ONE?

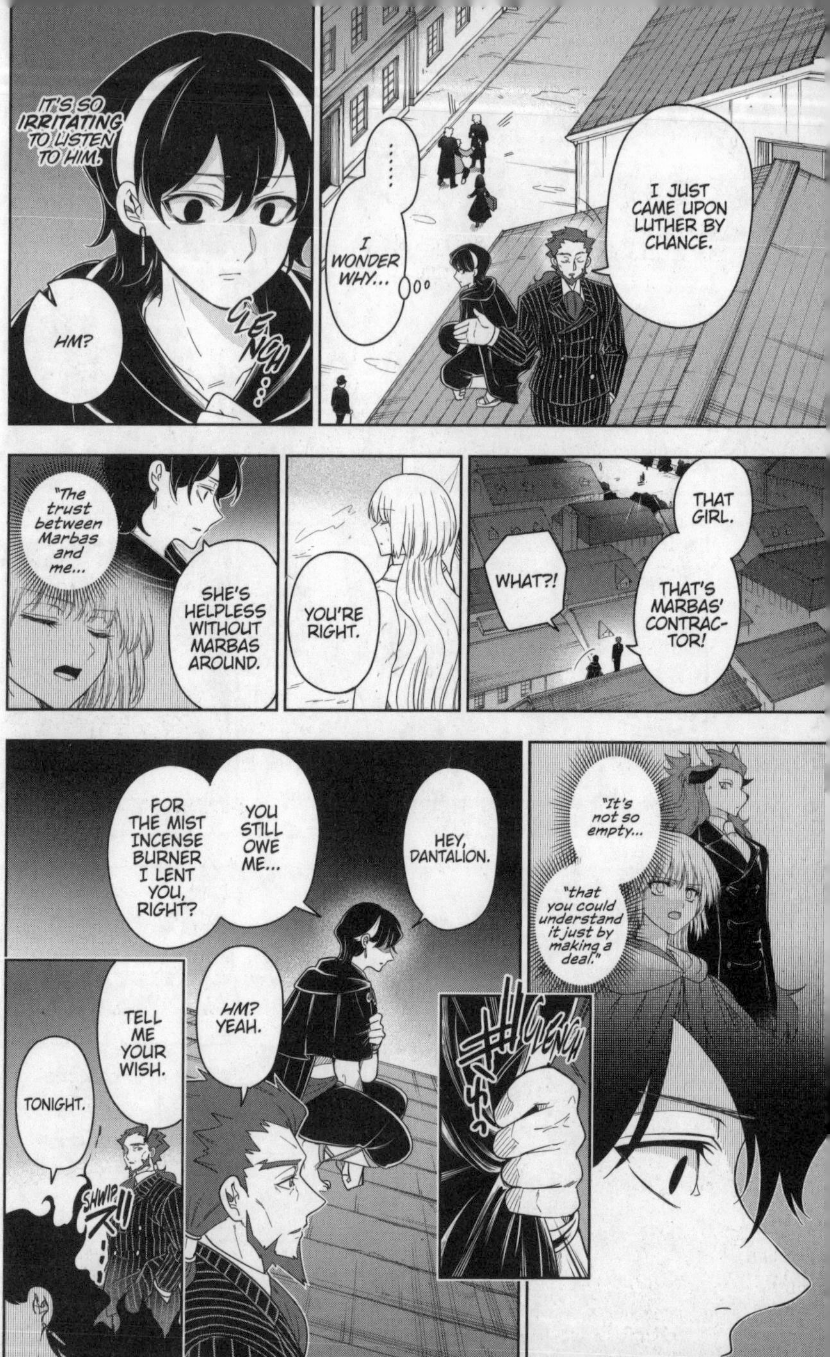
I JUST CAME UPON LUTHER BY CHANCE.
......
I WONDER WHY...
IT'S SO IRRITATING TO LISTEN TO HIM.
HM?
CLENCH...
THAT GIRL.
THAT'S MARBAS' CONTRACTOR!
WHAT?!
YOU'RE RIGHT.
SHE'S HELPLESS WITHOUT MARBAS AROUND.
"The trust between Marbas and me...
"It's not so empty...
"that you could understand it just by making a deal."
HEY, DANTALION.
YOU STILL OWE ME...
FOR THE MIST INCENSE BURNER I LENT YOU, RIGHT?
HM? YEAH.
CLENCH
TELL ME YOUR WISH.
TONIGHT.
SHWIP!!

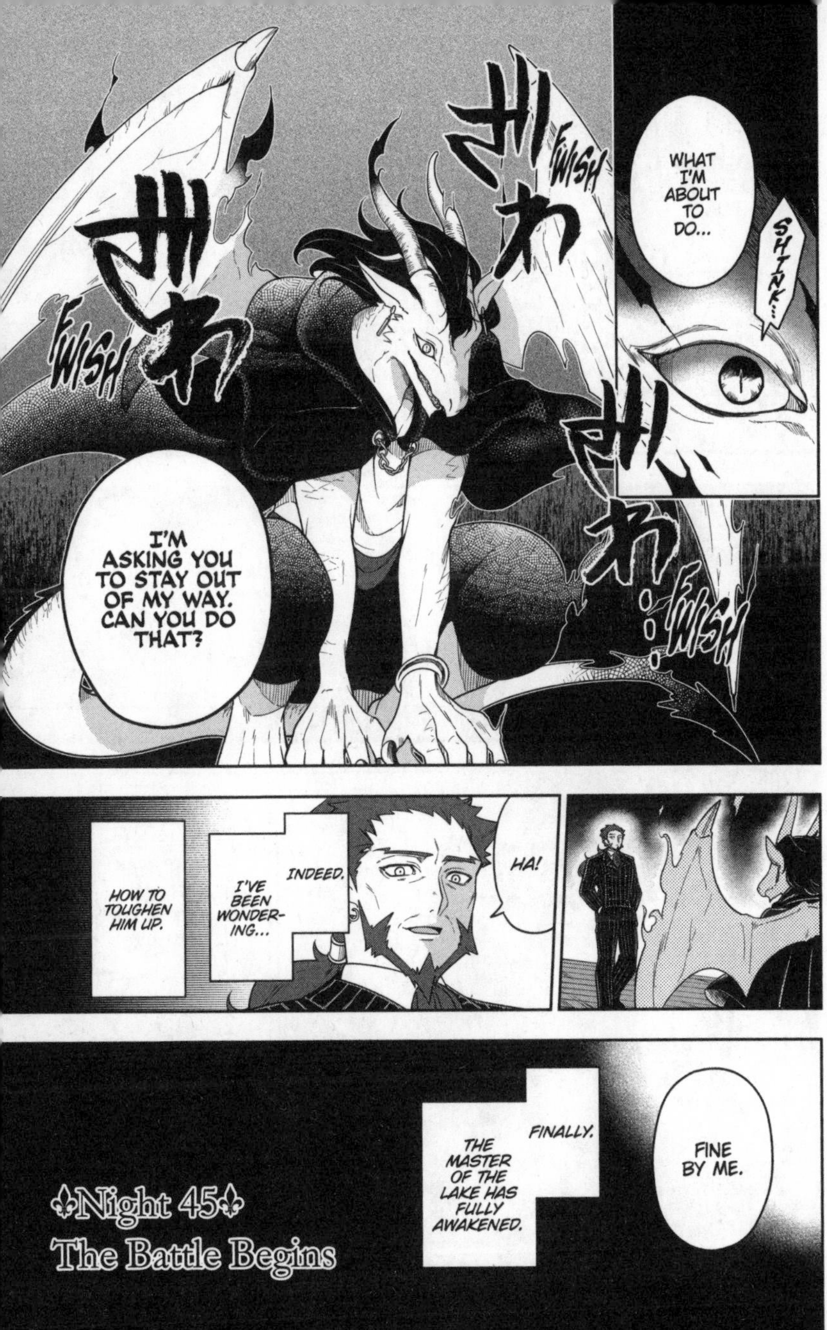
WHAT I'M ABOUT TO DO...
SHINK...
FWISH
FWISH
FWISH
FWISH
I'M ASKING YOU TO STAY OUT OF MY WAY. CAN YOU DO THAT?
HA!
INDEED.
I'VE BEEN WONDER-ING...
HOW TO TOUGHEN HIM UP.
FINE BY ME.
FINALLY.
THE MASTER OF THE LAKE HAS FULLY AWAKENED.
Night 45
The Battle Begins

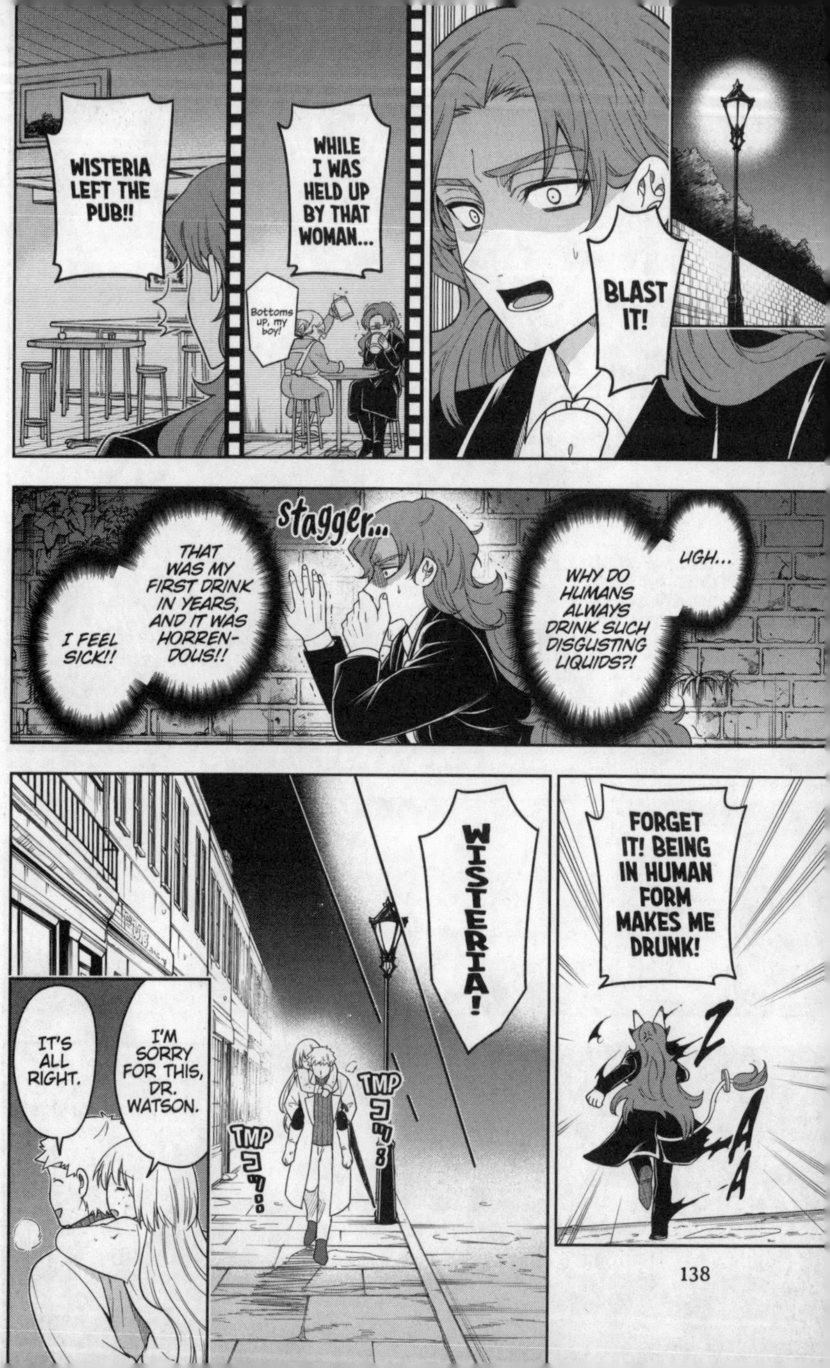
BLAST IT!
WHILE I WAS HELD UP BY THAT WOMAN...
Bottoms up, my boy!
WISTERIA LEFT THE PUB!!
UGH...
WHY DO HUMANS ALWAYS DRINK SUCH DISGUSTING LIQUIDS?!
stagger...
THAT WAS MY FIRST DRINK IN YEARS, AND IT WAS HORREN-DOUS!!
I FEEL SICK!!
FORGET IT! BEING IN HUMAN FORM MAKES ME DRUNK!
ZAA
WISTERIA!
TMP
TMP
I'M SORRY FOR THIS, DR. WATSON.
IT'S ALL RIGHT.

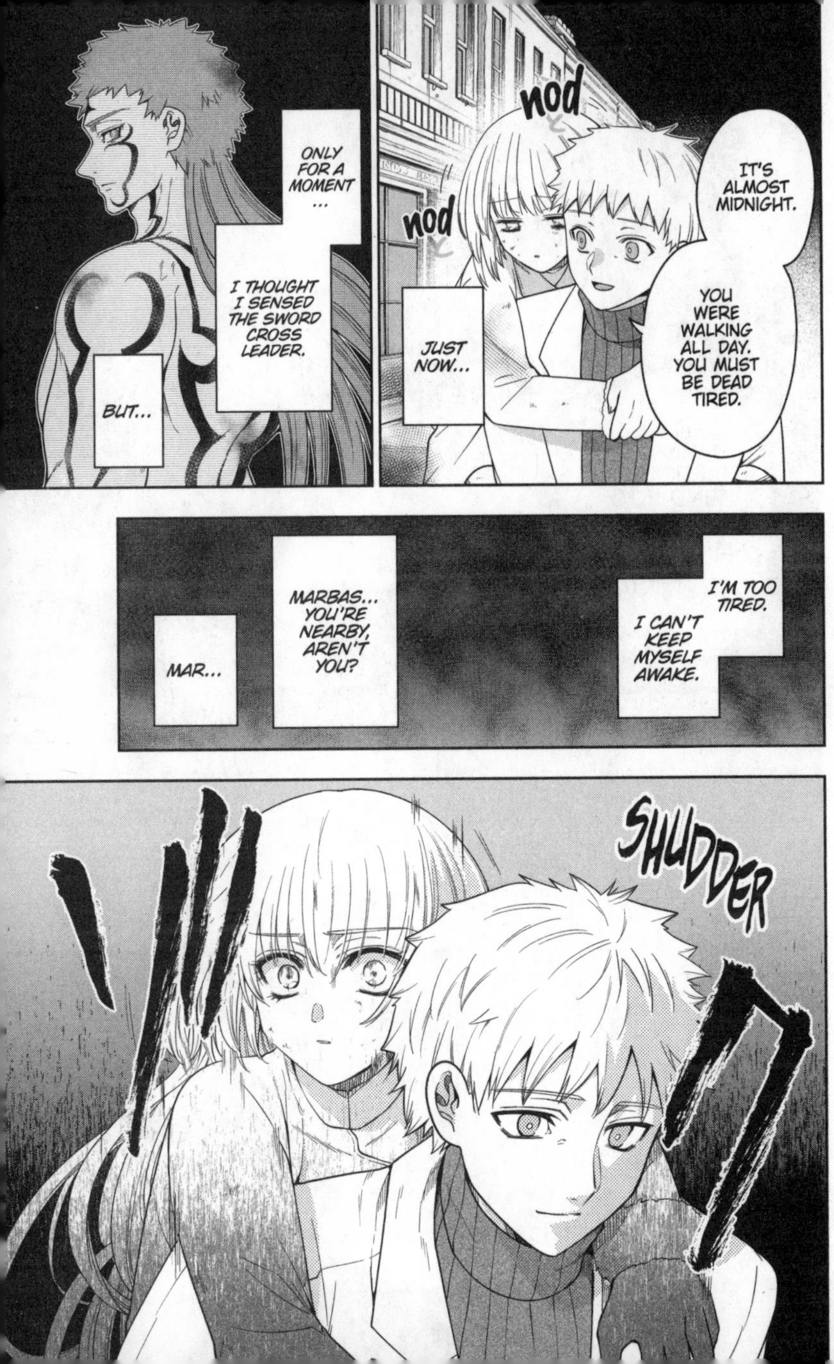

IT'S ALMOST MIDNIGHT.
YOU WERE WALKING ALL DAY. YOU MUST BE DEAD TIRED.
nod
nod
JUST NOW...
ONLY FOR A MOMENT ...
I THOUGHT I SENSED THE SWORD CROSS LEADER.
BUT...
I'M TOO TIRED.
I CAN'T KEEP MYSELF AWAKE.
MARBAS... YOU'RE NEARBY, AREN'T YOU?
MAR...
SHUDDER

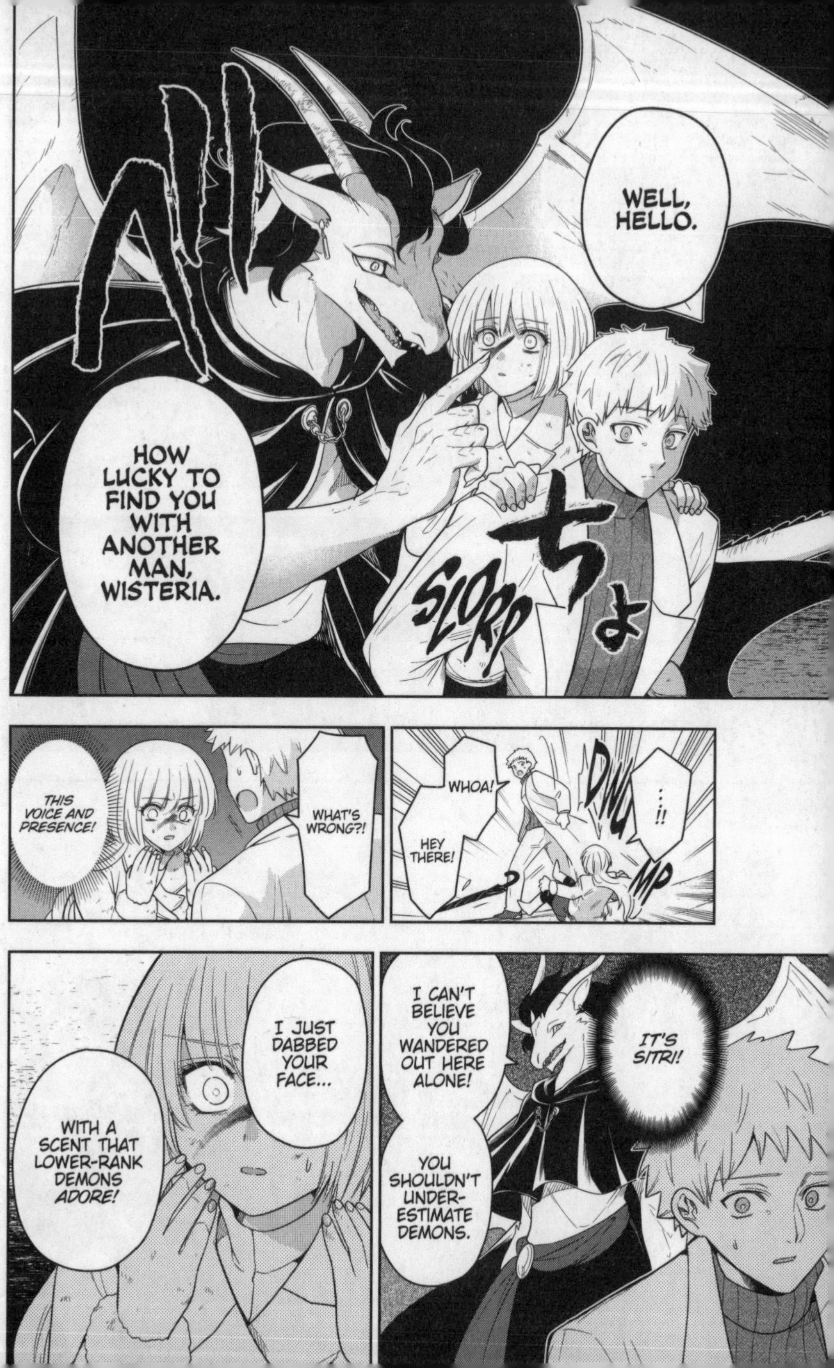
WELL, HELLO.
HOW LUCKY TO FIND YOU WITH ANOTHER MAN, WISTERIA.
ちょ
SLORP
...!!
WHOA!
HEY THERE!
DWUMP
WHAT'S WRONG?!
THIS VOICE AND PRESENCE!
IT'S SITRI!
I CAN'T BELIEVE YOU WANDERED OUT HERE ALONE!
YOU SHOULDN'T UNDER-ESTIMATE DEMONS.
I JUST DABBED YOUR FACE...
WITH A SCENT THAT LOWER-RANK DEMONS ADORE!

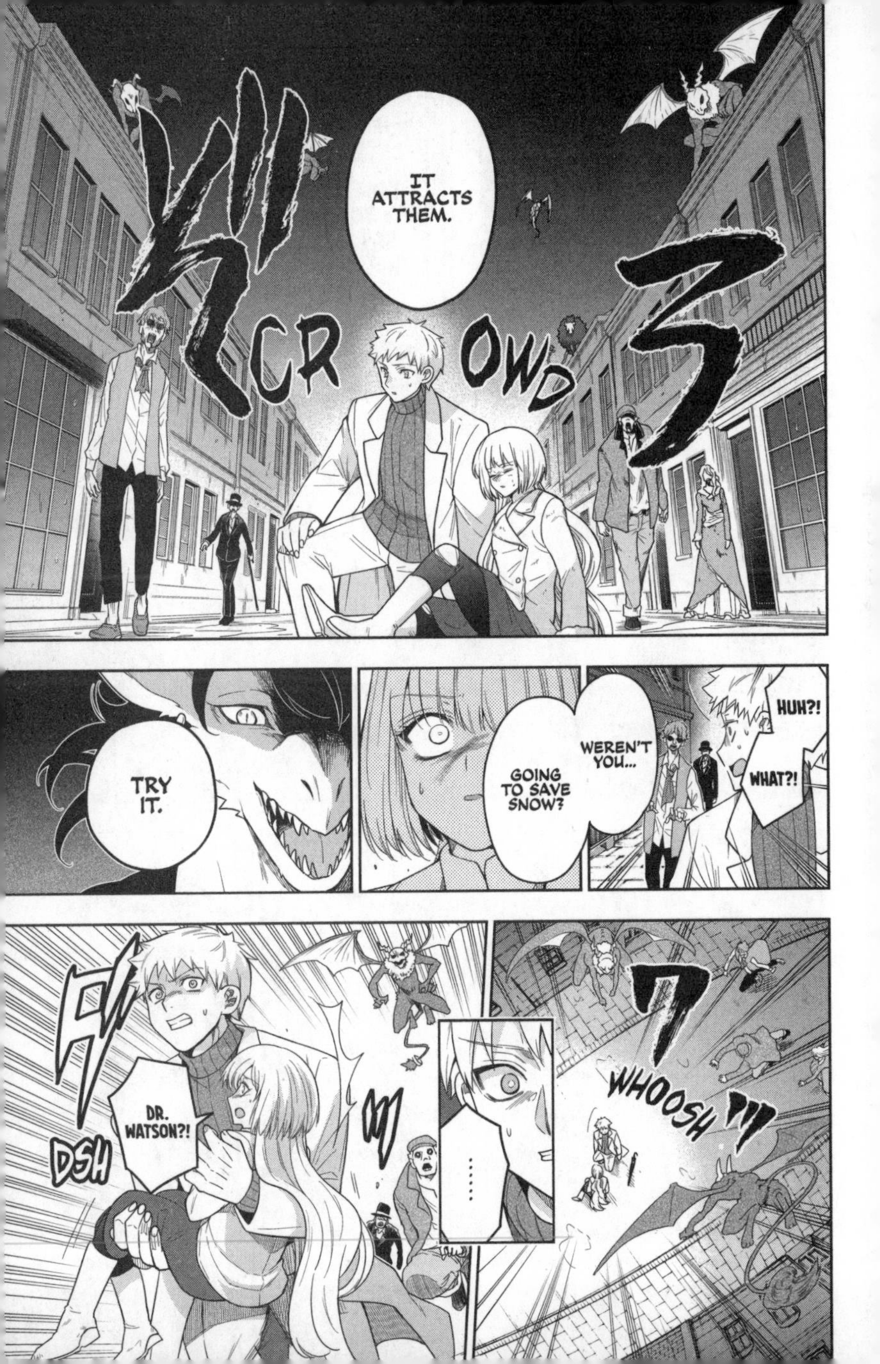
IT ATTRACTS THEM.
CROWD
HUH?!
WHAT?!
WEREN'T YOU...
GOING TO SAVE SNOW?
TRY IT.
WHOOSH
......
DR. WATSON?!
DSH

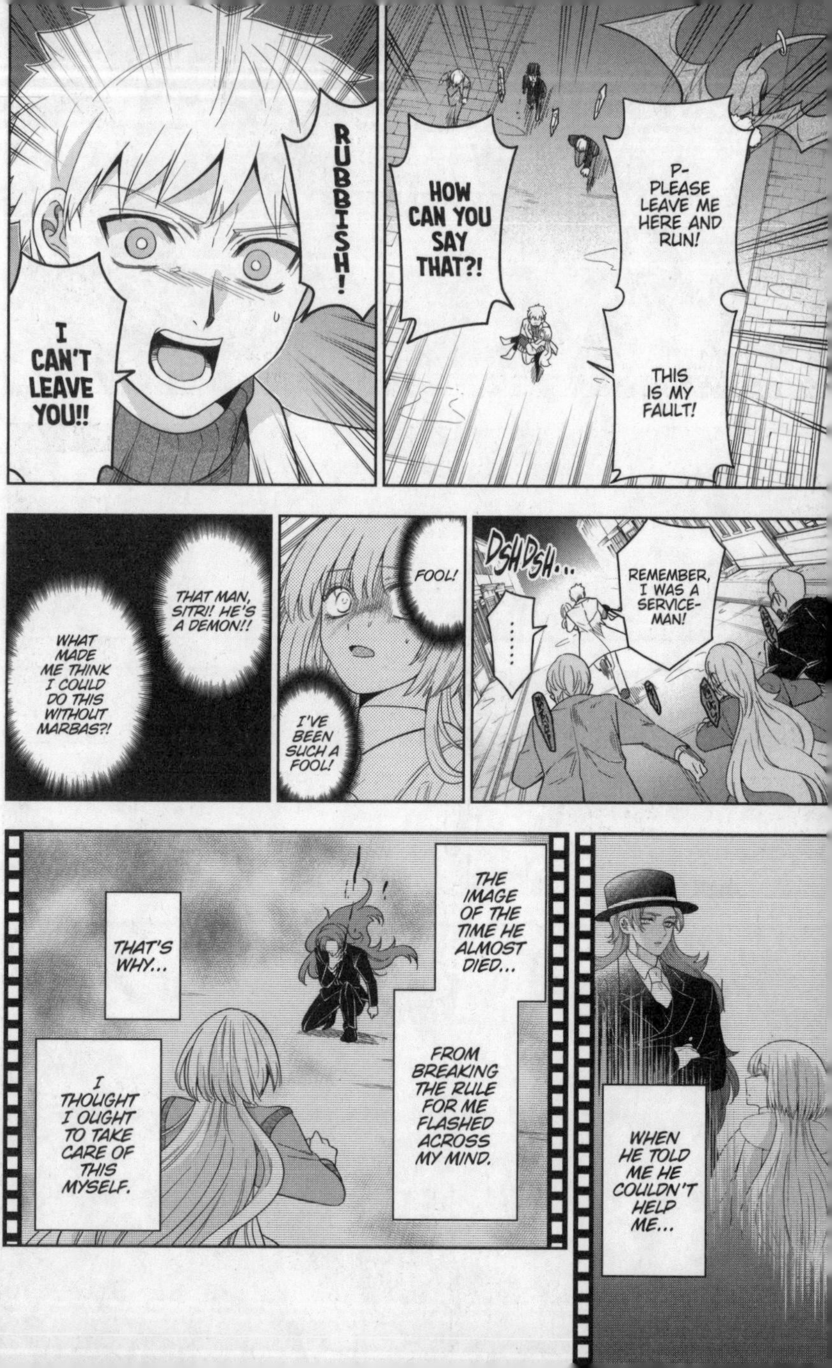
P- PLEASE LEAVE ME HERE AND RUN!
THIS IS MY FAULT!
HOW CAN YOU SAY THAT?!
RUBBISH!
I CAN'T LEAVE YOU!!
DSHDSH...
REMEMBER, I WAS A SERVICE-MAN!
......
FOOL!
I'VE BEEN SUCH A FOOL!
THAT MAN, SITRI! HE'S A DEMON!!
WHAT MADE ME THINK I COULD DO THIS WITHOUT MARBAS?!
WHEN HE TOLD ME HE COULDN'T HELP ME...
THE IMAGE OF THE TIME HE ALMOST DIED...
FROM BREAKING THE RULE FOR ME FLASHED ACROSS MY MIND.
THAT'S WHY...
I THOUGHT I OUGHT TO TAKE CARE OF THIS MYSELF.

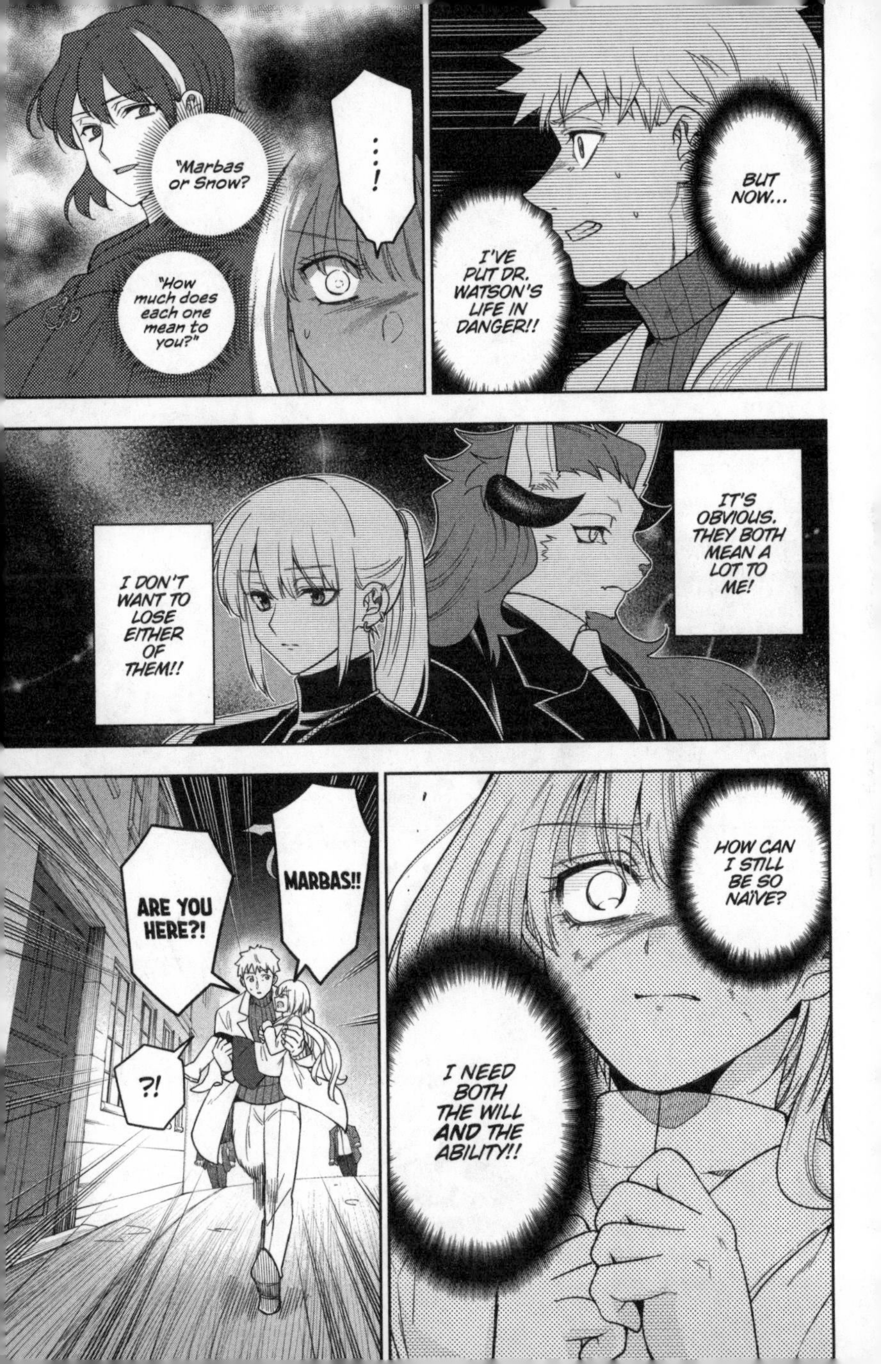
BUT NOW...
I'VE PUT DR. WATSON'S LIFE IN DANGER!!
...!
"Marbas or Snow?
"How much does each one mean to you?"
IT'S OBVIOUS. THEY BOTH MEAN A LOT TO ME!
I DON'T WANT TO LOSE EITHER OF THEM!!
HOW CAN I STILL BE SO NAÏVE?
I NEED BOTH THE WILL AND THE ABILITY!!
MARBAS!!
ARE YOU HERE?!
?!

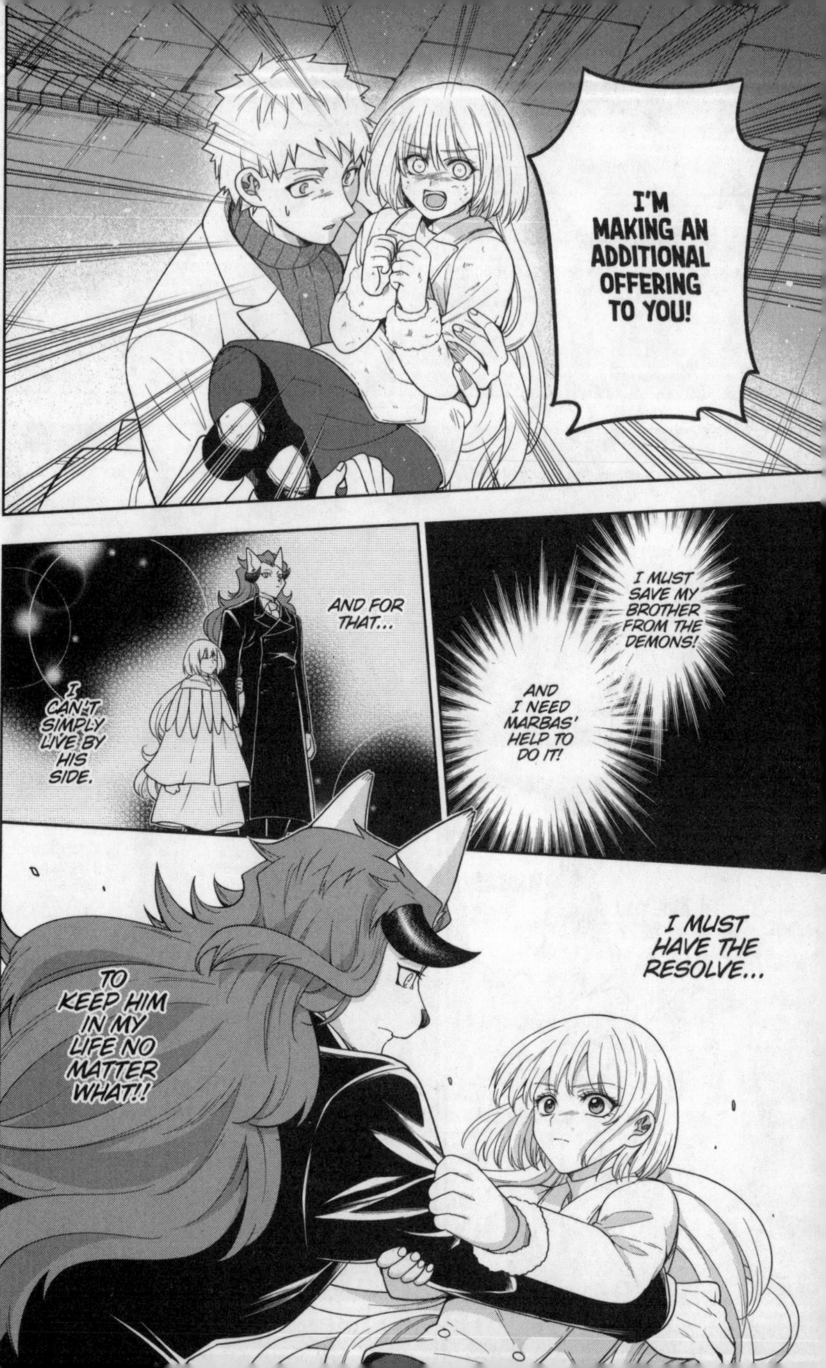
I'M MAKING AN ADDITIONAL OFFERING TO YOU!
I MUST SAVE MY BROTHER FROM THE DEMONS!
AND I NEED MARBAS' HELP TO DO IT!
AND FOR THAT...
I CAN'T SIMPLY LIVE BY HIS SIDE.
I MUST HAVE THE RESOLVE...
TO KEEP HIM IN MY LIFE NO MATTER WHAT!!

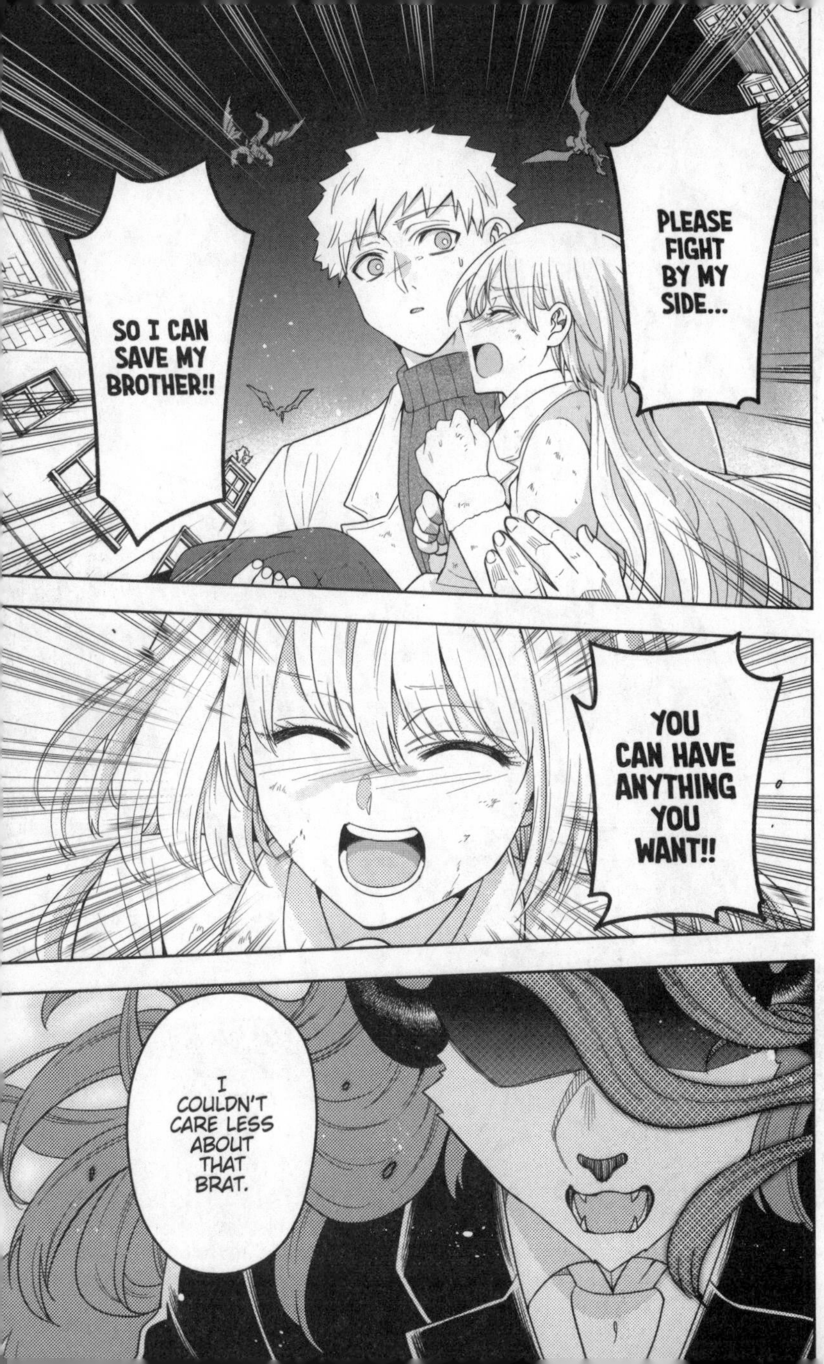
PLEASE FIGHT BY MY SIDE...
SO I CAN SAVE MY BROTHER!!
YOU CAN HAVE ANYTHING YOU WANT!!
I COULDN'T CARE LESS ABOUT THAT BRAT.

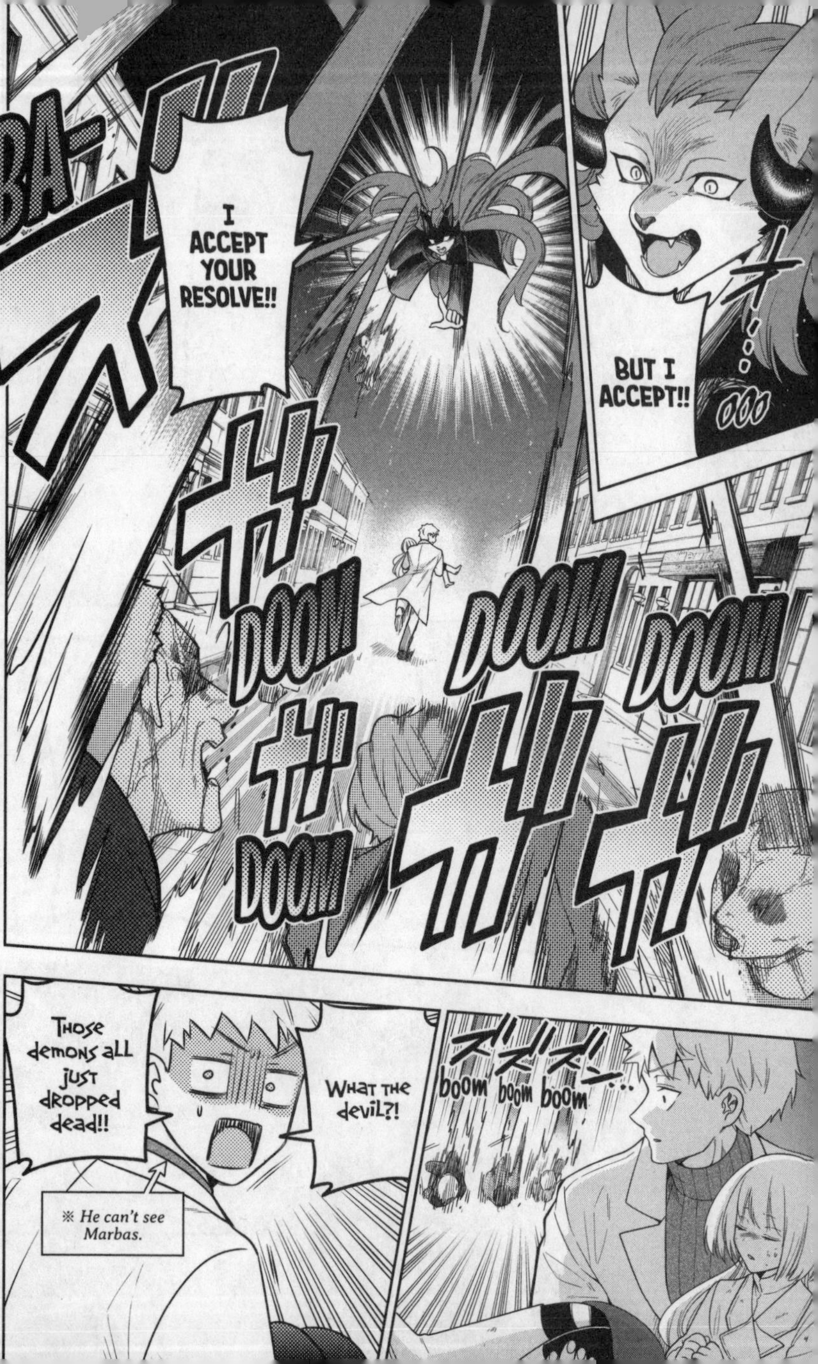
BUT I ACCEPT!!
ooo
BA-
I ACCEPT YOUR RESOLVE!!
DOOM
DOOM
DOOM
DOOM
boom boom boom
What the devil?!
Those demons all just dropped dead!!
※ He can't see Marbas.

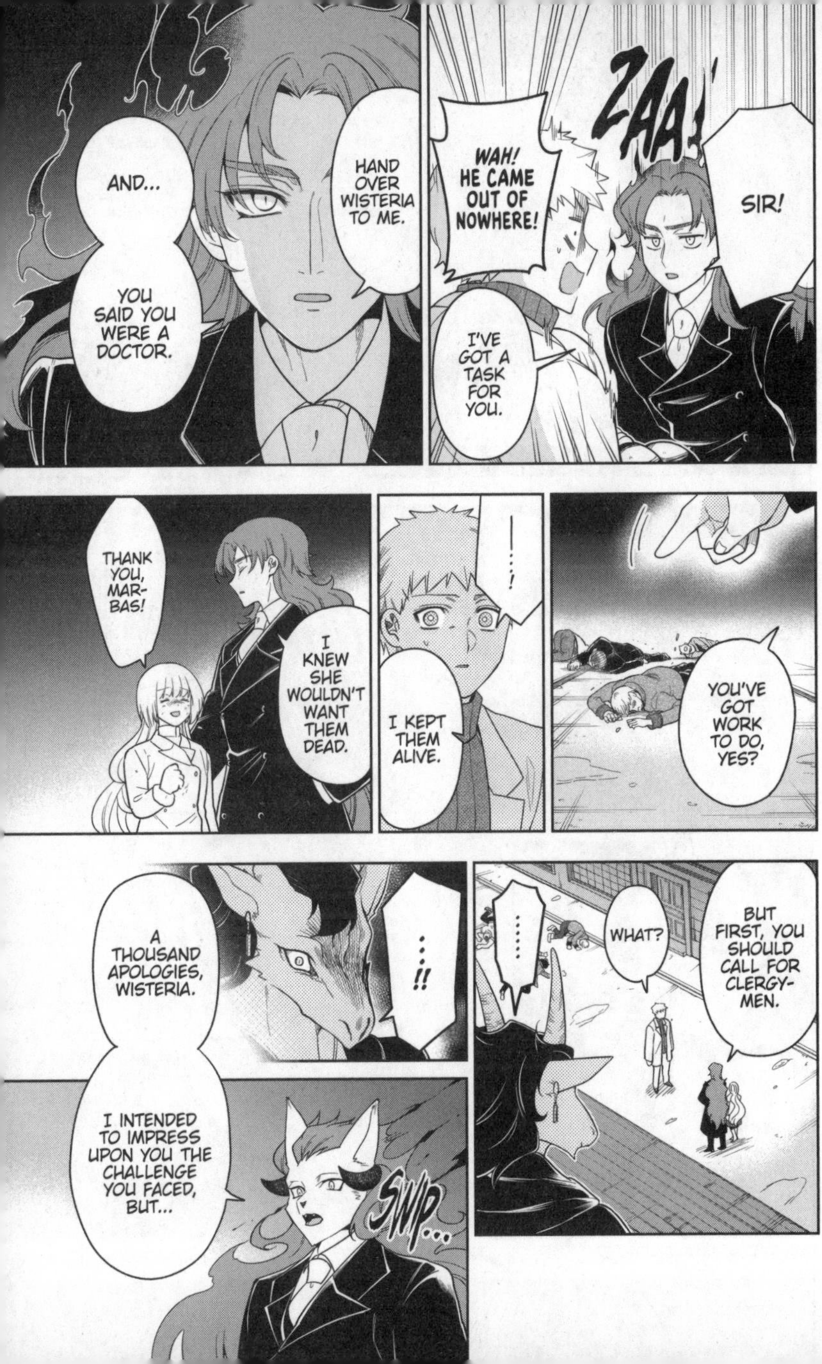
ZAA!
SIR!
WAH! HE CAME OUT OF NOWHERE!
I'VE GOT A TASK FOR YOU.
HAND OVER WISTERIA TO ME.
AND...
YOU SAID YOU WERE A DOCTOR.
YOU'VE GOT WORK TO DO, YES?
...!
I KEPT THEM ALIVE.
I KNEW SHE WOULDN'T WANT THEM DEAD.
THANK YOU, MAR-BAS!
BUT FIRST, YOU SHOULD CALL FOR CLERGY-MEN.
WHAT?
......
...!!
A THOUSAND APOLOGIES, WISTERIA.
I INTENDED TO IMPRESS UPON YOU THE CHALLENGE YOU FACED, BUT...
SWIP...

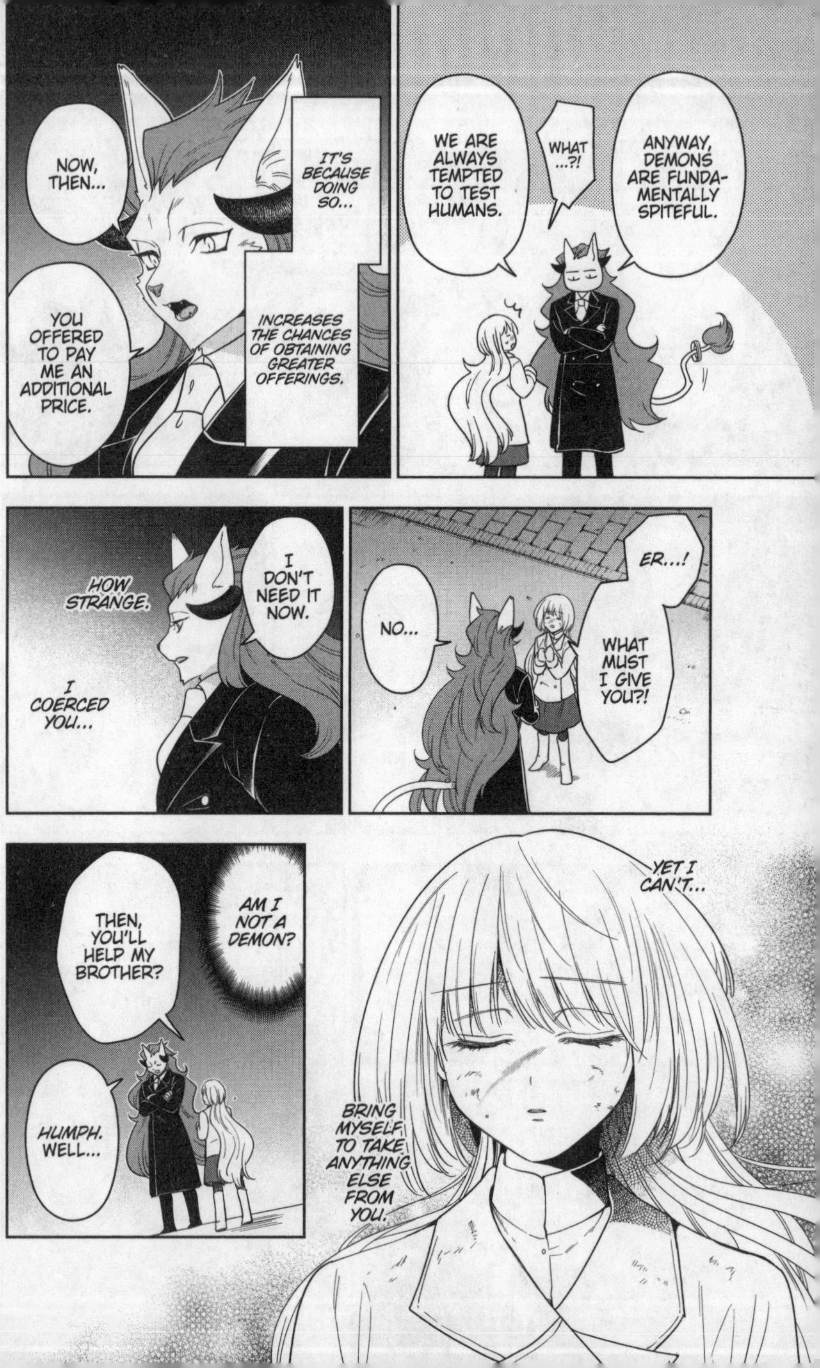
ANYWAY, DEMONS ARE FUNDA-MENTALLY SPITEFUL.
WHAT ...?!
WE ARE ALWAYS TEMPTED TO TEST HUMANS.
IT'S BECAUSE DOING SO...
INCREASES THE CHANCES OF OBTAINING GREATER OFFERINGS.
NOW, THEN...
YOU OFFERED TO PAY ME AN ADDITIONAL PRICE.
ER...!
WHAT MUST I GIVE YOU?!
NO...
I DON'T NEED IT NOW.
HOW STRANGE.
I COERCED YOU...
YET I CAN'T...
BRING MYSELF TO TAKE ANYTHING ELSE FROM YOU.
AM I NOT A DEMON?
THEN, YOU'LL HELP MY BROTHER?
HUMPH. WELL...

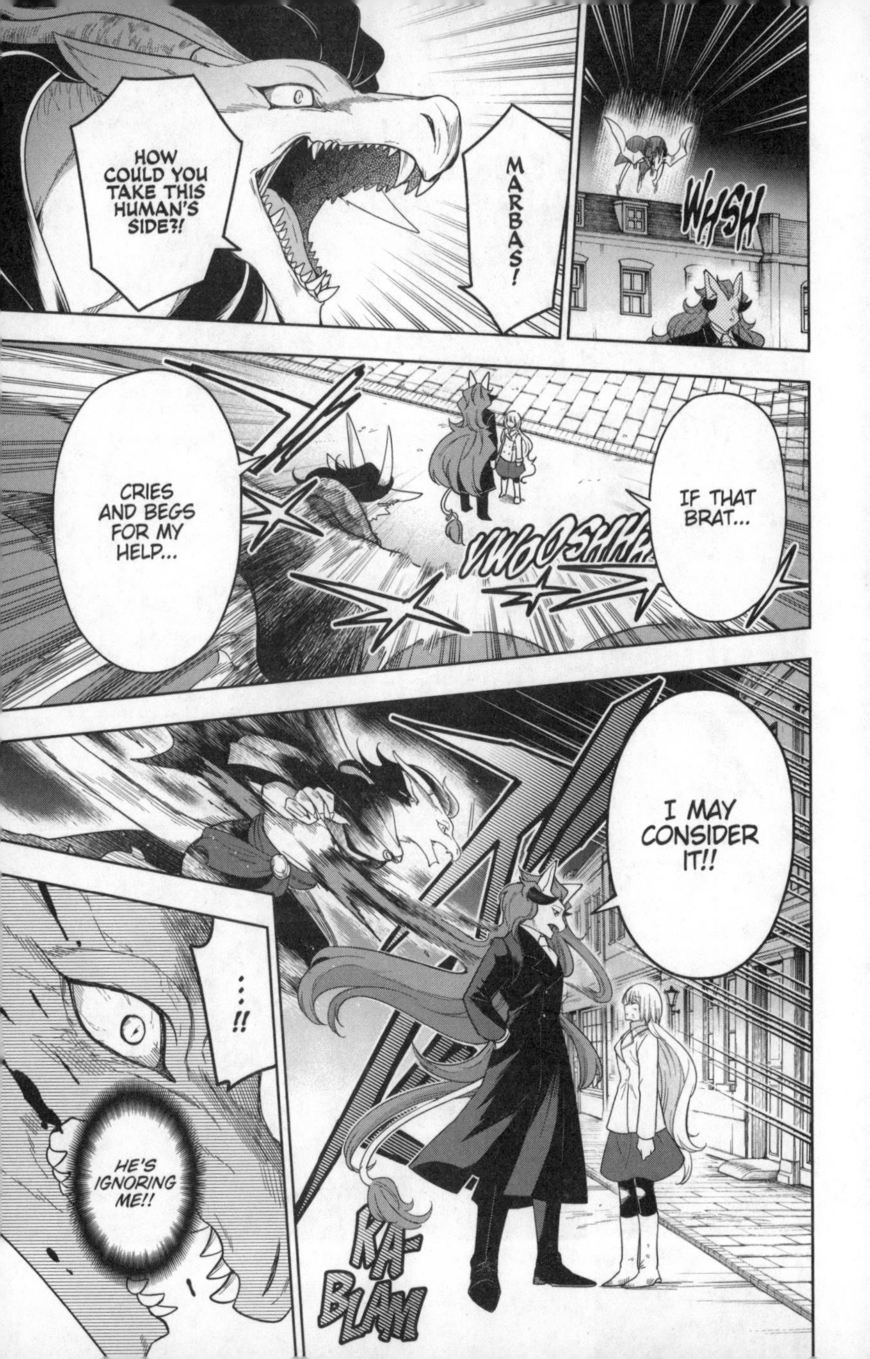
WHSH
MARBAS!
HOW COULD YOU TAKE THIS HUMAN'S SIDE?!
IF THAT BRAT...
VWOOSHHH
CRIES AND BEGS FOR MY HELP...
I MAY CONSIDER IT!!
KA-BLAM
...!!
HE'S IGNORING ME!!

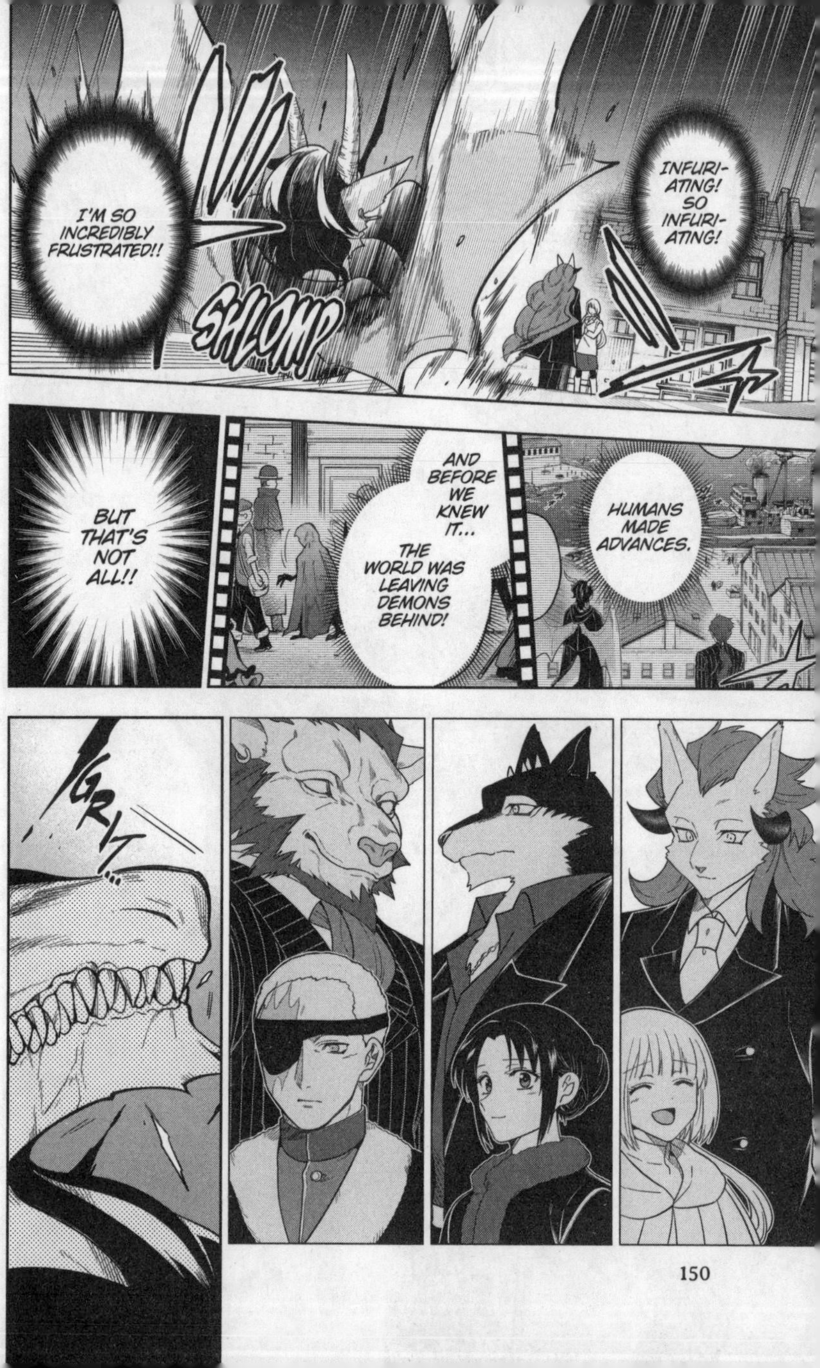
INFURIATING! SO INFURIATING!
I'M SO INCREDIBLY FRUSTRATED!!
SHLOMP
HUMANS MADE ADVANCES.
AND BEFORE WE KNEW IT...
THE WORLD WAS LEAVING DEMONS BEHIND!
BUT THAT'S NOT ALL!!
GRIT...

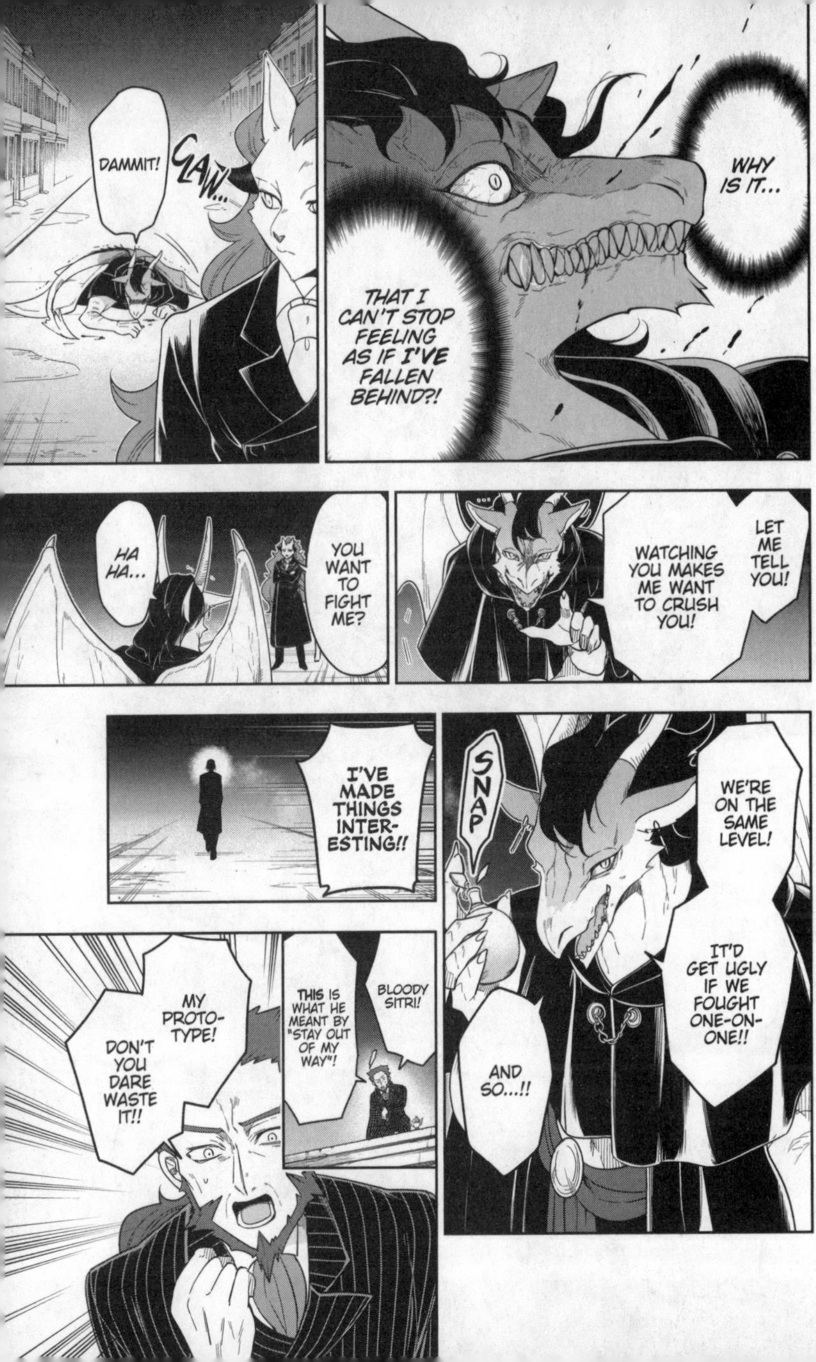
WHY IS IT...
THAT I CAN'T STOP FEELING AS IF I'VE FALLEN BEHIND?!
CLAW...
DAMMIT!
LET ME TELL YOU!
WATCHING YOU MAKES ME WANT TO CRUSH YOU!
YOU WANT TO FIGHT ME?
HA HA...
WE'RE ON THE SAME LEVEL!
SNAP
IT'D GET UGLY IF WE FOUGHT ONE-ON-ONE!!
AND SO...!!
I'VE MADE THINGS INTER-ESTING!!
BLOODY SITRI!
THIS IS WHAT HE MEANT BY "STAY OUT OF MY WAY"!
MY PROTO-TYPE!
DON'T YOU DARE WASTE IT!!

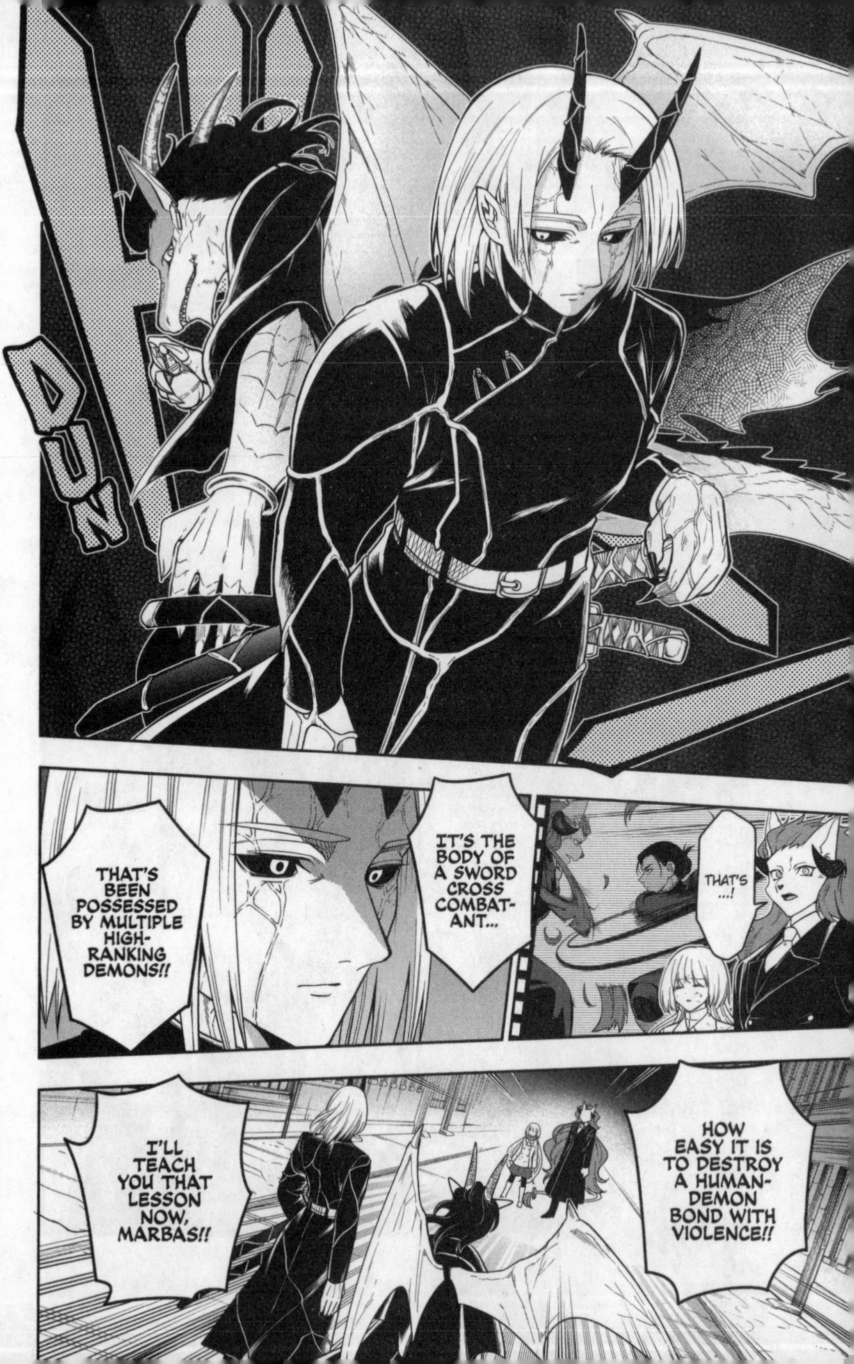
DUN
THAT'S ...!
IT'S THE BODY OF A SWORD CROSS COMBATANT...
THAT'S BEEN POSSESSED BY MULTIPLE HIGH-RANKING DEMONS!!
HOW EASY IT IS TO DESTROY A HUMAN-DEMON BOND WITH VIOLENCE!!
I'LL TEACH YOU THAT LESSON NOW, MARBAS!!

⚜Night 46⚜ Possessed

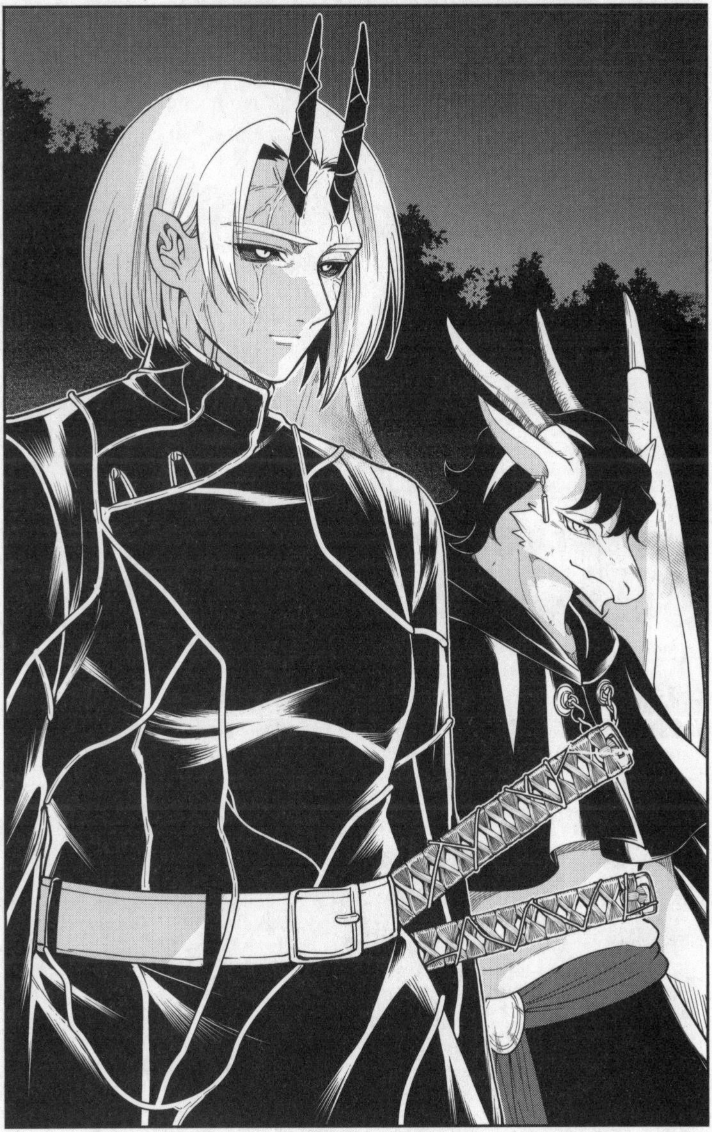

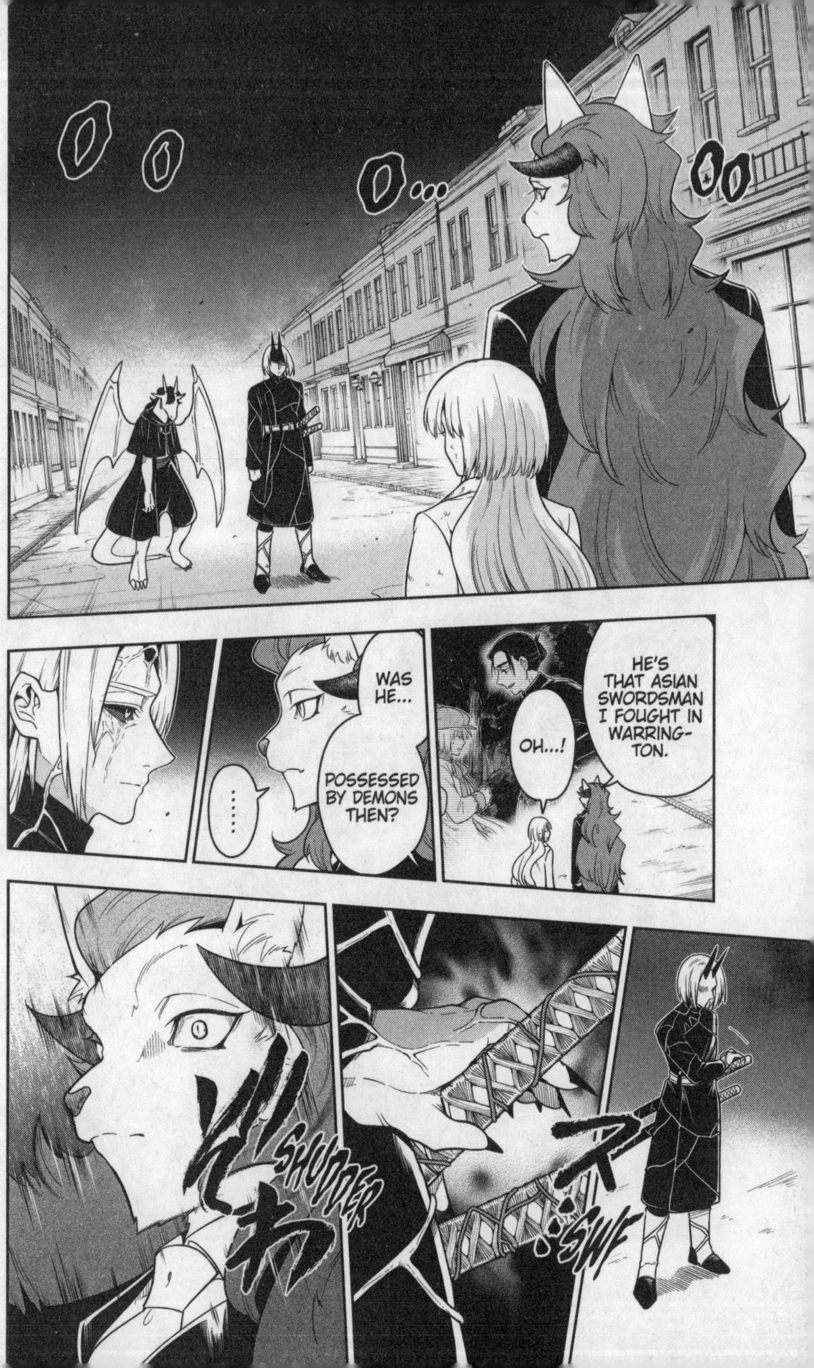
OO
O...
O
O
HE'S THAT ASIAN SWORDSMAN I FOUGHT IN WARRING-TON.
OH...!
WAS HE...
POSSESSED BY DEMONS THEN?
......
SWF
SHUDDER

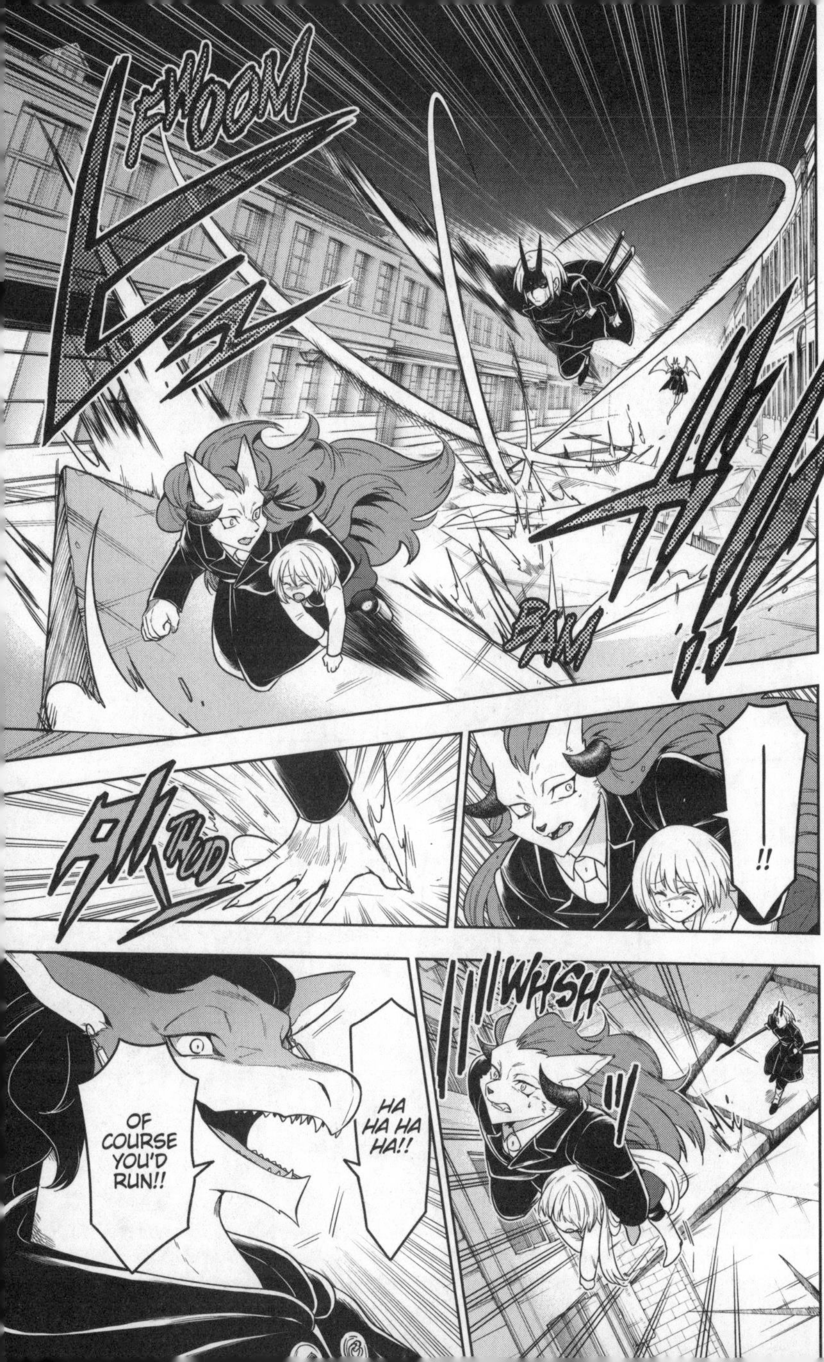
FWOOM
BAM
!!
—
!!
THUD
WHSH
!!
HA HA HA HA!!
OF COURSE YOU'D RUN!!

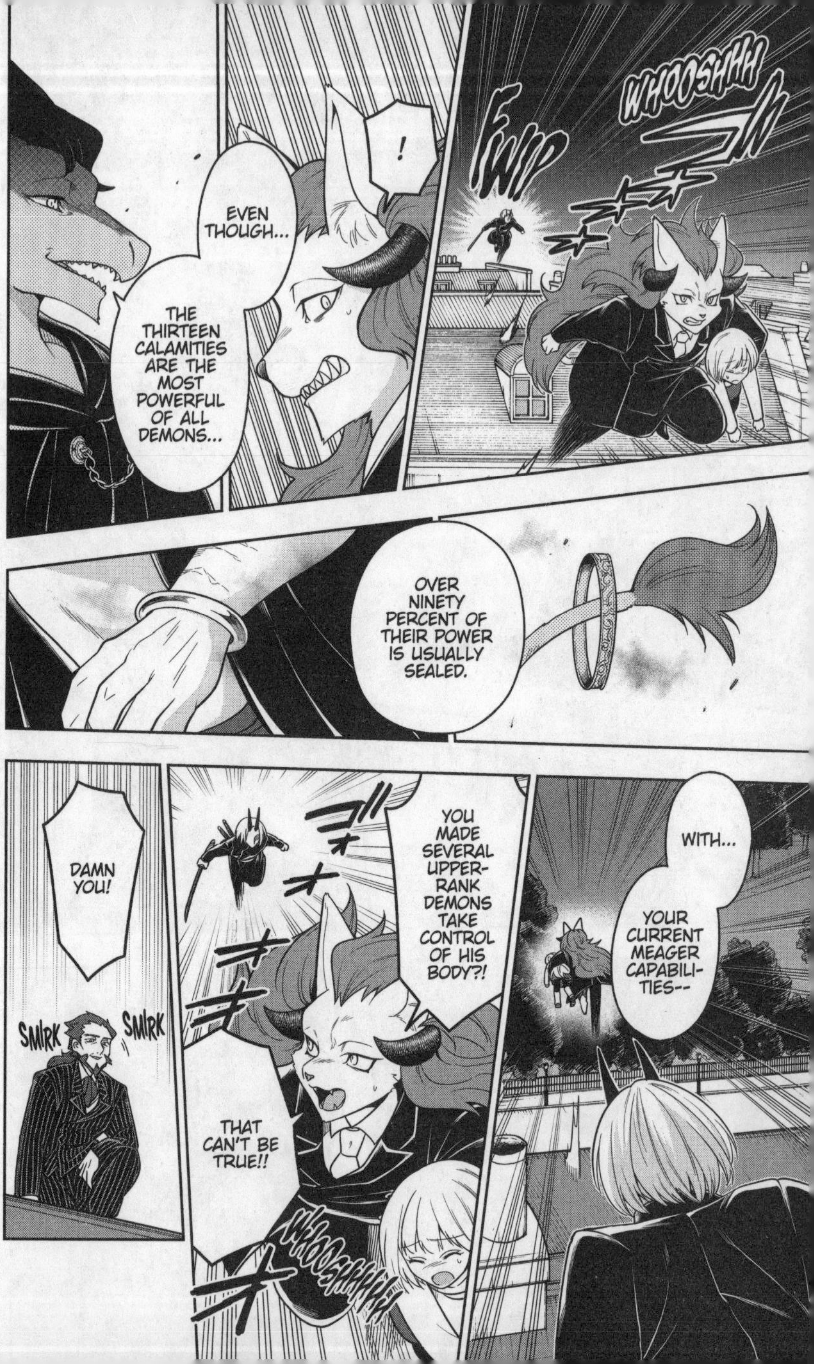
WHOOSHHH
FWIP
!
EVEN THOUGH...
THE THIRTEEN CALAMITIES ARE THE MOST POWERFUL OF ALL DEMONS...
OVER NINETY PERCENT OF THEIR POWER IS USUALLY SEALED.
WITH...
YOUR CURRENT MEAGER CAPABILI-TIES--
YOU MADE SEVERAL UPPER-RANK DEMONS TAKE CONTROL OF HIS BODY?!
THAT CAN'T BE TRUE!!
WHOOSHHHH
DAMN YOU!
SMIRK
SMIRK

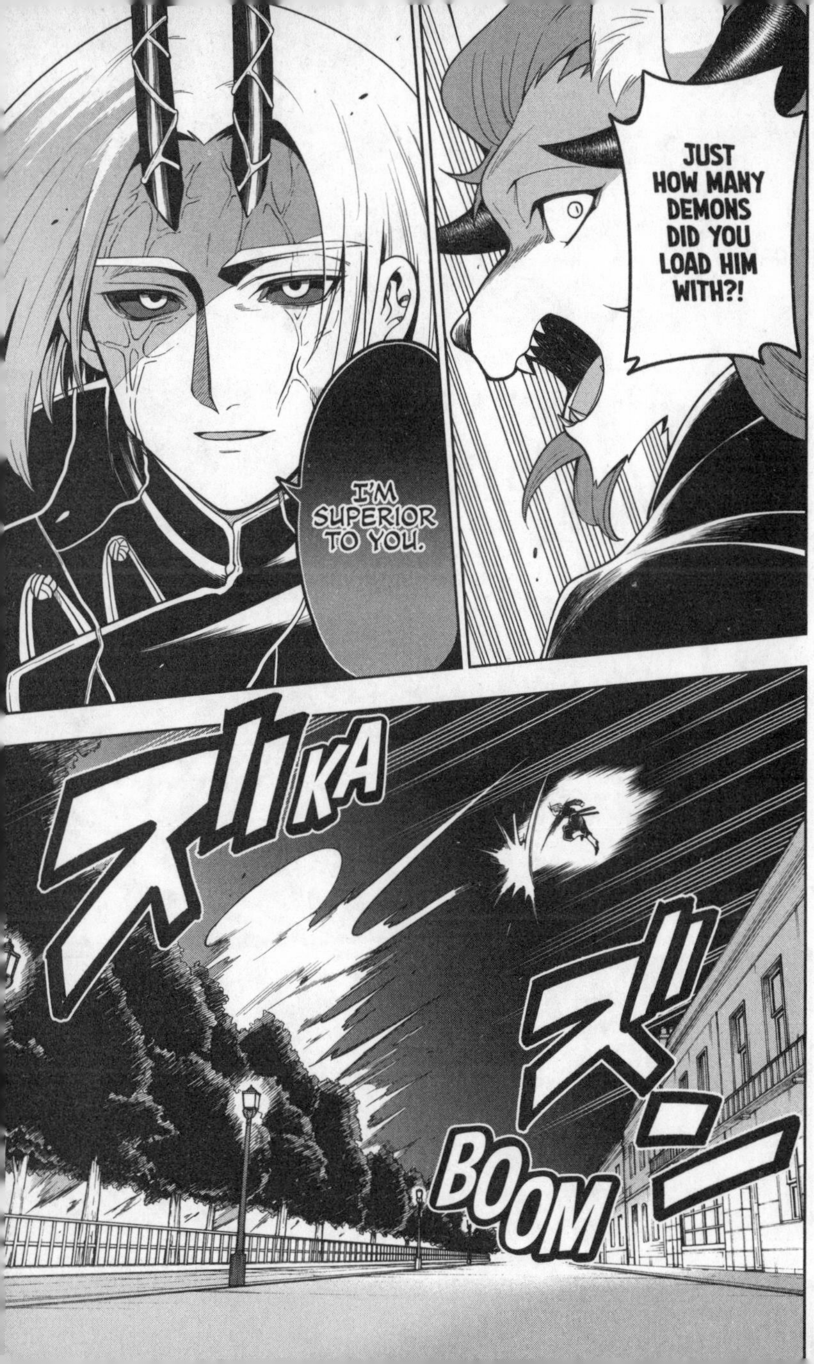
JUST HOW MANY DEMONS DID YOU LOAD HIM WITH?!
I'M SUPERIOR TO YOU.
KA
BOOM

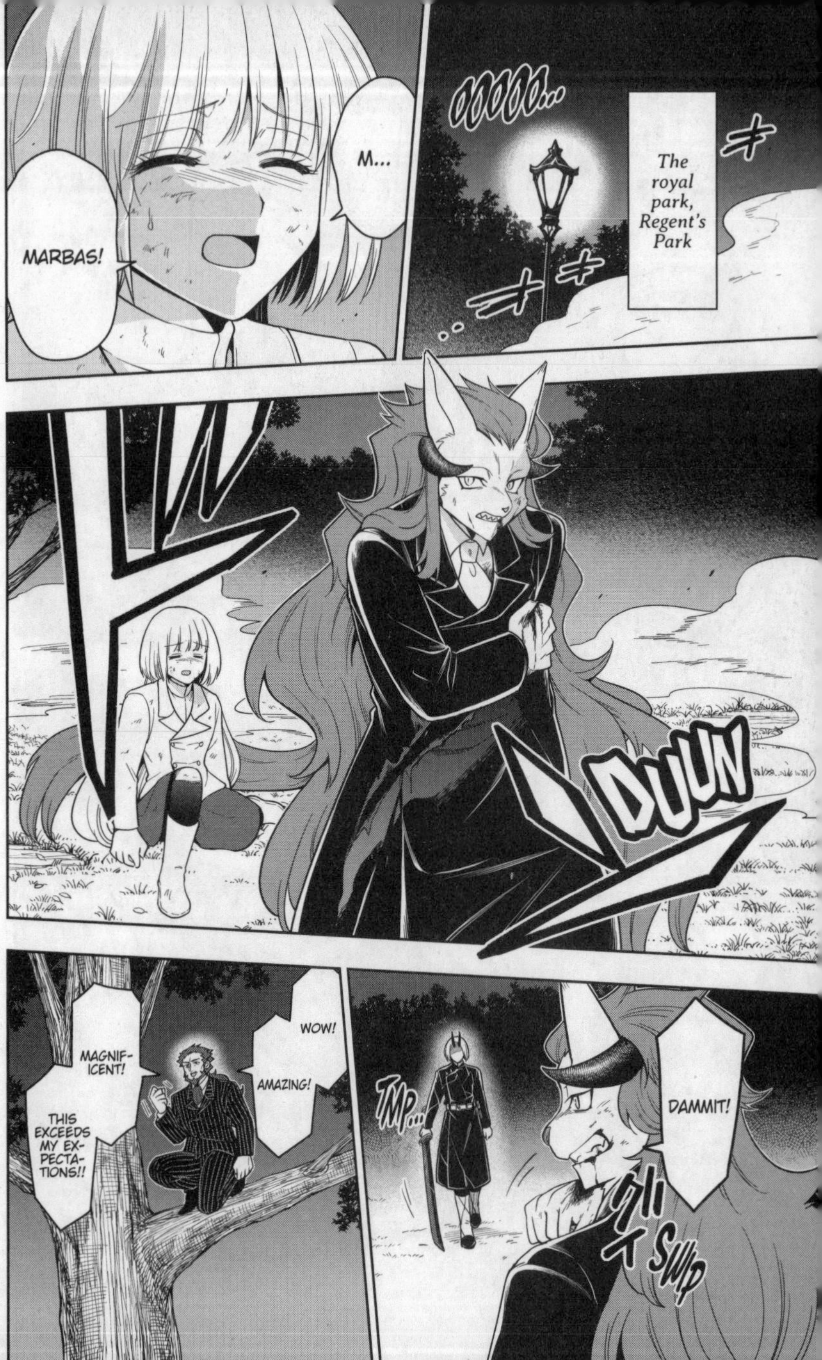
OOOOO...
The royal park, Regent's Park
M...
MARBAS!
DUUN
DAMMIT!
TMP...
グイ
SWIP
WOW!
AMAZING!
MAGNIFICENT!
THIS EXCEEDS MY EXPECTATIONS!!

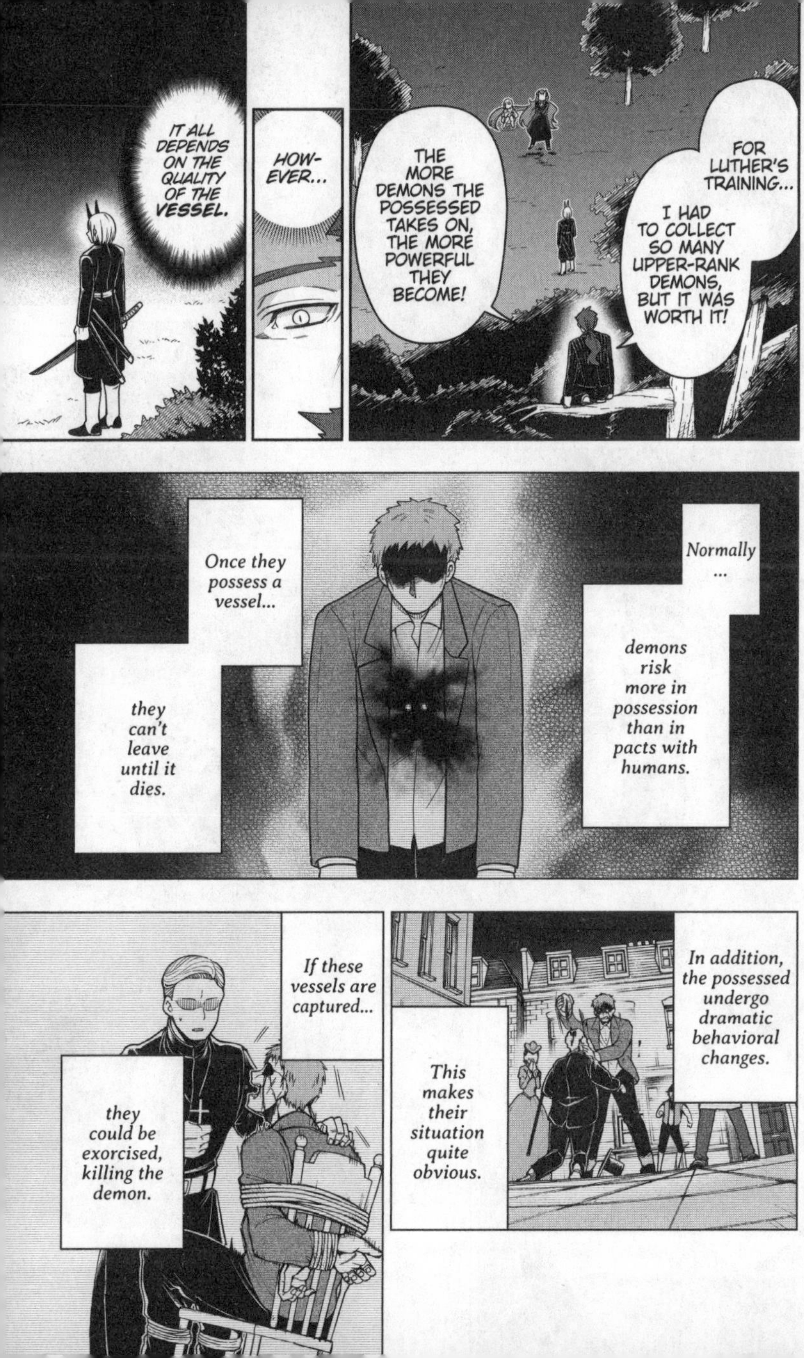
FOR LUTHER'S TRAINING...
I HAD TO COLLECT SO MANY UPPER-RANK DEMONS, BUT IT WAS WORTH IT!
THE MORE DEMONS THE POSSESSED TAKES ON, THE MORE POWERFUL THEY BECOME!
HOW-EVER...
IT ALL DEPENDS ON THE QUALITY OF THE VESSEL.
Normally...
demons risk more in possession than in pacts with humans.
Once they possess a vessel...
they can't leave until it dies.
In addition, the possessed undergo dramatic behavioral changes.
This makes their situation quite obvious.
If these vessels are captured...
they could be exorcised, killing the demon.

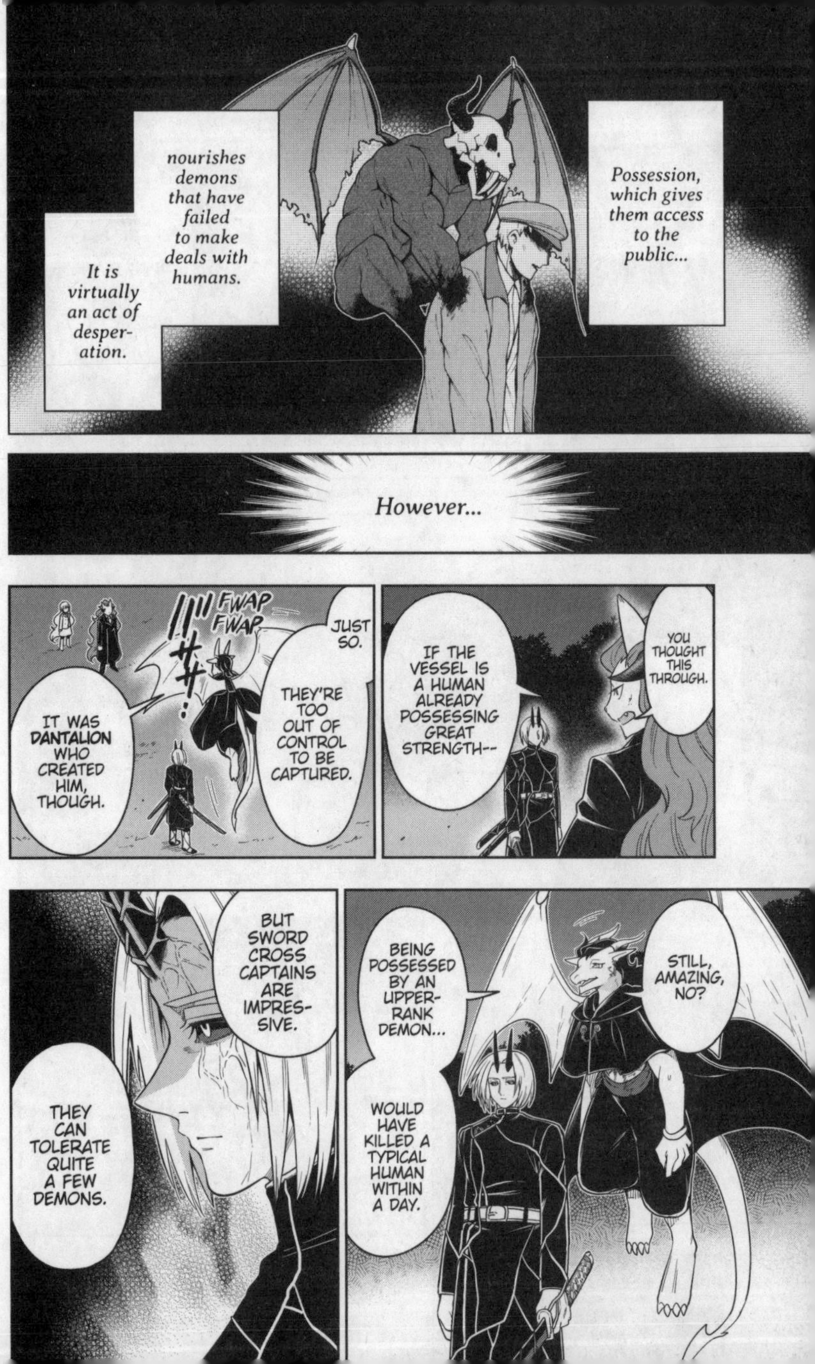
Possession, which gives them access to the public...
nourishes demons that have failed to make deals with humans.
It is virtually an act of desperation.
However...
YOU THOUGHT THIS THROUGH.
IF THE VESSEL IS A HUMAN ALREADY POSSESSING GREAT STRENGTH--
JUST SO.
THEY'RE TOO OUT OF CONTROL TO BE CAPTURED.
FWAP FWAP
IT WAS DANTALION WHO CREATED HIM, THOUGH.
STILL, AMAZING, NO?
BEING POSSESSED BY AN UPPER-RANK DEMON...
WOULD HAVE KILLED A TYPICAL HUMAN WITHIN A DAY.
BUT SWORD CROSS CAPTAINS ARE IMPRESSIVE.
THEY CAN TOLERATE QUITE A FEW DEMONS.

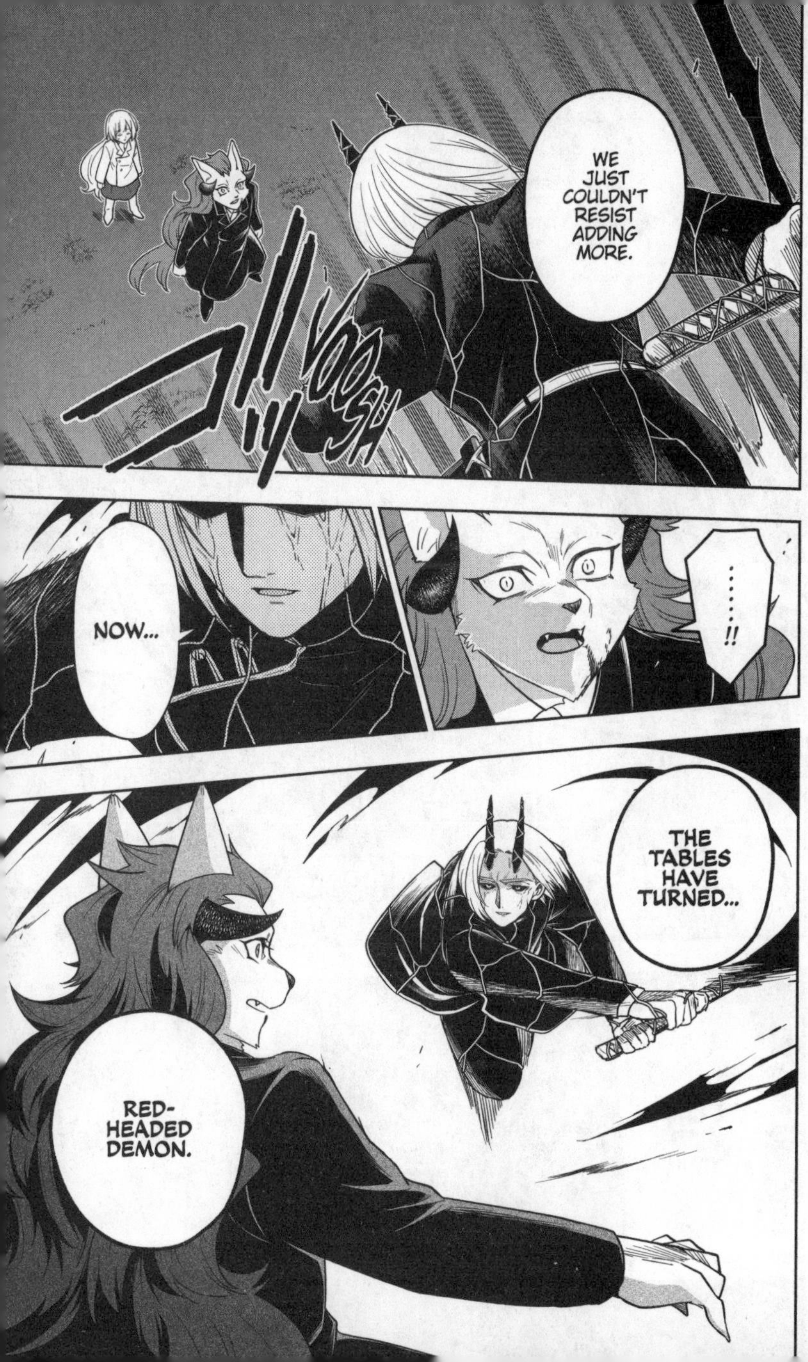
WE JUST COULDN'T RESIST ADDING MORE.
VOOSH
......!!
NOW...
THE TABLES HAVE TURNED...
RED-HEADED DEMON.

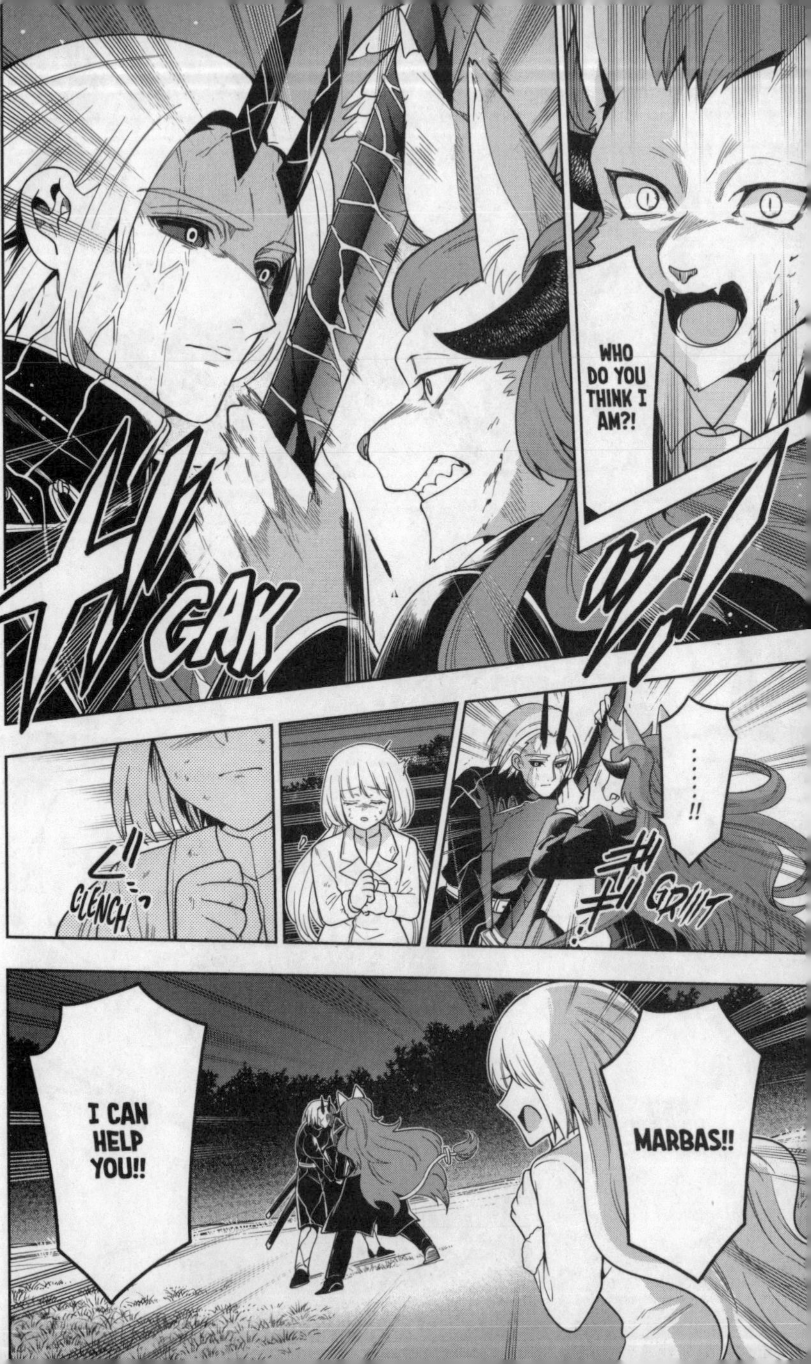
WHO DO YOU THINK I AM?!
GAK
......!!
GRIIT
CLENCH
MARBAS!!
I CAN HELP YOU!!

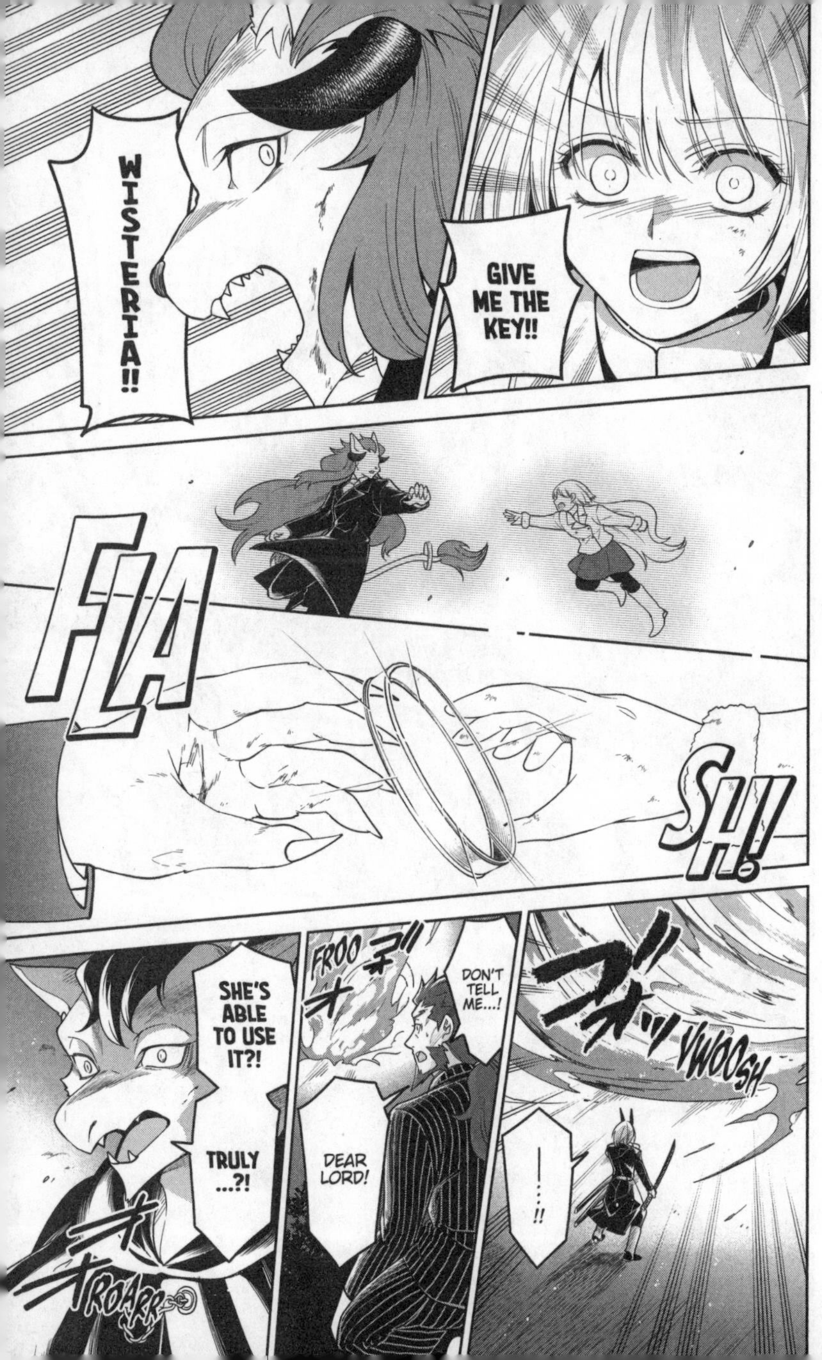
GIVE ME THE KEY!!
WISTERIA!!
FLA
SH!
VWOOSH
...!!
DON'T TELL ME...!
FROO
DEAR LORD!
SHE'S ABLE TO USE IT?!
TRULY ...?!
ROARR

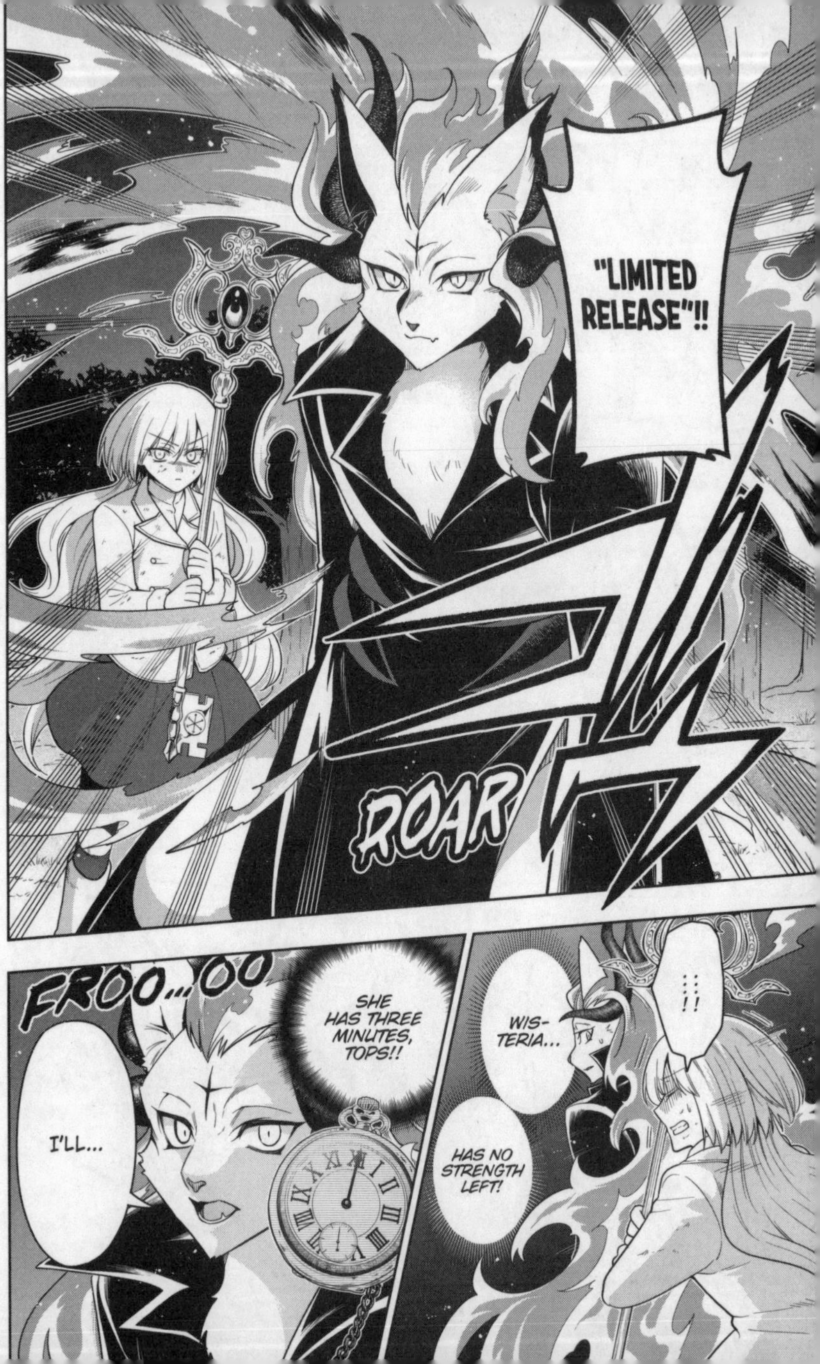
"LIMITED RELEASE"!!
ROAR
...!!
WIS-TERIA...
HAS NO STRENGTH LEFT!
SHE HAS THREE MINUTES, TOPS!!
FROO...OO
I'LL...

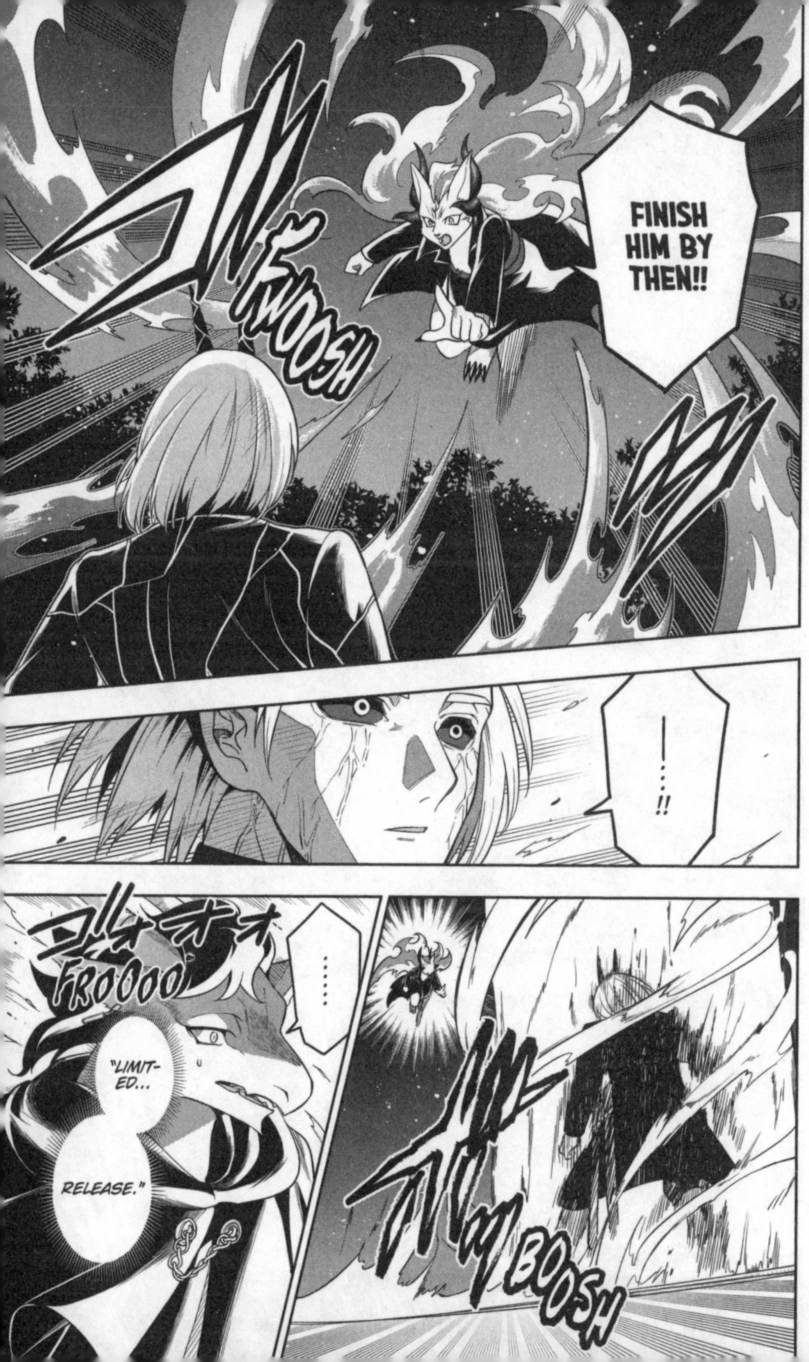
WHOOSH
FINISH HIM BY THEN!!
......!!
BOOSH
......
FROOOO
"LIMITED...
RELEASE."

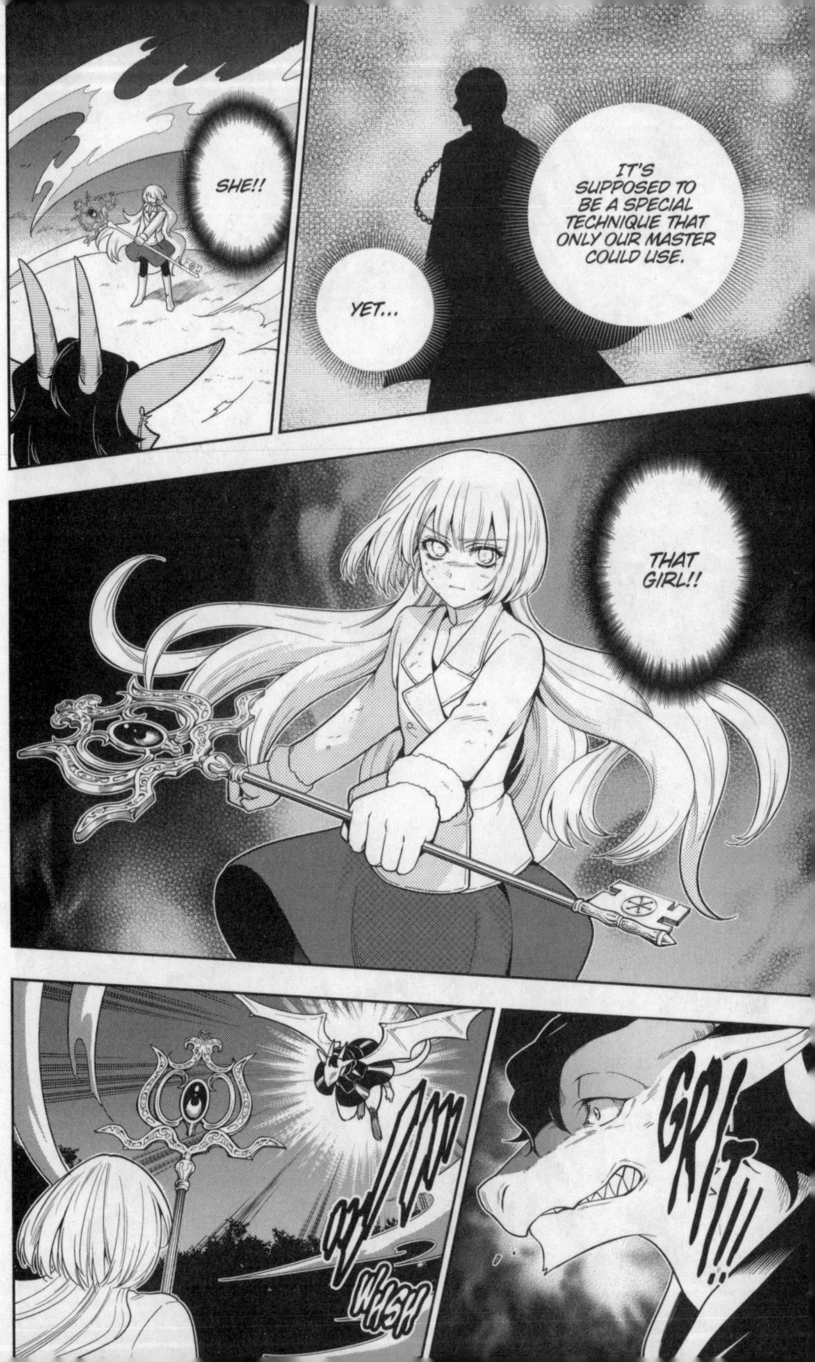
IT'S SUPPOSED TO BE A SPECIAL TECHNIQUE THAT ONLY OUR MASTER COULD USE.
YET...
SHE!!
THAT GIRL!!
WHSH

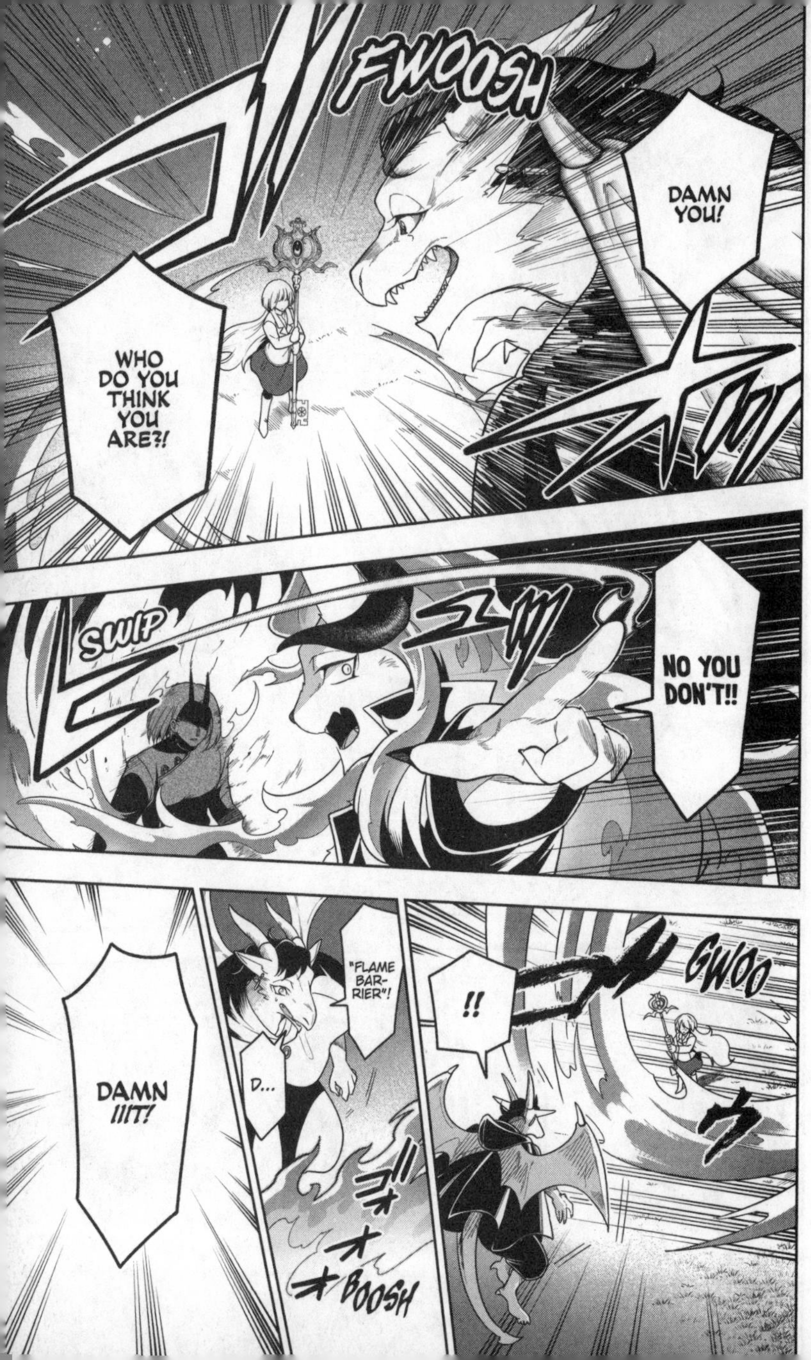
FWOOSH
DAMN YOU!
WHO DO YOU THINK YOU ARE?!
NO YOU DON'T!!
SWIP
GWOO
!!
"FLAME BAR-RIER"!
D...
BOOSH
DAMN IIIT!

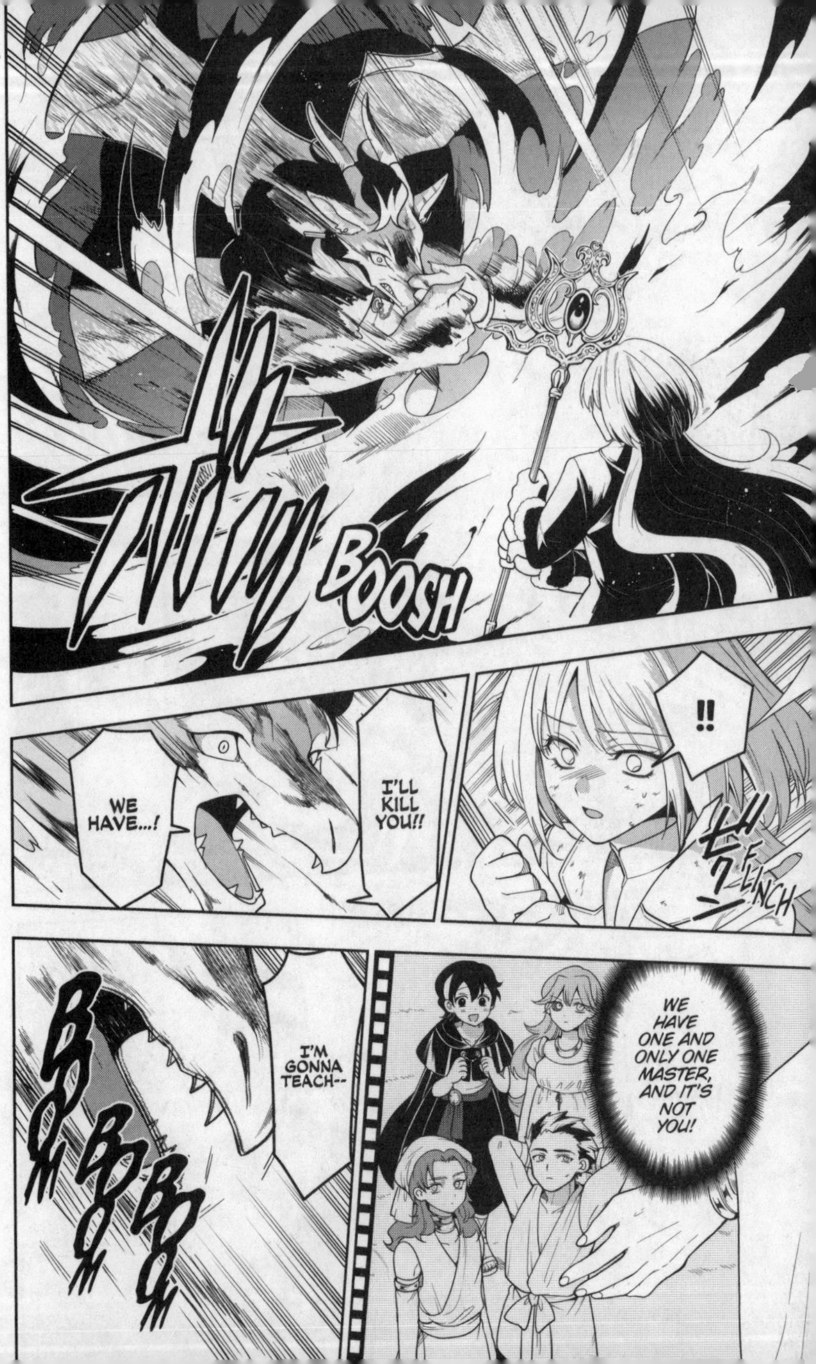
BOOSH
!!
FLINCH
I'LL KILL YOU!!
WE HAVE...!
WE HAVE ONE AND ONLY ONE MASTER, AND IT'S NOT YOU!
I'M GONNA TEACH--

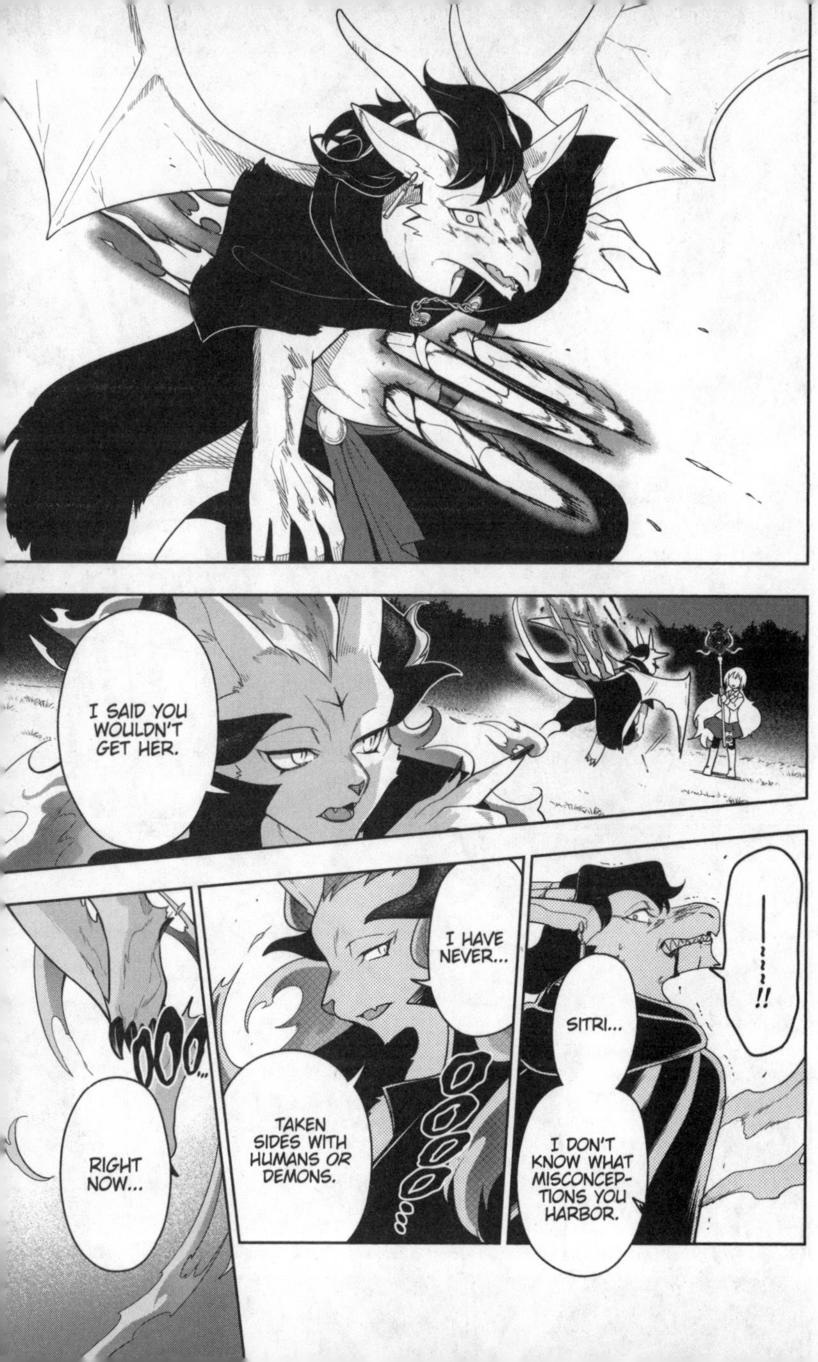
I SAID YOU WOULDN'T GET HER.
—???!!
SITRI...
I DON'T KNOW WHAT MISCONCEPTIONS YOU HARBOR.
I HAVE NEVER...
TAKEN SIDES WITH HUMANS OR DEMONS.
RIGHT NOW...

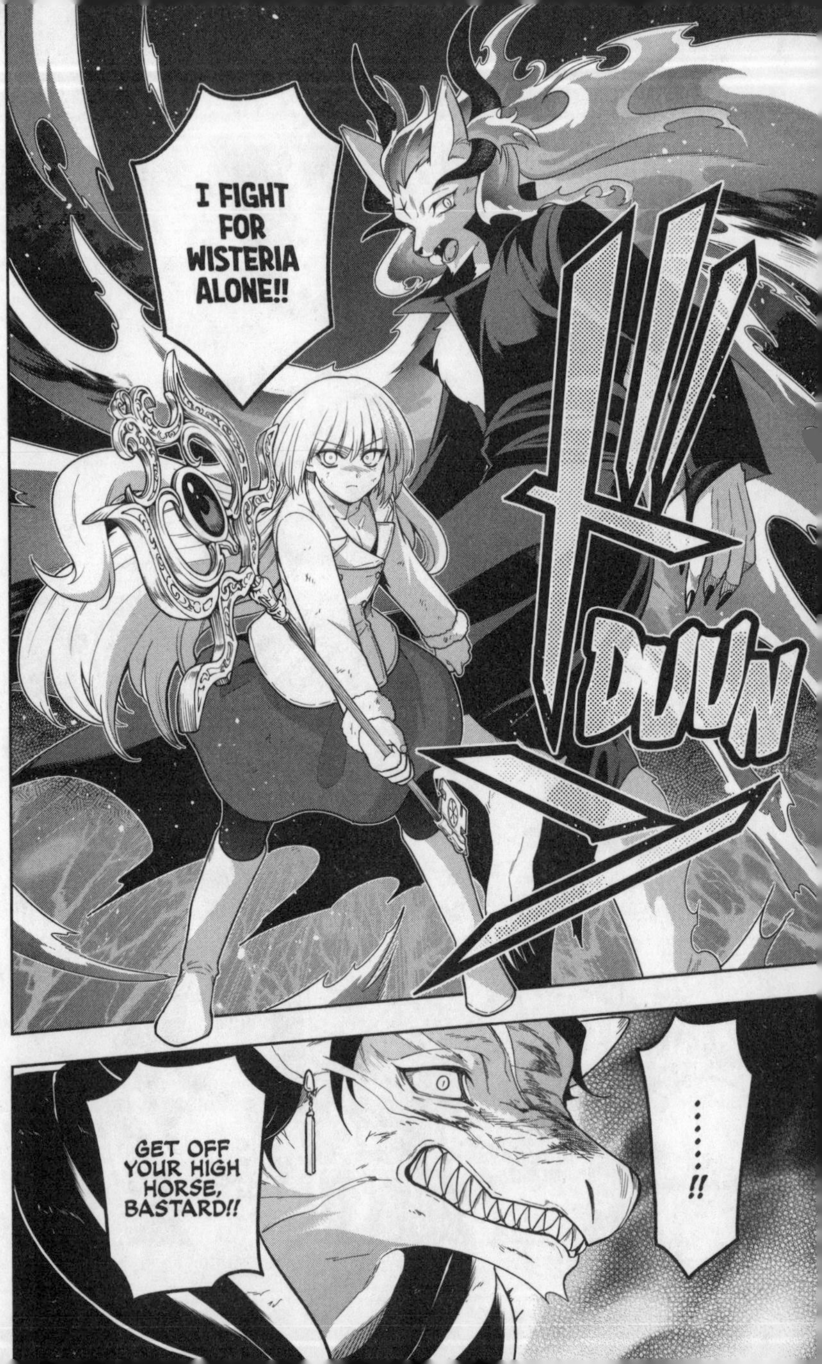
I FIGHT FOR WISTERIA ALONE!!
DUUN
......!!
GET OFF YOUR HIGH HORSE, BASTARD!!

The Tale of the Outcasts

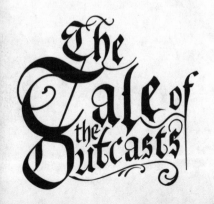

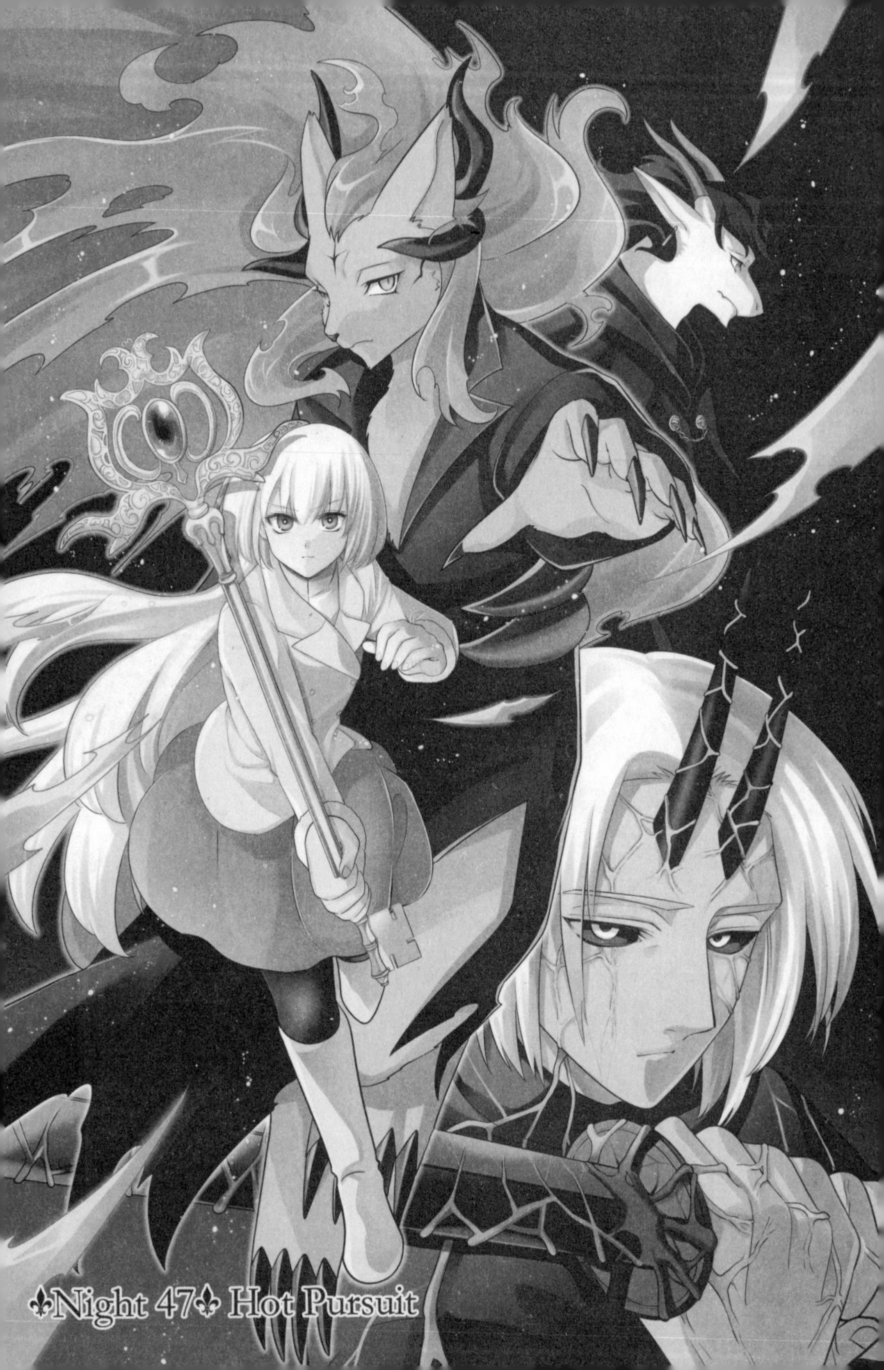

Night 47 Hot Pursuit

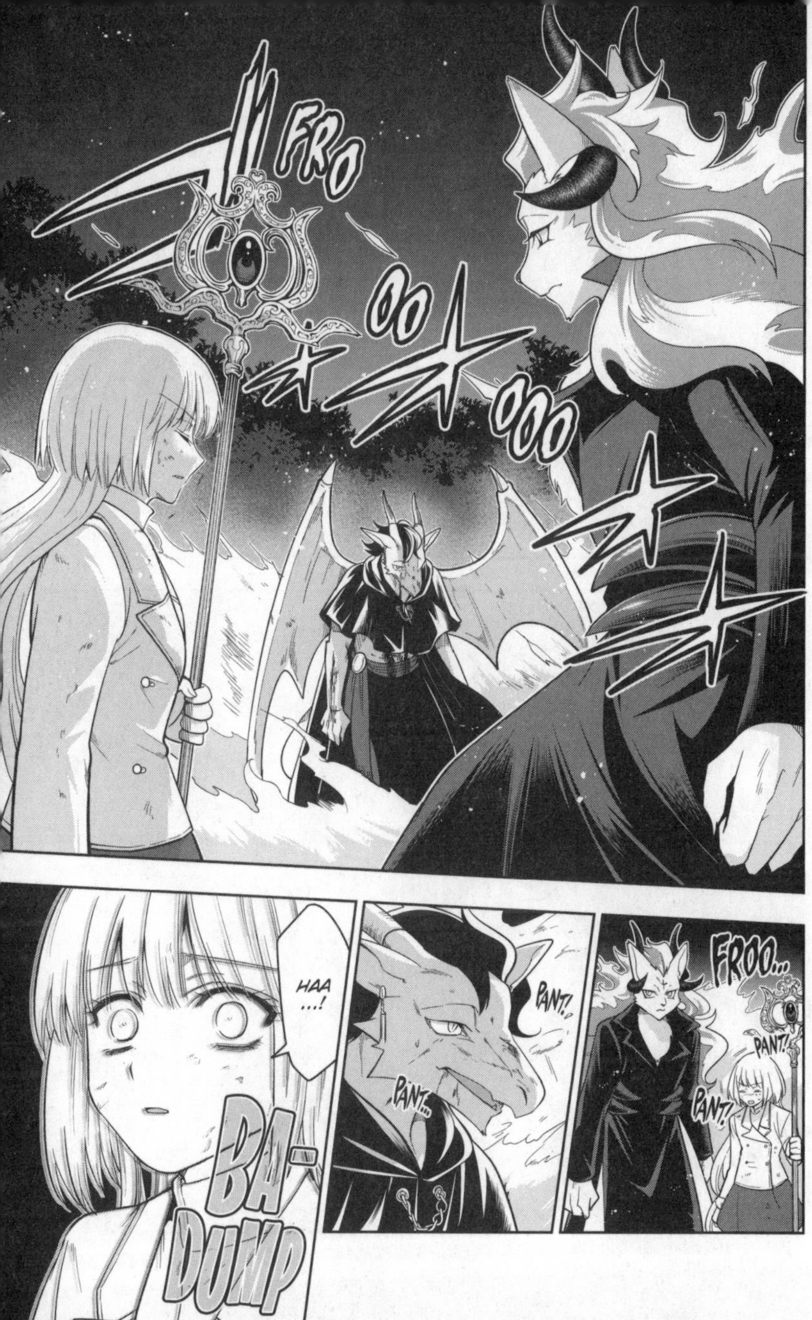
FROOOOOOOO
FROO...
PANT!
PANT!
PANT!
PANT...
HAA...!
BA-DUMP

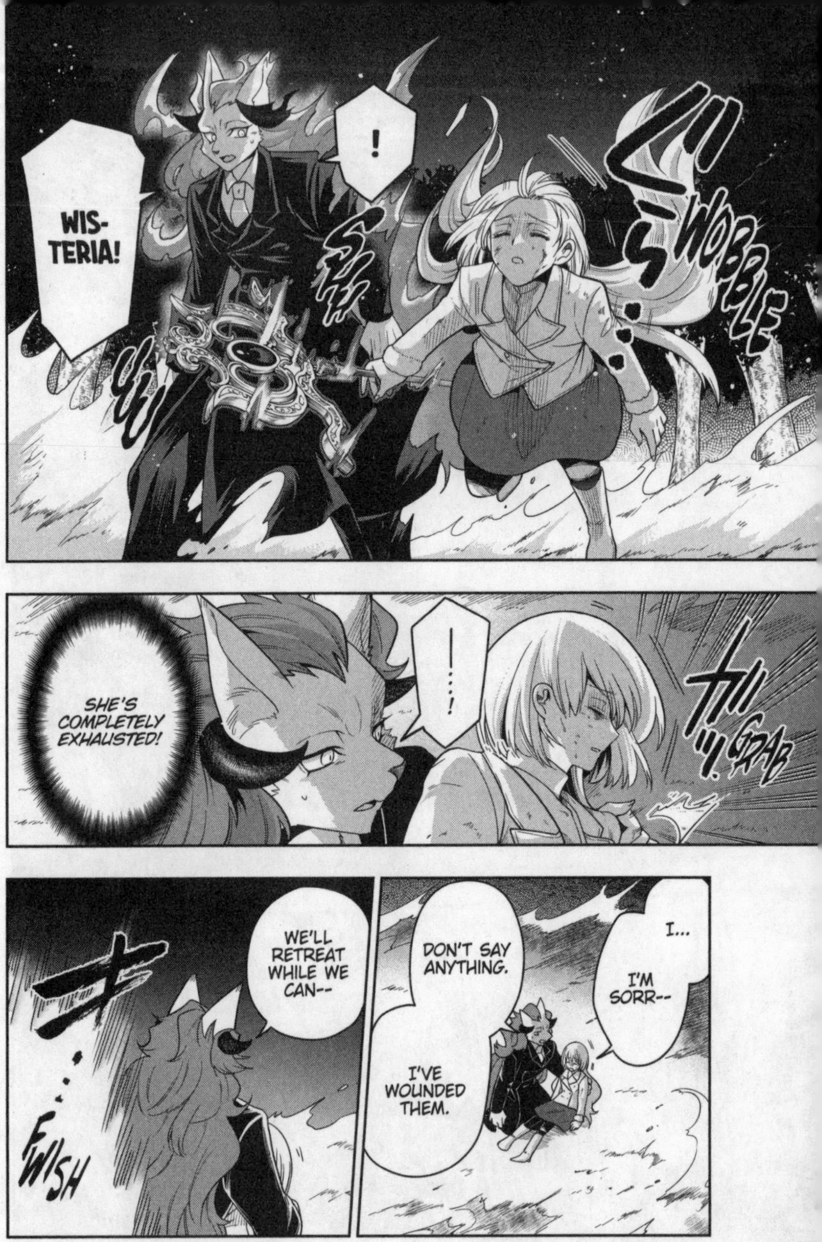
WOBBLE
!
WIS-TERIA!
GRAB
...!
SHE'S COMPLETELY EXHAUSTED!
I... I'M SORR--
DON'T SAY ANYTHING.
I'VE WOUNDED THEM.
WE'LL RETREAT WHILE WE CAN--
FWISH

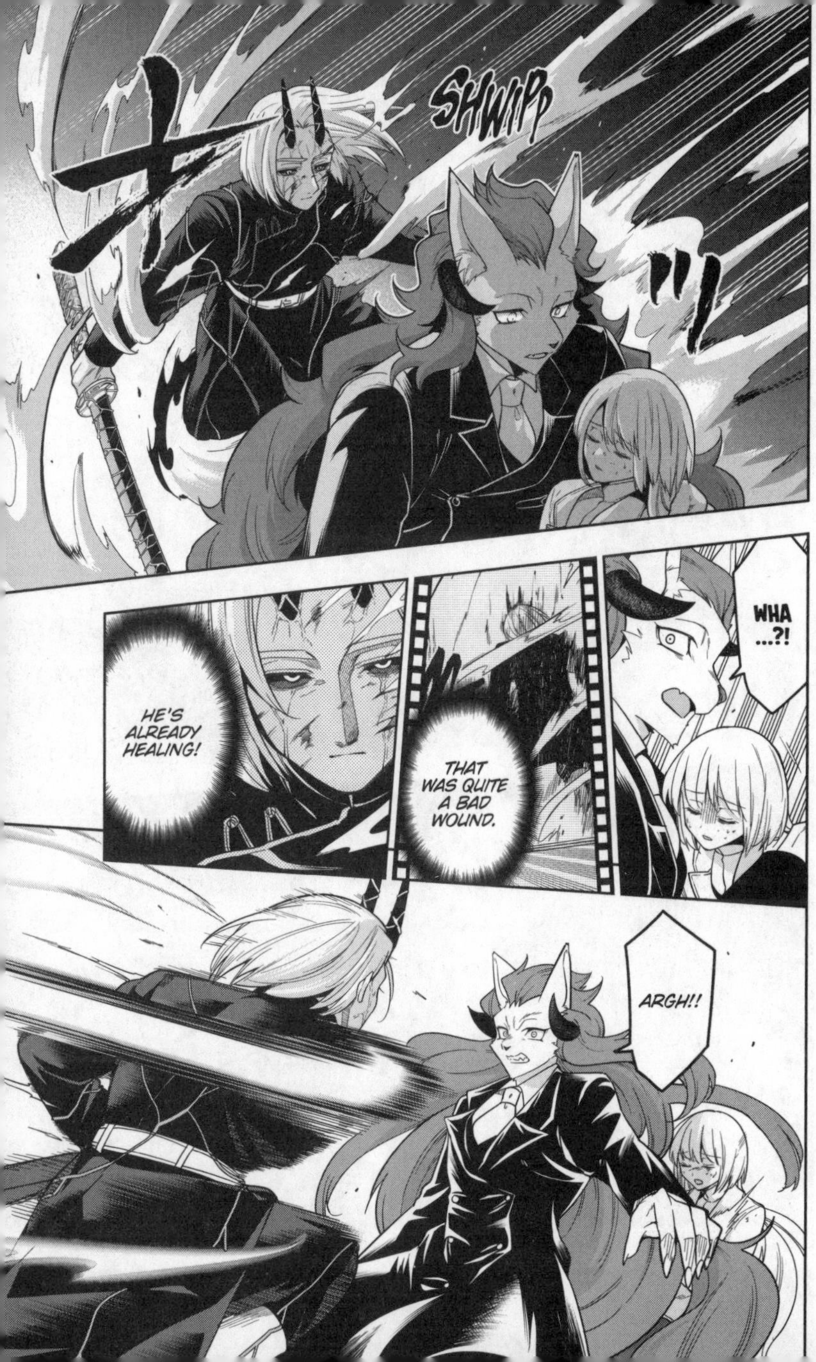
SHWIPP
WHA ...?!
THAT WAS QUITE A BAD WOUND.
HE'S ALREADY HEALING!
ARGH!!

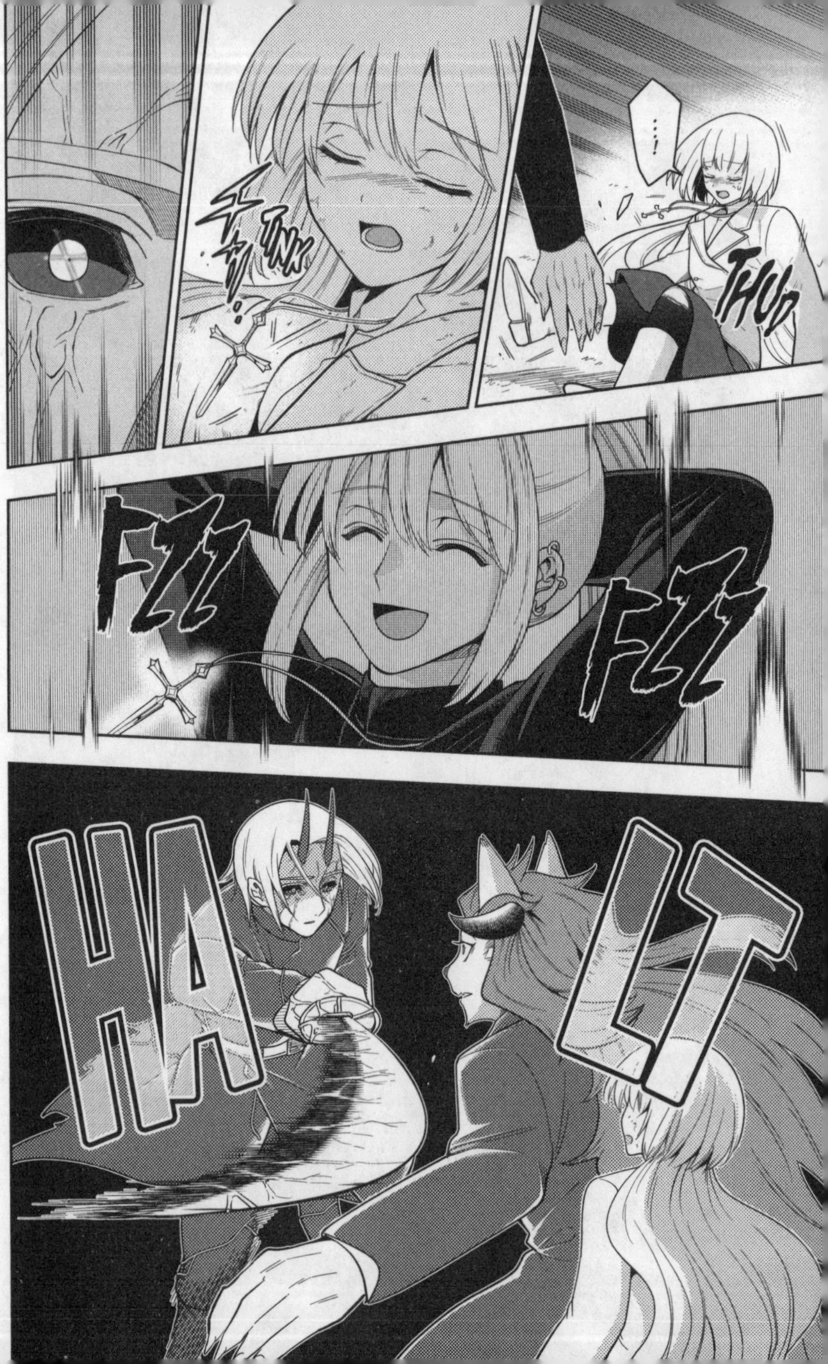

...!
THUD
TINK
FZZ
FZZ
HALT

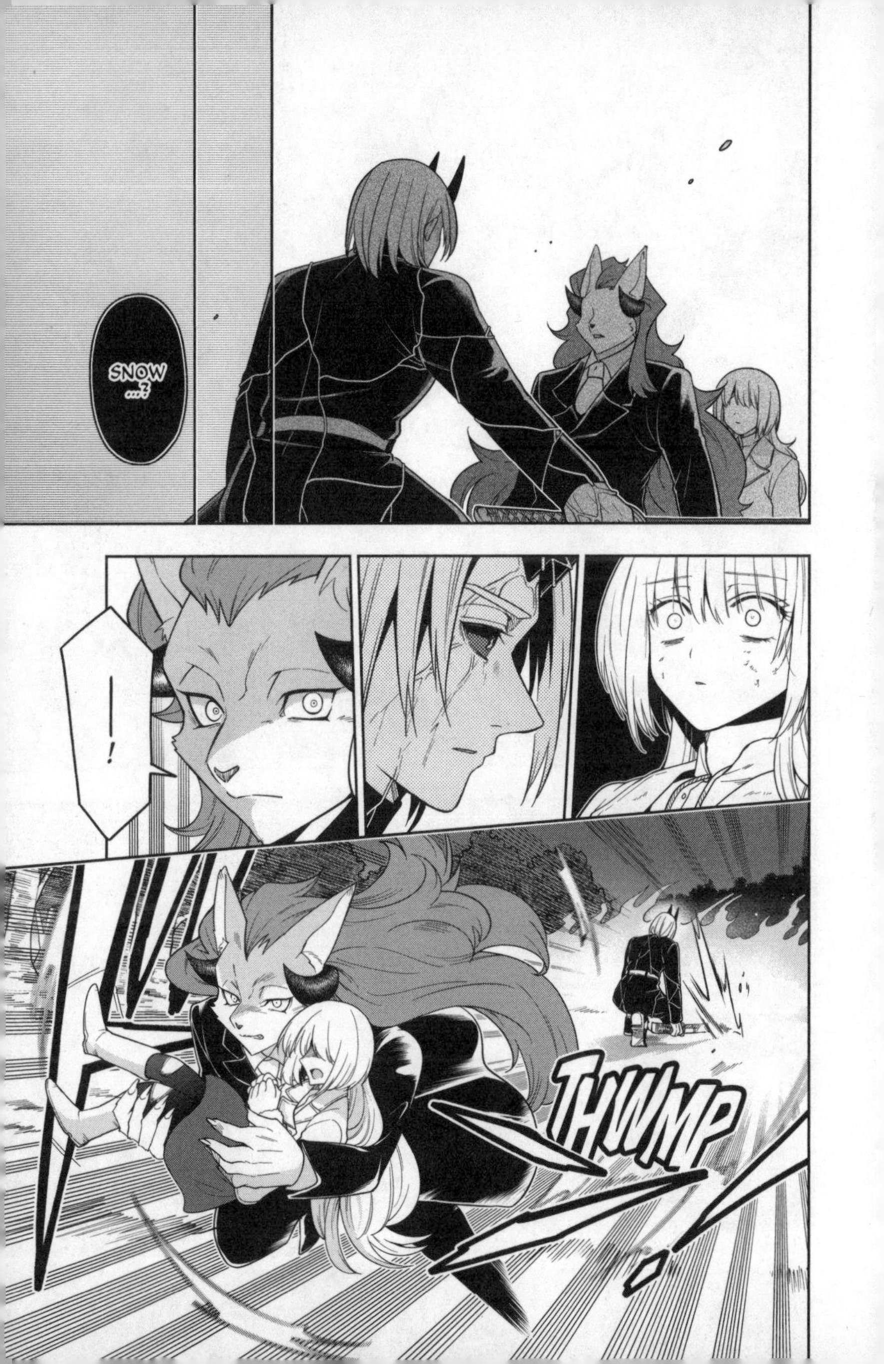
SNOW ...?
!!
THWMP

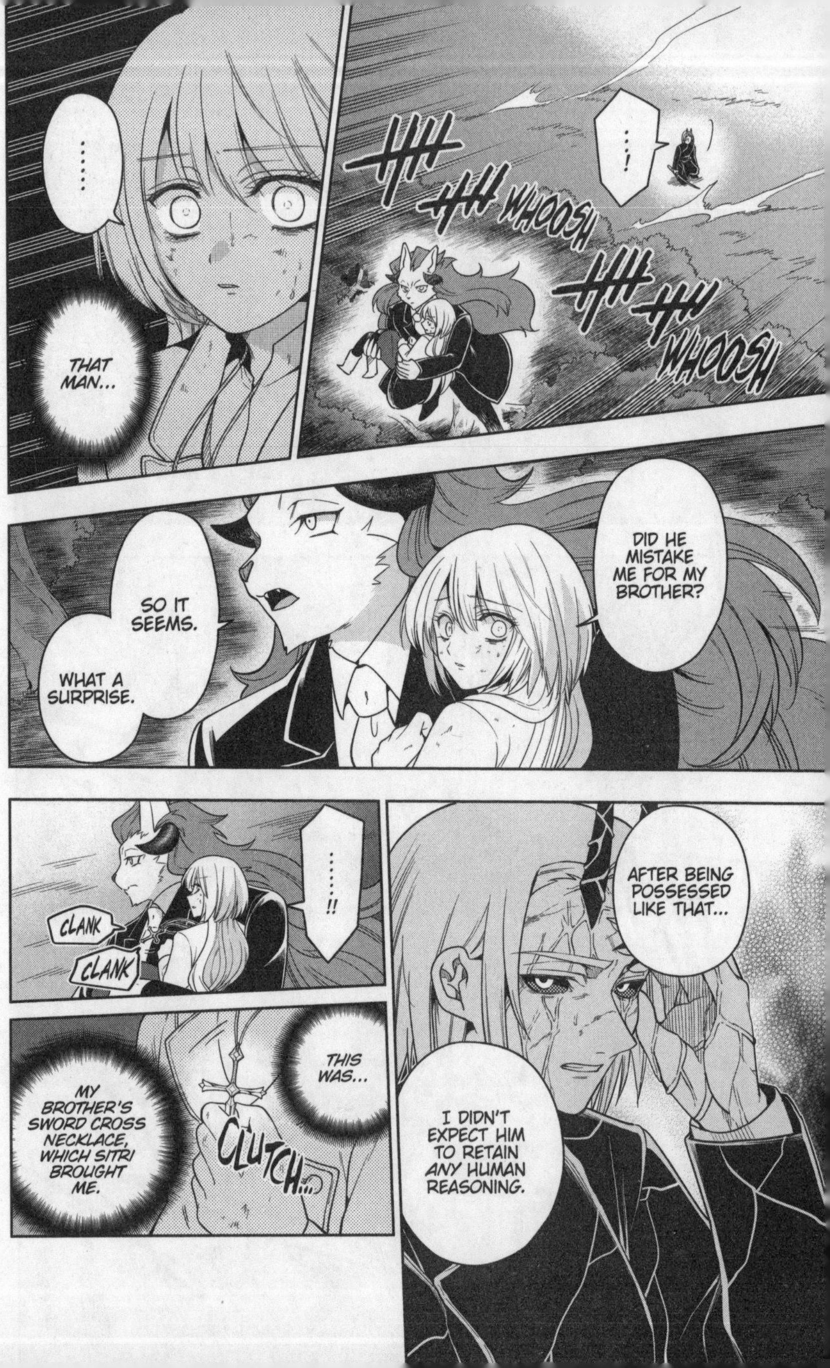

...!
WHOOSH
WHOOSH
......
THAT MAN...
DID HE MISTAKE ME FOR MY BROTHER?
SO IT SEEMS.
WHAT A SURPRISE.
AFTER BEING POSSESSED LIKE THAT...
I DIDN'T EXPECT HIM TO RETAIN ANY HUMAN REASONING.
......!!
CLANK
CLANK
THIS WAS...
MY BROTHER'S SWORD CROSS NECKLACE, WHICH SITRI BROUGHT ME.
CLUTCH...

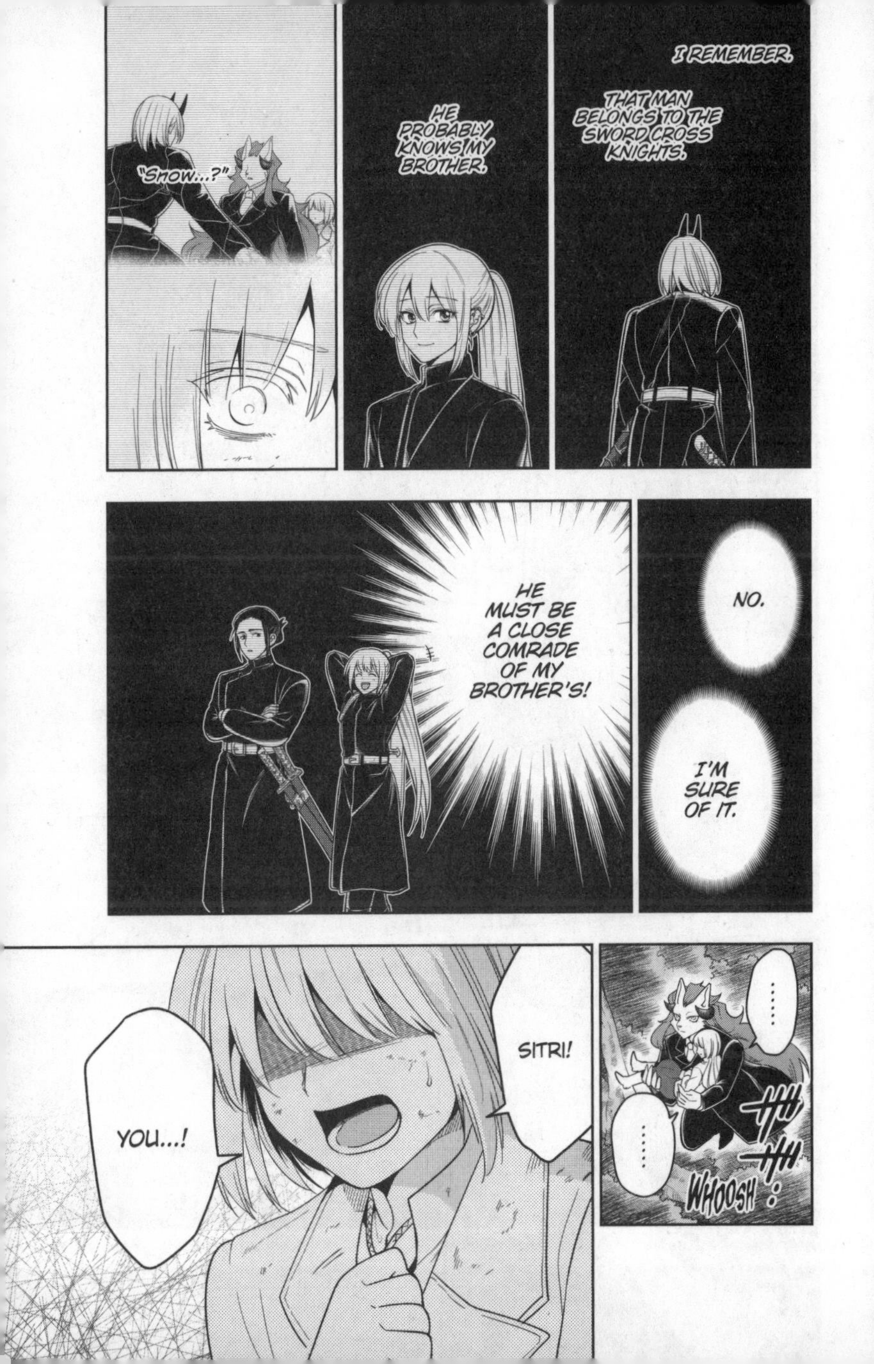
I REMEMBER.
THAT MAN BELONGS TO THE SWORD CROSS KNIGHTS.
HE PROBABLY KNOWS MY BROTHER.
"Snow...?"
NO.
I'M SURE OF IT.
HE MUST BE A CLOSE COMRADE OF MY BROTHER'S!
......
......
WHOOSH
SITRI!
YOU...!

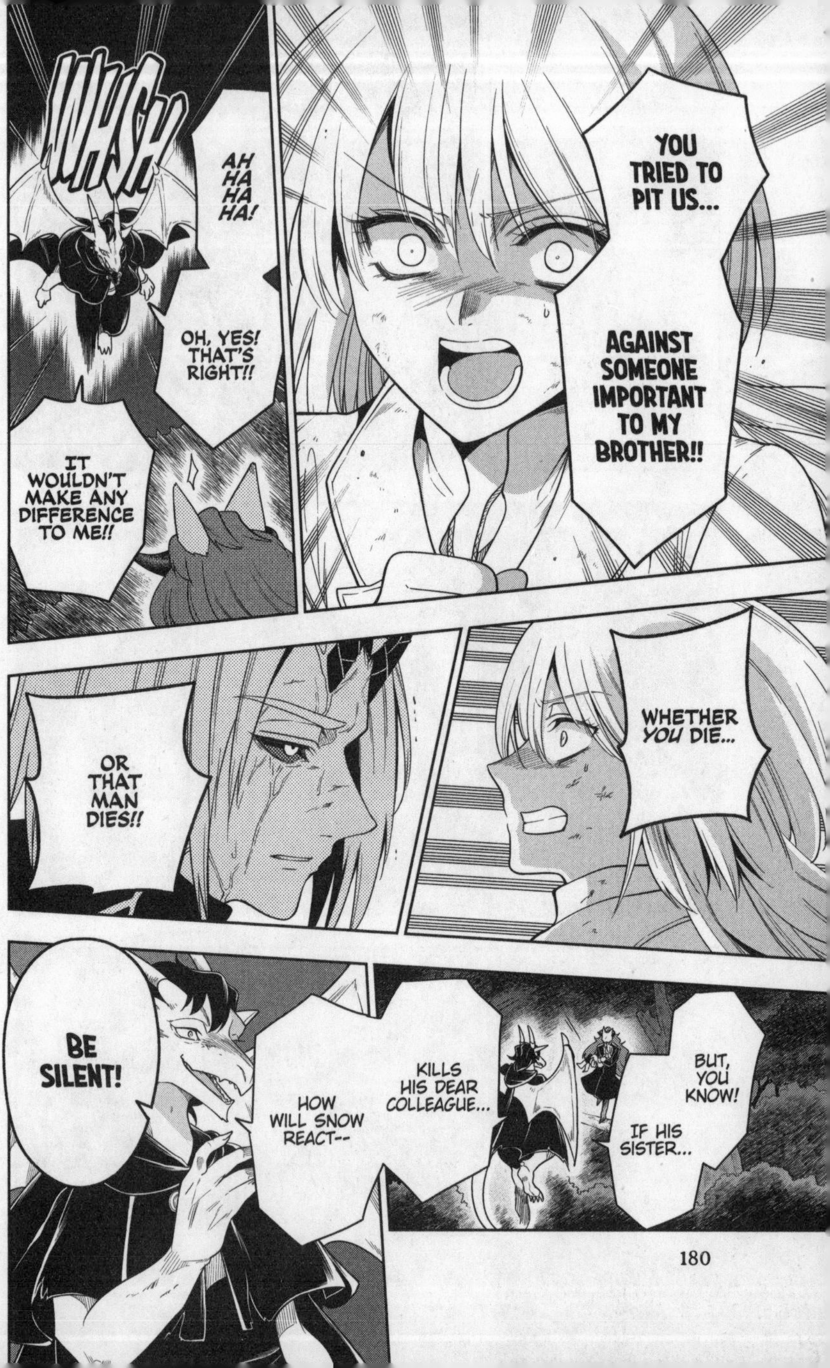
YOU TRIED TO PIT US...
AGAINST SOMEONE IMPORTANT TO MY BROTHER!!
WHSH
AH HA HA HA!
OH, YES! THAT'S RIGHT!!
IT WOULDN'T MAKE ANY DIFFERENCE TO ME!!
WHETHER *YOU* DIE...
OR THAT MAN DIES!!
BUT, YOU KNOW!
IF HIS SISTER...
KILLS HIS DEAR COLLEAGUE...
HOW WILL SNOW REACT--
BE SILENT!

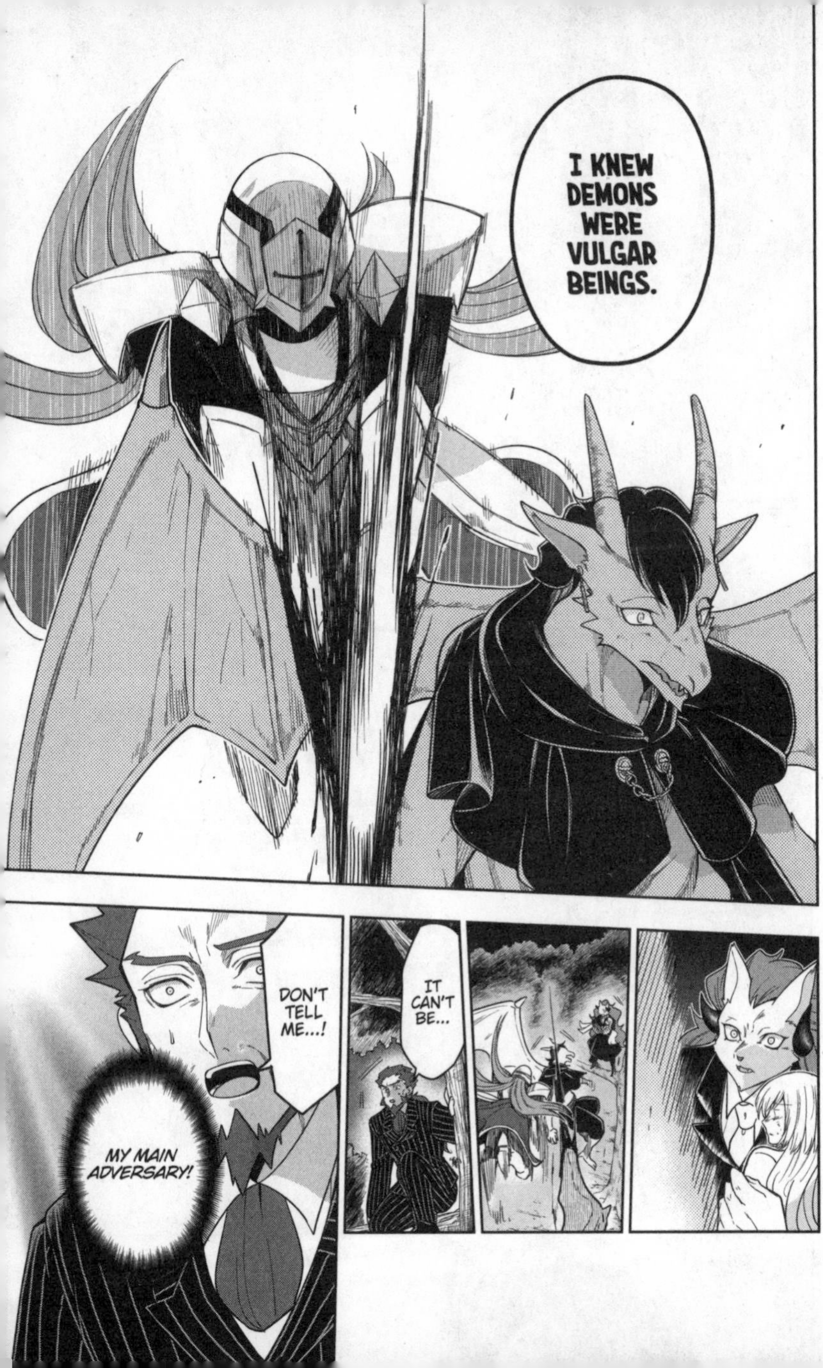
I KNEW DEMONS WERE VULGAR BEINGS.
IT CAN'T BE...
DON'T TELL ME...!
MY MAIN ADVERSARY!

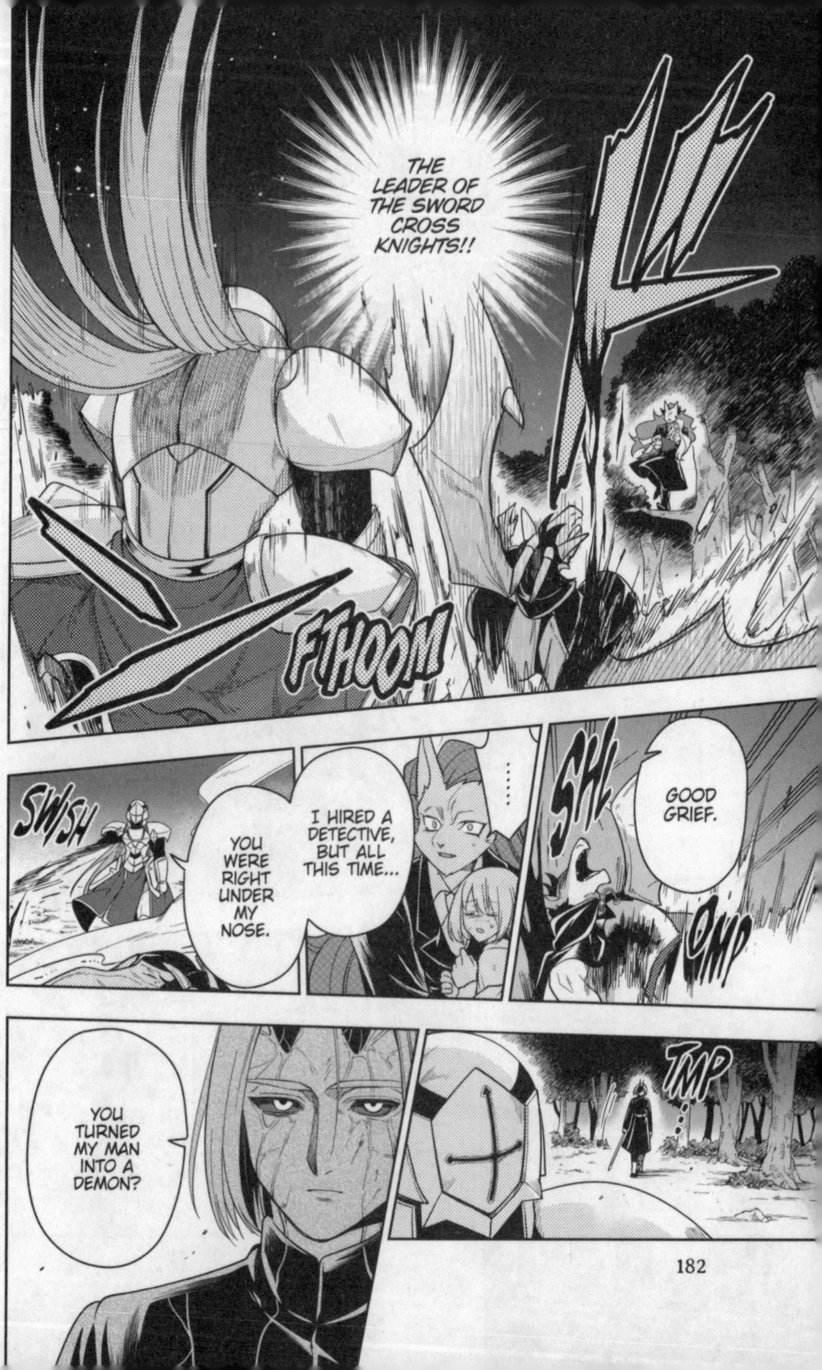
THE LEADER OF THE SWORD CROSS KNIGHTS!!
FTHOOM
GOOD GRIEF.
SHL
OMP
......
I HIRED A DETECTIVE, BUT ALL THIS TIME...
YOU WERE RIGHT UNDER MY NOSE.
SWISH
TMP
...
YOU TURNED MY MAN INTO A DEMON?

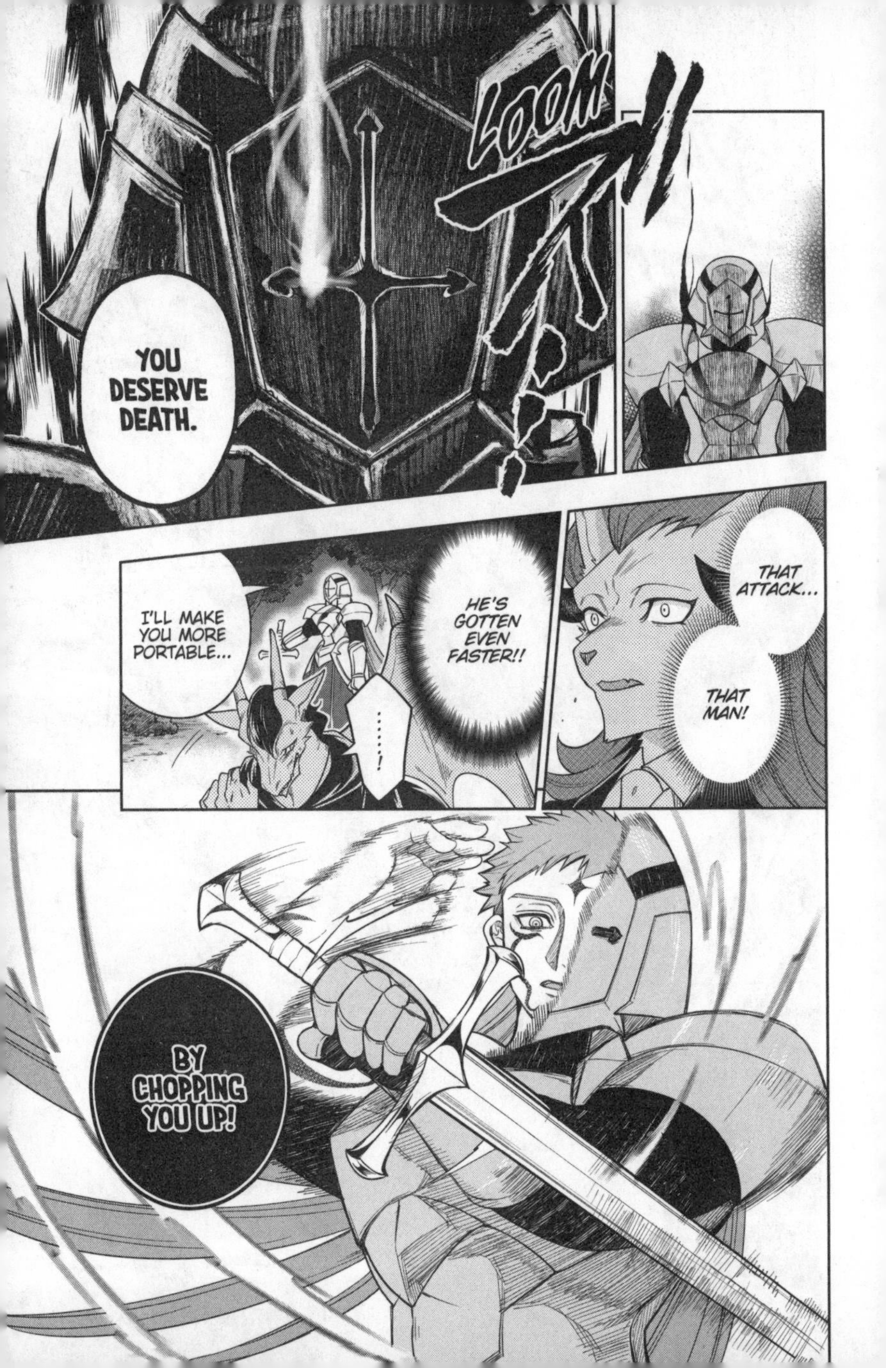
LOOM
YOU DESERVE DEATH.
THAT ATTACK...
THAT MAN!
HE'S GOTTEN EVEN FASTER!!
......!
I'LL MAKE YOU MORE PORTABLE...
BY CHOPPING YOU UP!

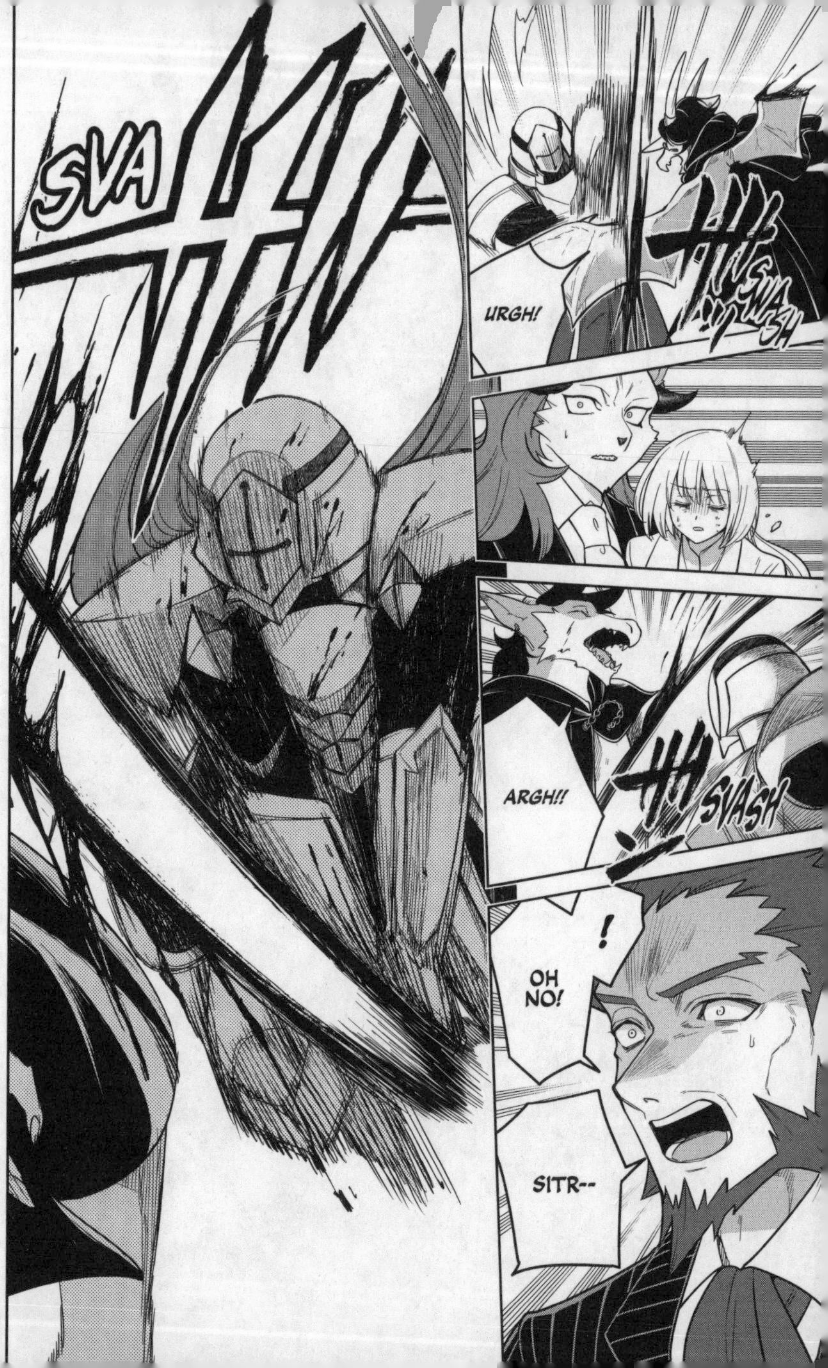
URGH!
SWASH
ARGH!!
SVASH
!
OH NO!
SITR--
SVA

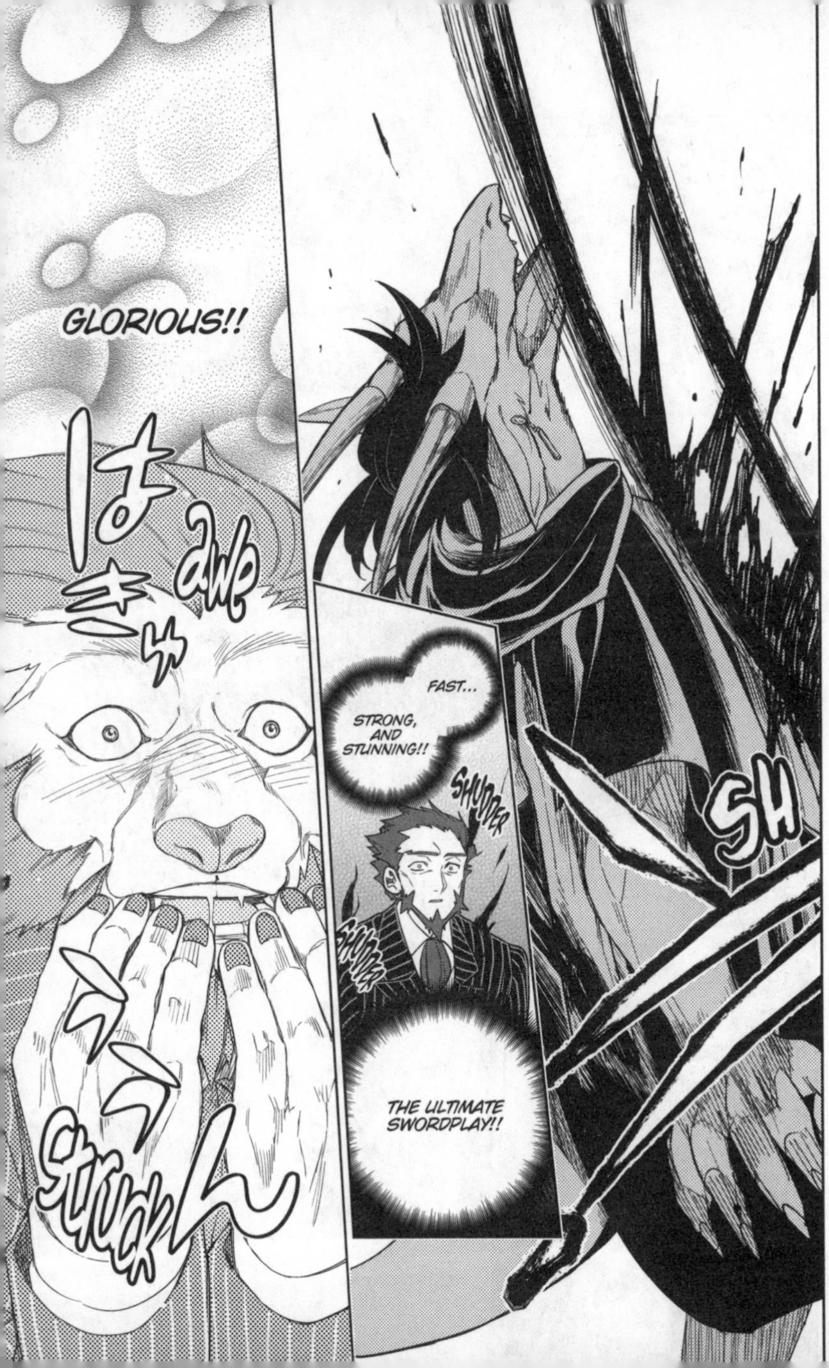
SH
FAST...
STRONG, AND STUNNING!!
SHUDDER
SHUDDER
THE ULTIMATE SWORDPLAY!!
GLORIOUS!!
はきゅうん
awe
struck

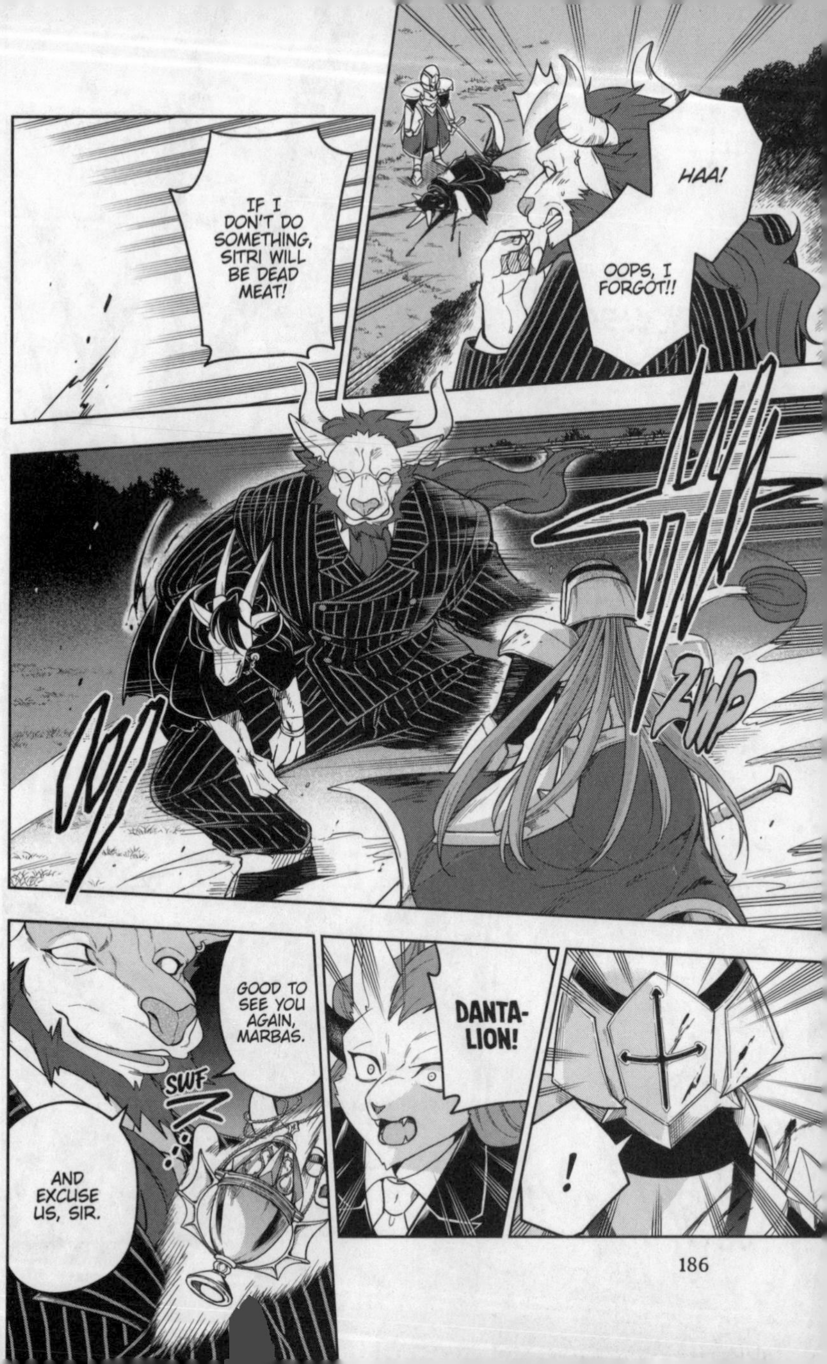
HAA!
OOPS, I FORGOT!!
IF I DON'T DO SOMETHING, SITRI WILL BE DEAD MEAT!
ZWP
!
DANTA-LION!
GOOD TO SEE YOU AGAIN, MARBAS.
SWF
AND EXCUSE US, SIR.

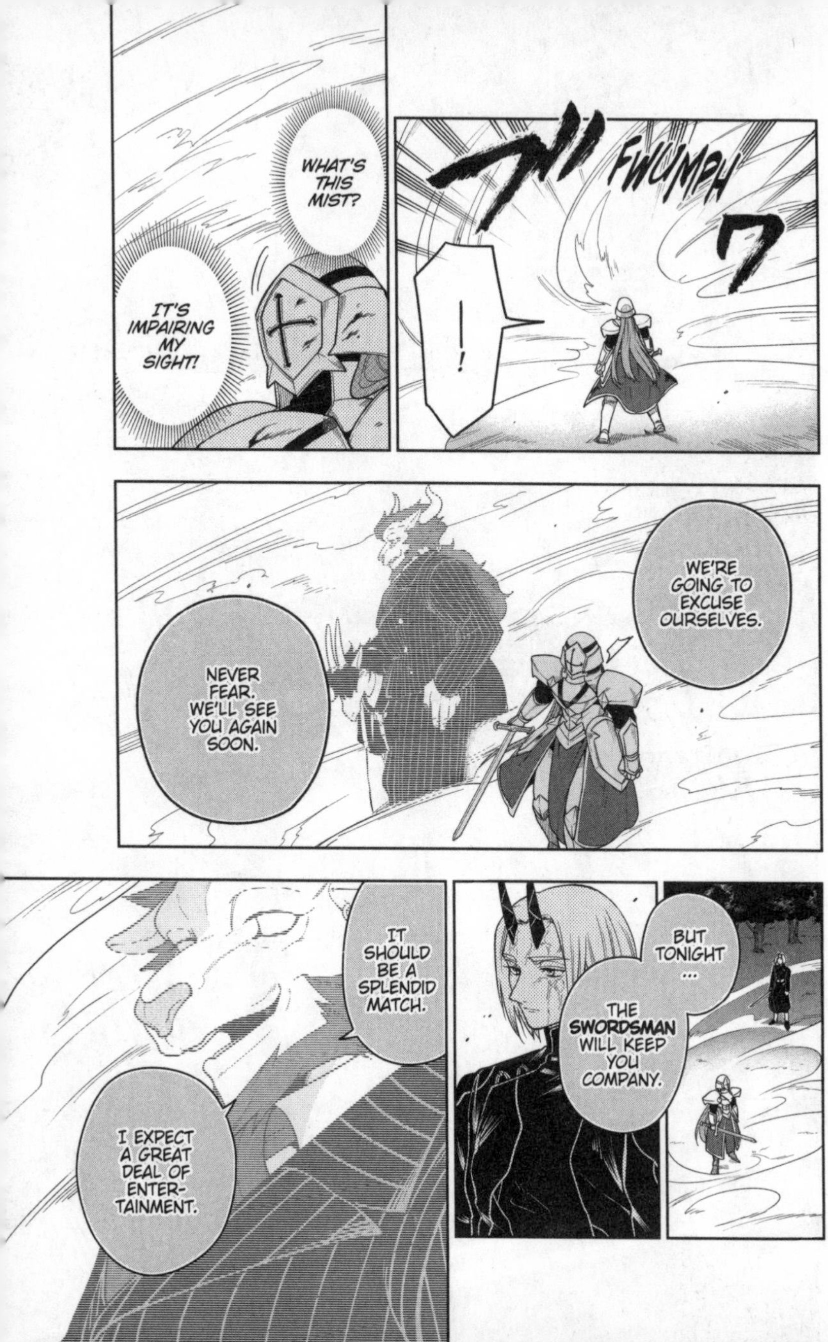
FWUMPH
!
WHAT'S THIS MIST?
IT'S IMPAIRING MY SIGHT!
WE'RE GOING TO EXCUSE OURSELVES.
NEVER FEAR. WE'LL SEE YOU AGAIN SOON.
BUT TONIGHT...
THE **SWORDSMAN** WILL KEEP YOU COMPANY.
IT SHOULD BE A SPLENDID MATCH.
I EXPECT A GREAT DEAL OF ENTER-TAINMENT.

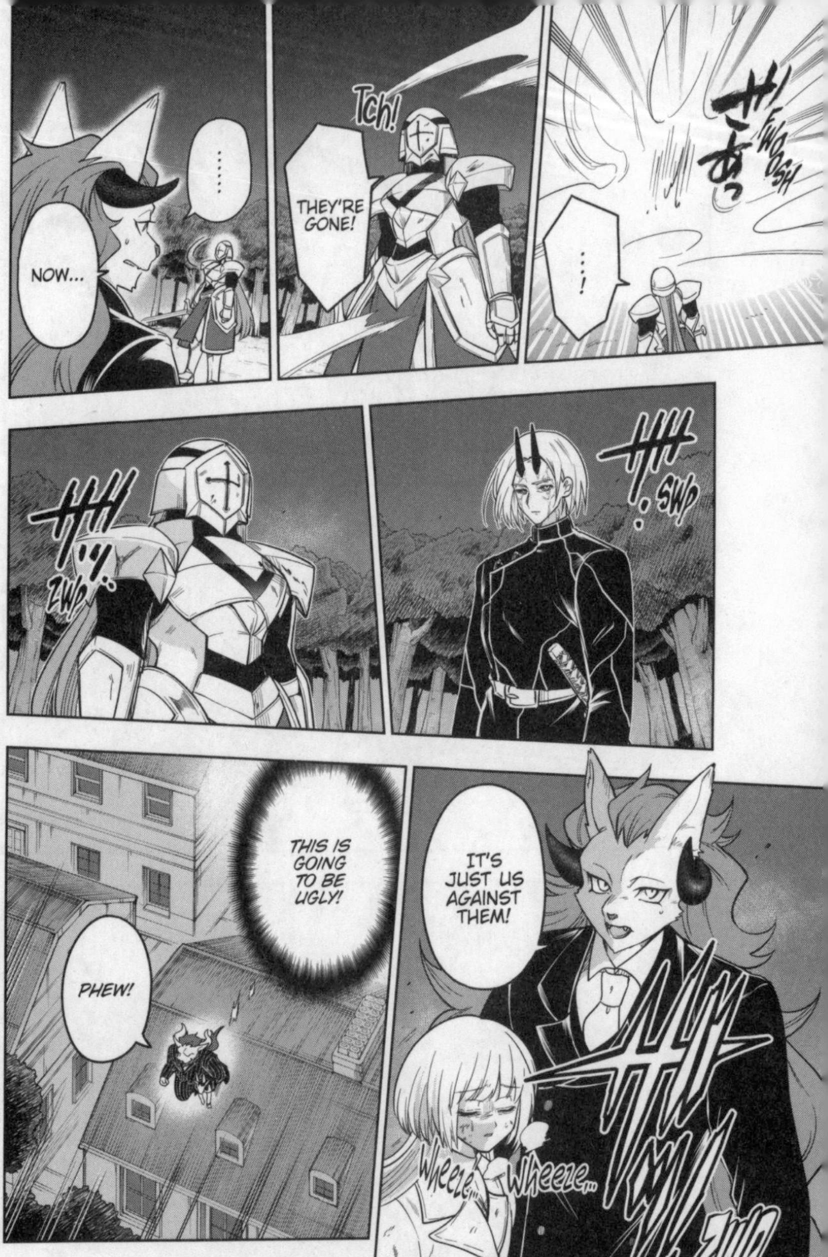

FWOOSH
...!
Tch!
THEY'RE GONE!
......
NOW...
SWP
ZWP
IT'S JUST US AGAINST THEM!
wheeze... wheeze...
ZIP
THIS IS GOING TO BE UGLY!
PHEW!

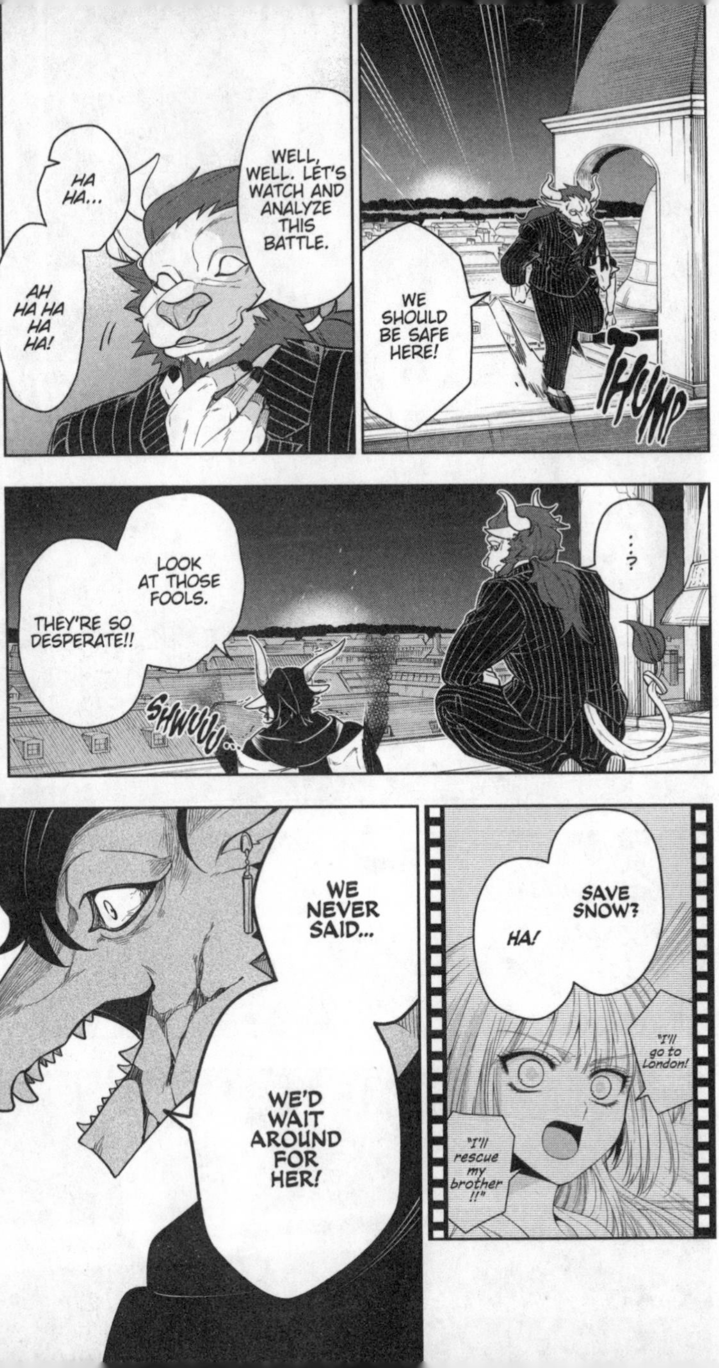
WE SHOULD BE SAFE HERE!
THUMP
WELL, WELL. LET'S WATCH AND ANALYZE THIS BATTLE.
HA HA...
AH HA HA HA HA!
...?
LOOK AT THOSE FOOLS.
THEY'RE SO DESPERATE!!
SHWUUU...
SAVE SNOW?
HA!
"I'll go to London!
"I'll rescue my brother!!"
WE NEVER SAID...
WE'D WAIT AROUND FOR HER!

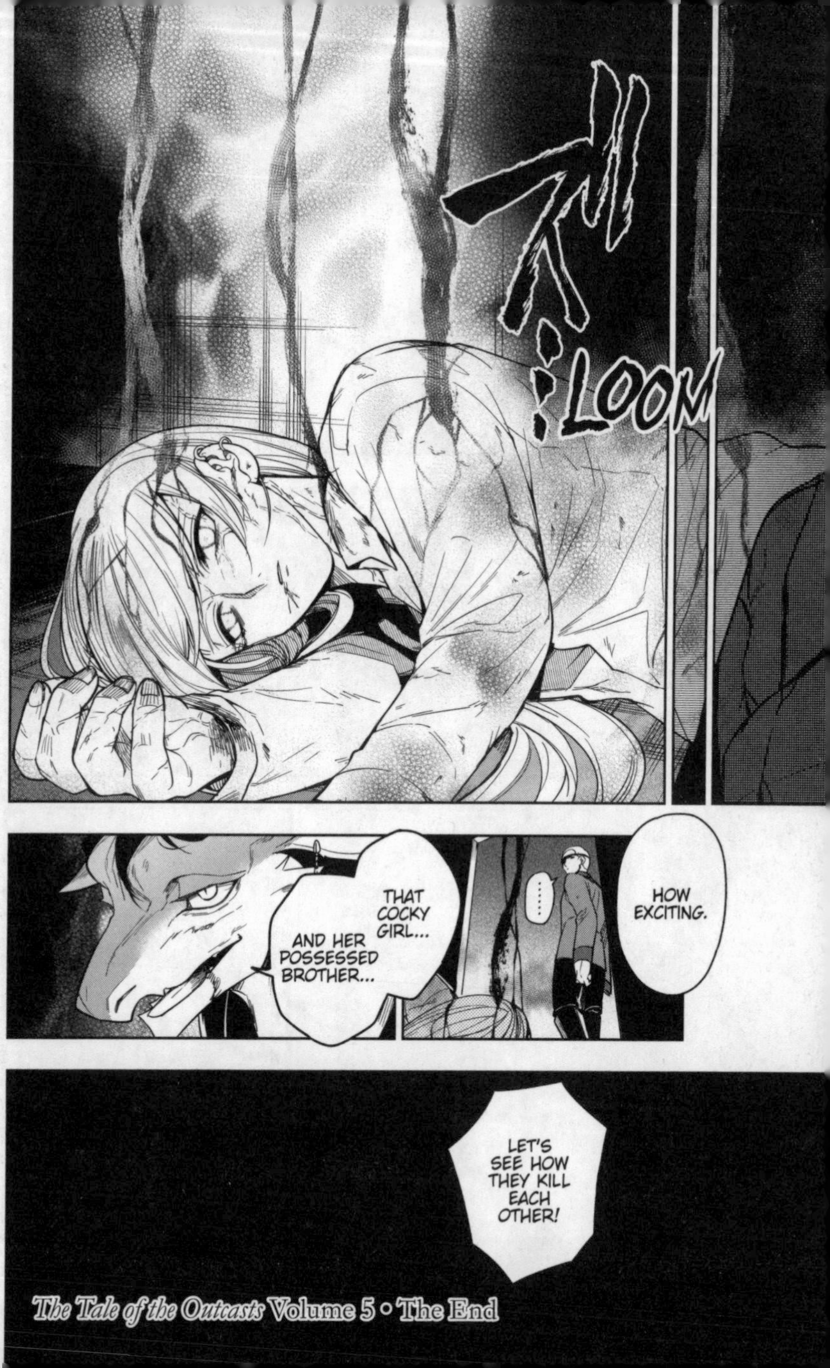
LOOM
HOW EXCITING.
......
THAT COCKY GIRL...
AND HER POSSESSED BROTHER...
LET'S SEE HOW THEY KILL EACH OTHER!
The Tale of the Outcasts Volume 5 • The End

SEVEN SEAS ENTERTAINMENT PRESENTS

The Tale of the Outcasts

Vol. 5

story and art by **MAKOTO HOSHINO**

TRANSLATION
Elina Ishikawa

ADAPTATION
M. Lyn Hall

LETTERING
Brendon Hull

COVER DESIGN
H. Qi

PROOFREADER
Krista Grandy

SENIOR EDITOR
Shanti Whitesides

PRODUCTION DESIGNER
Christa Miesner

PRODUCTION MANAGER
Lissa Pattillo

PREPRESS TECHNICIAN
Rhiannon Rasmussen-Silverstein

PRINT MANAGER
Melanie Ujimori

EDITOR-IN-CHIEF
Julie Davis

ASSOCIATE PUBLISHER
Adam Arnold

PUBLISHER
Jason DeAngelis

NOKEMONO-TACHI NO YORU Vol.5
by Makoto HOSHINO
© 2019 Makoto HOSHINO
All rights reserved.
Original Japanese edition published by SHOGAKUKAN.
English translation rights in the United States of America, Canada, and the United
Kingdom arranged with SHOGAKUKAN through Tuttle-Mori Agency, Inc.

Seven Seas press and purchase enquiries can be sent to Marketing Manager Lianne
Sentar at press@gomanga.com. Information regarding the distribution and purchase of
digital editions is available from Digital Manager CK Russell at digital@gomanga.com.

Seven Seas and the Seven Seas logo are trademarks of
Seven Seas Entertainment. All rights reserved.

ISBN: 978-1-63858-205-2
Printed in Canada
First Printing: June 2022
10 9 8 7 6 5 4 3 2 1

▨▨▨ READING DIRECTIONS ▨▨▨

This book reads from *right to left*,
Japanese style. If this is your first time
reading manga, you start reading from
the top right panel on each page and
take it from there. If you get lost, just
follow the numbered diagram here.
It may seem backwards at first,
but you'll get the hang of it! Have fun!!

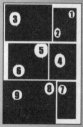

Follow us online: www.SevenSeasEntertainment.com

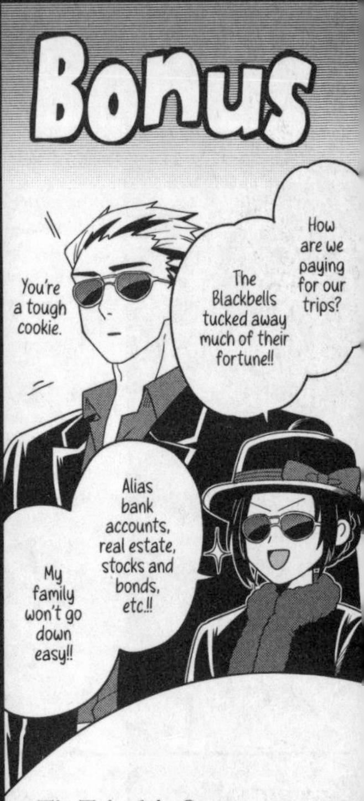
Bonus
How are we paying for our trips?
The Blackbells tucked away much of their fortune!!
You're a tough cookie.
Alias bank accounts, real estate, stocks and bonds, etc.!!
My family won't go down easy!!

The Tale of the Outcasts Volume 5

<Special Thanks>

Chihiro Makiguchi
Akihisa Maki
Sanshi Fujita
Ugebeso Hatsumaru
Zakuro Mizuhara
Hirorin

<Editors>

Shiotani-san
Ogura-san
Hayashi-san

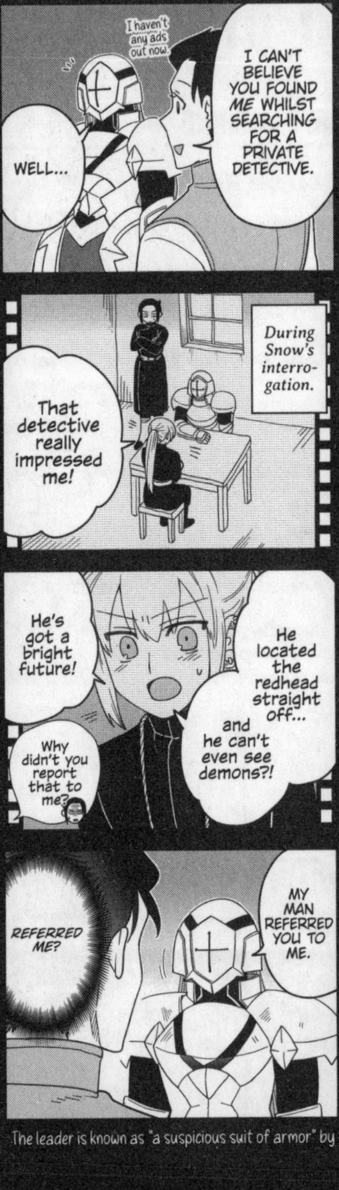
I CAN'T BELIEVE YOU FOUND *ME* WHILST SEARCHING FOR A PRIVATE DETECTIVE.
I haven't any ads out now.
WELL...
During Snow's interrogation.
That detective really impressed me!
He located the redhead straight off...
and he can't even see demons?!
He's got a bright future!
Why didn't you report that to me?
MY MAN REFERRED YOU TO ME.
REFERRED ME?

The leader is known as "a suspicious suit of armor" by townspeople. See you in the next volume!